子連れ狼

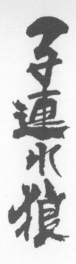

LONE
WOLF
AND
子連れ狼 CUB

story
KAZUO KOIKE

art
GOSEKI KOJIMA

DARK HORSE COMICS

translation
DANA LEWIS

lettering & retouch
DIGITAL CHAMELEON

cover artwork
FRANK MILLER with **LYNN VARLEY**

publisher
MIKE RICHARDSON

editor
MIKE HANSEN

assistant editor
TIM ERVIN-GORE

consulting editor
TOREN SMITH for **STUDIO PROTEUS**

book design
DARIN FABRICK

art director
MARK COX

Published by Dark Horse Comics, Inc. in association
with MegaHouse and Koike Shoin Publishing Company.

Dark Horse Comics, Inc.
10956 SE Main Street, Milwaukie, OR 97222
www.darkhorse.com

First edition: March 2001
ISBN: 1-56971-508-4

1 3 5 7 9 10 8 6 4 2

Printed in Canada

To find a comics shop in your area, call the
Comic Shop Locator Service toll-free at 1-888-266-4226

CLOUD DRAGON, WIND TIGER

子連れ狼

By KAZUO KOIKE
& GOSEKI KOJIMA

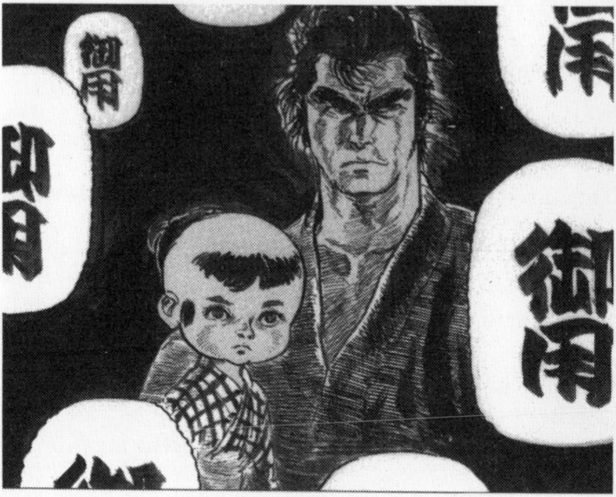
御用

VOLUME

7

A NOTE TO READERS

Lone Wolf and Cub is famous for its carefully researched re-creation of Edo-Period Japan. To preserve the flavor of the work, we have chosen to retain many Edo-Period terms that have no direct equivalents in English. Japanese is written in a mix of Chinese ideograms and a syllabic writing system, resulting in numerous synonyms. In the glossary, you may encounter words with multiple meanings. These are words written with Chinese ideograms that are pronounced the same but carry different meanings. A Japanese reader seeing the different ideograms would know instantly which meaning it is, but these synonyms can cause confusion when Japanese is spelled out in our alphabet. *O-yurushi o* (please forgive us)!

LONE WOLF AND CUB

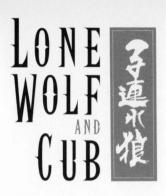

TABLE OF CONTENTS

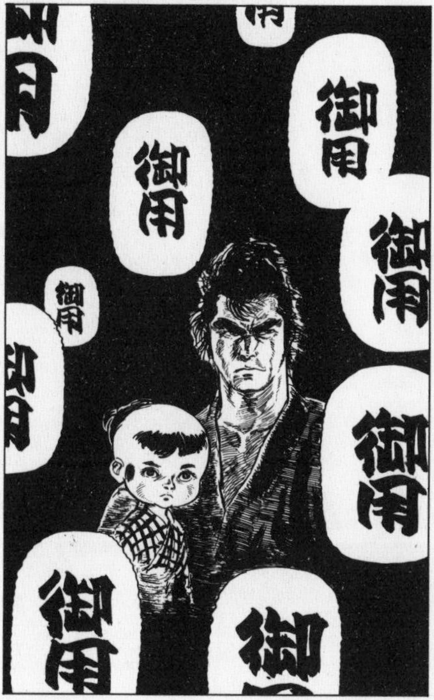
御用
御用
御用
御用
御用
御用

the thirty-fourth

Dragnet

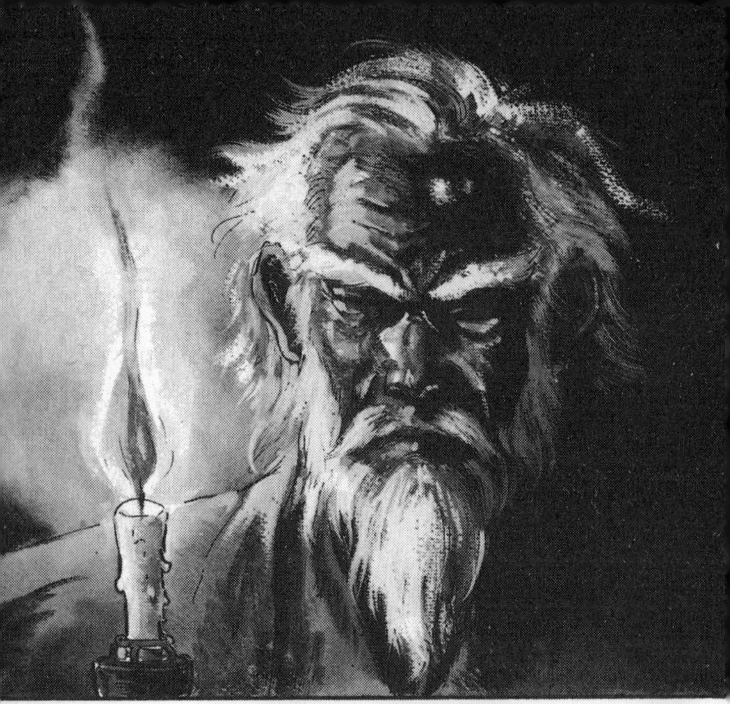

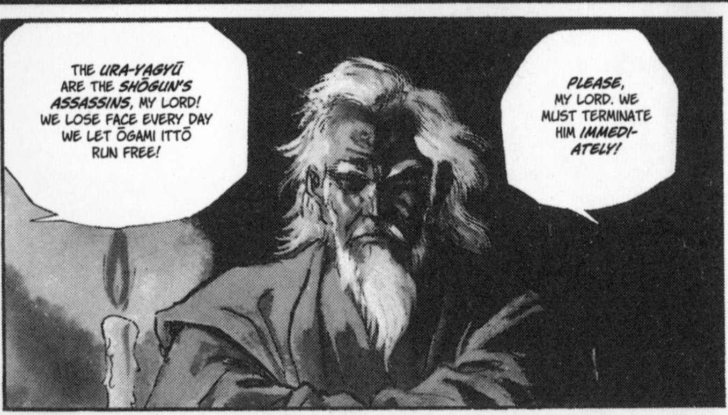

THE *URA-YAGYŪ* ARE THE *SHŌGUN'S ASSASSINS*, MY LORD! WE LOSE FACE EVERY DAY WE LET ŌGAMI ITTŌ RUN FREE!
PLEASE, MY LORD. WE MUST TERMINATE HIM *IMMEDI-ATELY!*

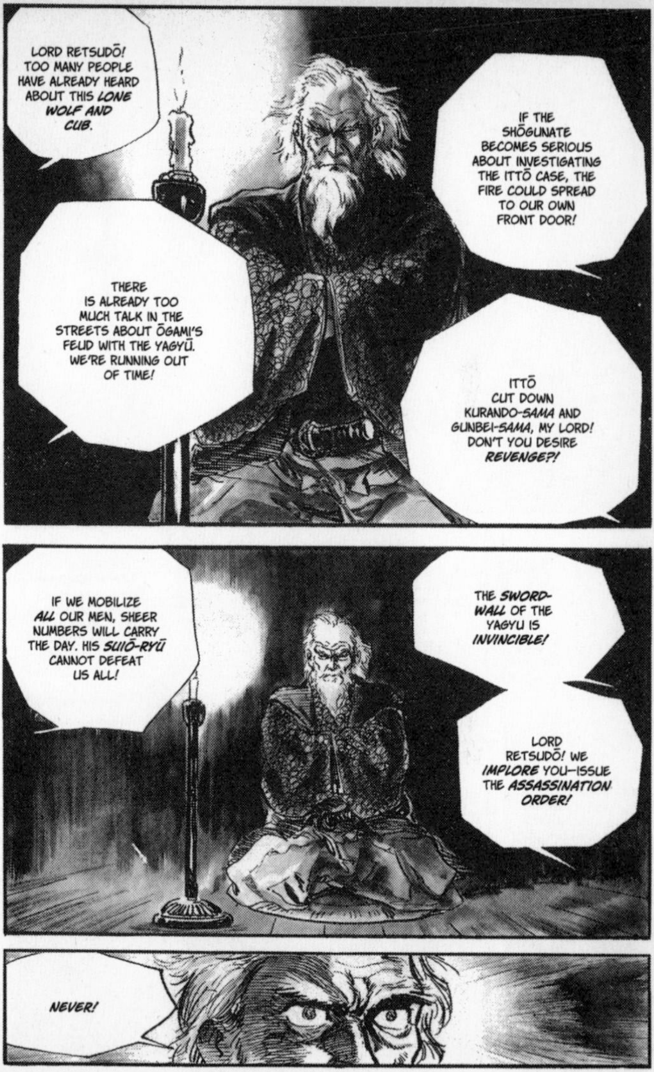
LORD RETSUDŌ! TOO MANY PEOPLE HAVE ALREADY HEARD ABOUT THIS *LONE WOLF AND CUB*.
IF THE SHŌGUNATE BECOMES SERIOUS ABOUT INVESTIGATING THE ITTŌ CASE, THE FIRE COULD SPREAD TO OUR OWN FRONT DOOR!
THERE IS ALREADY TOO MUCH TALK IN THE STREETS ABOUT ŌGAMI'S FEUD WITH THE YAGYŪ. WE'RE RUNNING OUT OF TIME!
ITTŌ CUT DOWN KURANDO-*SAMA* AND GUNBEI-*SAMA*, MY LORD! DON'T YOU DESIRE *REVENGE?!*
IF WE MOBILIZE *ALL* OUR MEN, SHEER NUMBERS WILL CARRY THE DAY. HIS *SUIŌ-RYŪ* CANNOT DEFEAT US ALL!
THE *SWORD-WALL* OF THE YAGYU IS *INVINCIBLE!*
LORD RETSUDŌ! WE *IMPLORE* YOU—ISSUE THE *ASSASSINATION ORDER!*
NEVER!

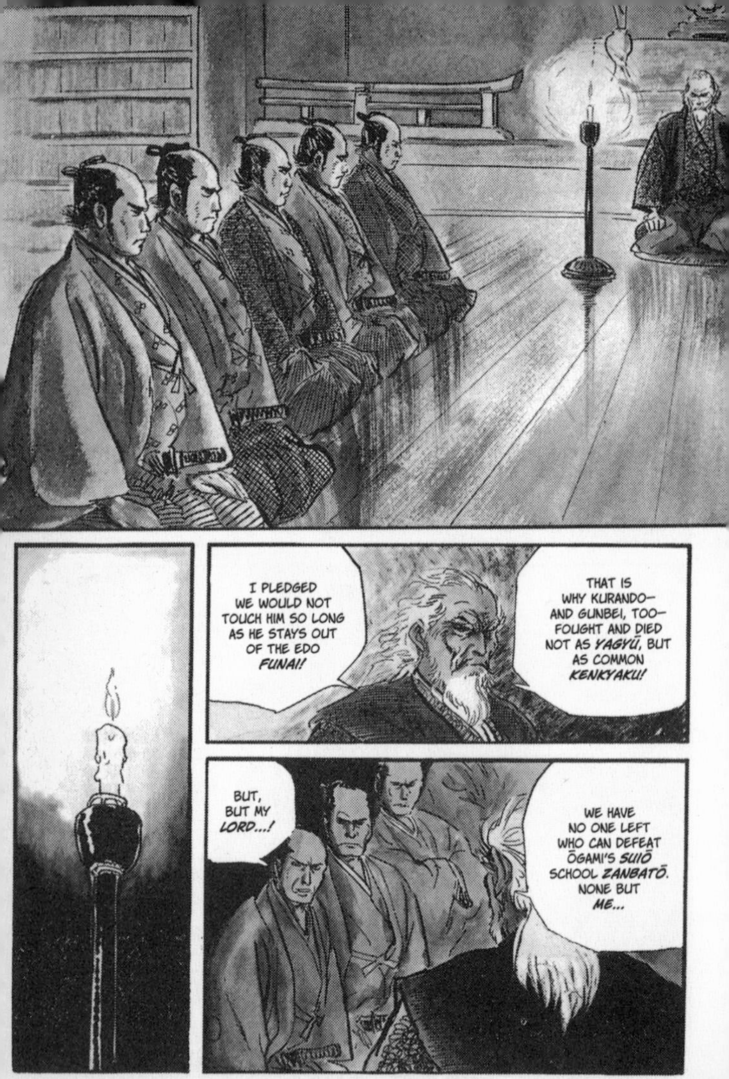
I PLEDGED WE WOULD NOT TOUCH HIM SO LONG AS HE STAYS OUT OF THE EDO FUNAI!
THAT IS WHY KURANDO— AND GUNBEI, TOO— FOUGHT AND DIED NOT AS YAGYŪ, BUT AS COMMON KENKYAKU!
BUT, BUT MY LORD...!
WE HAVE NO ONE LEFT WHO CAN DEFEAT ŌGAMI'S SUIŌ SCHOOL ZANBATŌ. NONE BUT ME...

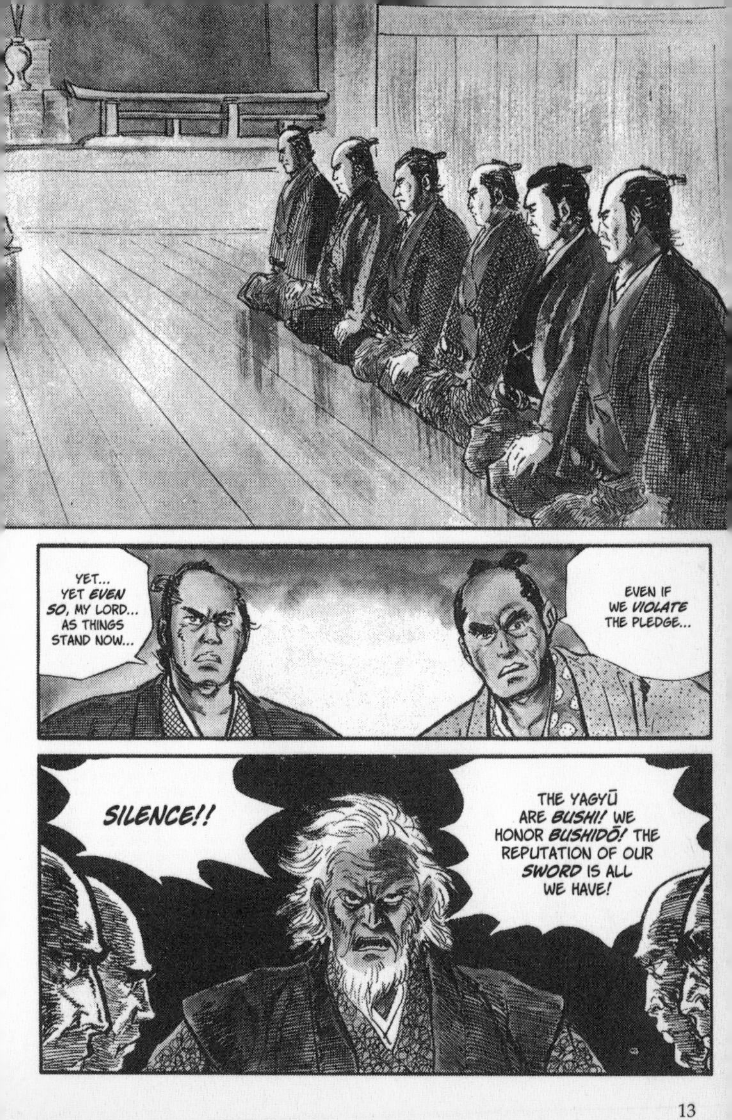
YET... YET *EVEN SO*, MY LORD... AS THINGS STAND NOW...
EVEN IF WE *VIOLATE* THE PLEDGE...
SILENCE!!
THE YAGYŪ ARE *BUSHI!* WE HONOR *BUSHIDŌ!* THE REPUTATION OF OUR *SWORD* IS ALL WE HAVE!

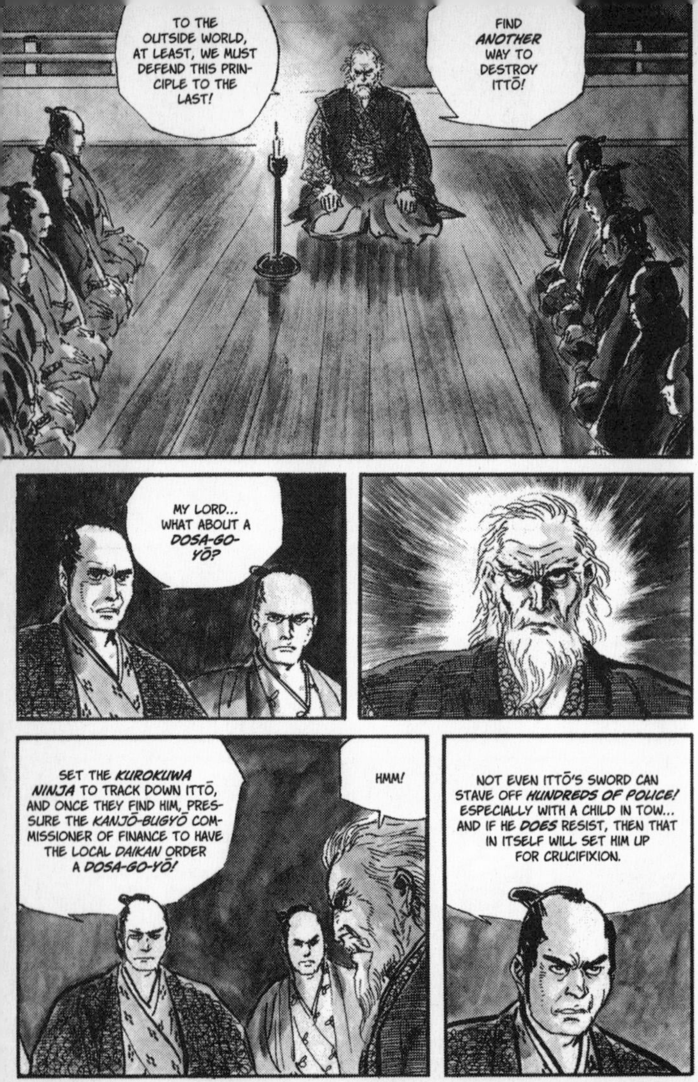
TO THE OUTSIDE WORLD, AT LEAST, WE MUST DEFEND THIS PRINCIPLE TO THE LAST!
FIND ANOTHER WAY TO DESTROY ITTŌ!
MY LORD... WHAT ABOUT A DOSA-GO-YŌ?
SET THE KUROKUWA NINJA TO TRACK DOWN ITTŌ, AND ONCE THEY FIND HIM, PRESSURE THE KANJŌ-BUGYŌ COMMISSIONER OF FINANCE TO HAVE THE LOCAL DAIKAN ORDER A DOSA-GO-YŌ!
HMM!
NOT EVEN ITTŌ'S SWORD CAN STAVE OFF HUNDREDS OF POLICE! ESPECIALLY WITH A CHILD IN TOW... AND IF HE DOES RESIST, THEN THAT IN ITSELF WILL SET HIM UP FOR CRUCIFIXION.

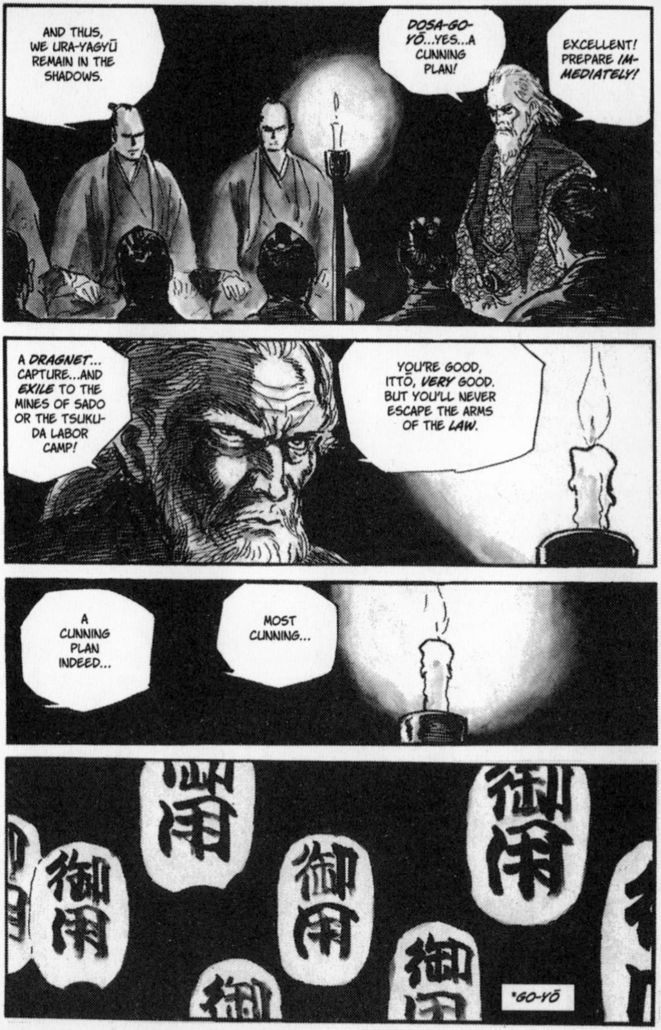
AND THUS, WE URA-YAGYŪ REMAIN IN THE SHADOWS.
DOSA-GO-YŌ...YES...A CUNNING PLAN!
EXCELLENT! PREPARE IM-MEDIATELY!
A DRAGNET... CAPTURE...AND EXILE TO THE MINES OF SADO OR THE TSUKUDA LABOR CAMP!
YOU'RE GOOD, ITTŌ, VERY GOOD. BUT YOU'LL NEVER ESCAPE THE ARMS OF THE LAW.
A CUNNING PLAN INDEED...
MOST CUNNING...
御用
*GO-YŌ

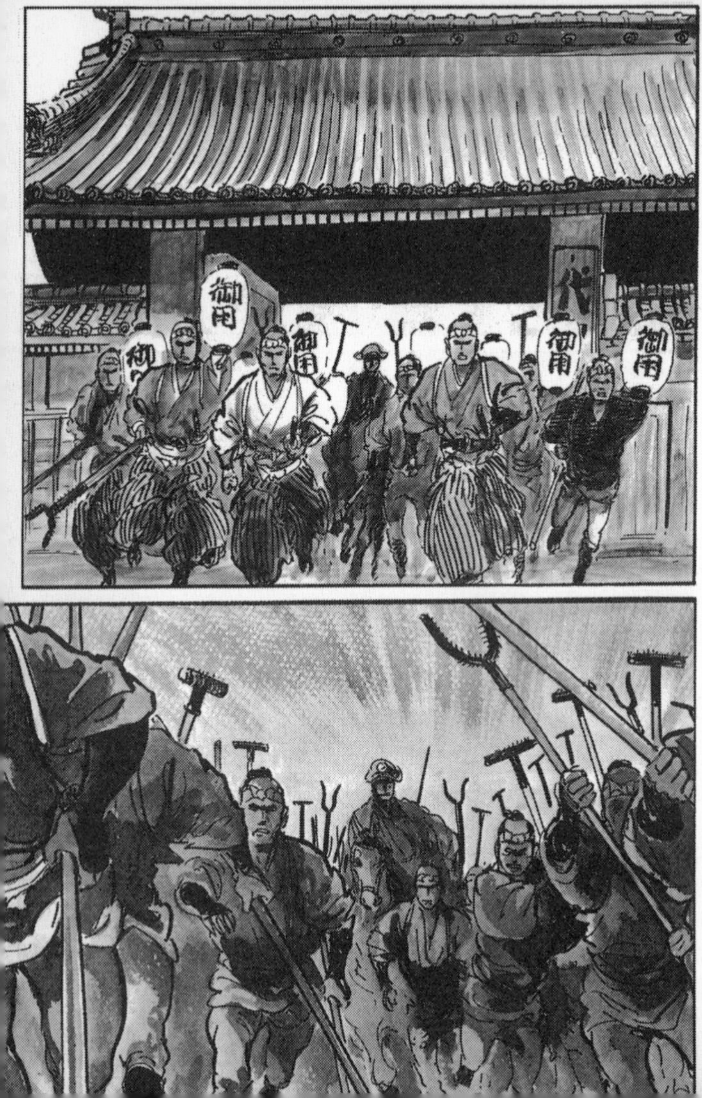

御
御用
御用
御用
代
御用

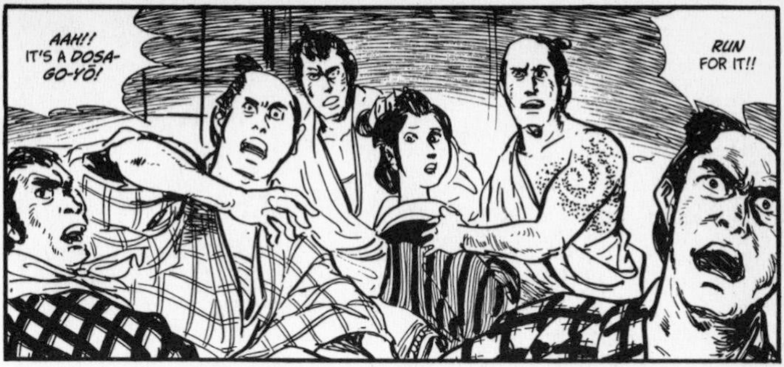
AAH!! IT'S A DOSA-GO-YŌ!
RUN FOR IT!!

SEEKING TO EMPLOY AND "REFORM" THE TENS OF THOUSANDS OF *MUSHUKU-MONO* HOMELESS, THEIR NAMES FOREVER REMOVED FROM THE RECORDS OF THE *NINBETSU-CHO* CENSUS FOR CRIMES AND OTHER IRREGULARITIES, THE TOKUGAWA SHŌGUNATE INSTITUTED A POLICY OF ROUNDING UP VAGRANTS FOR EXILE TO THE GOLD MINES OF SADO ISLAND OR THE BRUTISH LABOR CAMPS OF TSUKUDA ISLAND.

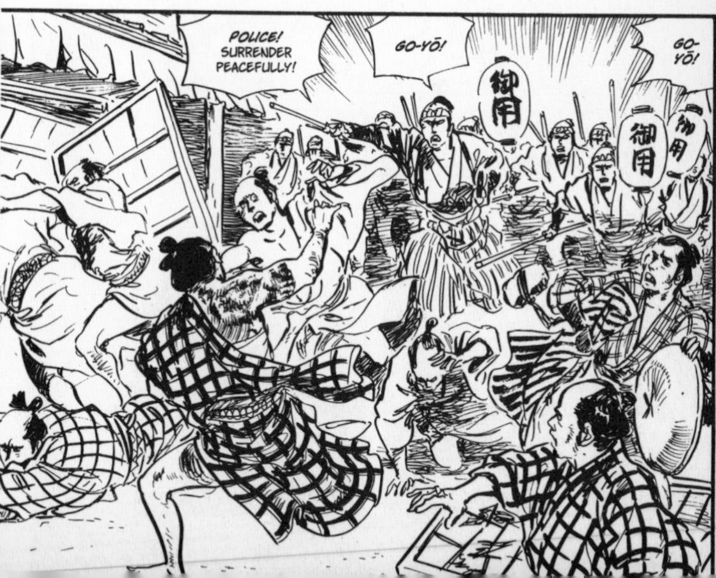
POLICE! SURRENDER PEACEFULLY!
GO-YŌ!
GO-YŌ!
御用
御用
御用

MUSHUKU-MONO: THE VAST MAJORITY OF THESE ROOTLESS PEOPLE HAD BEEN EXPELLED FROM SOCIETY FOR THEIR POVERTY OR "IMMORAL BEHAVIOR," OR HAD BEEN DISOWNED BY PARENTS, EXILED FOR CRIMES, AND OTHERWISE DRIVEN FROM THEIR PLACES OF BIRTH.

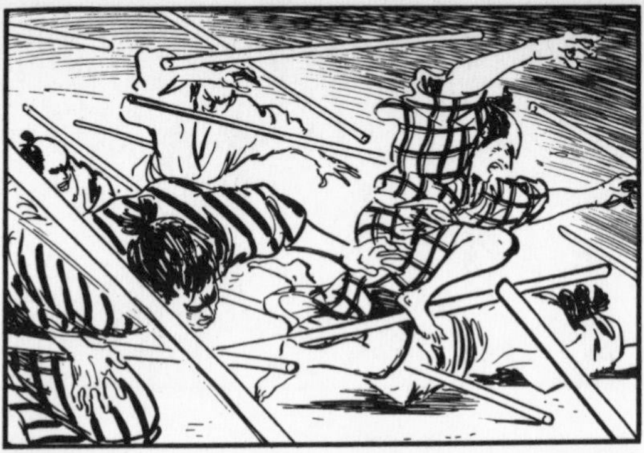

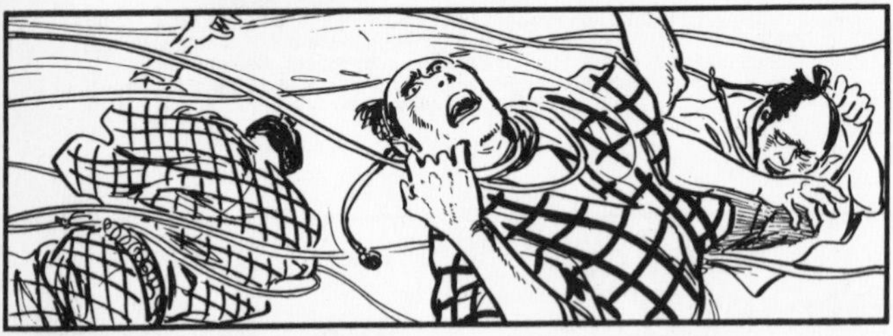

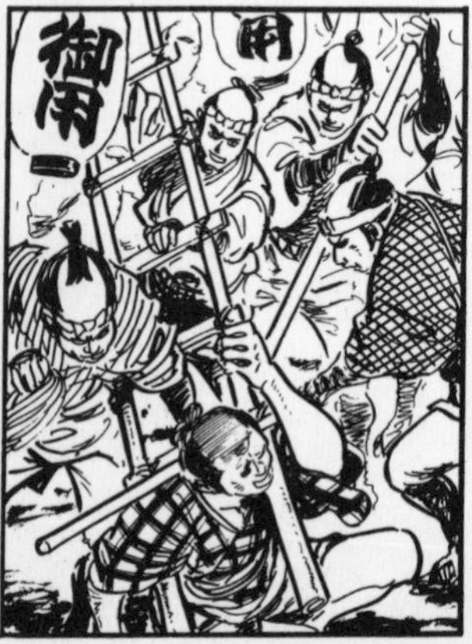
御用—
用

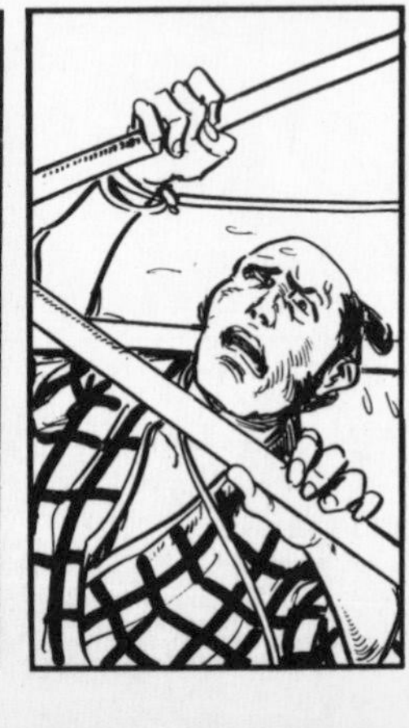

THE DRAGNETS FOR IMPRESSMENT, FROM WHICH FEW RETURNED ALIVE, WERE KNOWN AS *DOSA-GO-YŌ*, AND STRUCK TERROR INTO THE HEARTS OF THE DISPOSSESSED.

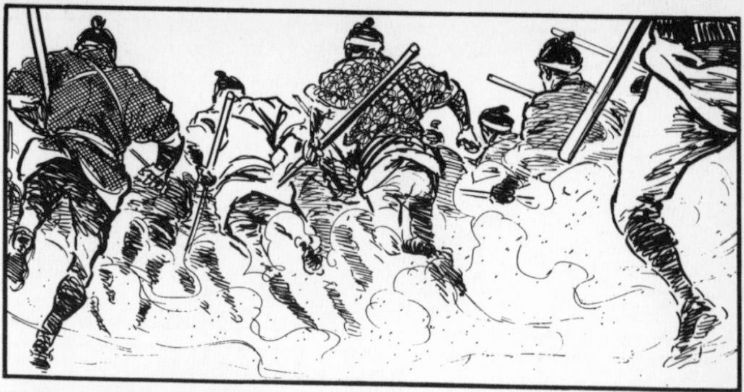

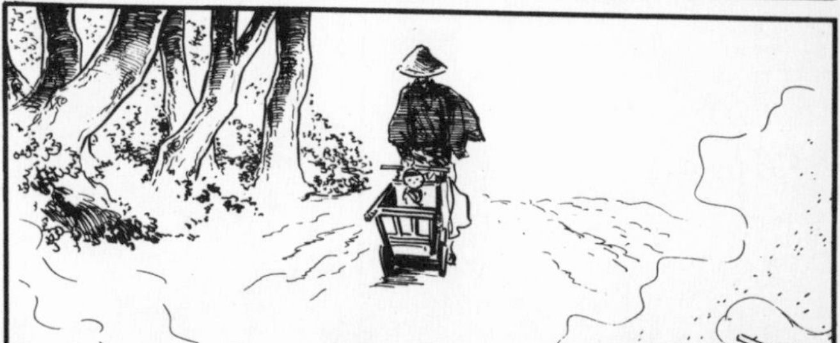

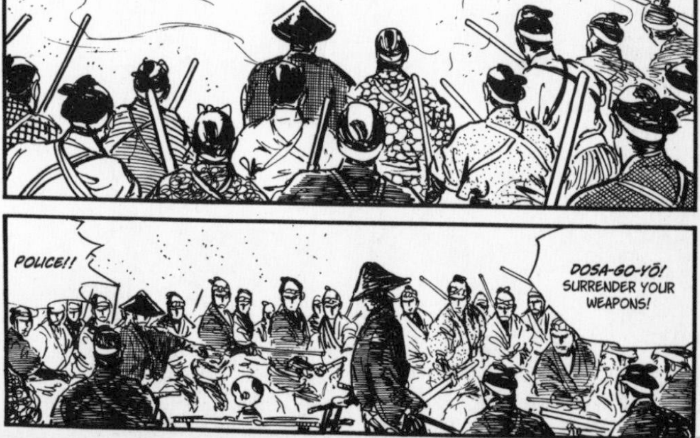
POLICE!!
DOSA-GO-YŌ! SURRENDER YOUR WEAPONS!

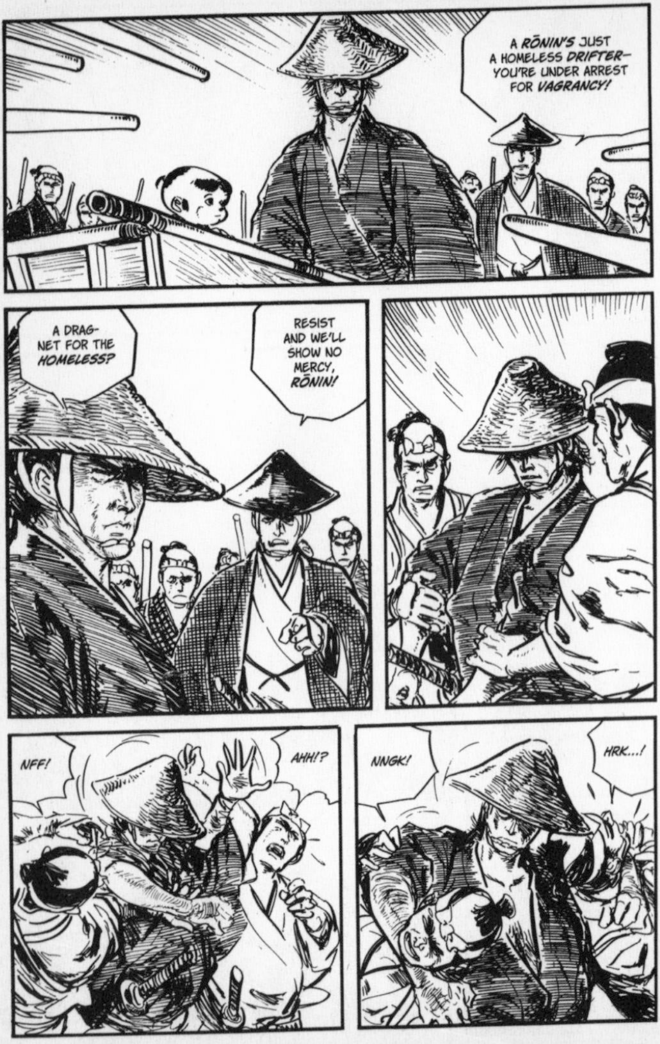
A RŌNIN'S JUST A HOMELESS DRIFTER— YOU'RE UNDER ARREST FOR VAGRANCY!
A DRAG-NET FOR THE HOMELESS?
RESIST AND WE'LL SHOW NO MERCY, RŌNIN!
NFF!
AHH!?
NNGK!
HRK...!

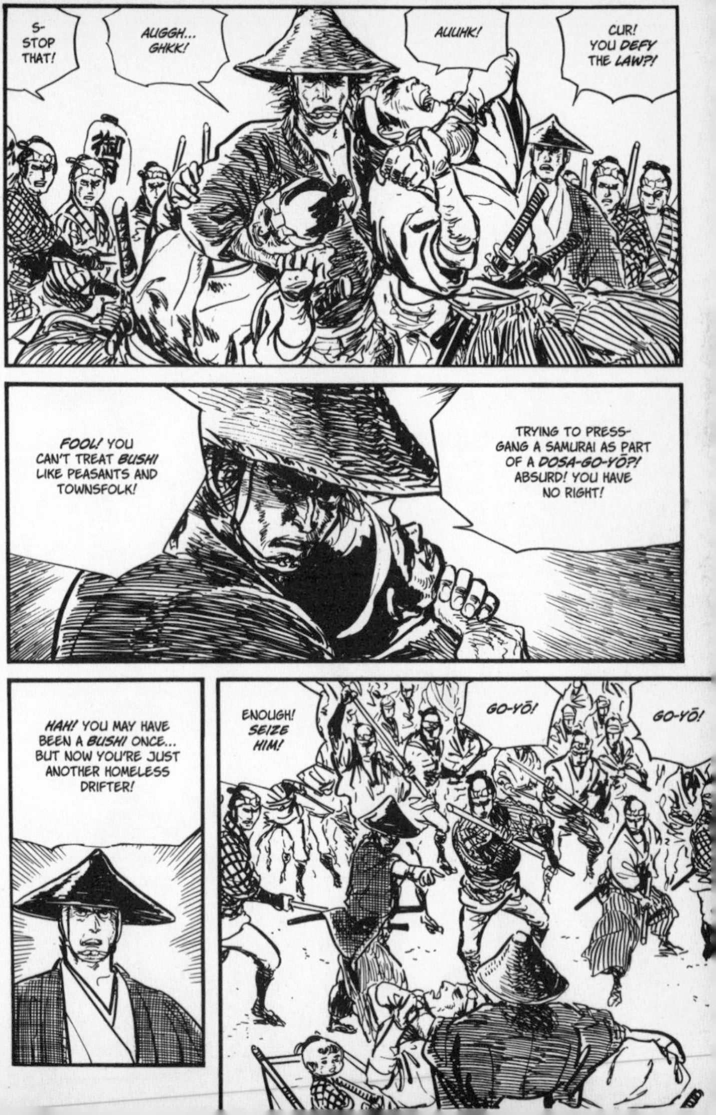
S-STOP THAT!
AUGGH... GHKK!
AUUHK!
CUR! YOU DEFY THE LAW?!
FOOL! YOU CAN'T TREAT BUSHI LIKE PEASANTS AND TOWNSFOLK!
TRYING TO PRESS-GANG A SAMURAI AS PART OF A DOSA-GO-YŌ?! ABSURD! YOU HAVE NO RIGHT!
HAH! YOU MAY HAVE BEEN A BUSHI ONCE... BUT NOW YOU'RE JUST ANOTHER HOMELESS DRIFTER!
ENOUGH! SEIZE HIM!
GO-YŌ!
GO-YŌ!

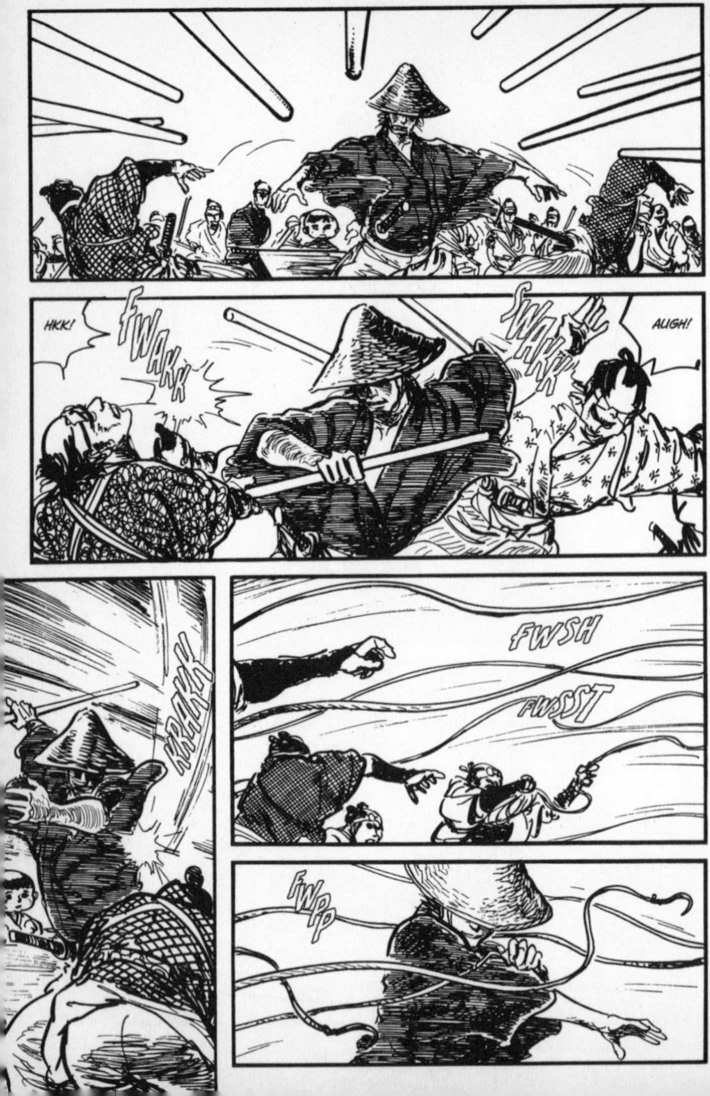
HKK!
FWAKK
FWAKK
AUGH!
KRAKK
FWSH
FWSST
FWPP

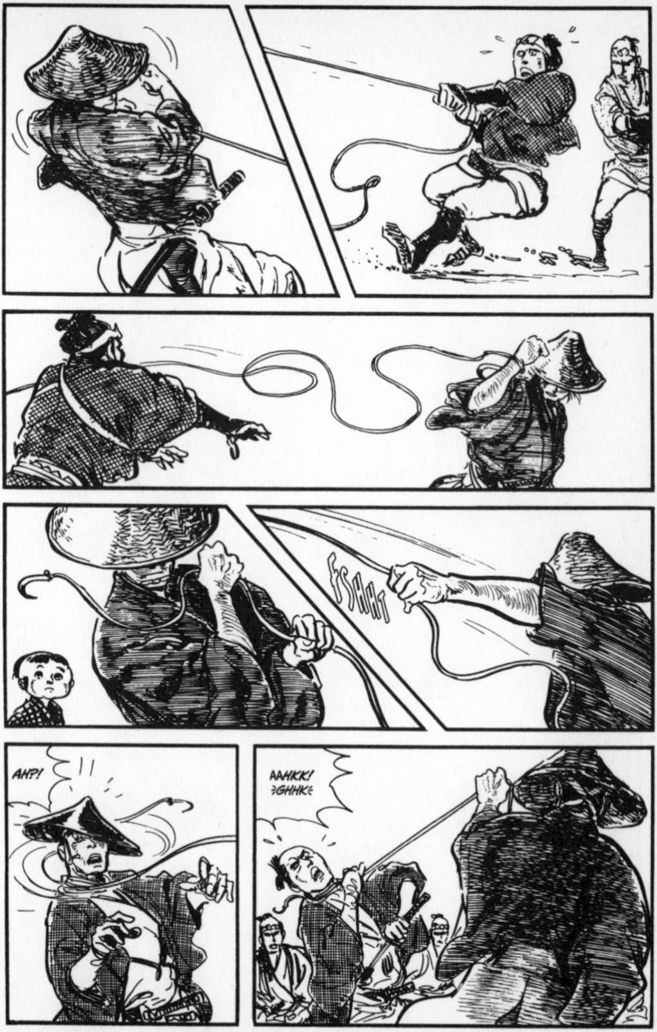
FSHHT
AH?!
AAHKK!
GHHK

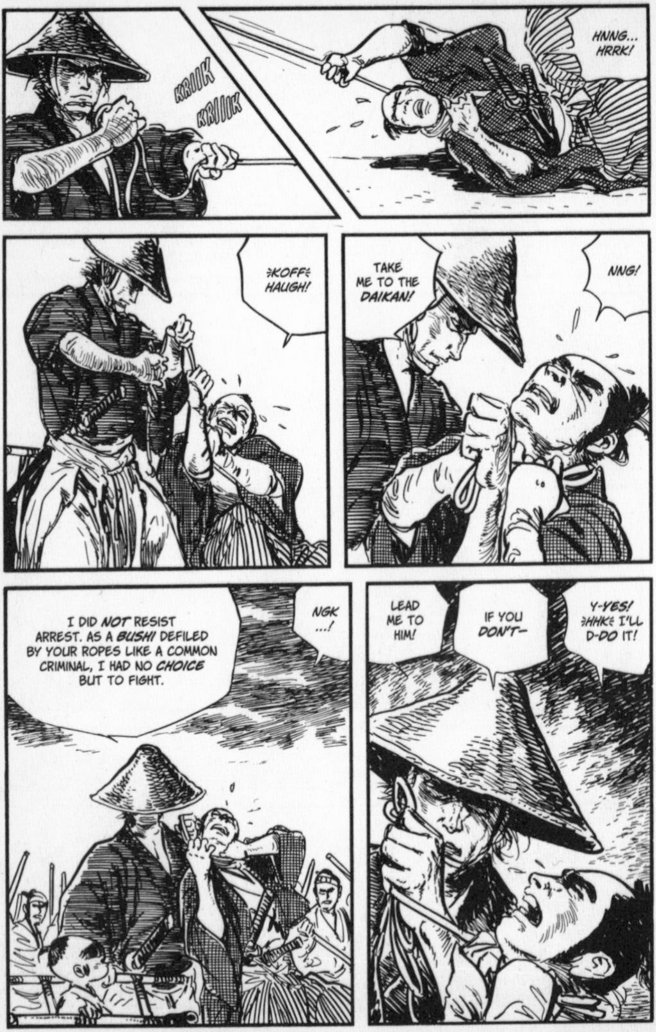
KRIIIK
KRIIIK
HNNG... HRRK!
≶KOFF≷ HAUGH!
TAKE ME TO THE DAIKAN!
NNG!
I DID NOT RESIST ARREST. AS A BUSHI DEFILED BY YOUR ROPES LIKE A COMMON CRIMINAL, I HAD NO CHOICE BUT TO FIGHT.
NGK ...!
LEAD ME TO HIM!
IF YOU DON'T–
Y-YES! ≶HHK≷ I'LL D-DO IT!

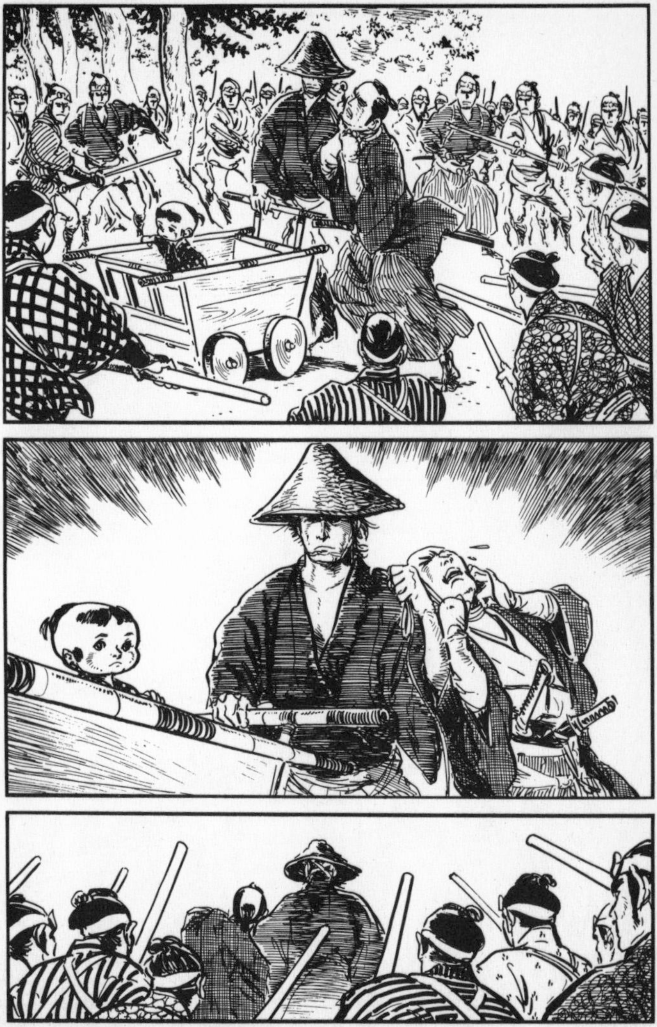

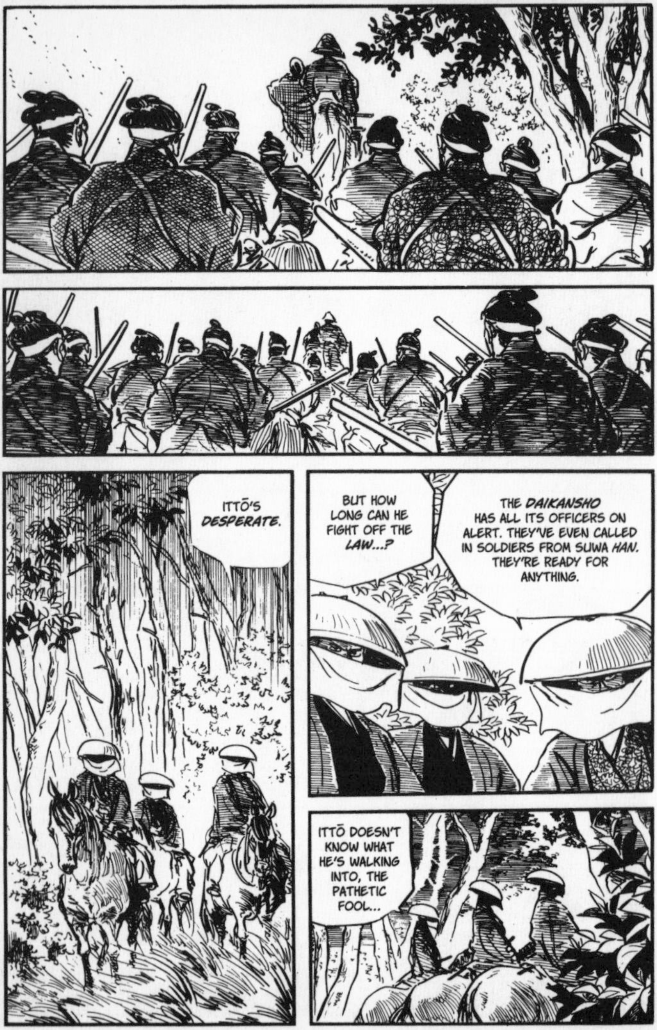
ITTŌ'S *DESPERATE.*
BUT HOW LONG CAN HE FIGHT OFF THE *LAW...?*
THE *DAIKANSHO* HAS ALL ITS OFFICERS ON ALERT. THEY'VE EVEN CALLED IN SOLDIERS FROM SUWA *HAN.* THEY'RE READY FOR ANYTHING.
ITTŌ DOESN'T KNOW WHAT HE'S WALKING INTO, THE PATHETIC FOOL...

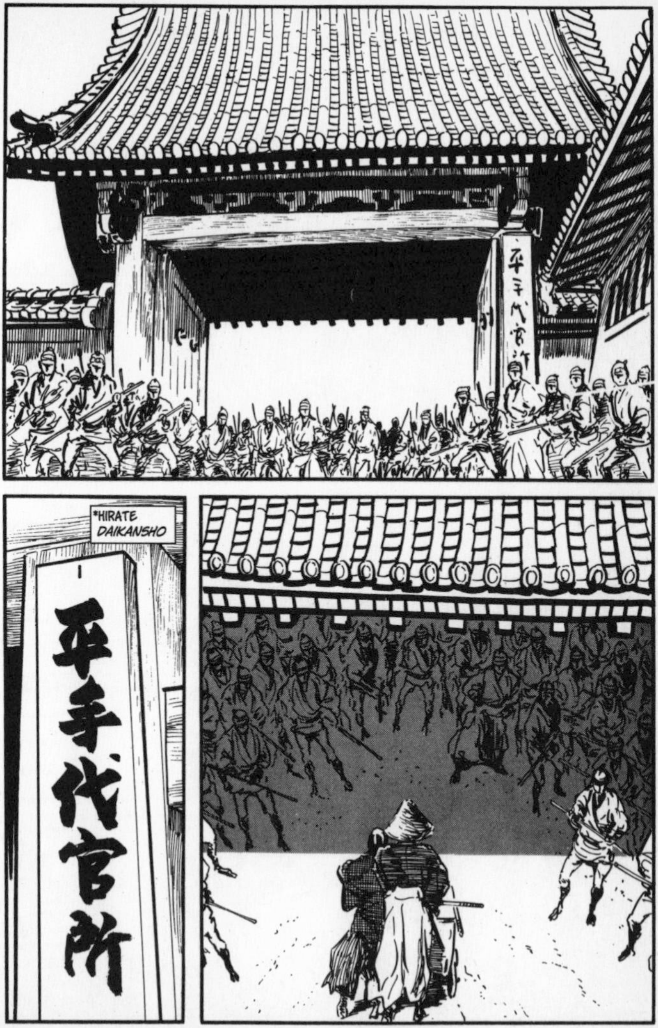
平手代官所
*HIRATE DAIKANSHO
平手代官所

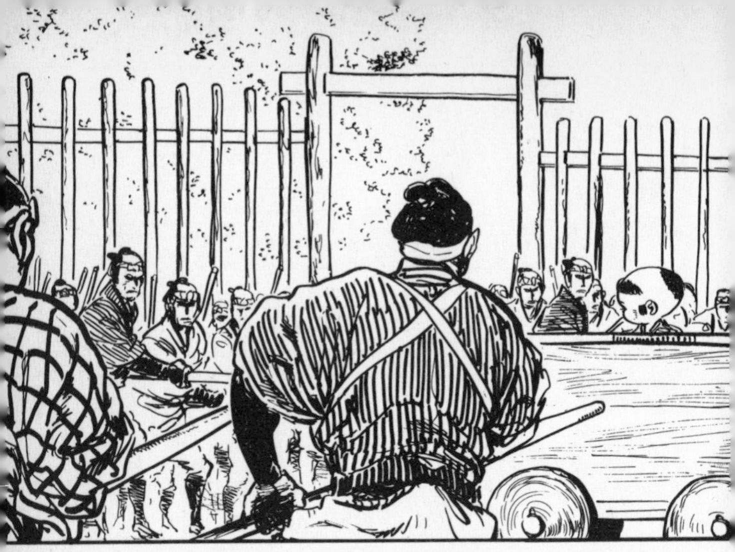

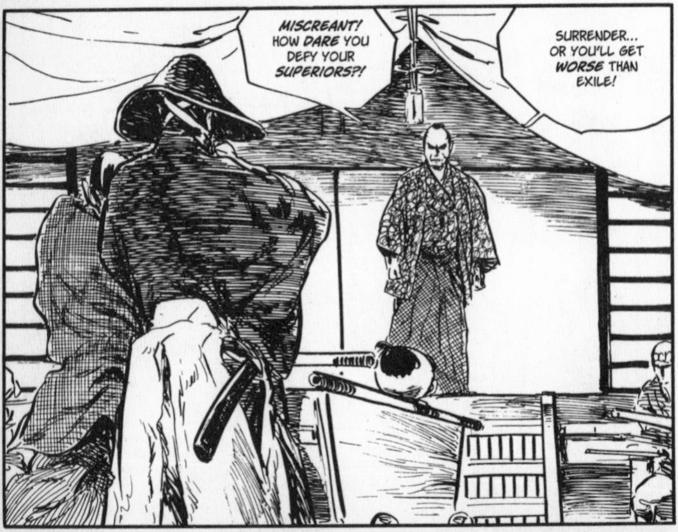
MISCREANT! HOW DARE YOU DEFY YOUR SUPERIORS?!
SURRENDER... OR YOU'LL GET WORSE THAN EXILE!

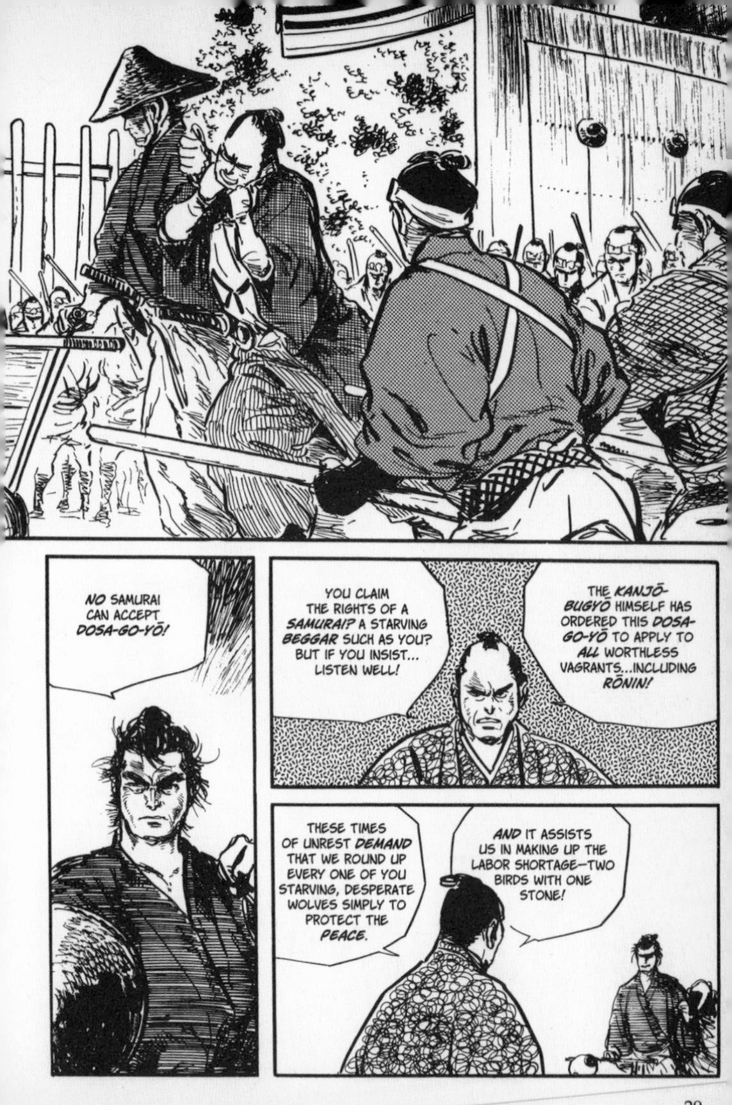
NO SAMURAI CAN ACCEPT DOSA-GO-YŌ!
YOU CLAIM THE RIGHTS OF A SAMURAI? A STARVING BEGGAR SUCH AS YOU? BUT IF YOU INSIST... LISTEN WELL!
THE KANJŌ-BUGYŌ HIMSELF HAS ORDERED THIS DOSA-GO-YŌ TO APPLY TO ALL WORTHLESS VAGRANTS...INCLUDING RŌNIN!
THESE TIMES OF UNREST DEMAND THAT WE ROUND UP EVERY ONE OF YOU STARVING, DESPERATE WOLVES SIMPLY TO PROTECT THE PEACE.
AND IT ASSISTS US IN MAKING UP THE LABOR SHORTAGE—TWO BIRDS WITH ONE STONE!

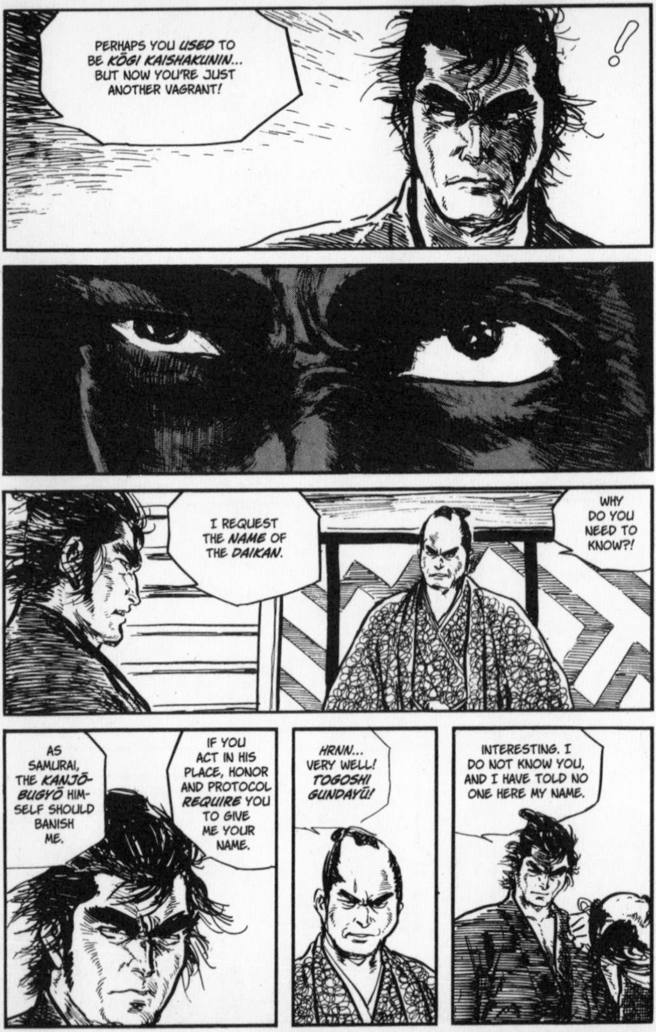
PERHAPS YOU *USED* TO BE *KŌGI KAISHAKUNIN*... BUT NOW YOU'RE JUST ANOTHER VAGRANT!
!
I REQUEST THE *NAME* OF THE *DAIKAN*.
WHY DO YOU NEED TO KNOW?!
AS SAMURAI, THE *KANJŌ-BUGYŌ* HIMSELF SHOULD BANISH ME.
IF YOU ACT IN HIS PLACE, HONOR AND PROTOCOL *REQUIRE* YOU TO GIVE ME YOUR NAME.
HRNN... VERY WELL! TOGOSHI GUNDAYŪ!
INTERESTING. I DO NOT KNOW YOU, AND I HAVE TOLD NO ONE HERE MY NAME.

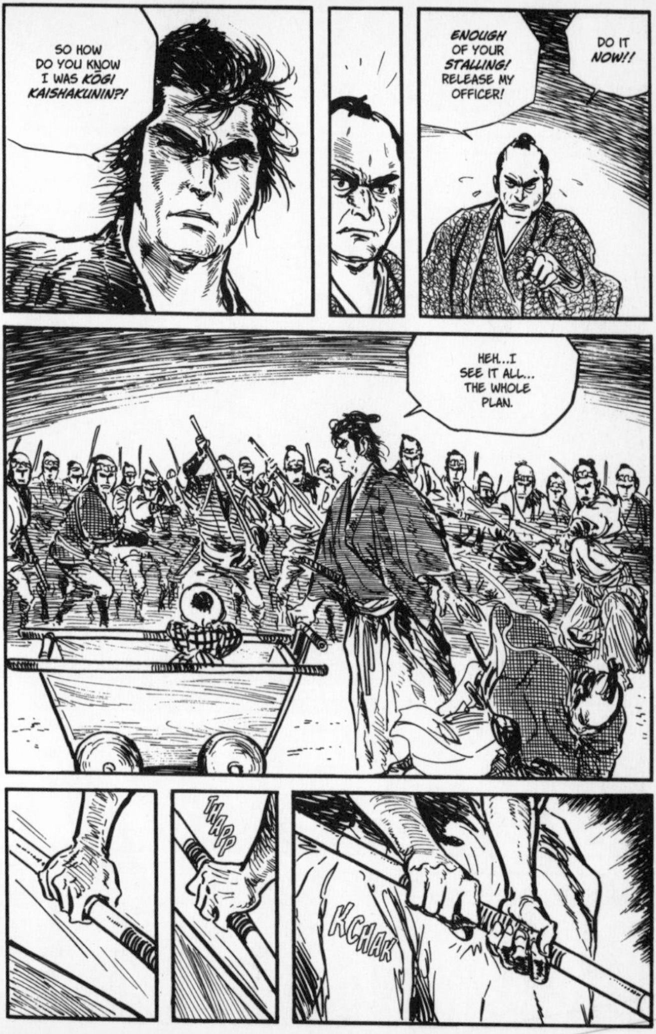
SO HOW DO YOU KNOW I WAS KŌGI KAISHAKUNIN?!
ENOUGH OF YOUR STALLING! RELEASE MY OFFICER!
DO IT NOW!!
HEH...I SEE IT ALL... THE WHOLE PLAN.
THAPP
KCHAK

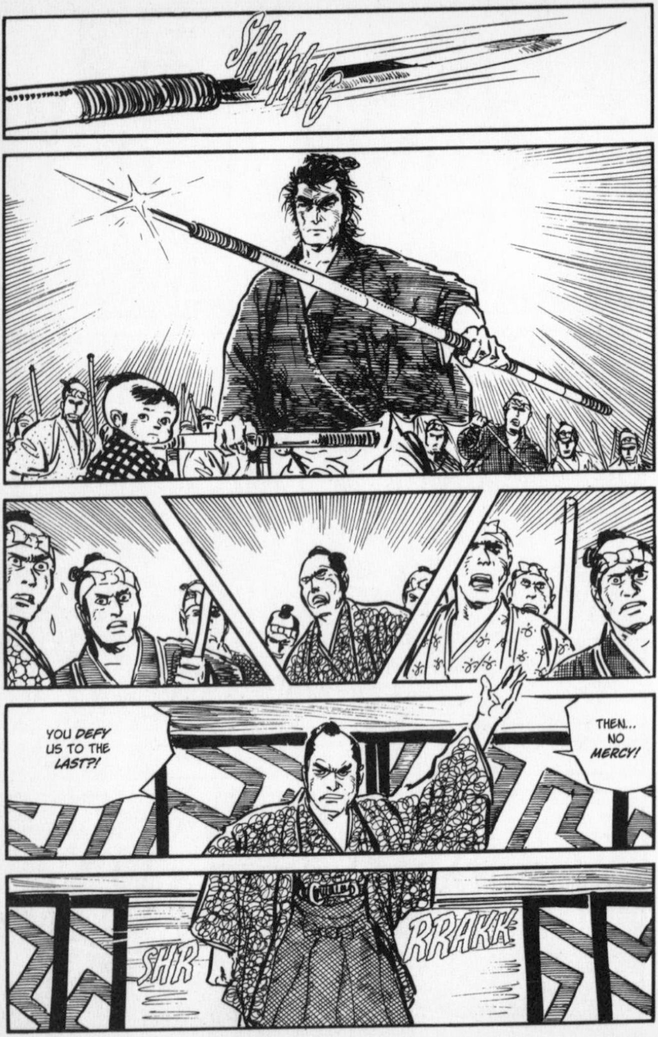
SHINNG
YOU DEFY US TO THE LAST?!
THEN... NO MERCY!
SHR
RRAKK

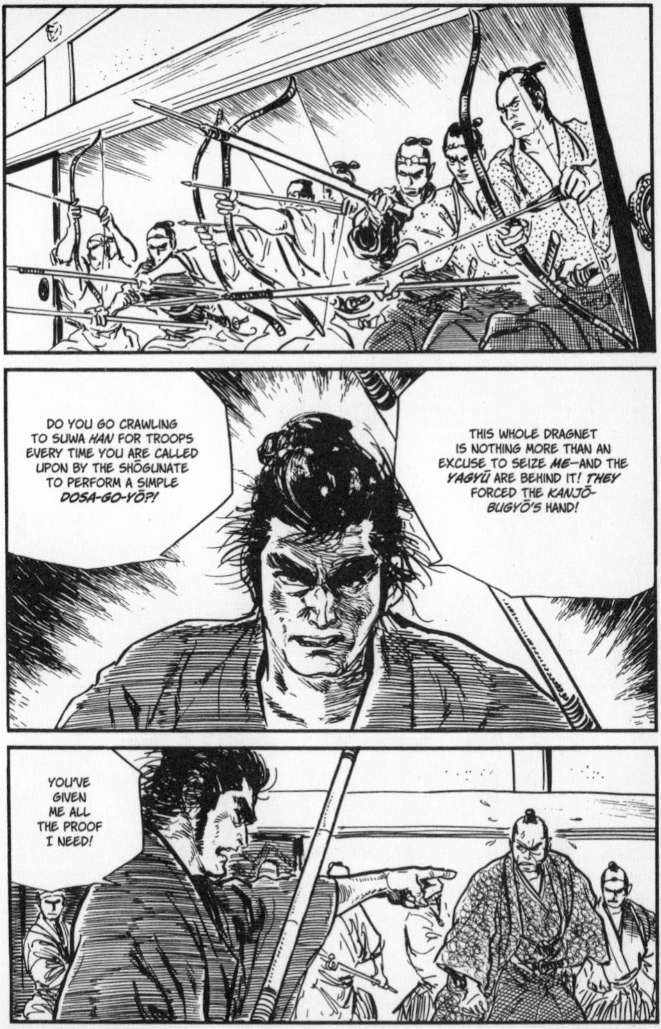
DO YOU GO CRAWLING TO SUWA *HAN* FOR TROOPS EVERY TIME YOU ARE CALLED UPON BY THE SHŌGUNATE TO PERFORM A SIMPLE *DOSA-GO-YŌ?!*
THIS WHOLE DRAGNET IS NOTHING MORE THAN AN EXCUSE TO SEIZE *ME*—AND THE *YAGYŪ* ARE BEHIND IT! *THEY* FORCED THE *KANJŌ-BUGYŌ'S* HAND!
YOU'VE GIVEN ME ALL THE PROOF I NEED!

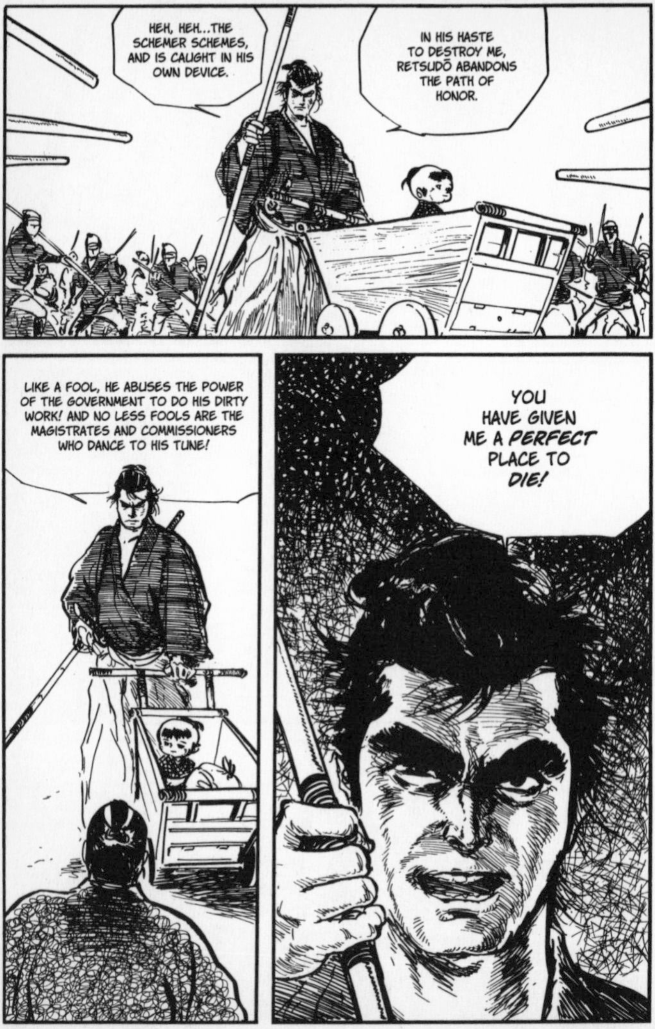
HEH, HEH...THE SCHEMER SCHEMES, AND IS CAUGHT IN HIS OWN DEVICE.
IN HIS HASTE TO DESTROY ME, RETSUDŌ ABANDONS THE PATH OF HONOR.
LIKE A FOOL, HE ABUSES THE POWER OF THE GOVERNMENT TO DO HIS DIRTY WORK! AND NO LESS FOOLS ARE THE MAGISTRATES AND COMMISSIONERS WHO DANCE TO HIS TUNE!
YOU HAVE GIVEN ME A *PERFECT* PLACE TO *DIE!*

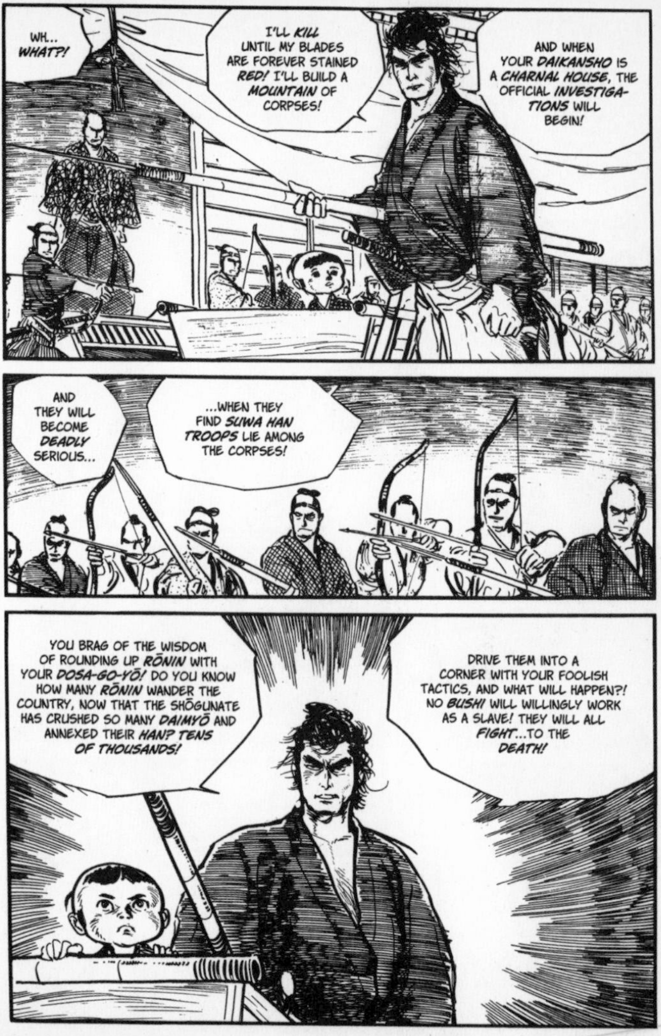
WH... WHAT?!
I'LL KILL UNTIL MY BLADES ARE FOREVER STAINED RED! I'LL BUILD A MOUNTAIN OF CORPSES!
AND WHEN YOUR DAIKANSHO IS A CHARNAL HOUSE, THE OFFICIAL INVESTIGATIONS WILL BEGIN!
AND THEY WILL BECOME DEADLY SERIOUS...
...WHEN THEY FIND SUWA HAN TROOPS LIE AMONG THE CORPSES!
YOU BRAG OF THE WISDOM OF ROUNDING UP RŌNIN WITH YOUR DOSA-GO-YŌ! DO YOU KNOW HOW MANY RŌNIN WANDER THE COUNTRY, NOW THAT THE SHŌGUNATE HAS CRUSHED SO MANY DAIMYŌ AND ANNEXED THEIR HAN? TENS OF THOUSANDS!
DRIVE THEM INTO A CORNER WITH YOUR FOOLISH TACTICS, AND WHAT WILL HAPPEN?! NO BUSHI WILL WILLINGLY WORK AS A SLAVE! THEY WILL ALL FIGHT...TO THE DEATH!

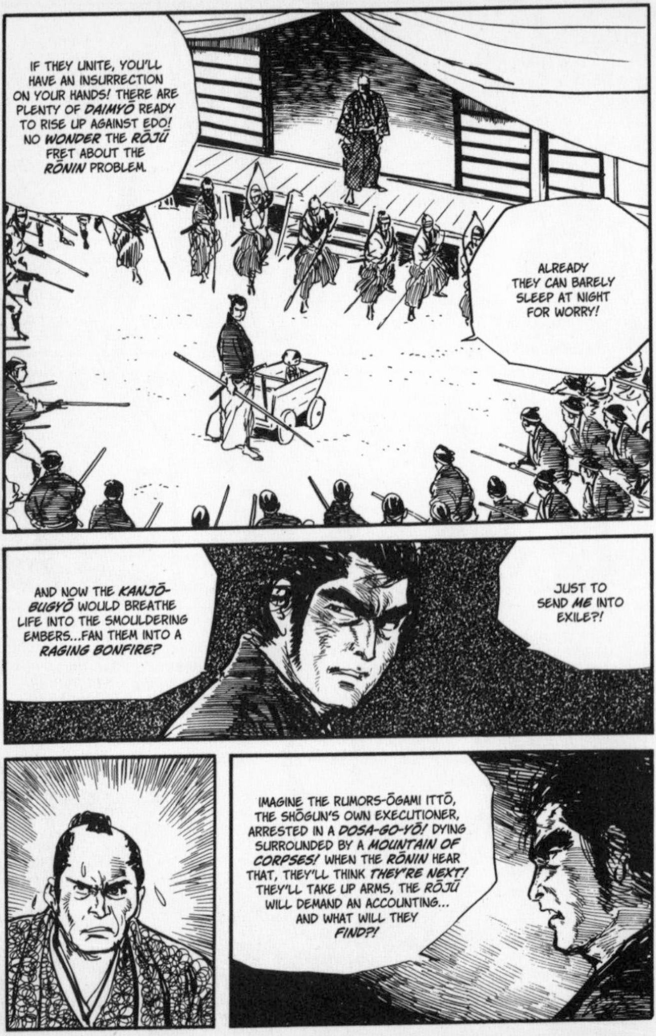
IF THEY UNITE, YOU'LL HAVE AN INSURRECTION ON YOUR HANDS! THERE ARE PLENTY OF DAIMYŌ READY TO RISE UP AGAINST EDO! NO WONDER THE RŌJŪ FRET ABOUT THE RŌNIN PROBLEM.
ALREADY THEY CAN BARELY SLEEP AT NIGHT FOR WORRY!
AND NOW THE KANJŌ-BUGYŌ WOULD BREATHE LIFE INTO THE SMOULDERING EMBERS...FAN THEM INTO A RAGING BONFIRE?
JUST TO SEND ME INTO EXILE?!
IMAGINE THE RUMORS-ŌGAMI ITTŌ, THE SHŌGUN'S OWN EXECUTIONER, ARRESTED IN A DOSA-GO-YŌ! DYING SURROUNDED BY A MOUNTAIN OF CORPSES! WHEN THE RŌNIN HEAR THAT, THEY'LL THINK THEY'RE NEXT! THEY'LL TAKE UP ARMS, THE RŌJŪ WILL DEMAND AN ACCOUNTING... AND WHAT WILL THEY FIND?!

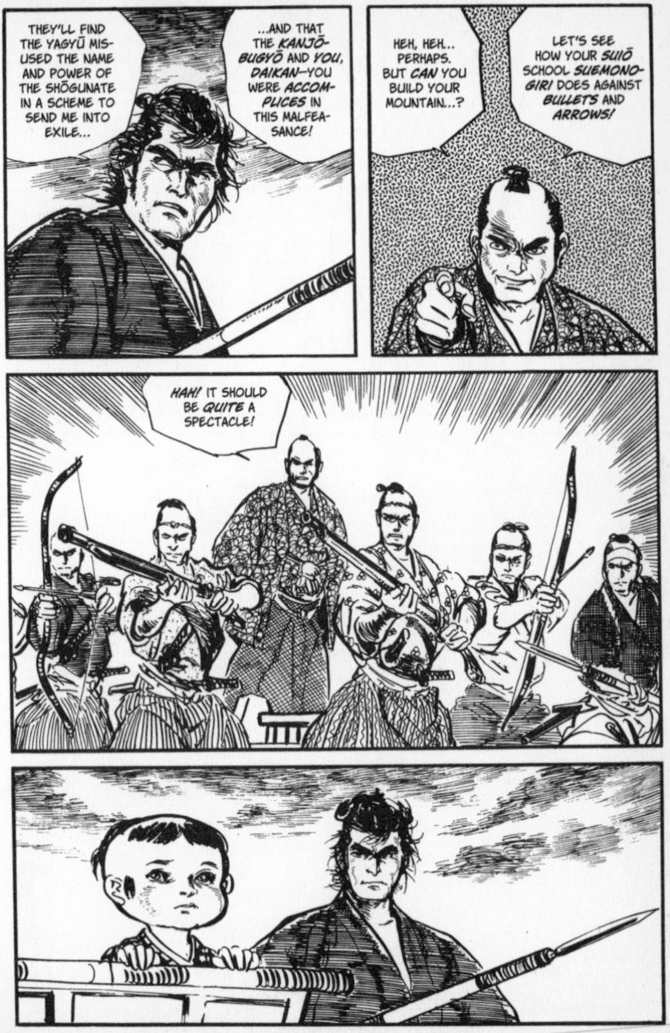
THEY'LL FIND THE YAGYŪ MIS-USED THE NAME AND POWER OF THE SHŌGUNATE IN A SCHEME TO SEND ME INTO EXILE...
...AND THAT THE KANJŌ-BUGYŌ AND YOU, DAIKAN—YOU WERE ACCOMPLICES IN THIS MALFEASANCE!
HEH, HEH.. PERHAPS. BUT CAN YOU BUILD YOUR MOUNTAIN...?
LET'S SEE HOW YOUR SUIŌ SCHOOL SUEMONO-GIRI DOES AGAINST BULLETS AND ARROWS!
HAH! IT SHOULD BE QUITE A SPECTACLE!

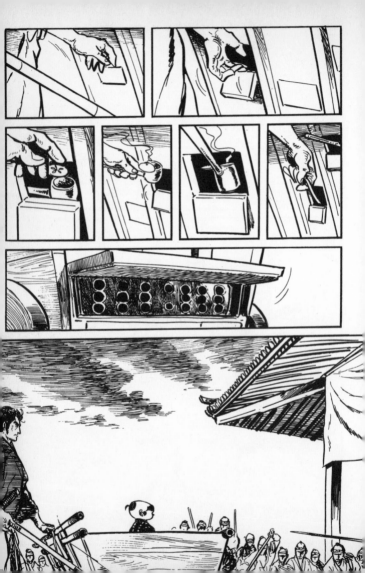

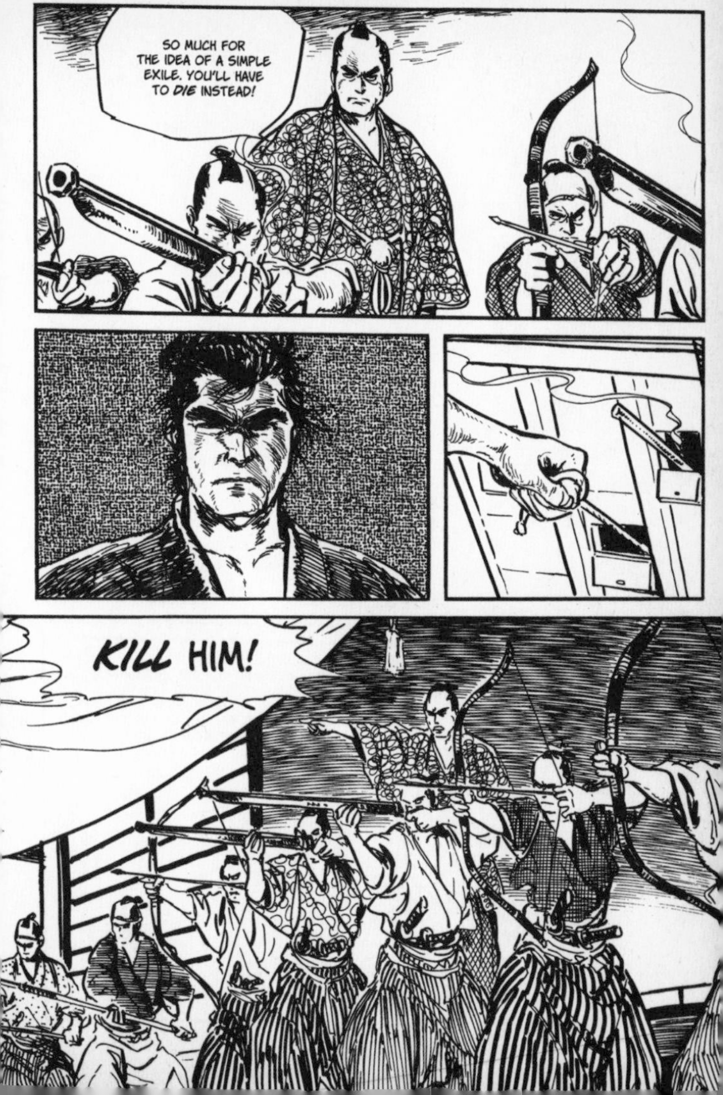
SO MUCH FOR THE IDEA OF A SIMPLE EXILE. YOU'LL HAVE TO *DIE* INSTEAD!
KILL HIM!

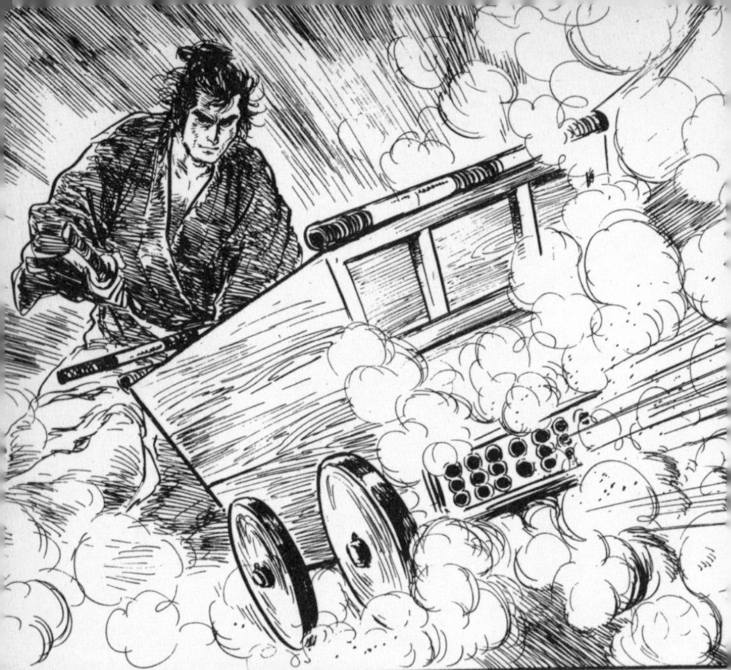

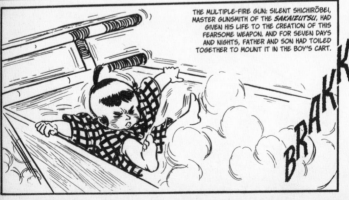

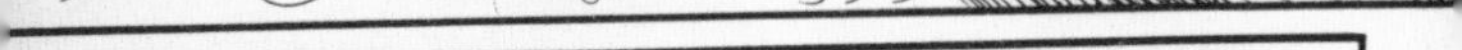
THE MULTIPLE-FIRE GUN: SILENT SHICHIRŌBEI, MASTER GUNSMITH OF THE *SAKAIZUTSU*, HAD GIVEN HIS LIFE TO THE CREATION OF THIS FEARSOME WEAPON. AND FOR SEVEN DAYS AND NIGHTS, FATHER AND SON HAD TOILED TOGETHER TO MOUNT IT IN THE BOY'S CART.
BRAKKA

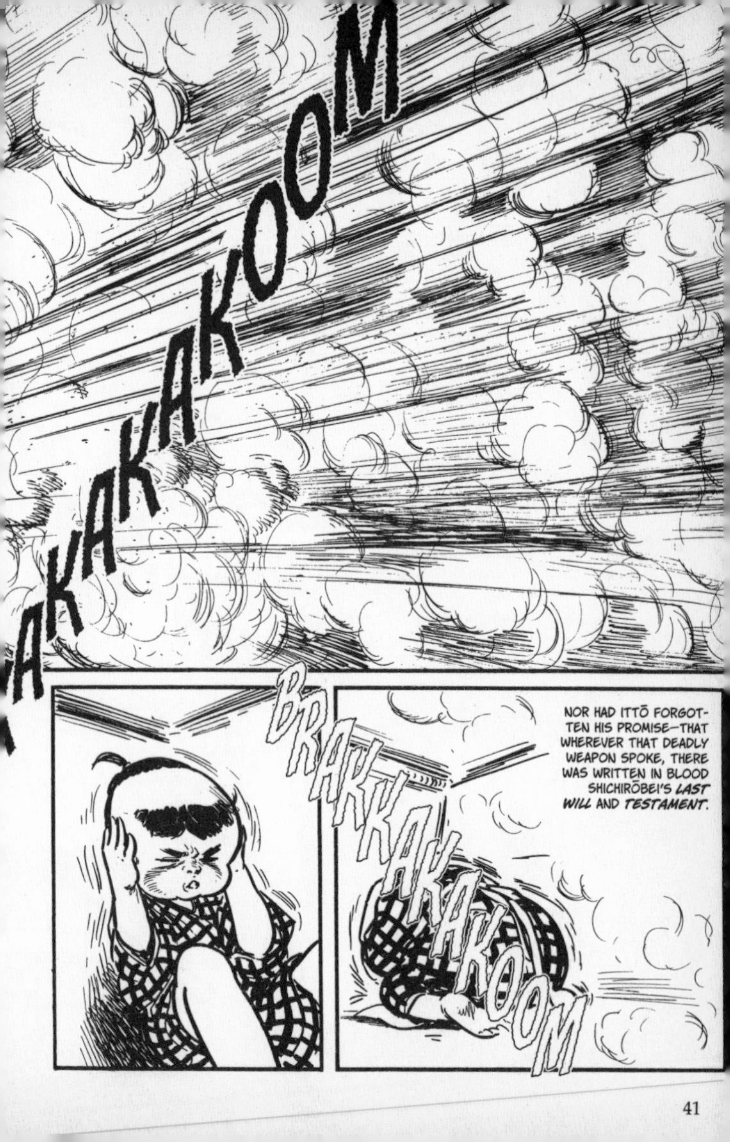
AKAKAKAKOOM
BRAKKAKAKAKOOM
NOR HAD ITTŌ FORGOTTEN HIS PROMISE—THAT WHEREVER THAT DEADLY WEAPON SPOKE, THERE WAS WRITTEN IN BLOOD SHICHIRŌBEI'S *LAST WILL* AND *TESTAMENT*.

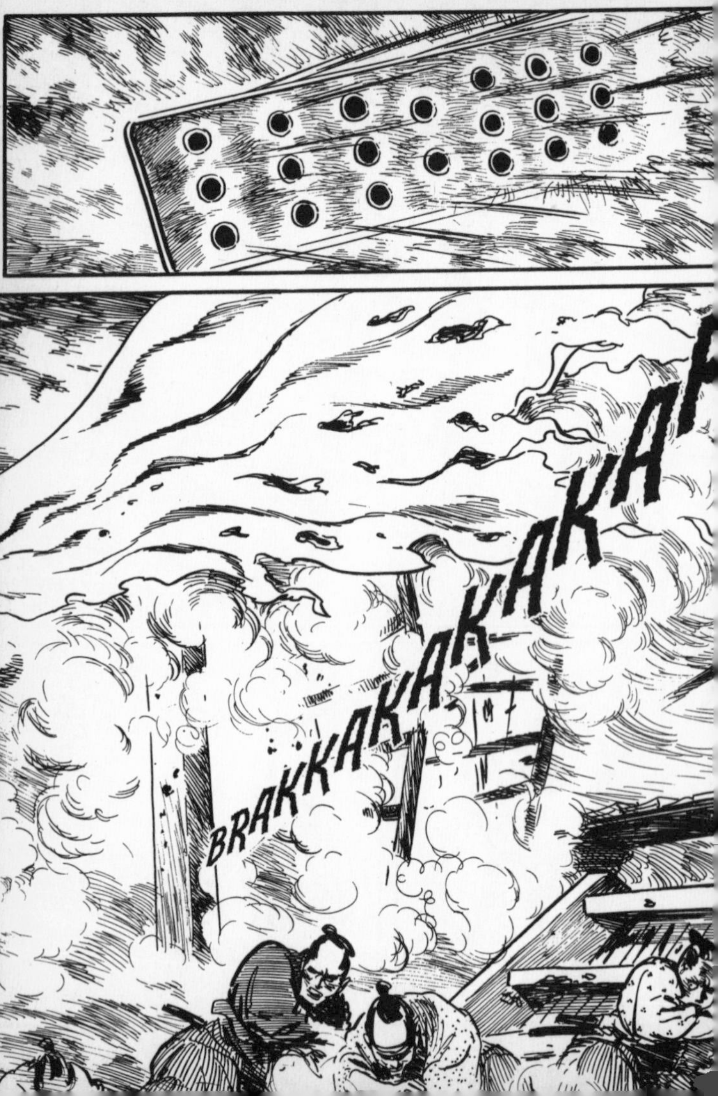
BRAKKAKAKAKAKAKA

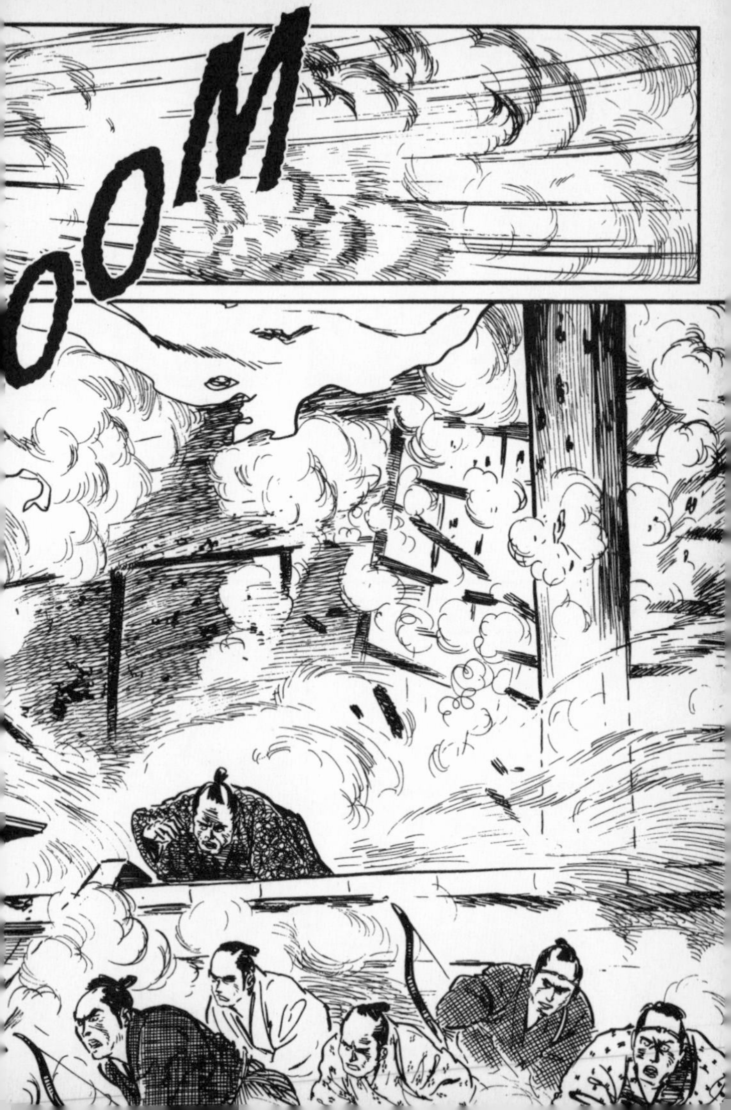
OOM

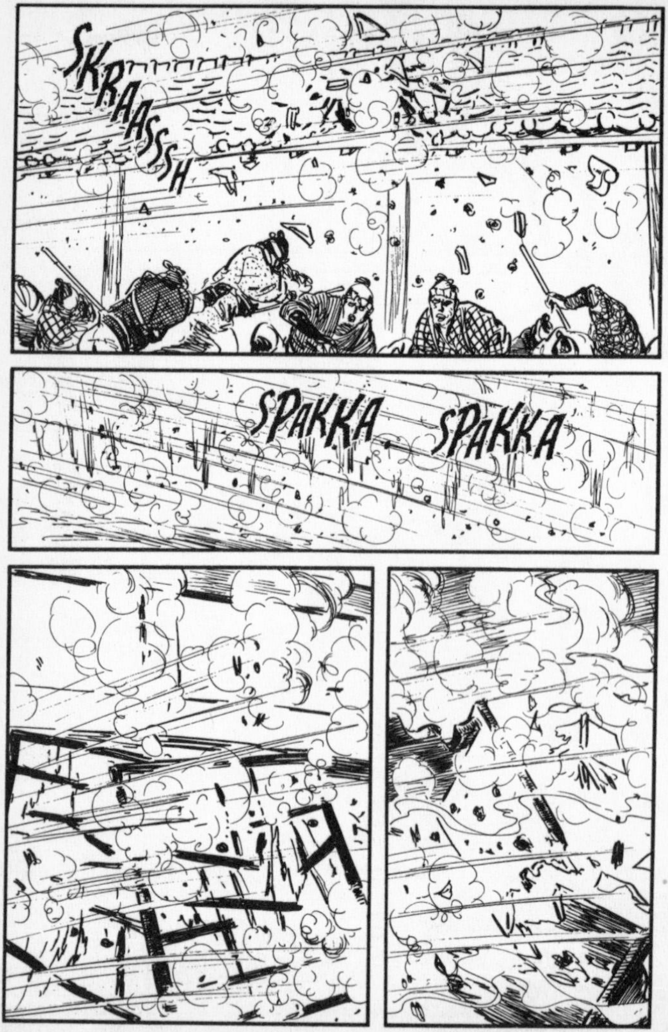
SKRAASSSH
SPAKKA SPAKKA

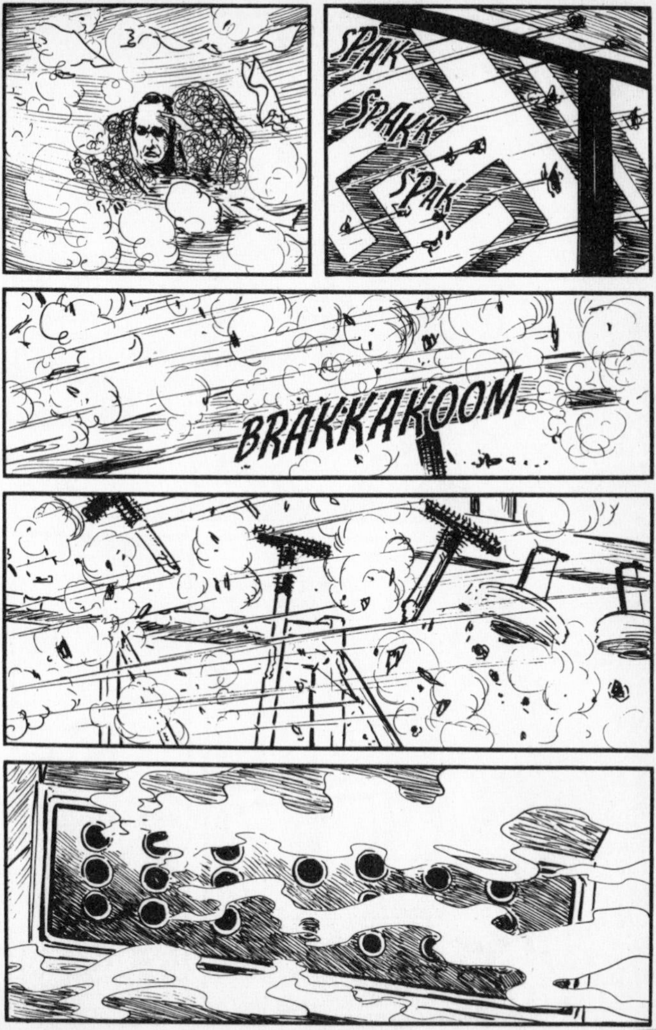
SPAK
SPAKK
SPAK
BRAKKAKOOM

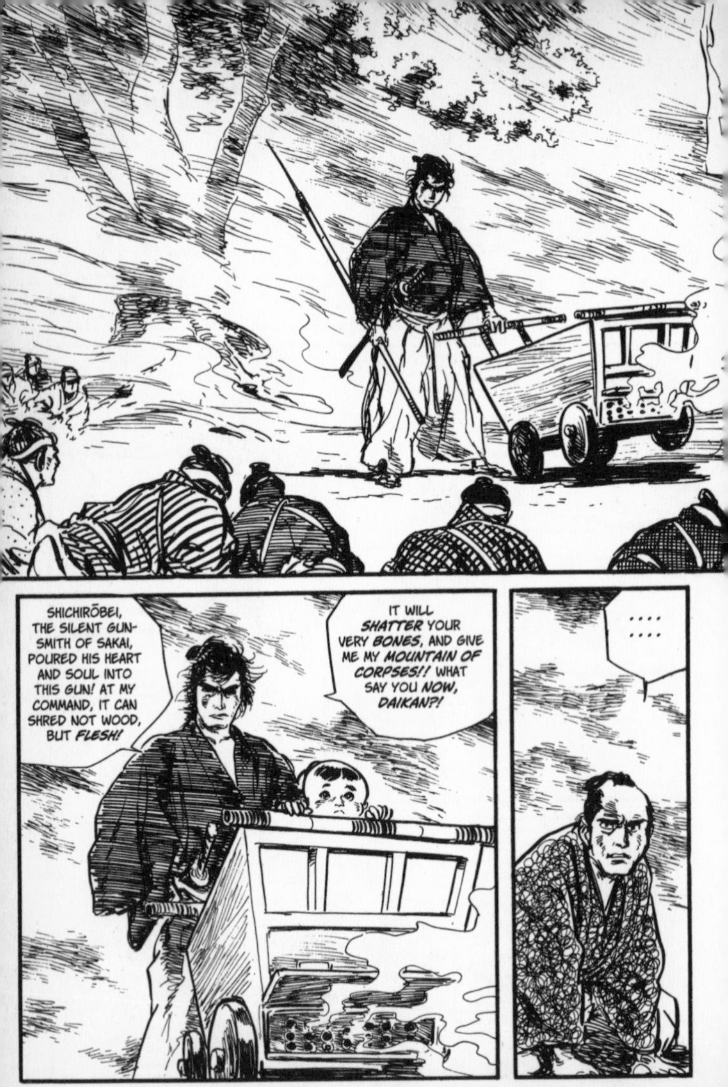
SHICHIRŌBEI, THE SILENT GUNSMITH OF SAKAI, POURED HIS HEART AND SOUL INTO THIS GUN! AT MY COMMAND, IT CAN SHRED NOT WOOD, BUT *FLESH!*
IT WILL *SHATTER* YOUR VERY *BONES,* AND GIVE ME MY *MOUNTAIN OF CORPSES!!* WHAT SAY YOU *NOW, DAIKAN?!*
....
....

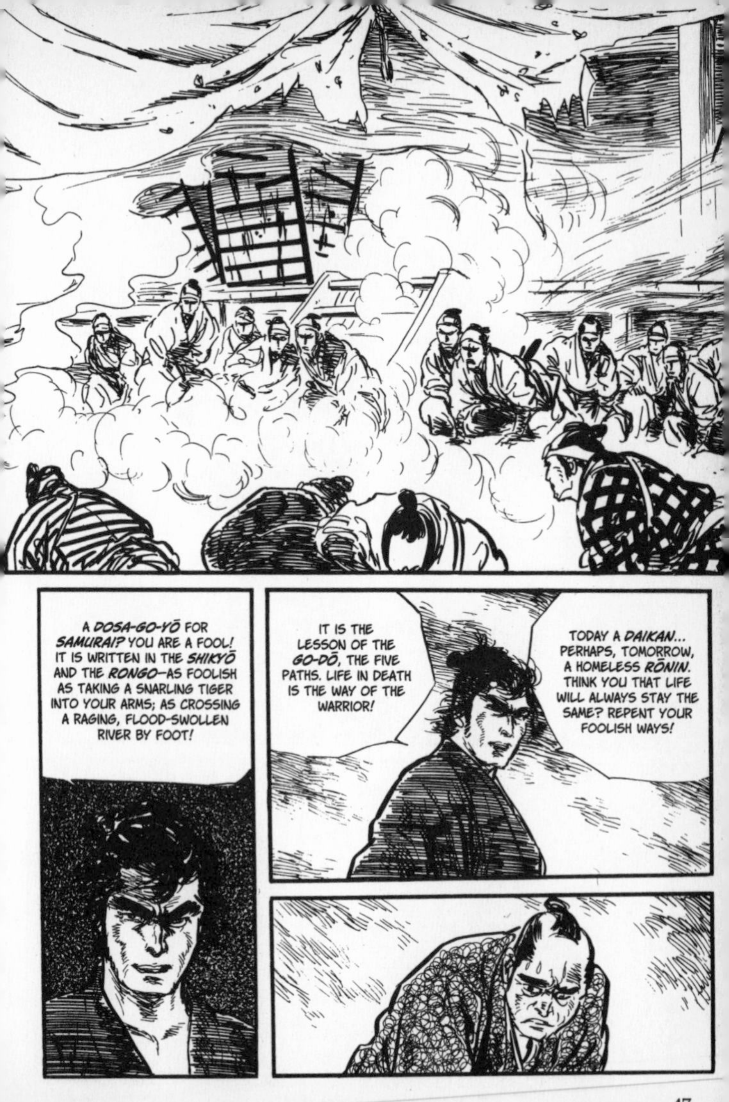
A *DOSA-GO-YŌ* FOR *SAMURAI?* YOU ARE A FOOL! IT IS WRITTEN IN THE *SHIKYŌ* AND THE *RONGO*—AS FOOLISH AS TAKING A SNARLING TIGER INTO YOUR ARMS; AS CROSSING A RAGING, FLOOD-SWOLLEN RIVER BY FOOT!
IT IS THE LESSON OF THE *GO-DŌ*, THE FIVE PATHS. LIFE IN DEATH IS THE WAY OF THE WARRIOR!
TODAY A *DAIKAN*... PERHAPS, TOMORROW, A HOMELESS *RŌNIN*. THINK YOU THAT LIFE WILL ALWAYS STAY THE SAME? REPENT YOUR FOOLISH WAYS!

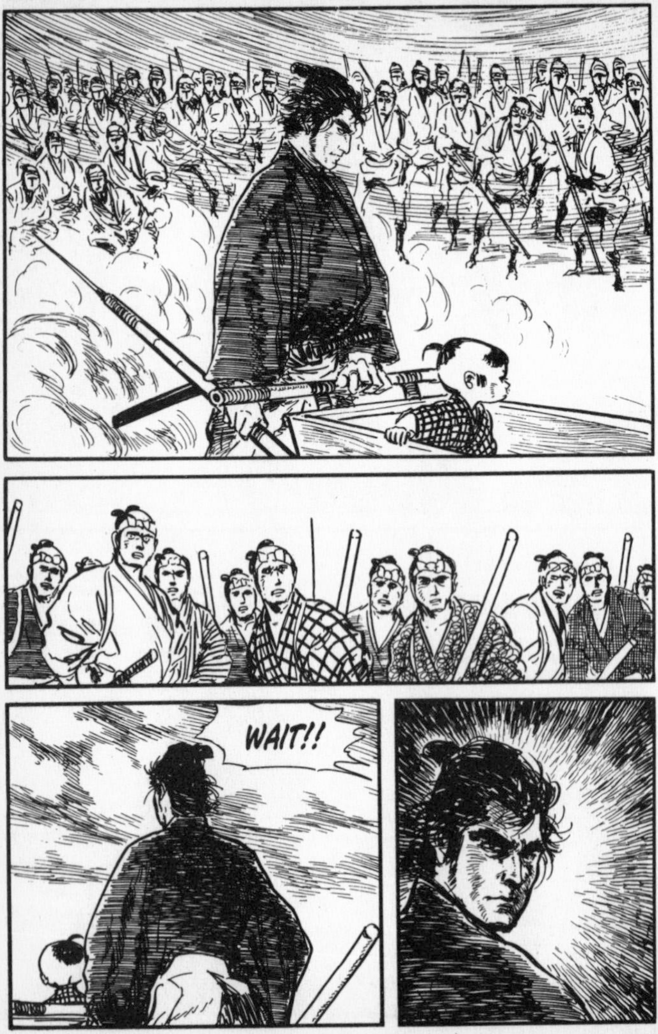
WAIT!!

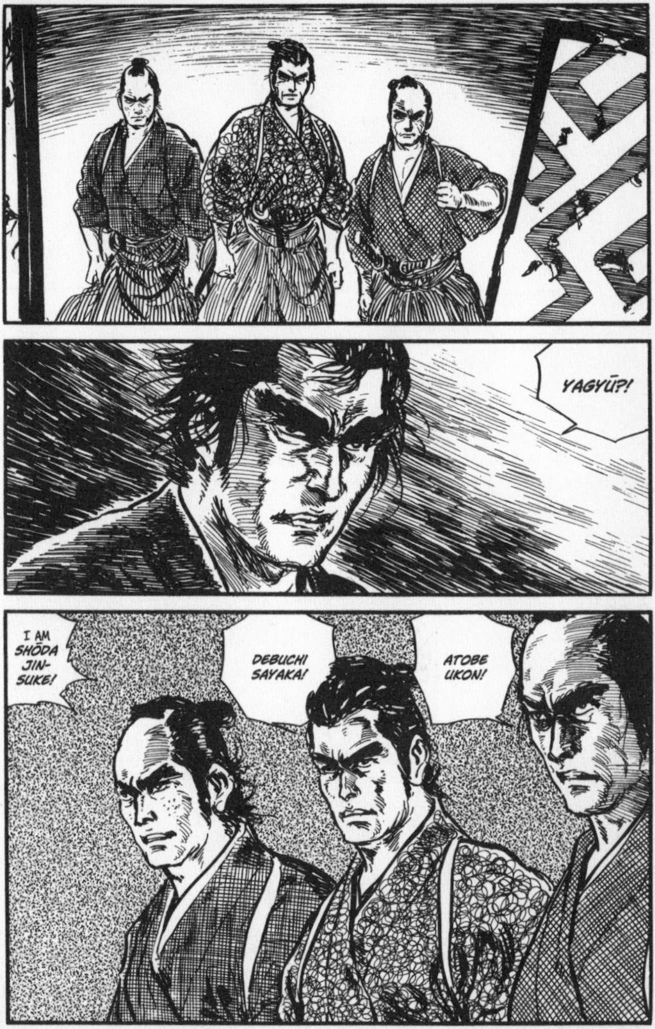
YAGYŪ?!
I AM SHŌDA JIN-SUKE!
DEBUCHI SAYAKA!
ATOBE UKON!

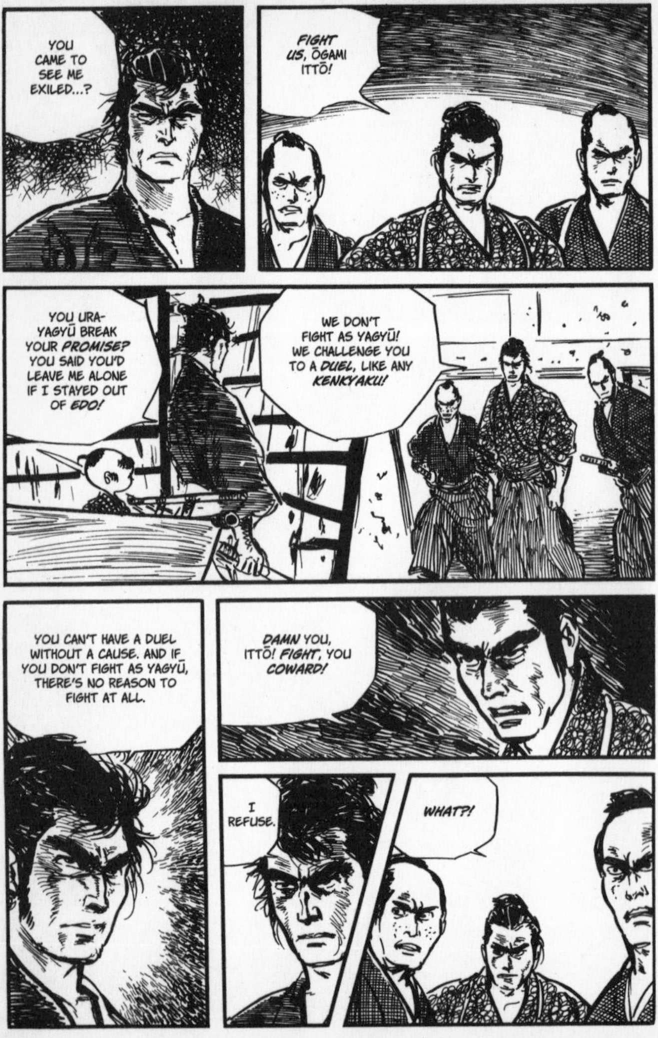
YOU CAME TO SEE ME EXILED...?
FIGHT US, ŌGAMI ITTŌ!
YOU URA-YAGYŪ BREAK YOUR PROMISE? YOU SAID YOU'D LEAVE ME ALONE IF I STAYED OUT OF EDO!
WE DON'T FIGHT AS YAGYŪ! WE CHALLENGE YOU TO A DUEL, LIKE ANY KENKYAKU!
YOU CAN'T HAVE A DUEL WITHOUT A CAUSE. AND IF YOU DON'T FIGHT AS YAGYŪ, THERE'S NO REASON TO FIGHT AT ALL.
DAMN YOU, ITTŌ! FIGHT, YOU COWARD!
I REFUSE.
WHAT?!

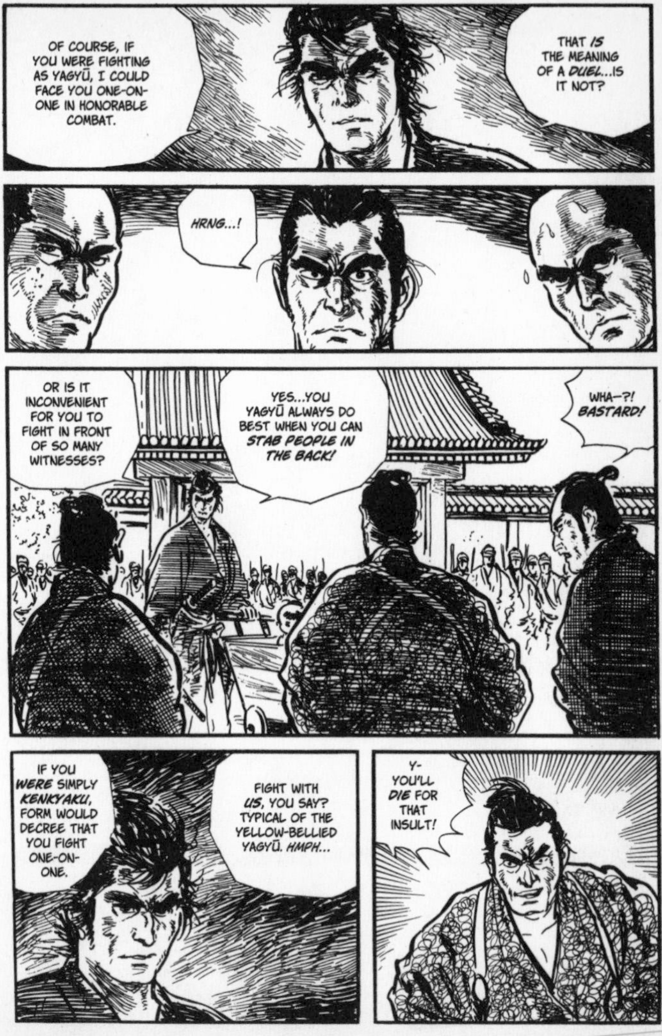
OF COURSE, IF YOU WERE FIGHTING AS YAGYŪ, I COULD FACE YOU ONE-ON-ONE IN HONORABLE COMBAT.
THAT *IS* THE MEANING OF A *DUEL*...IS IT NOT?
HRNG...!
OR IS IT INCONVENIENT FOR YOU TO FIGHT IN FRONT OF SO MANY WITNESSES?
YES...YOU YAGYŪ ALWAYS DO BEST WHEN YOU CAN *STAB PEOPLE IN THE BACK!*
WHA-?! *BASTARD!*
IF YOU *WERE* SIMPLY *KENKYAKU*, FORM WOULD DECREE THAT YOU FIGHT ONE-ON-ONE.
FIGHT WITH *US*, YOU SAY? TYPICAL OF THE YELLOW-BELLIED YAGYŪ. *HMPH...*
Y- YOU'LL *DIE* FOR THAT INSULT!

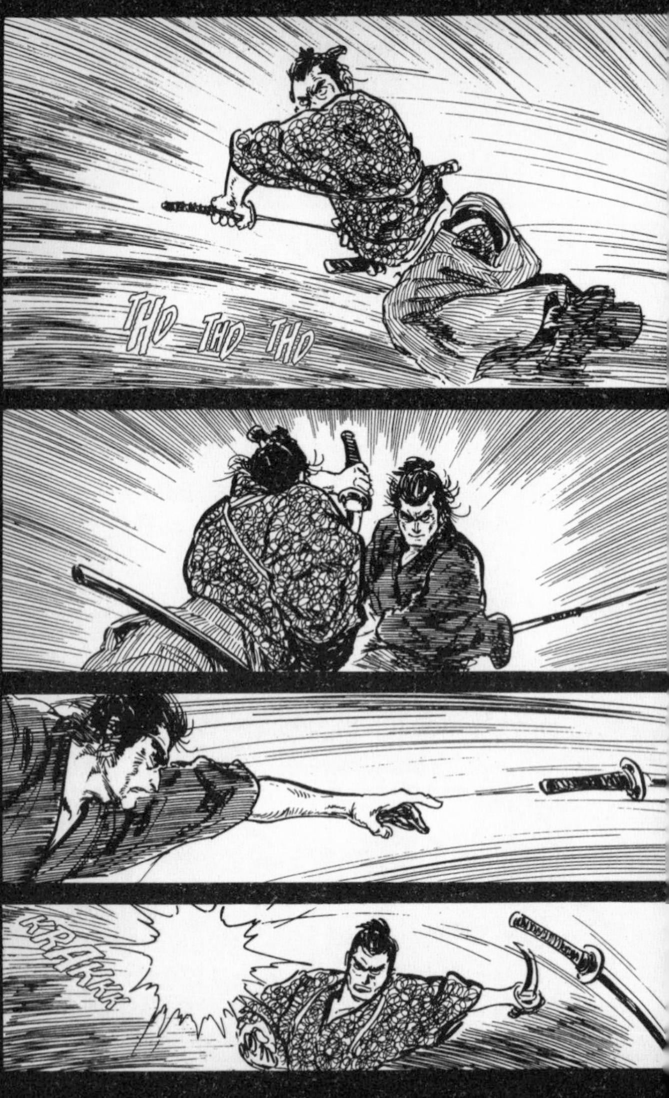
THD THD THD
KRAKKK

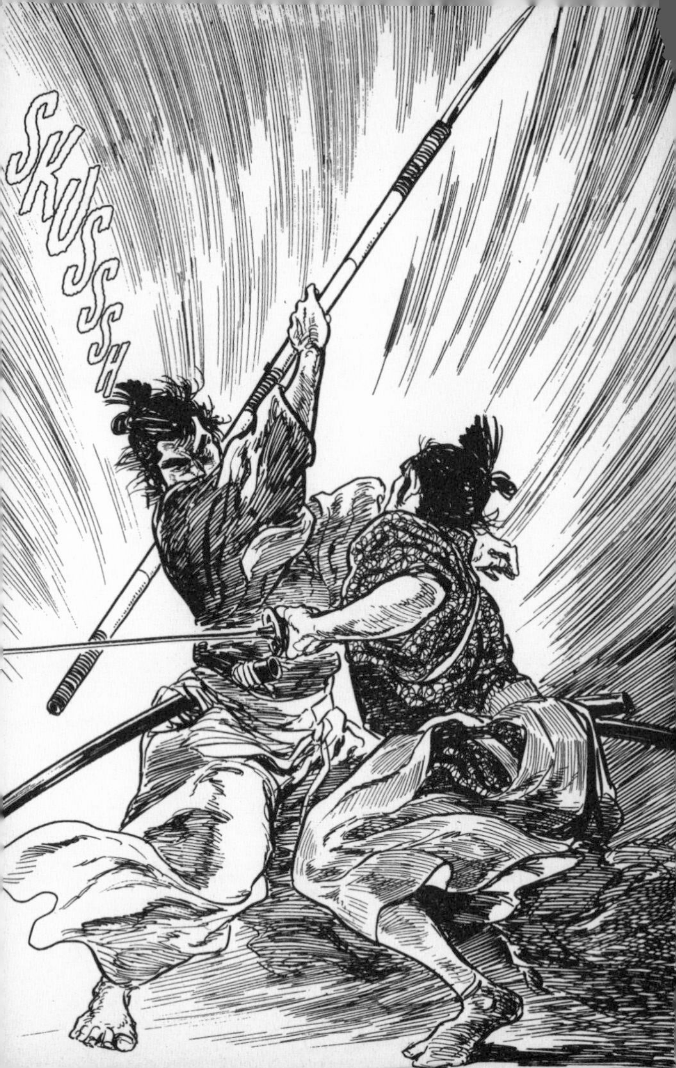
SKUSSSH

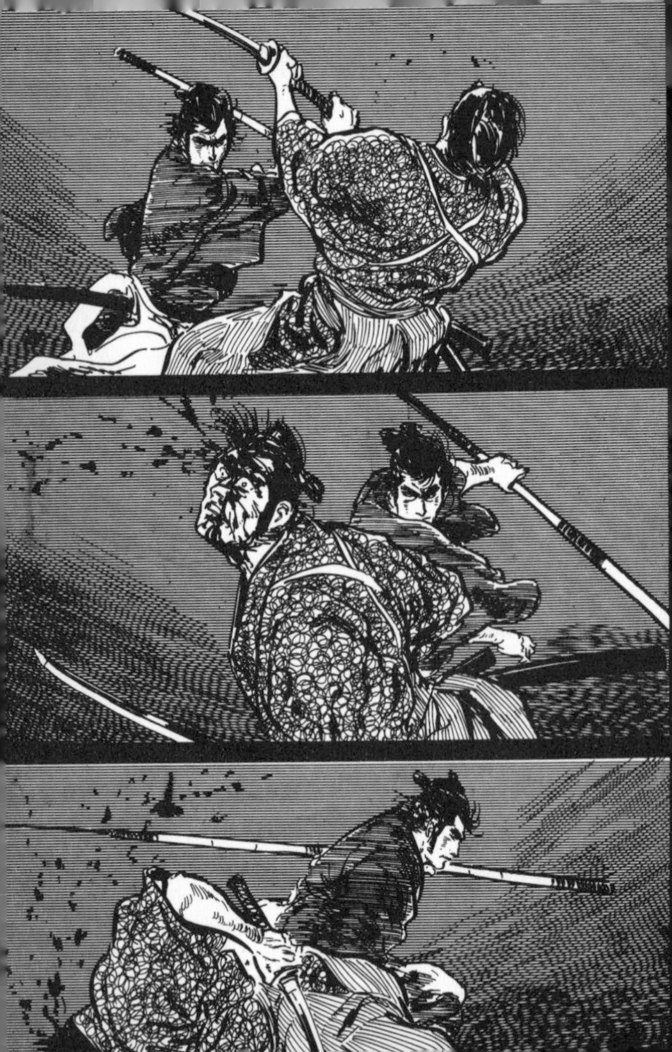

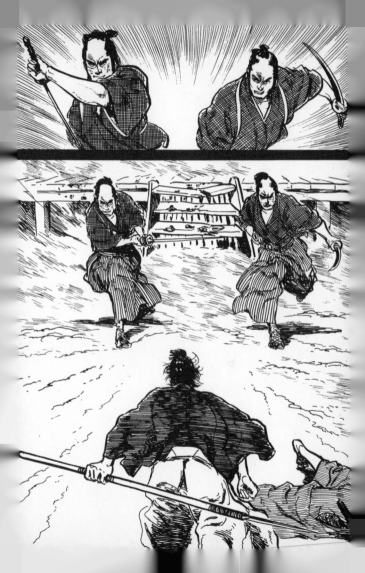

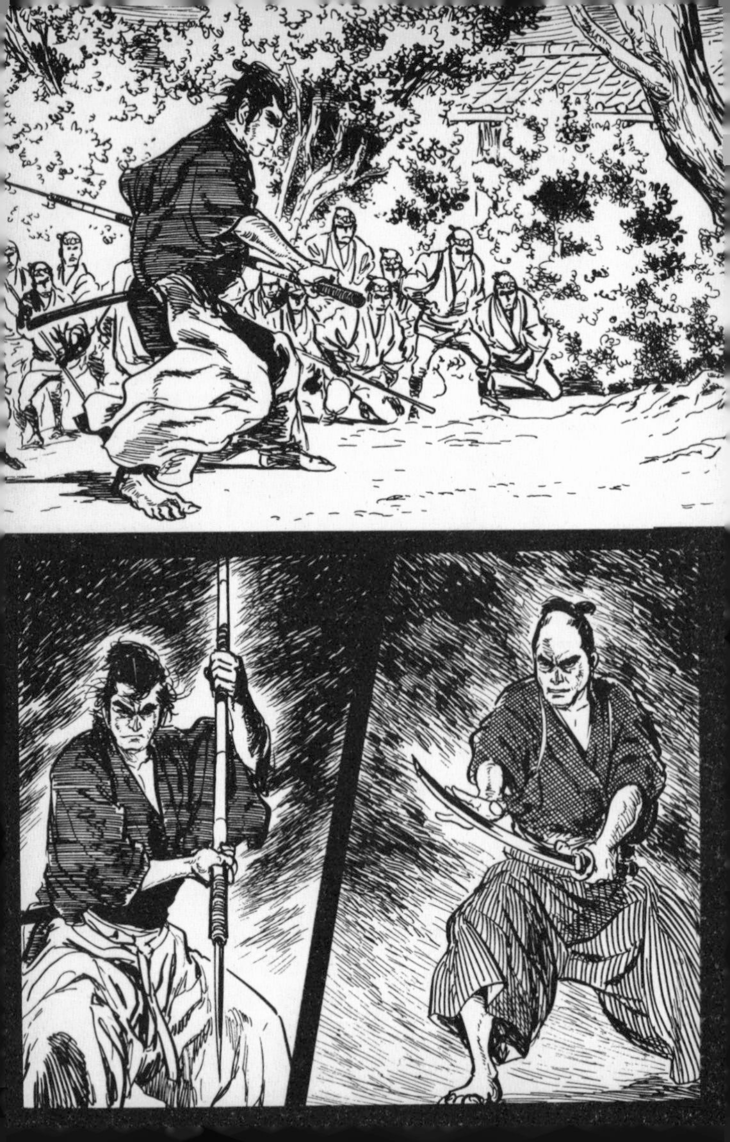

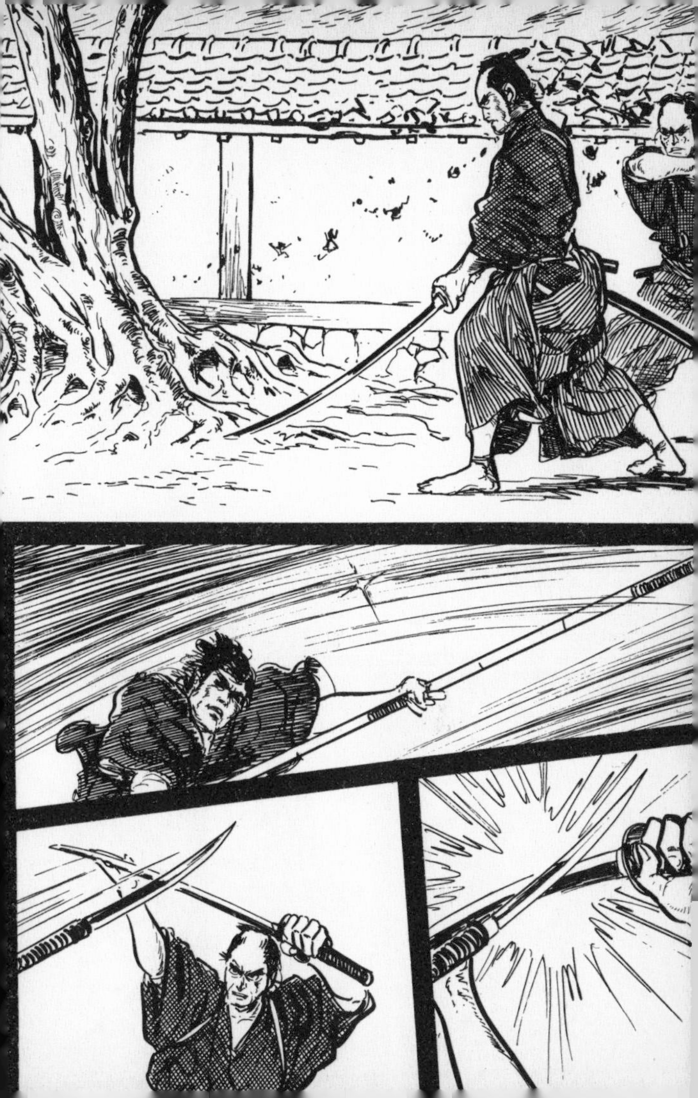

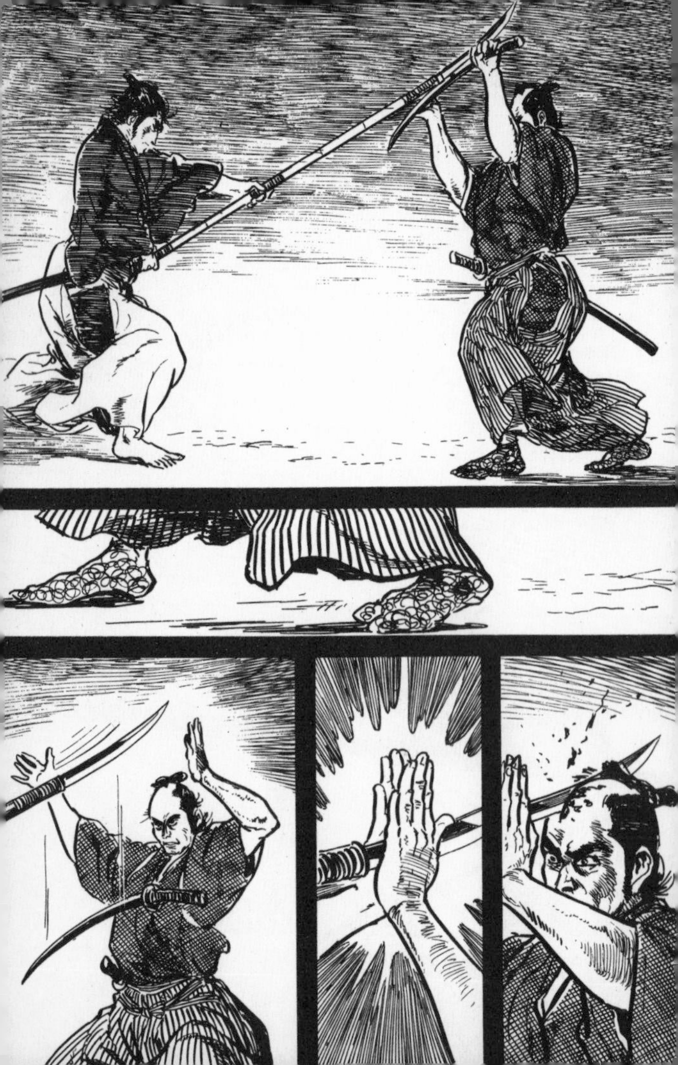

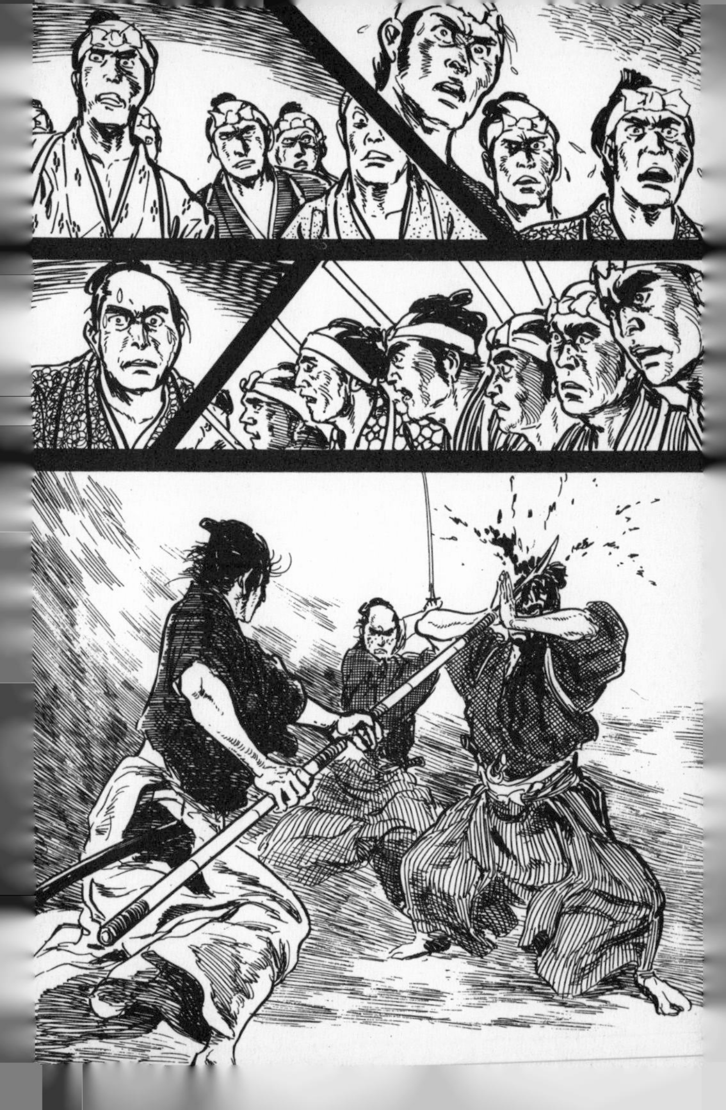

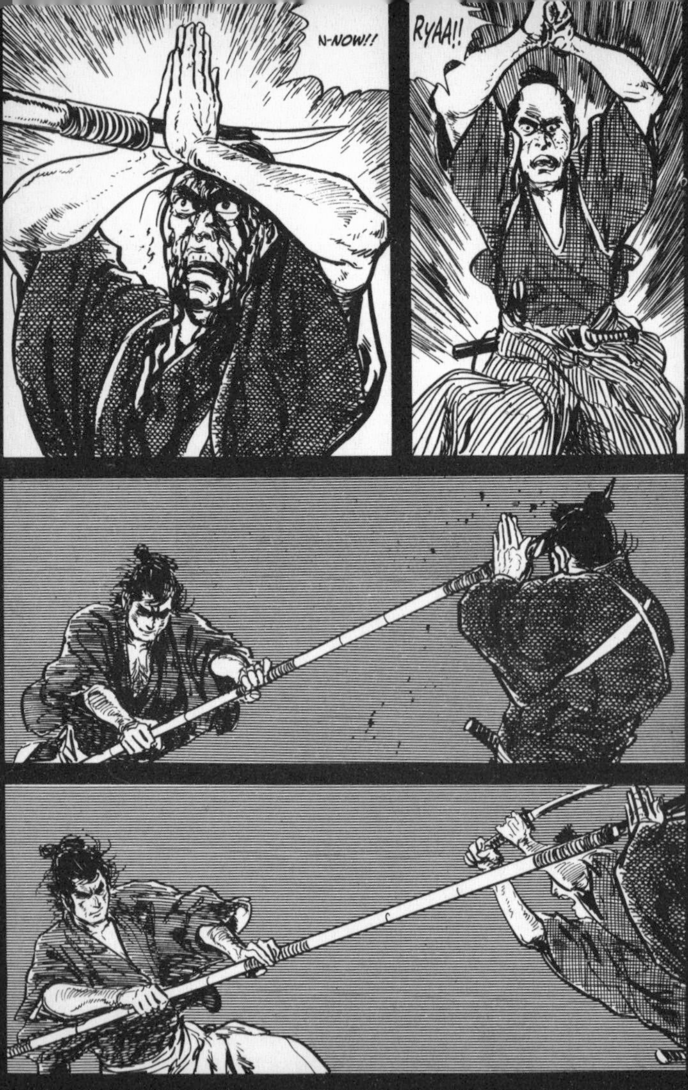
N-NOW!!
RyAA!!

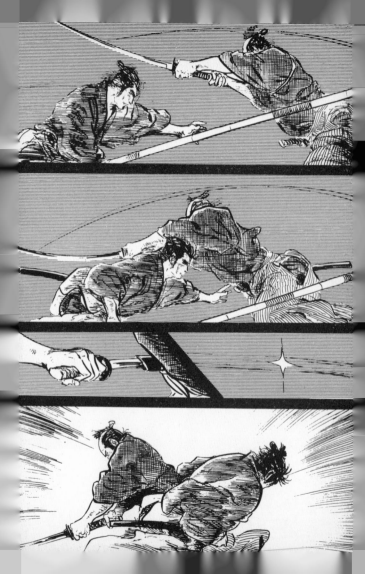

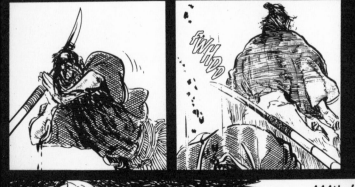

FWHOO

AAAH...!

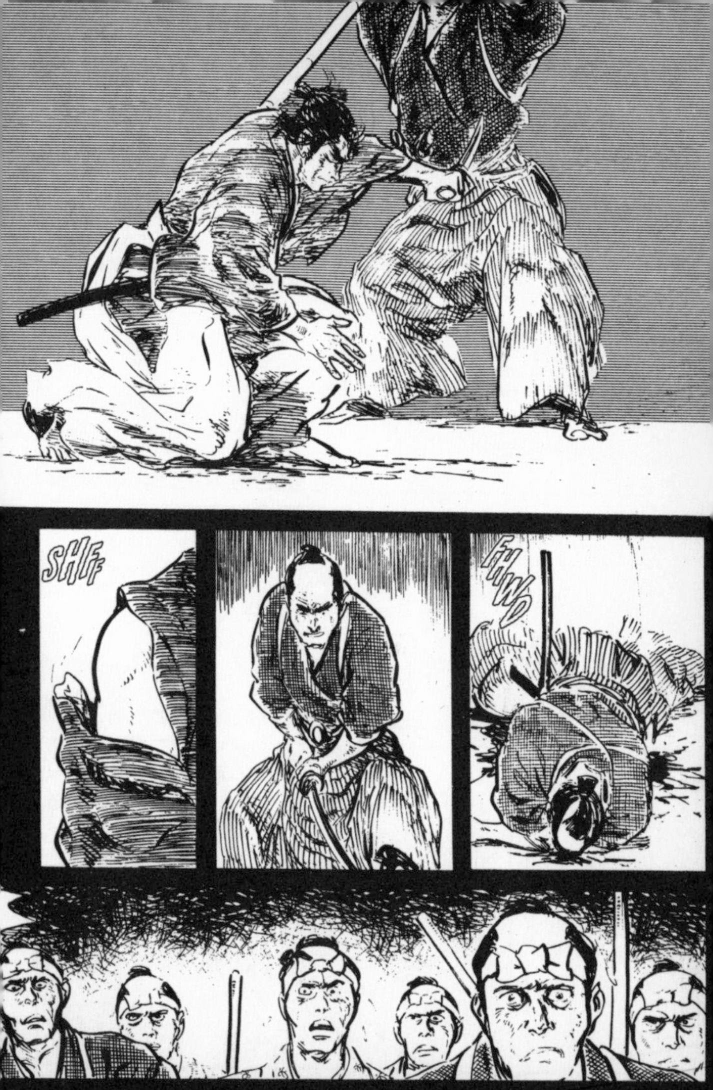
SHFF
FHWD

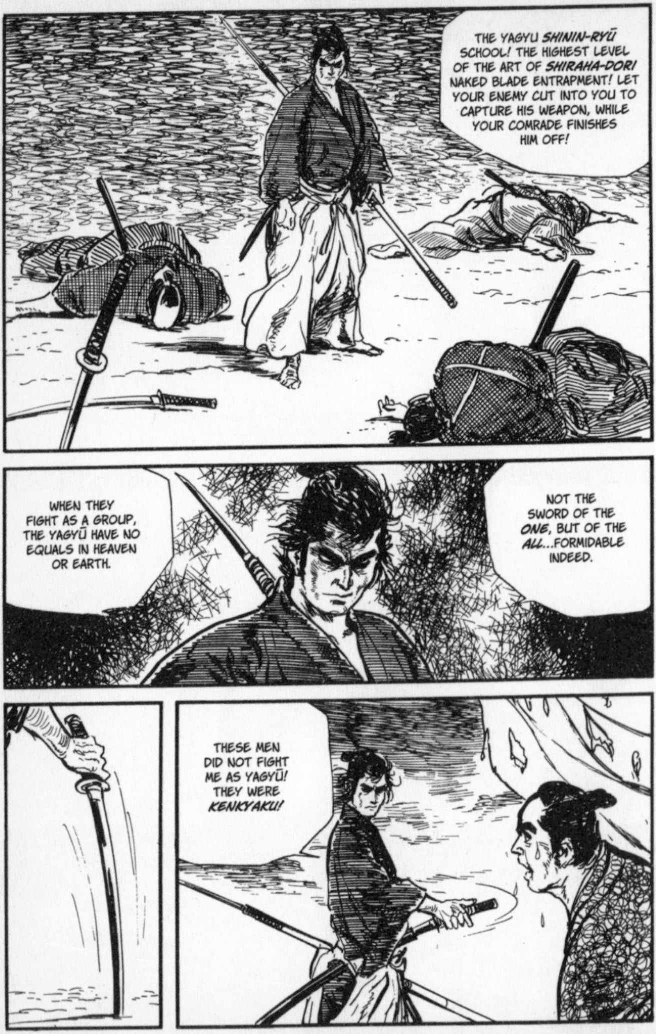
THE YAGYU SHININ-RYŪ SCHOOL! THE HIGHEST LEVEL OF THE ART OF SHIRAHA-DORI NAKED BLADE ENTRAPMENT! LET YOUR ENEMY CUT INTO YOU TO CAPTURE HIS WEAPON, WHILE YOUR COMRADE FINISHES HIM OFF!
WHEN THEY FIGHT AS A GROUP, THE YAGYŪ HAVE NO EQUALS IN HEAVEN OR EARTH.
NOT THE SWORD OF THE ONE, BUT OF THE ALL...FORMIDABLE INDEED.
THESE MEN DID NOT FIGHT ME AS YAGYŪ! THEY WERE KENKYAKU!

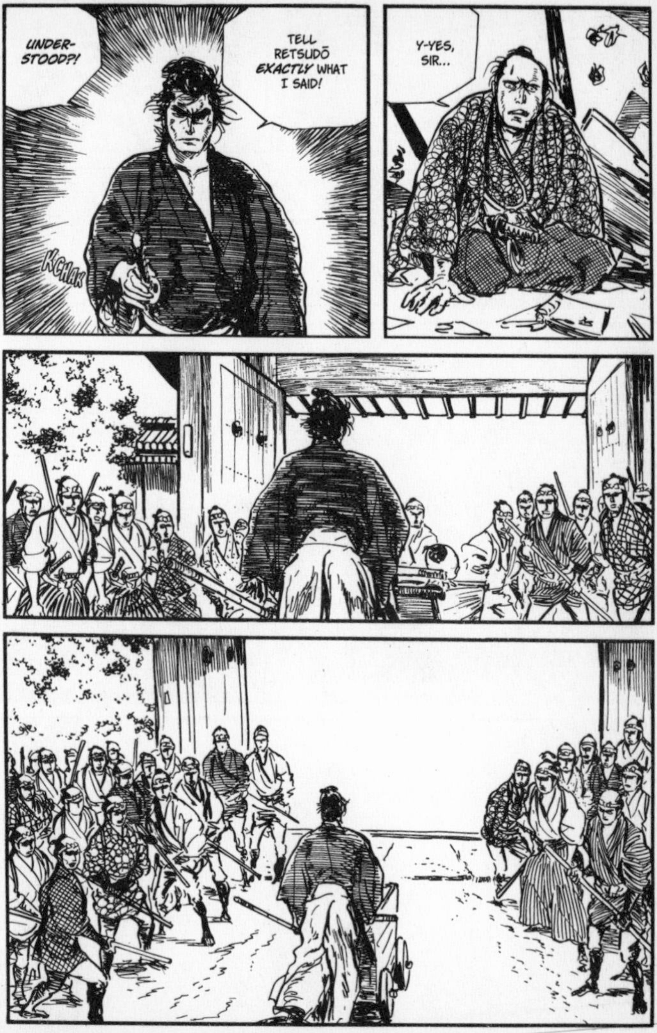
UNDER-STOOD?!
TELL RETSUDŌ *EXACTLY* WHAT I SAID!
KCHAK
Y-YES, SIR...

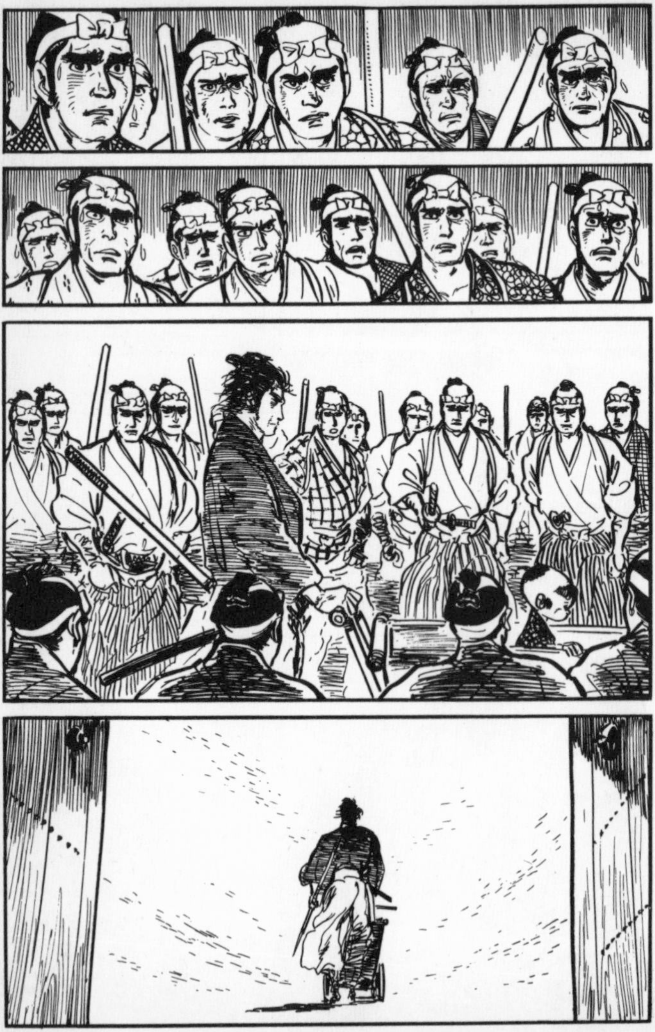

the thirty-fifth

Night Stalker

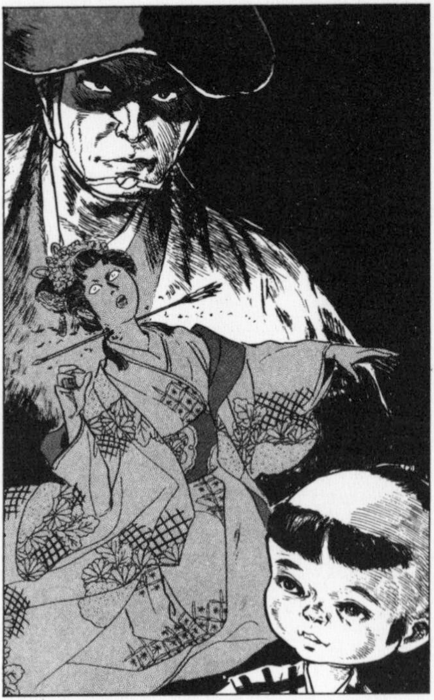

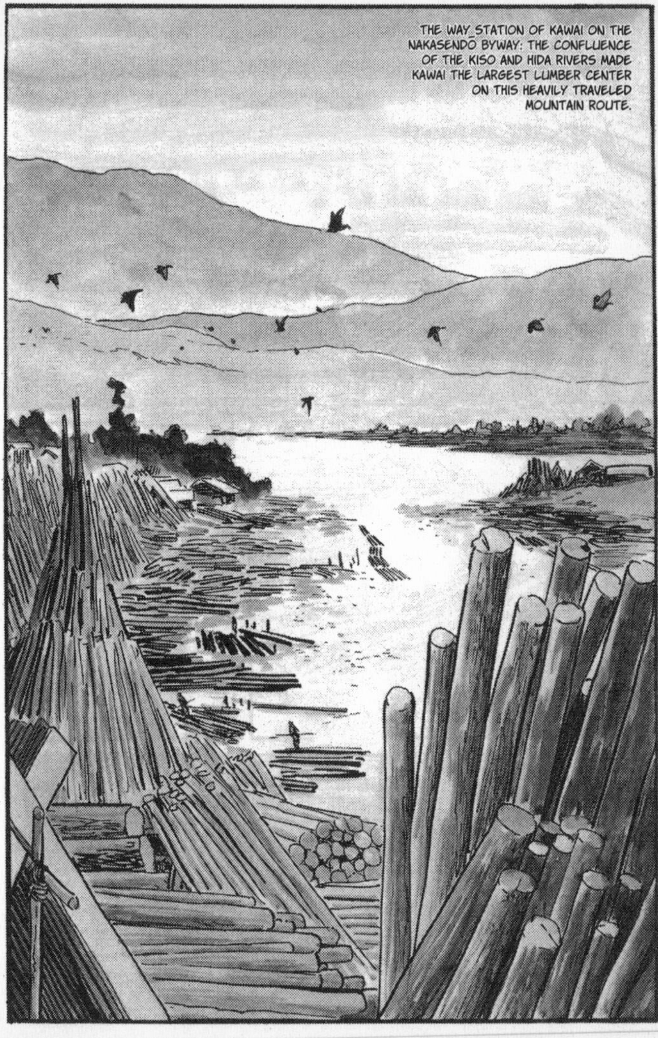
THE WAY STATION OF KAWAI ON THE NAKASENDŌ BYWAY: THE CONFLUENCE OF THE KISO AND HIDA RIVERS MADE KAWAI THE LARGEST LUMBER CENTER ON THIS HEAVILY TRAVELED MOUNTAIN ROUTE.

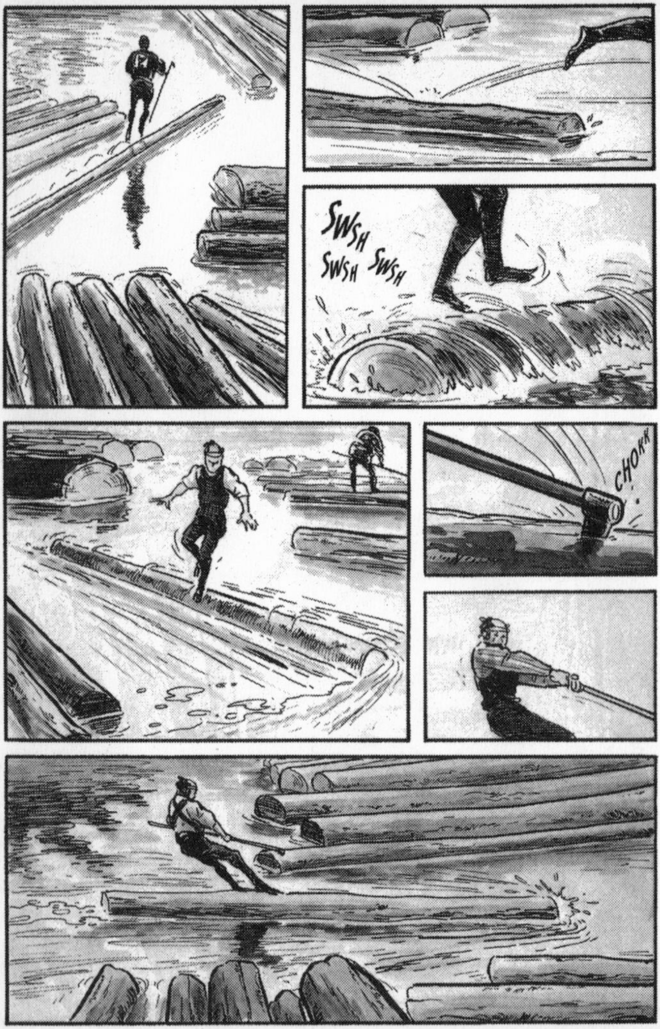
SWSH
SWSH SWSH
CHOKK

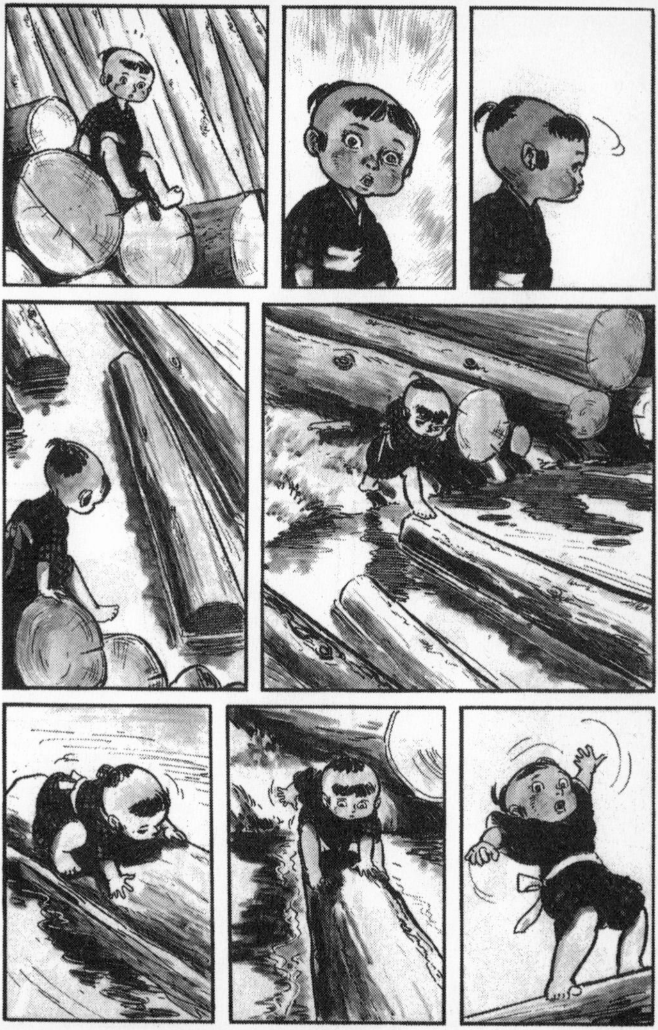

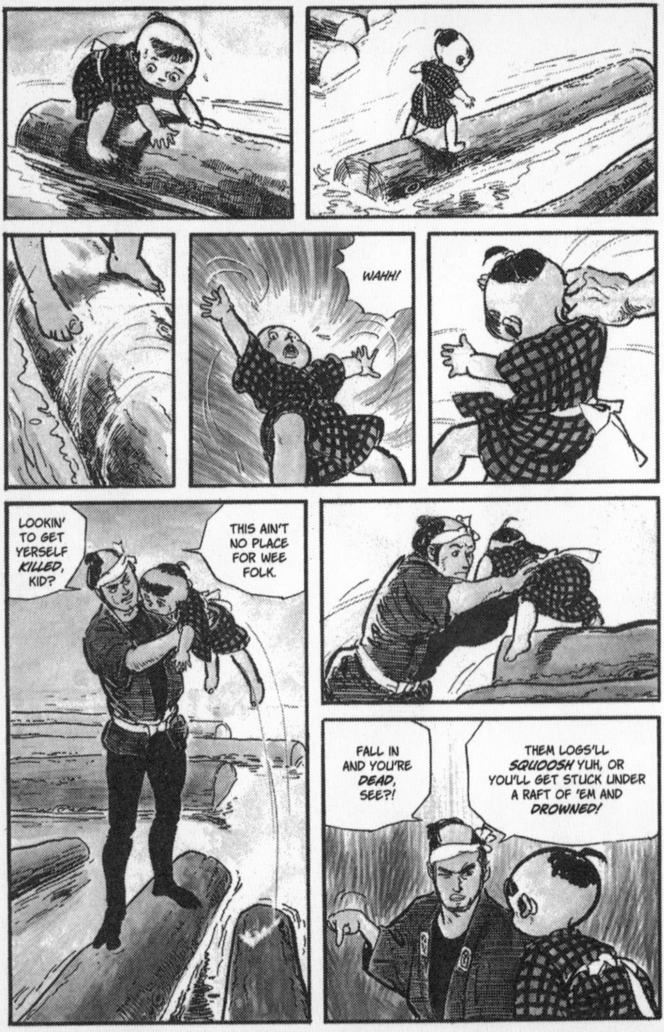
WAHH!
LOOKIN' TO GET YERSELF KILLED, KID?
THIS AIN'T NO PLACE FOR WEE FOLK.
FALL IN AND YOU'RE DEAD, SEE?!
THEM LOGS'LL SQUOOSH YUH, OR YOU'LL GET STUCK UNDER A RAFT OF 'EM AND DROWNED!

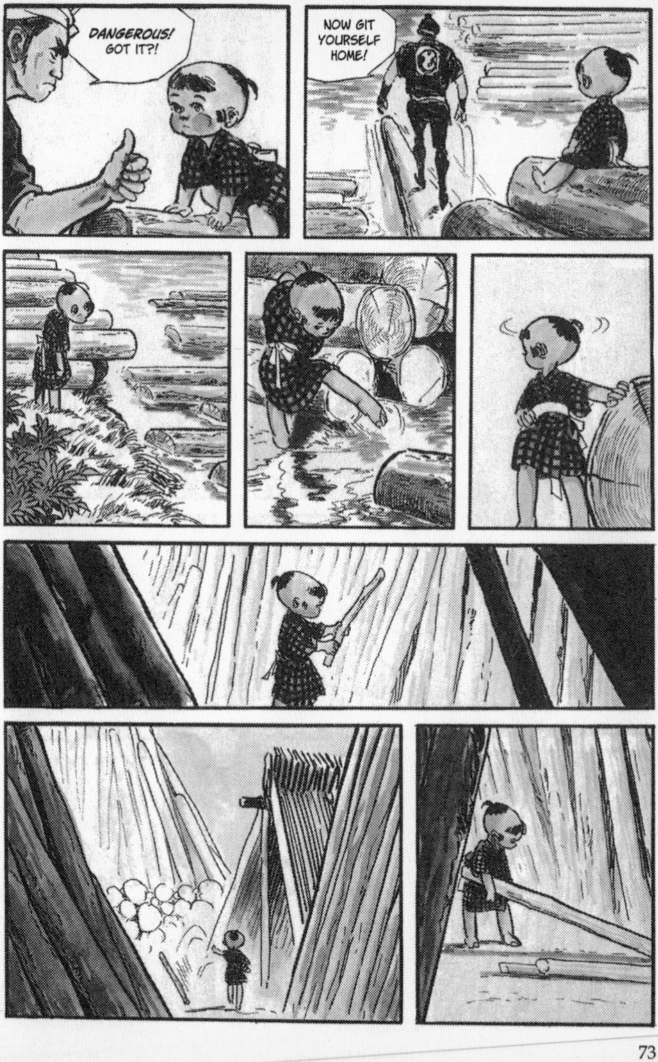
DANGEROUS! GOT IT?!
NOW GIT YOURSELF HOME!

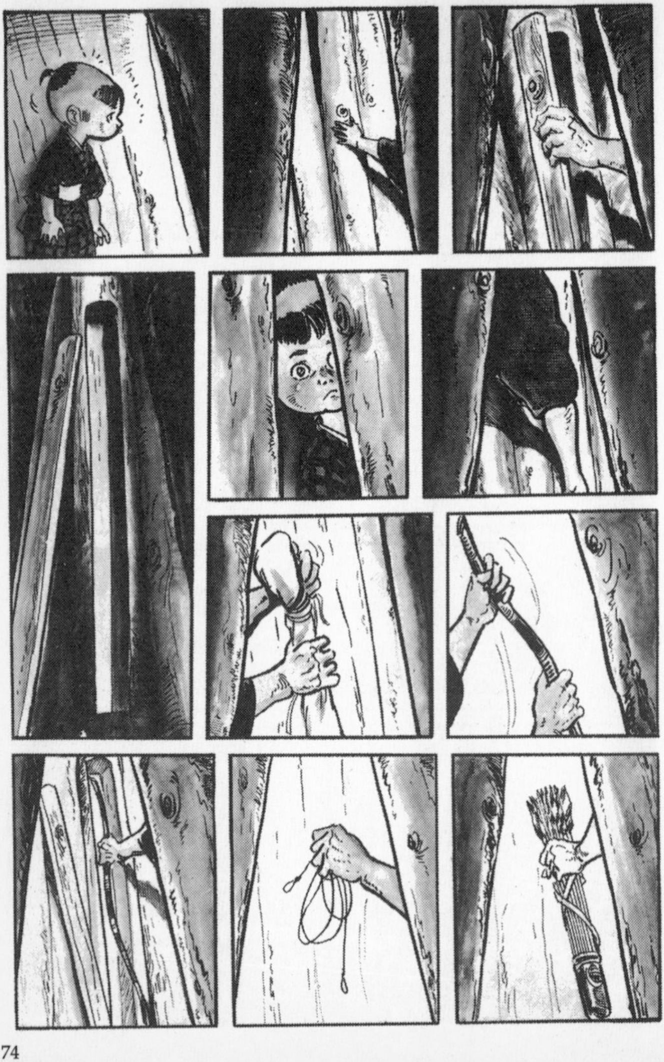

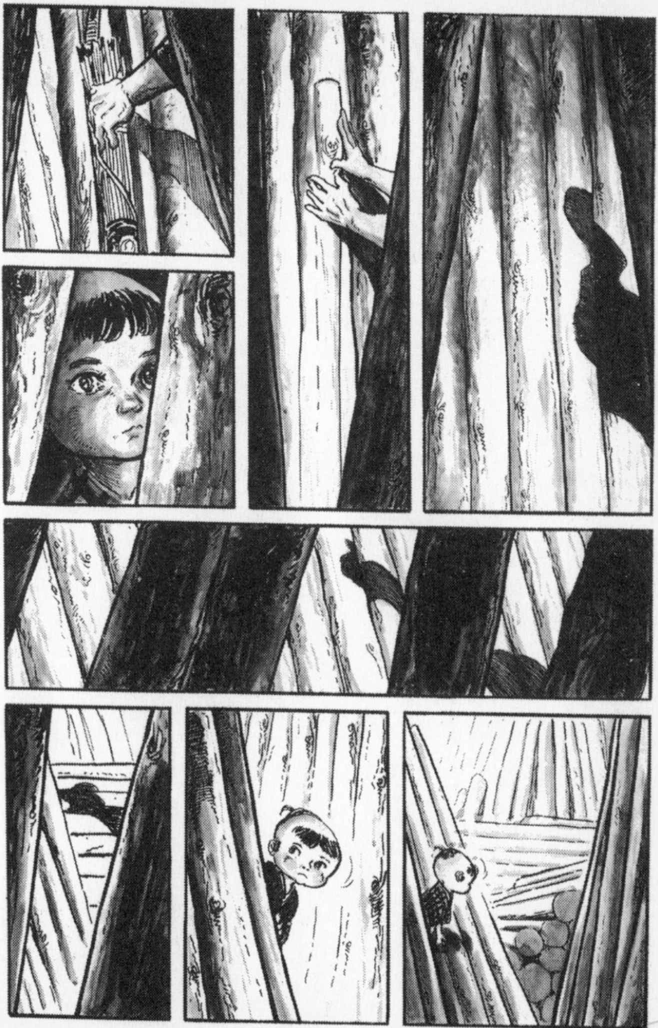

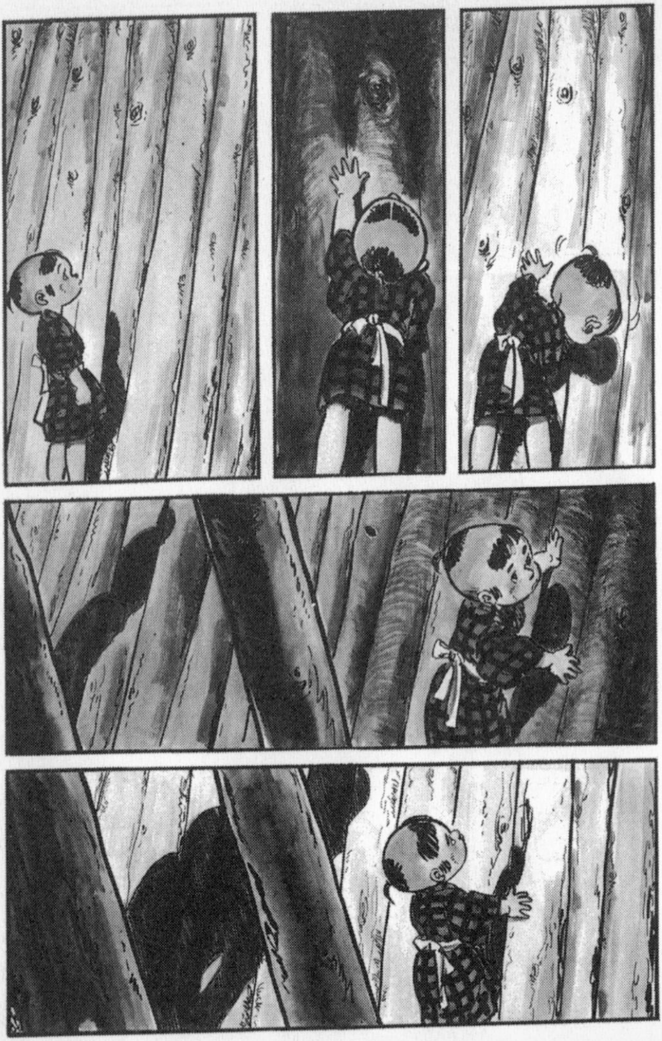

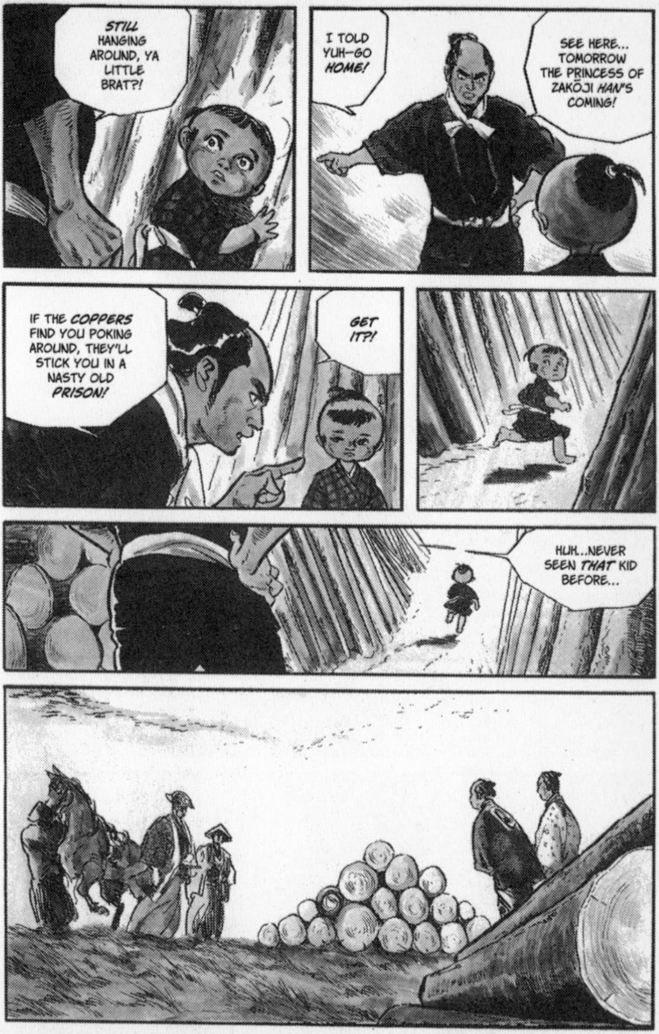
STILL HANGING AROUND, YA LITTLE BRAT?!
I TOLD YUH—GO HOME!
SEE HERE... TOMORROW THE PRINCESS OF ZAKŌJI HAN'S COMING!
IF THE COPPERS FIND YOU POKING AROUND, THEY'LL STICK YOU IN A NASTY OLD PRISON!
GET IT?!
HUH...NEVER SEEN THAT KID BEFORE...

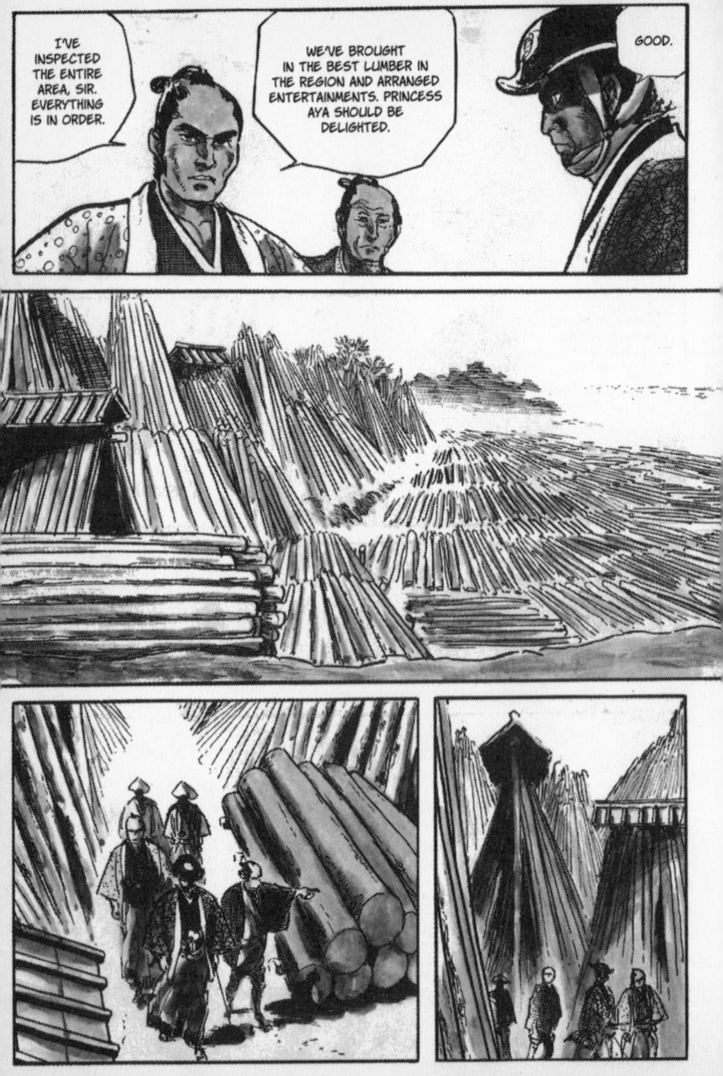
I'VE INSPECTED THE ENTIRE AREA, SIR. EVERYTHING IS IN ORDER.
WE'VE BROUGHT IN THE BEST LUMBER IN THE REGION AND ARRANGED ENTERTAINMENTS. PRINCESS AYA SHOULD BE DELIGHTED.
GOOD.

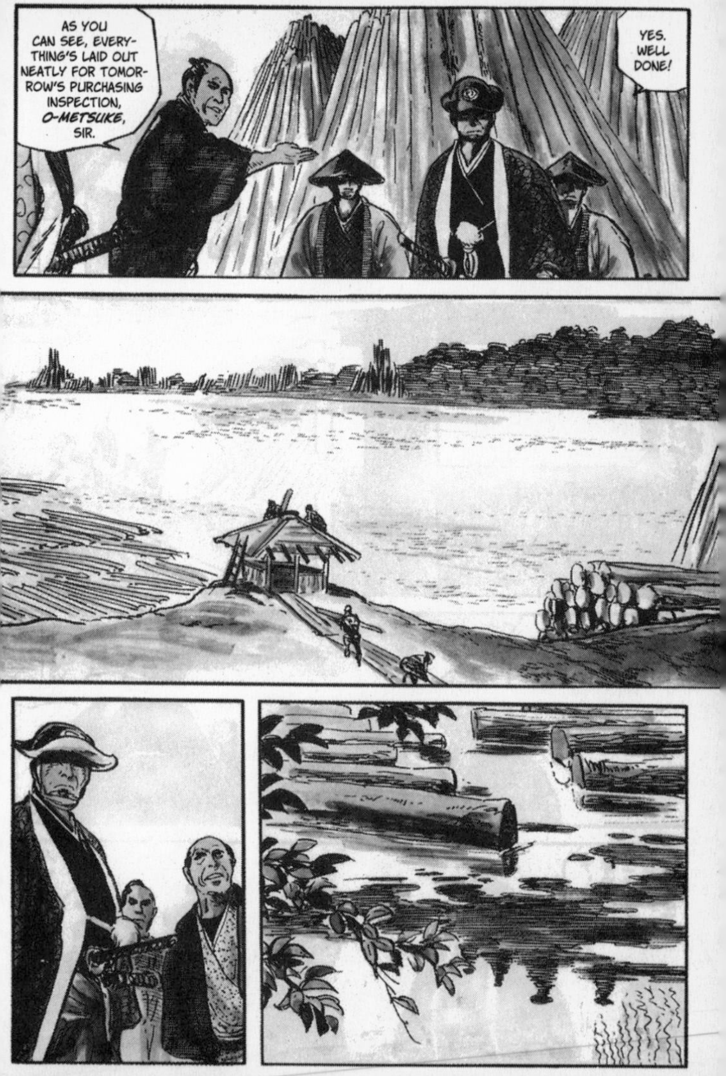
AS YOU CAN SEE, EVERYTHING'S LAID OUT NEATLY FOR TOMORROW'S PURCHASING INSPECTION, *O-METSUKE*, SIR.
YES. WELL DONE!

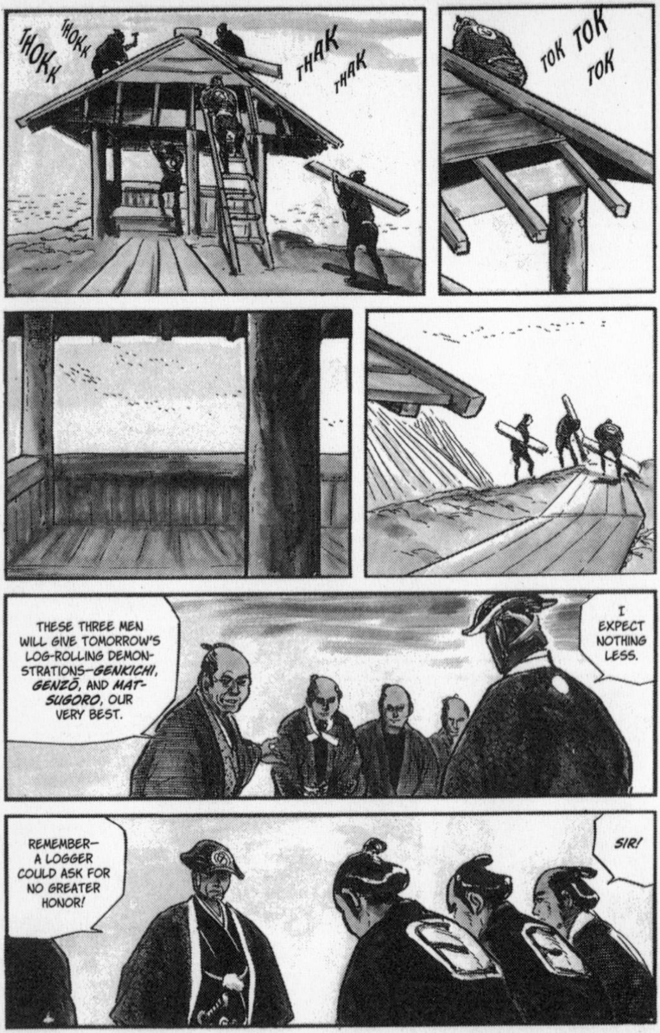
THOKK
THOKK
THAK
THAK
TOK TOK
TOK
THESE THREE MEN WILL GIVE TOMORROW'S LOG-ROLLING DEMONSTRATIONS—GENKICHI, GENZŌ, AND MATSUGORO, OUR VERY BEST.
I EXPECT NOTHING LESS.
REMEMBER— A LOGGER COULD ASK FOR NO GREATER HONOR!
SIR!

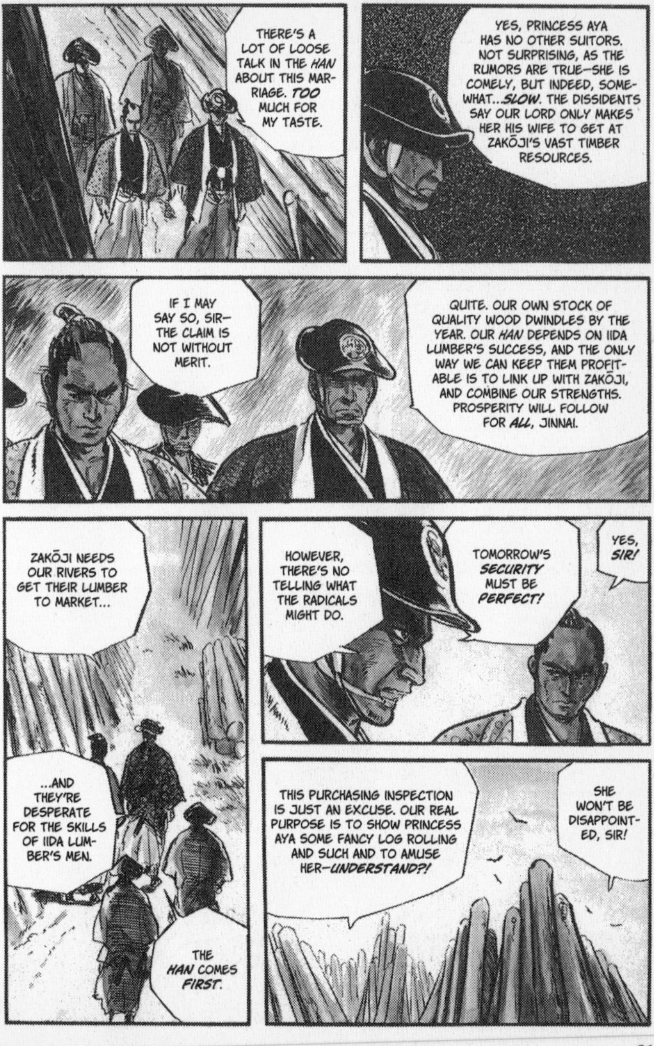
THERE'S A LOT OF LOOSE TALK IN THE *HAN* ABOUT THIS MARRIAGE. *TOO* MUCH FOR MY TASTE.
YES, PRINCESS AYA HAS NO OTHER SUITORS. NOT SURPRISING, AS THE RUMORS ARE TRUE—SHE IS COMELY, BUT INDEED, SOMEWHAT...*SLOW*. THE DISSIDENTS SAY OUR LORD ONLY MAKES HER HIS WIFE TO GET AT ZAKŌJI'S VAST TIMBER RESOURCES.
IF I MAY SAY SO, SIR—THE CLAIM IS NOT WITHOUT MERIT.
QUITE. OUR OWN STOCK OF QUALITY WOOD DWINDLES BY THE YEAR. OUR *HAN* DEPENDS ON IIDA LUMBER'S SUCCESS, AND THE ONLY WAY WE CAN KEEP THEM PROFITABLE IS TO LINK UP WITH ZAKŌJI, AND COMBINE OUR STRENGTHS. PROSPERITY WILL FOLLOW FOR *ALL*, JINNAI.
ZAKŌJI NEEDS OUR RIVERS TO GET THEIR LUMBER TO MARKET...
...AND THEY'RE DESPERATE FOR THE SKILLS OF IIDA LUMBER'S MEN.
THE *HAN* COMES *FIRST*.
HOWEVER, THERE'S NO TELLING WHAT THE RADICALS MIGHT DO.
TOMORROW'S *SECURITY* MUST BE *PERFECT!*
YES, *SIR!*
THIS PURCHASING INSPECTION IS JUST AN EXCUSE. OUR REAL PURPOSE IS TO SHOW PRINCESS AYA SOME FANCY LOG ROLLING AND SUCH AND TO AMUSE HER—*UNDERSTAND?!*
SHE WON'T BE DISAPPOINTED, SIR!

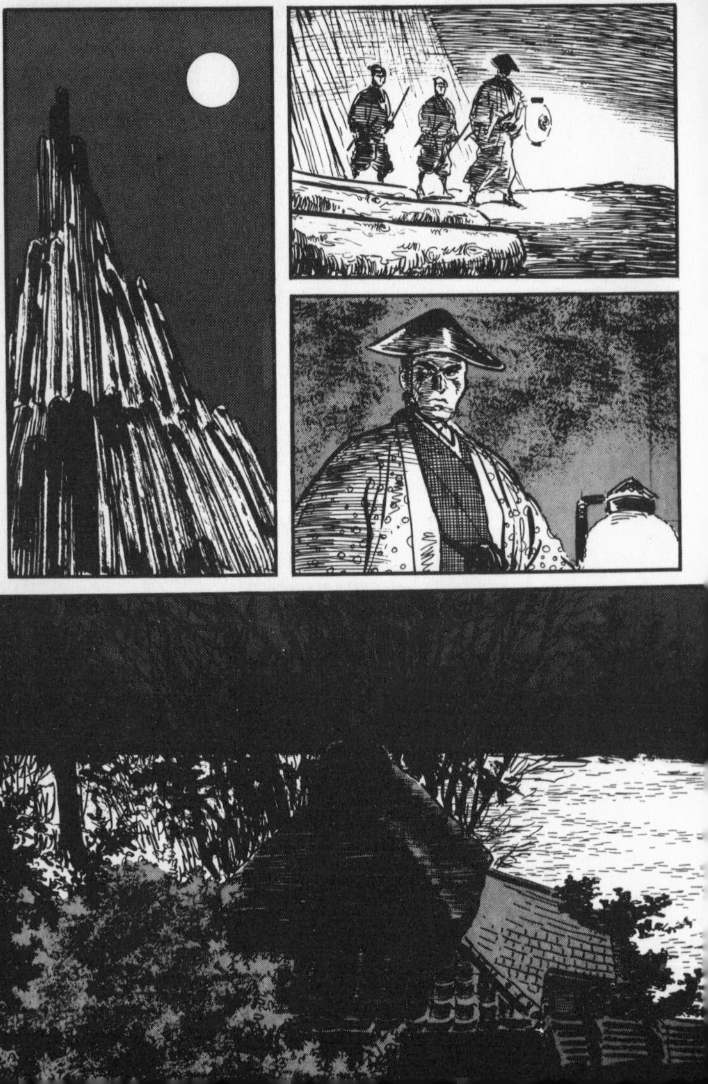

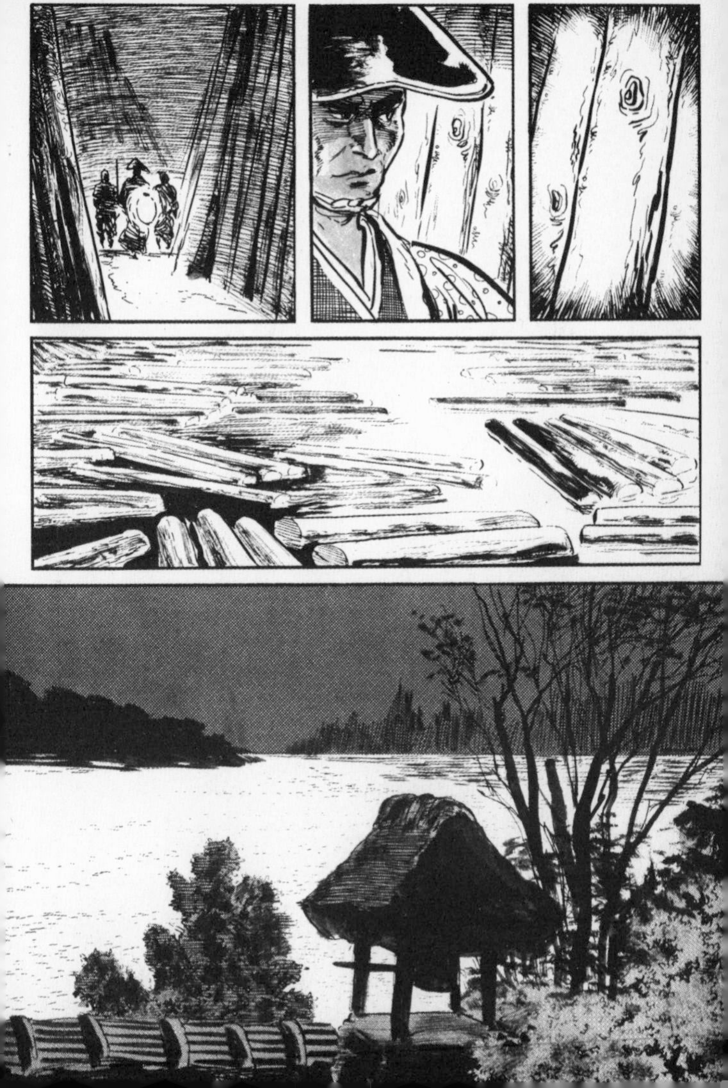

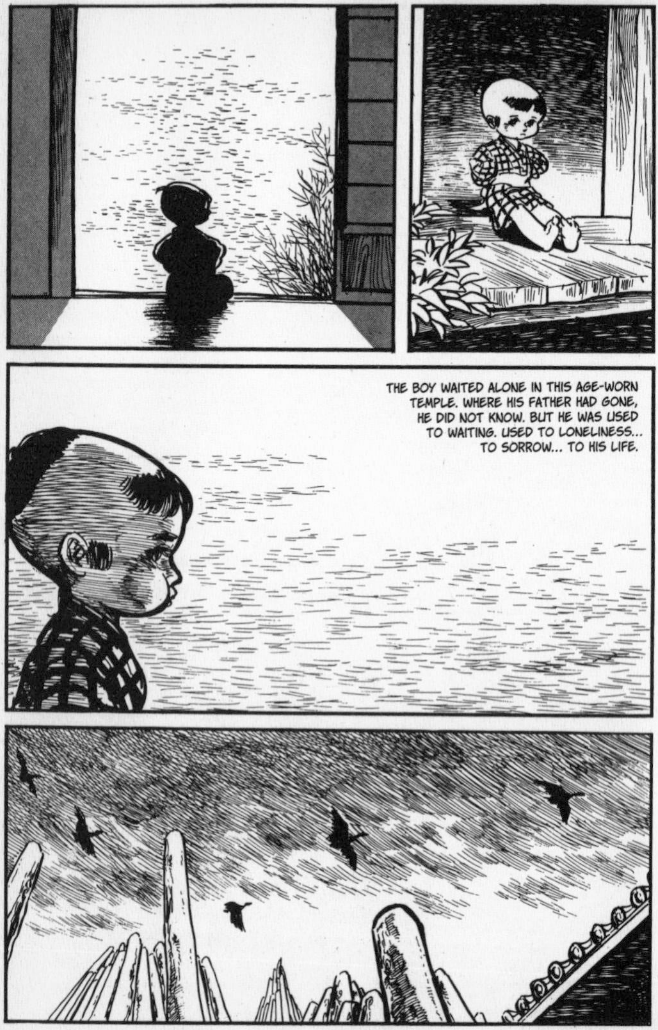
THE BOY WAITED ALONE IN THIS AGE-WORN TEMPLE. WHERE HIS FATHER HAD GONE, HE DID NOT KNOW. BUT HE WAS USED TO WAITING. USED TO LONELINESS... TO SORROW... TO HIS LIFE.

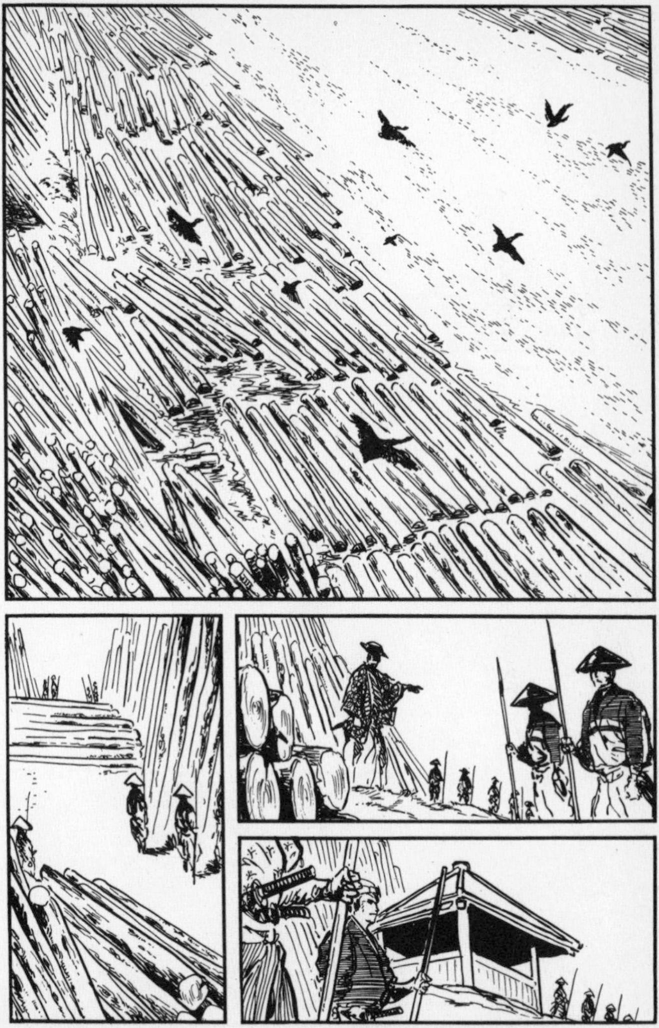

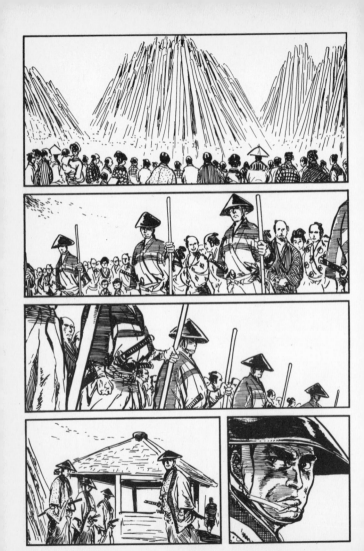

86

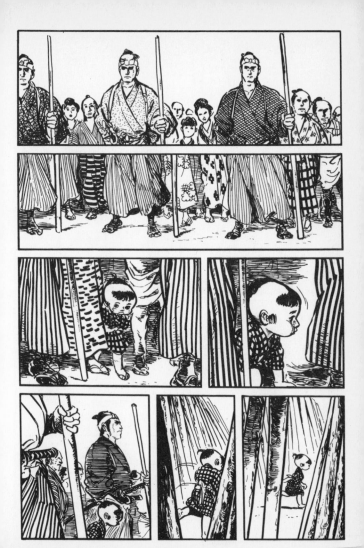

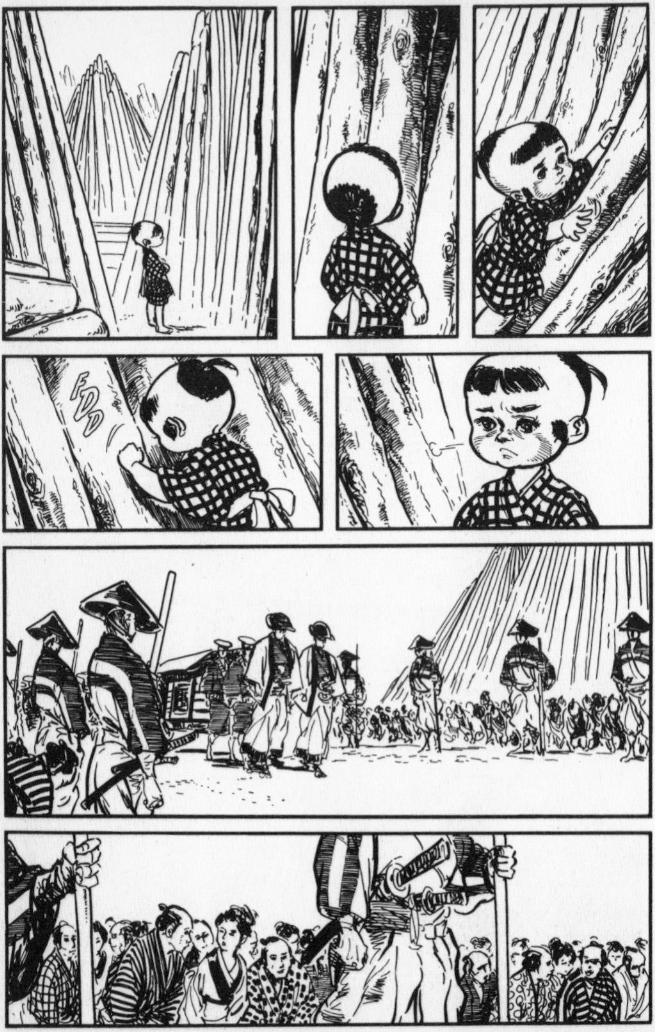
FDD

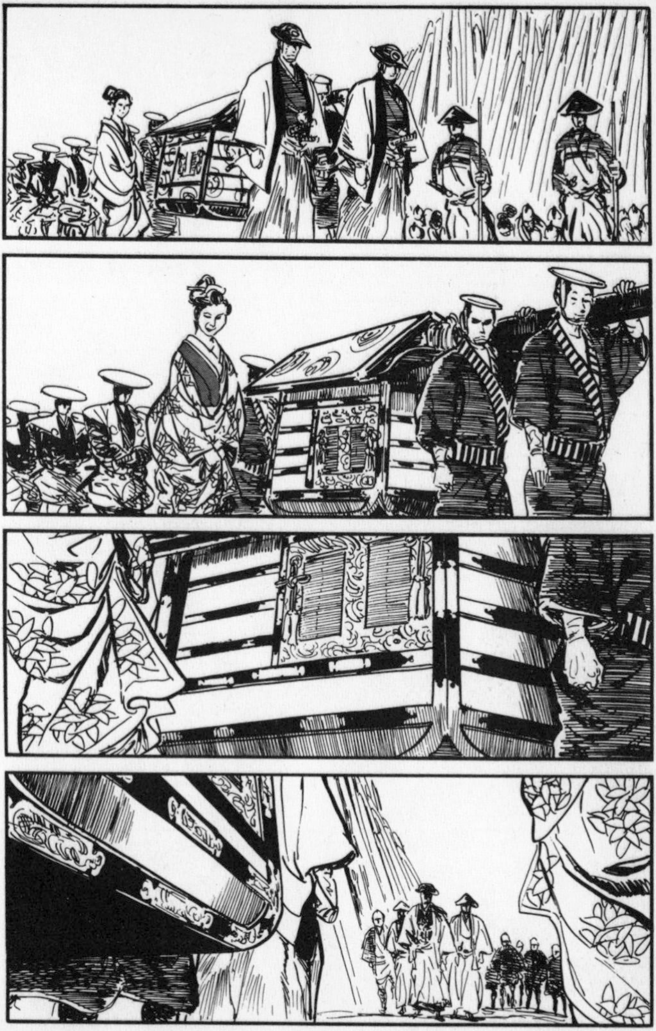

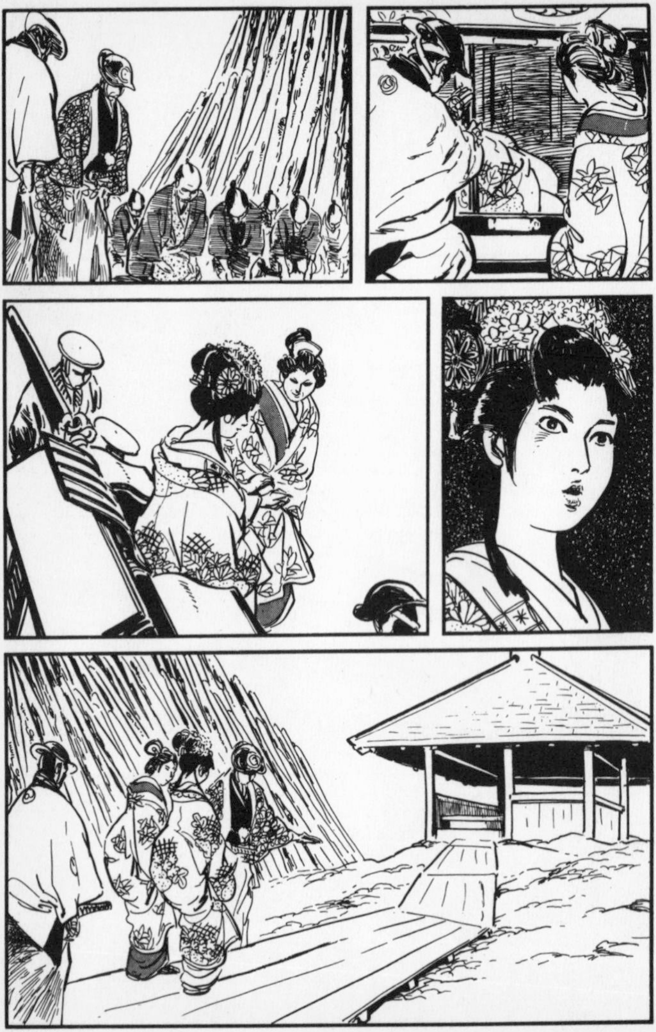

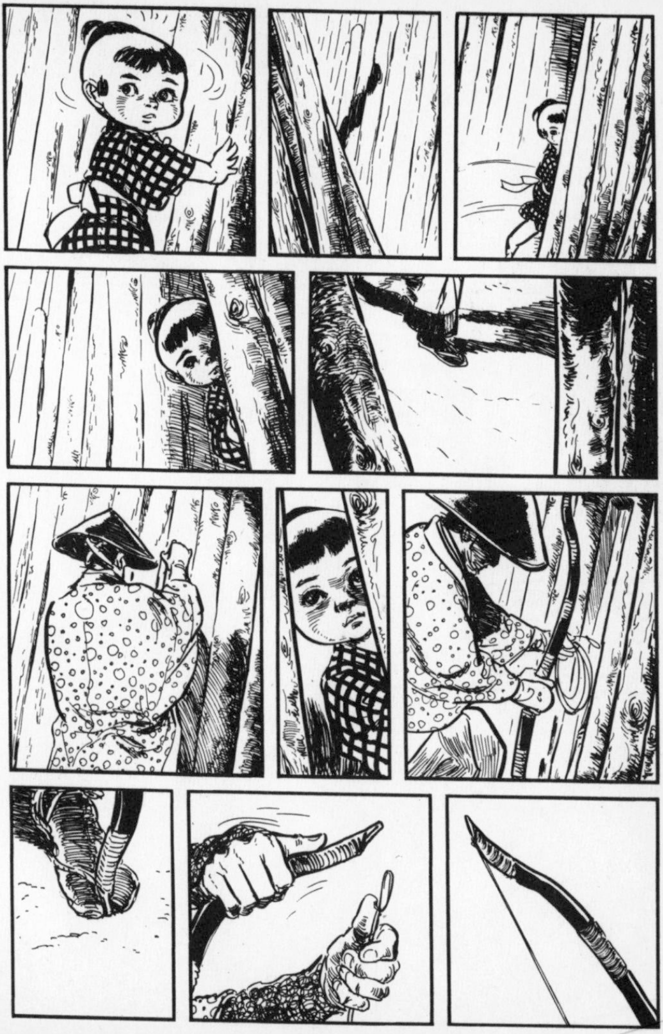

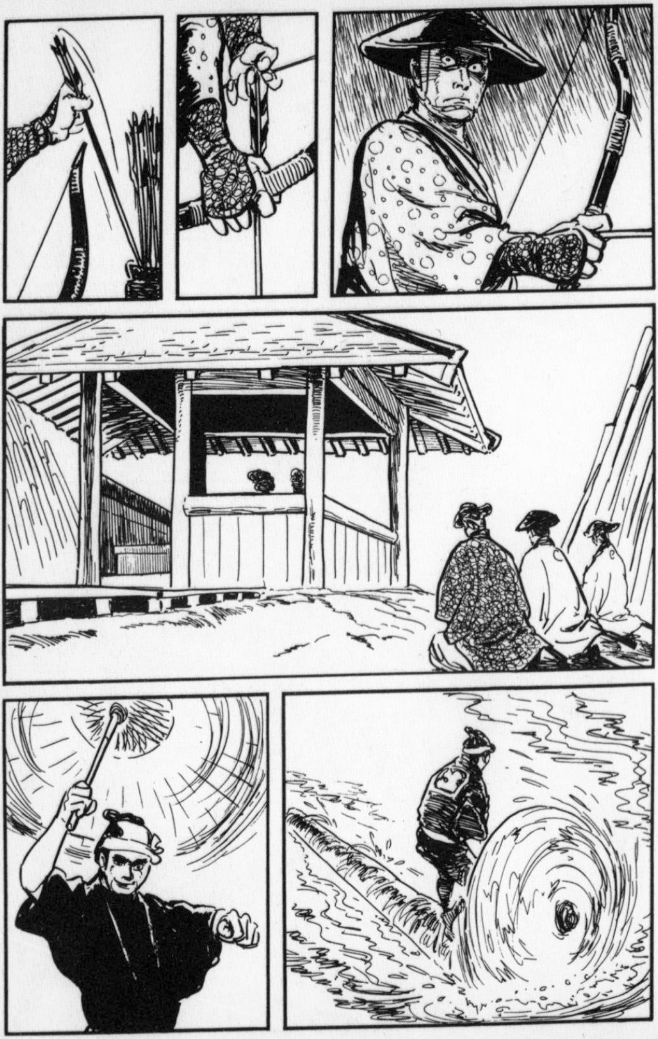

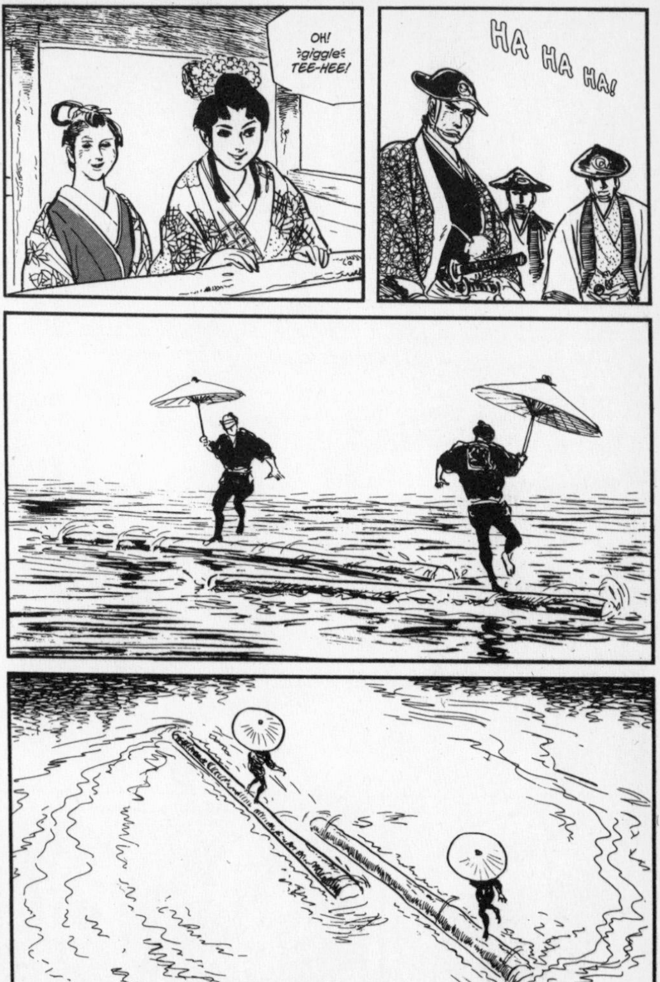
OH!
giggle
TEE-HEE!
HA HA HA!

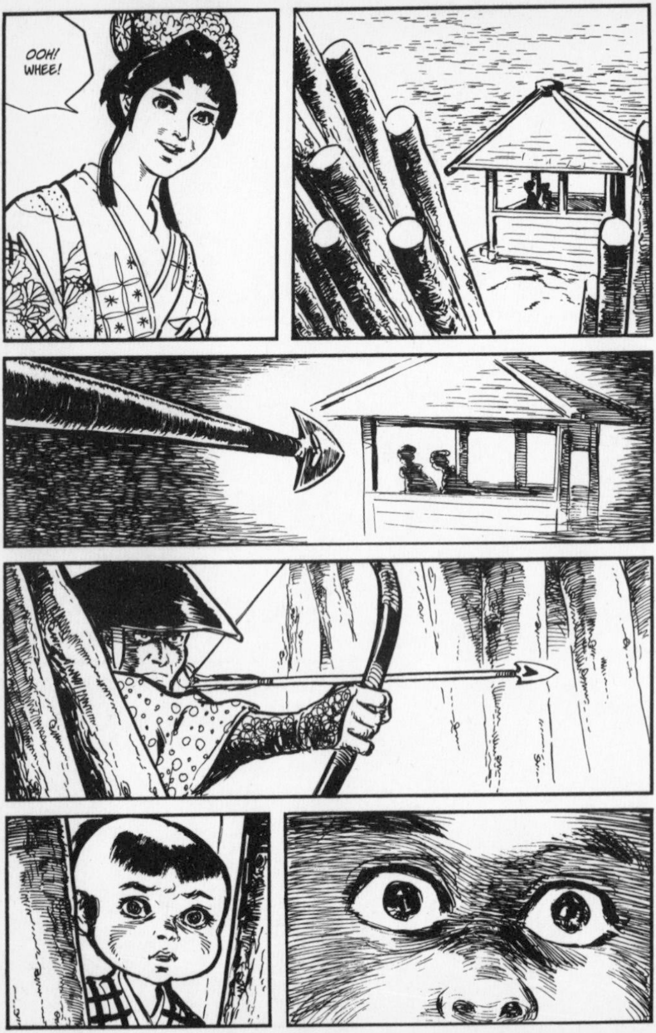
OOH! WHEE!

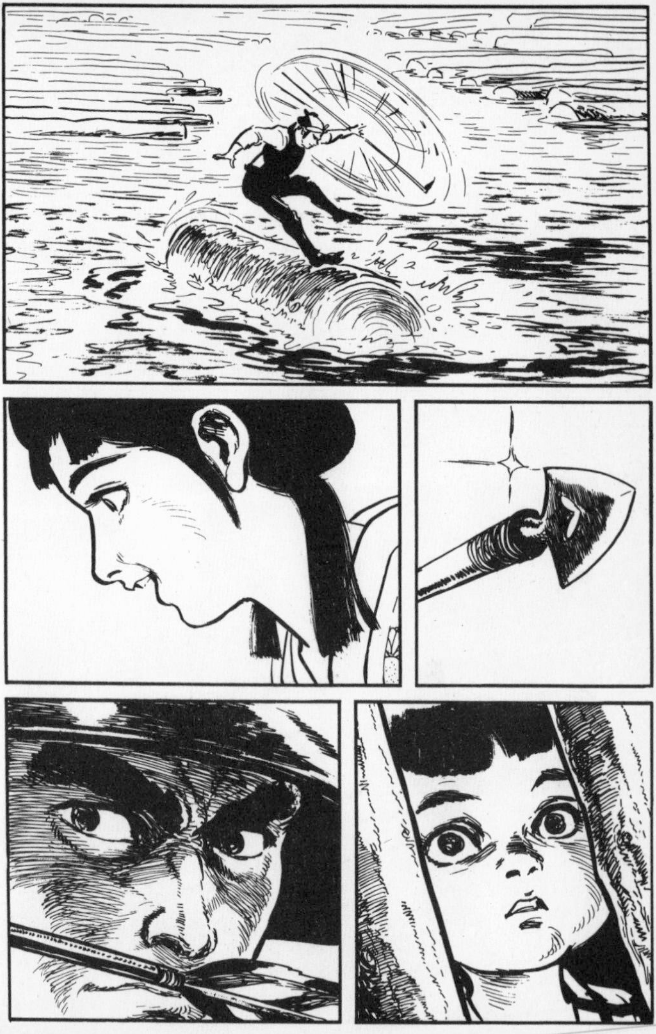

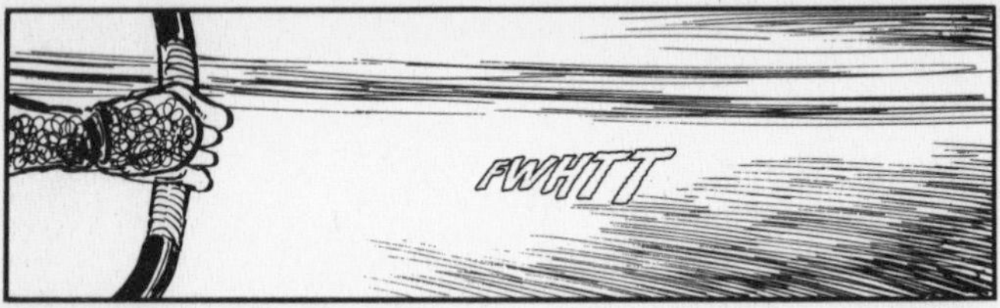
FWHTT
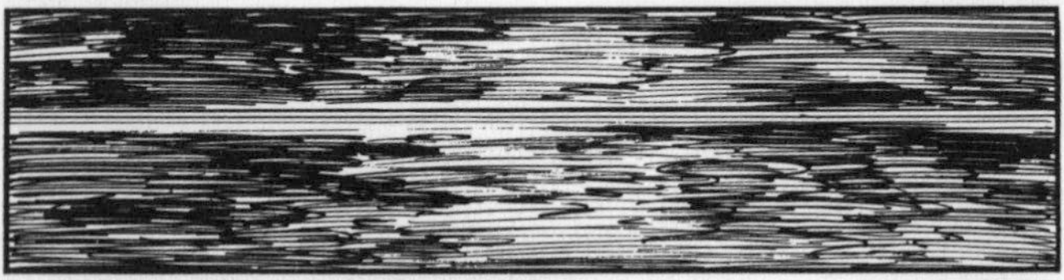
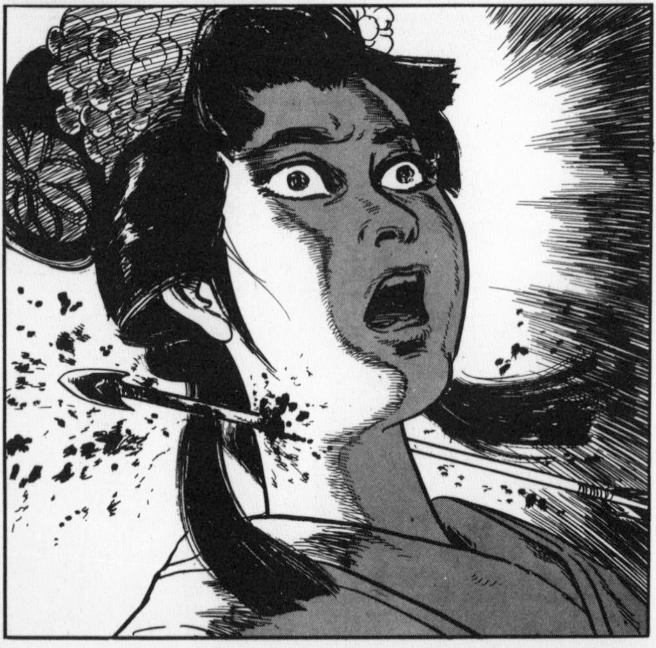

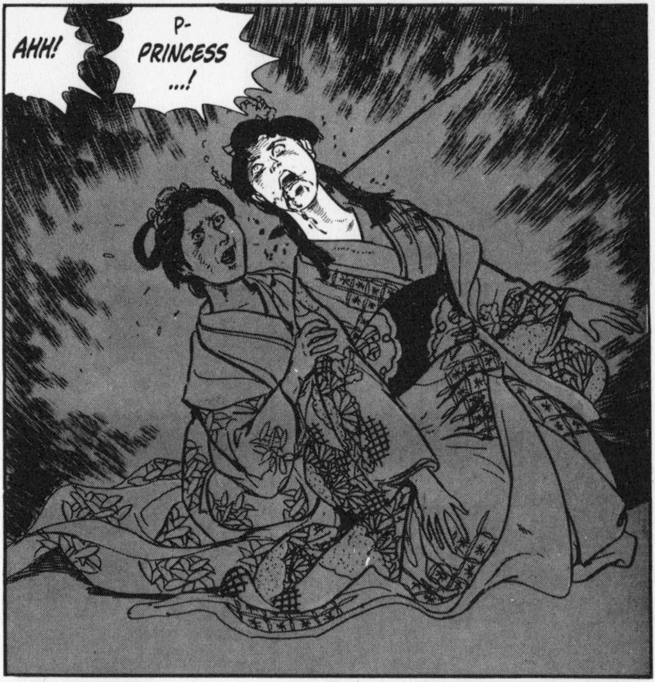
AHH!
P-
PRINCESS
...!

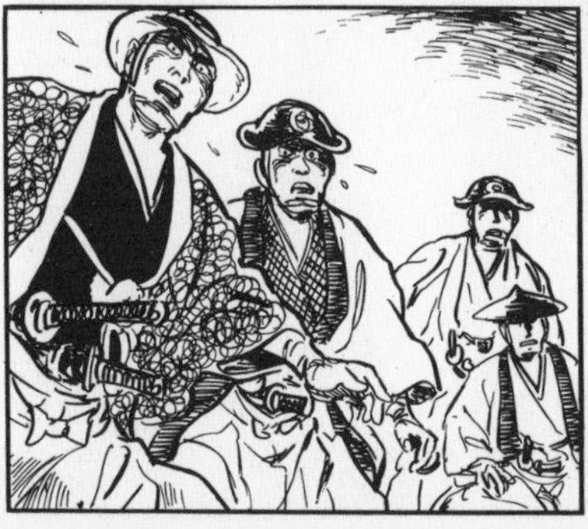

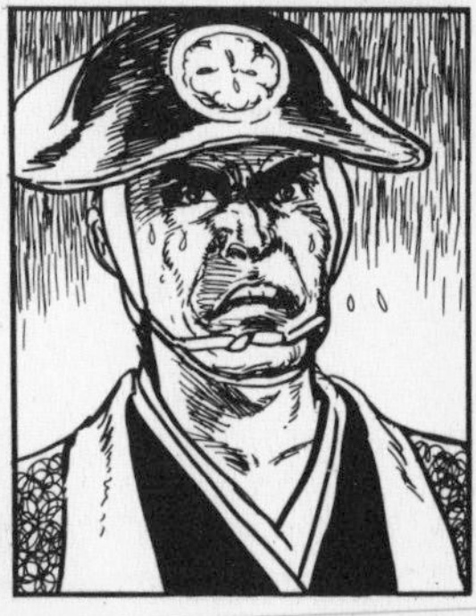

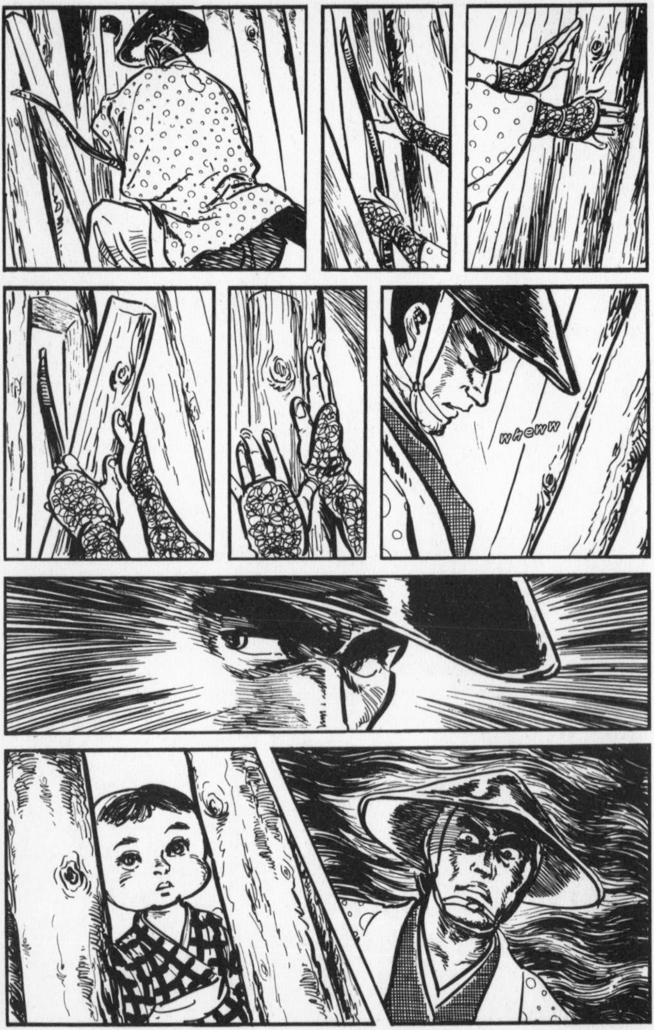
whewww

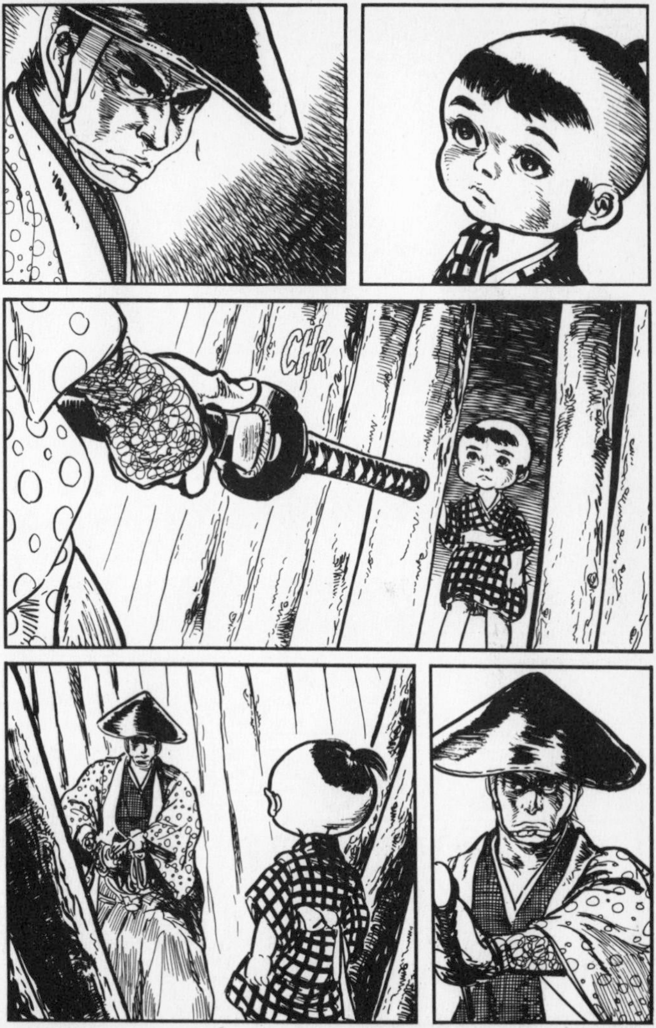
CHK

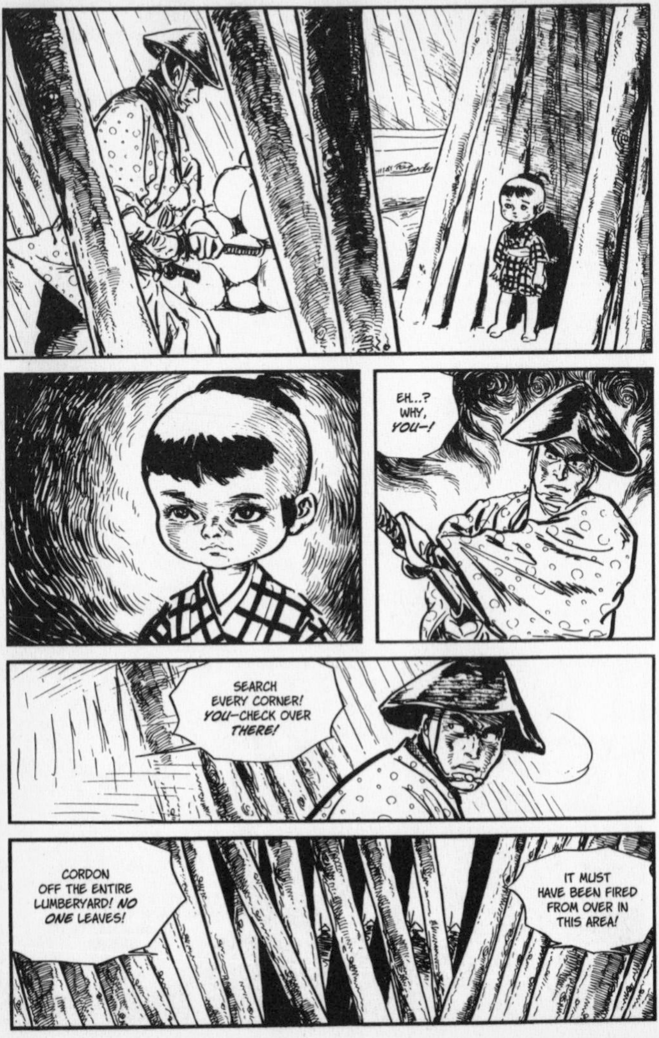
EH...? WHY, YOU-!
SEARCH EVERY CORNER! YOU-CHECK OVER THERE!
CORDON OFF THE ENTIRE LUMBERYARD! NO ONE LEAVES!
IT MUST HAVE BEEN FIRED FROM OVER IN THIS AREA!

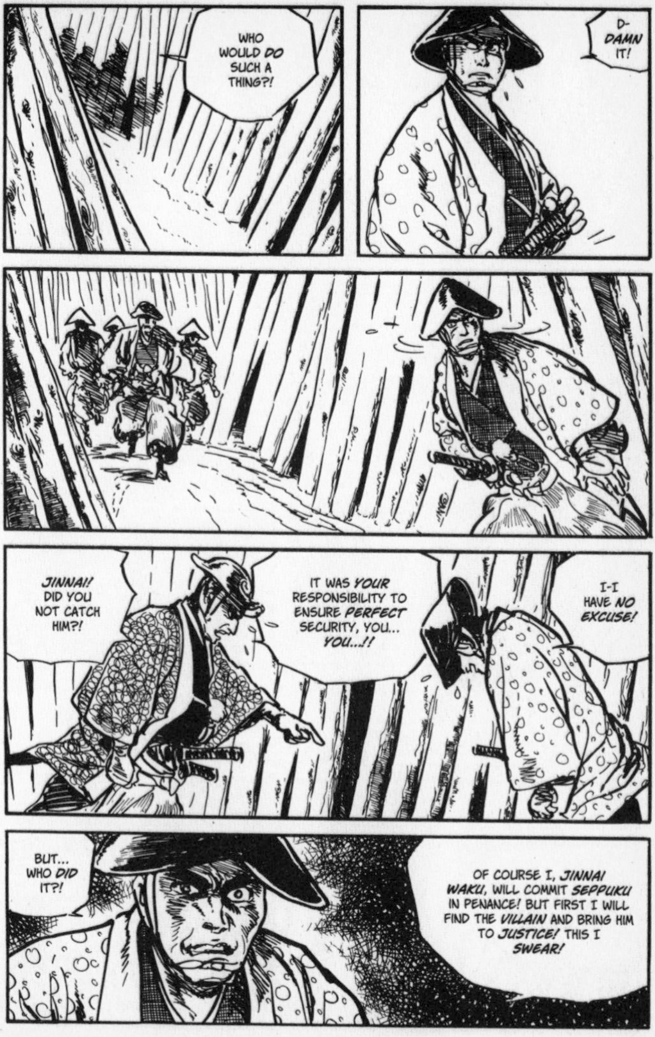
WHO WOULD *DO* SUCH A THING?!
D- *DAMN* IT!
JINNAI! DID YOU NOT CATCH HIM?!
IT WAS *YOUR* RESPONSIBILITY TO ENSURE *PERFECT* SECURITY, YOU... *YOU...!!*
I-I HAVE *NO EXCUSE!*
BUT... WHO *DID* IT?!
OF COURSE I, *JINNAI WAKU*, WILL COMMIT *SEPPUKU* IN PENANCE! BUT FIRST I WILL FIND THE *VILLAIN* AND BRING HIM TO *JUSTICE!* THIS I *SWEAR!*

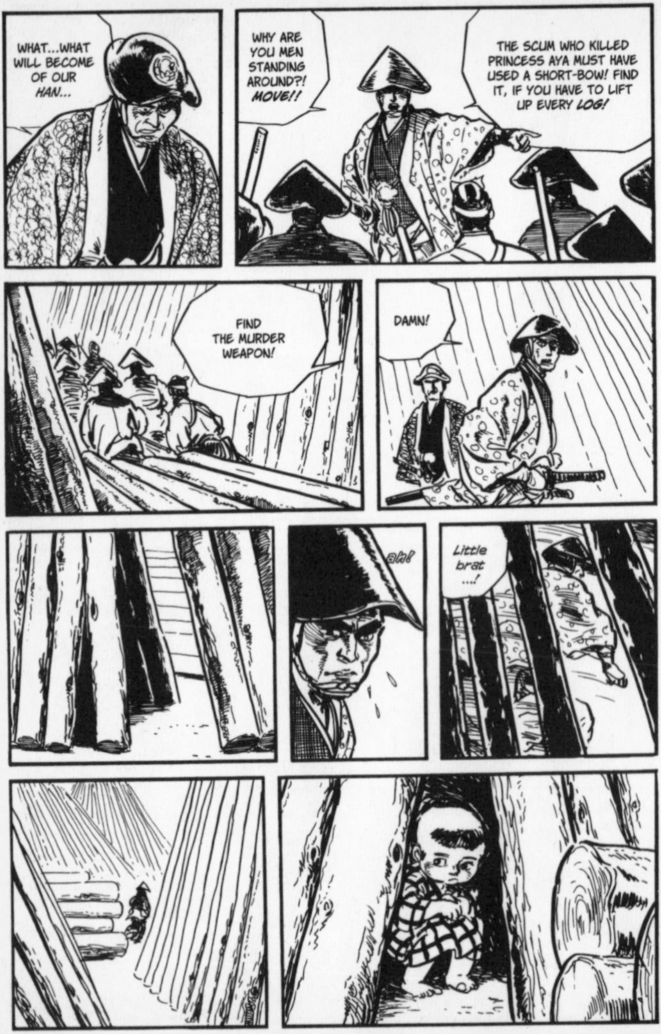
WHAT...WHAT WILL BECOME OF OUR *HAN*...
WHY ARE YOU MEN STANDING AROUND?! ***MOVE!!***
THE SCUM WHO KILLED PRINCESS AYA MUST HAVE USED A SHORT-BOW! FIND IT, IF YOU HAVE TO LIFT UP EVERY ***LOG!***
FIND THE MURDER WEAPON!
DAMN!
ah!
Little brat ...!

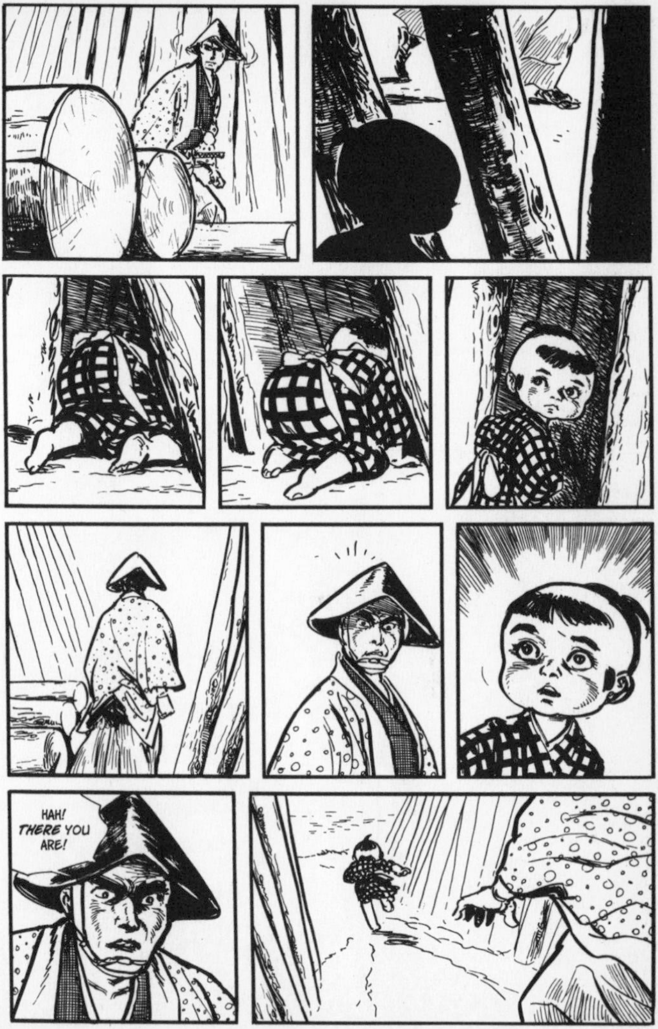
HAH! THERE YOU ARE!

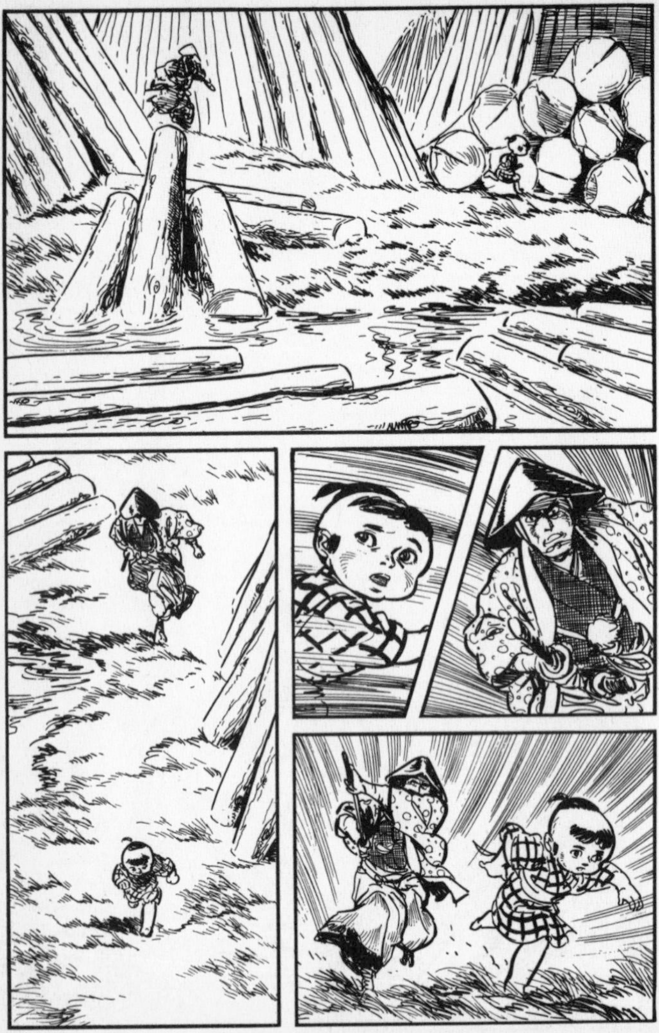

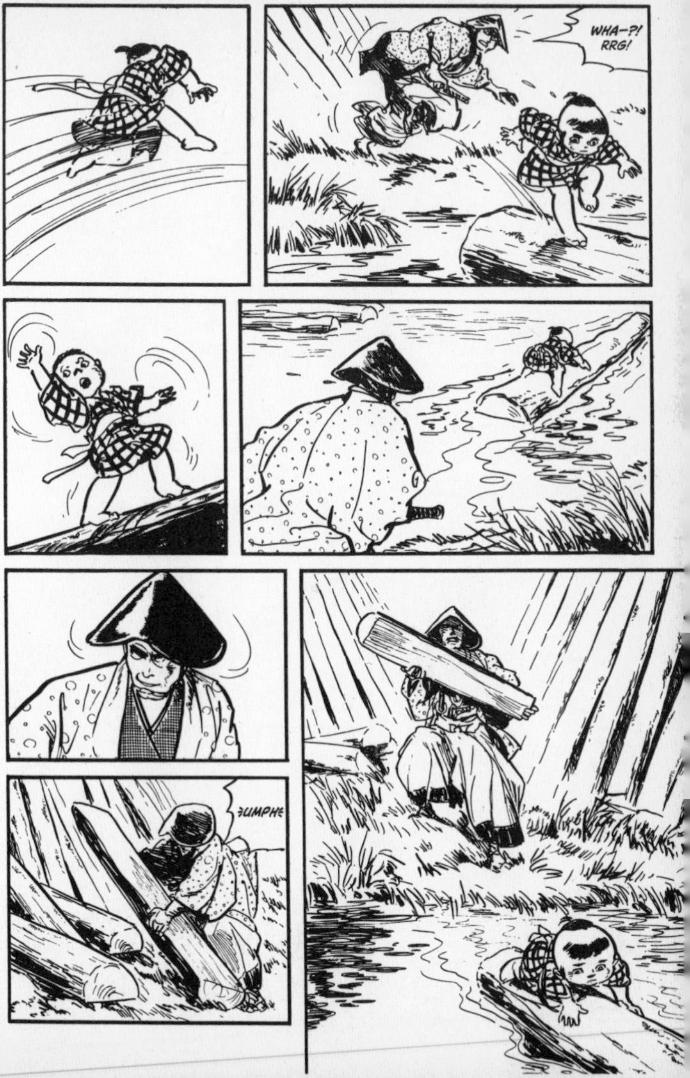
WHA-?! RRG!
UMPH

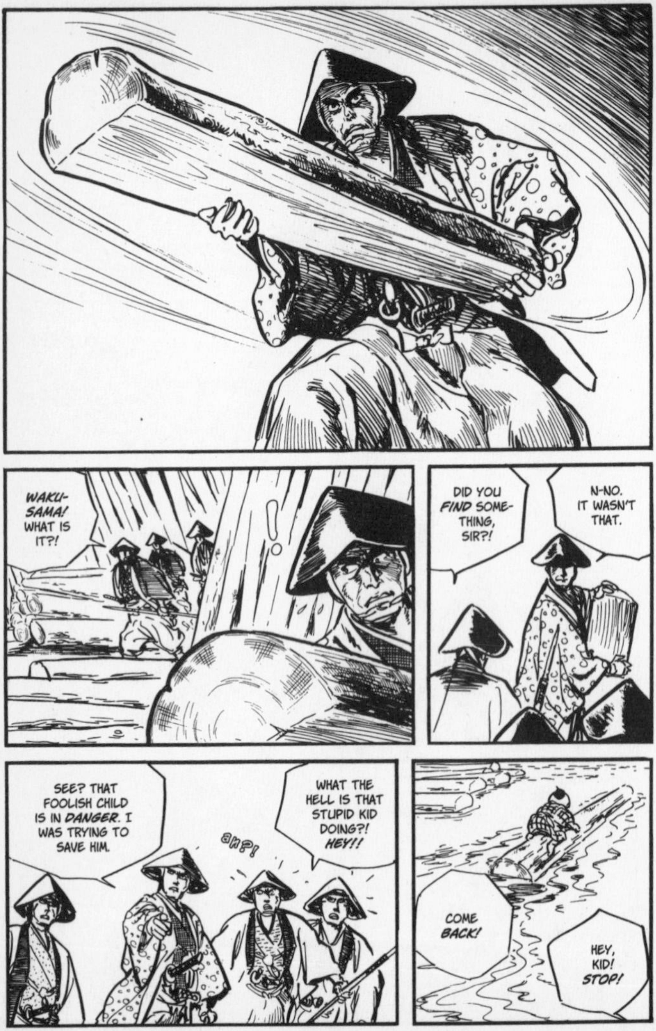
WAKU-SAMA! WHAT IS IT?!
!
DID YOU *FIND* SOME-THING, SIR?!
N-NO. IT WASN'T THAT.
SEE? THAT FOOLISH CHILD IS IN *DANGER*. I WAS TRYING TO SAVE HIM.
ah?!
WHAT THE HELL IS THAT STUPID KID DOING?! *HEY!!*
COME *BACK!*
HEY, KID! *STOP!*

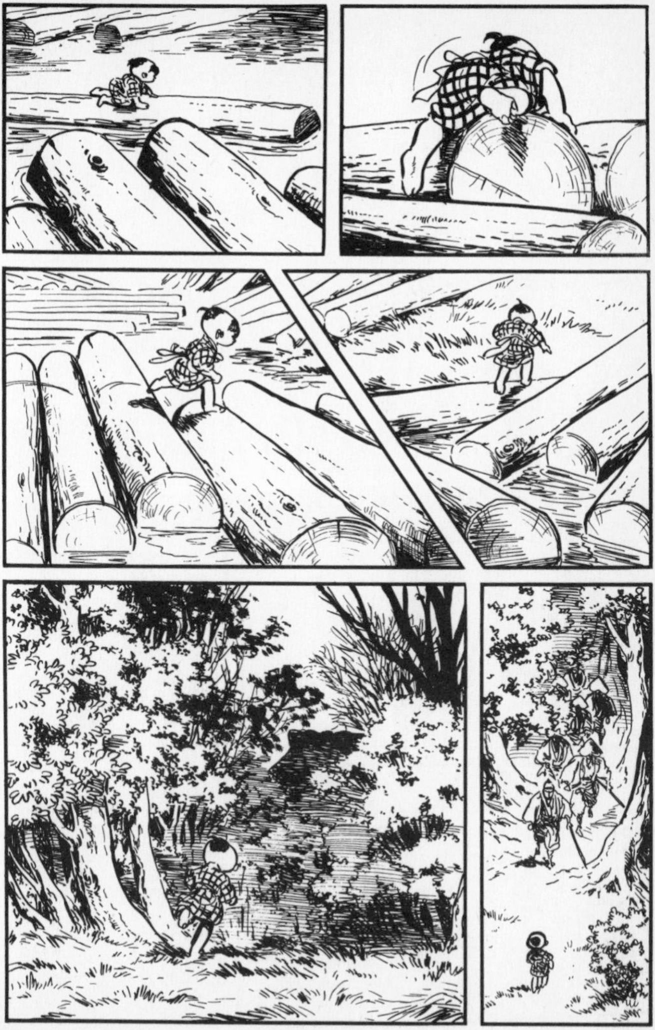

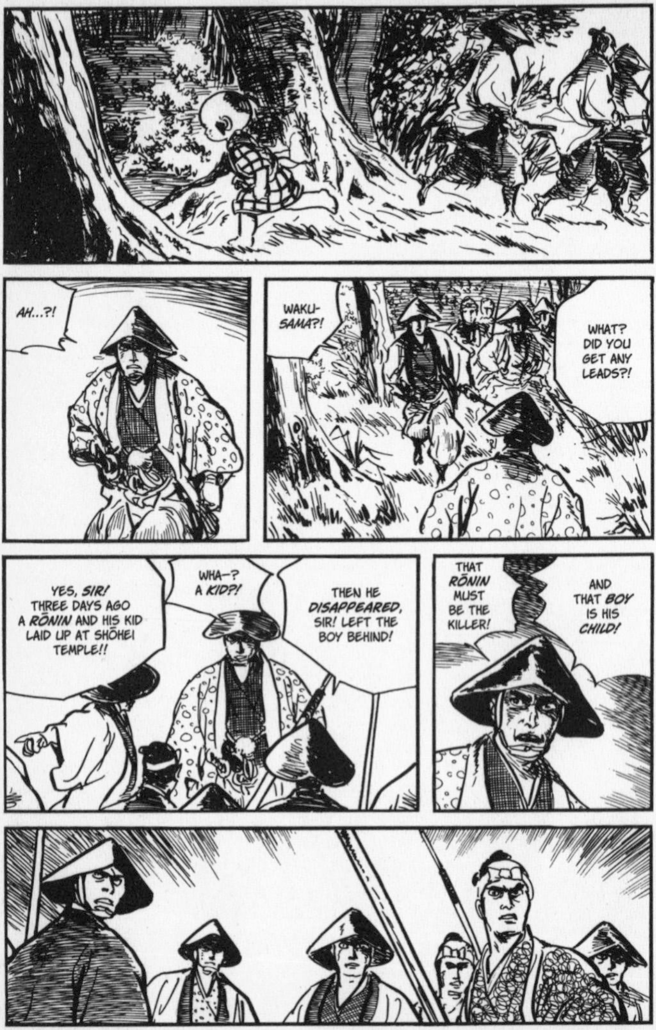
AH...?!
WAKU-SAMA?!
WHAT? DID YOU GET ANY LEADS?!
YES, *SIR!* THREE DAYS AGO A *RŌNIN* AND HIS KID LAID UP AT SHŌHEI TEMPLE!!
WHA–? A *KID?!*
THEN HE *DISAPPEARED,* SIR! LEFT THE BOY BEHIND!
THAT *RŌNIN* MUST BE THE KILLER!
AND THAT *BOY* IS HIS *CHILD!*

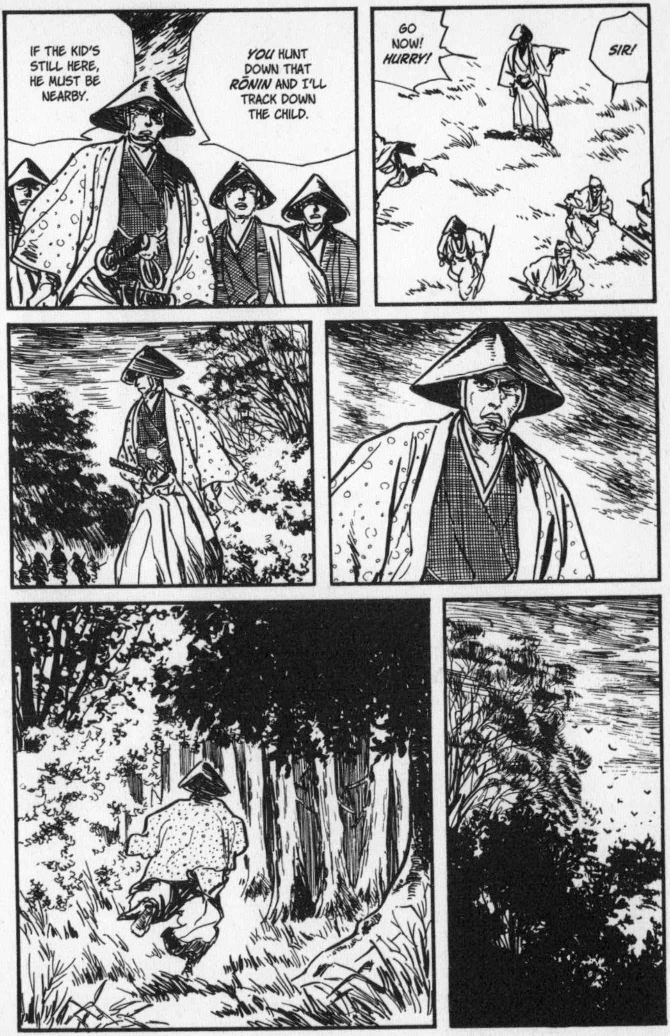
IF THE KID'S STILL HERE, HE MUST BE NEARBY.
YOU HUNT DOWN THAT RŌNIN AND I'LL TRACK DOWN THE CHILD.
GO NOW! HURRY!
SIR!

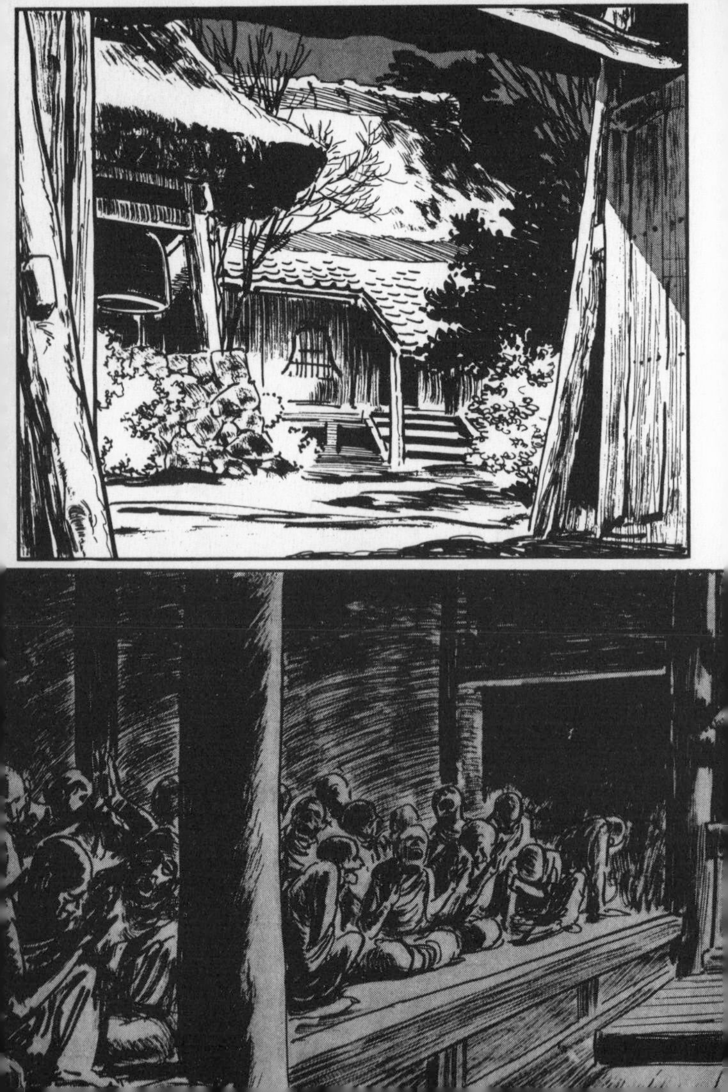

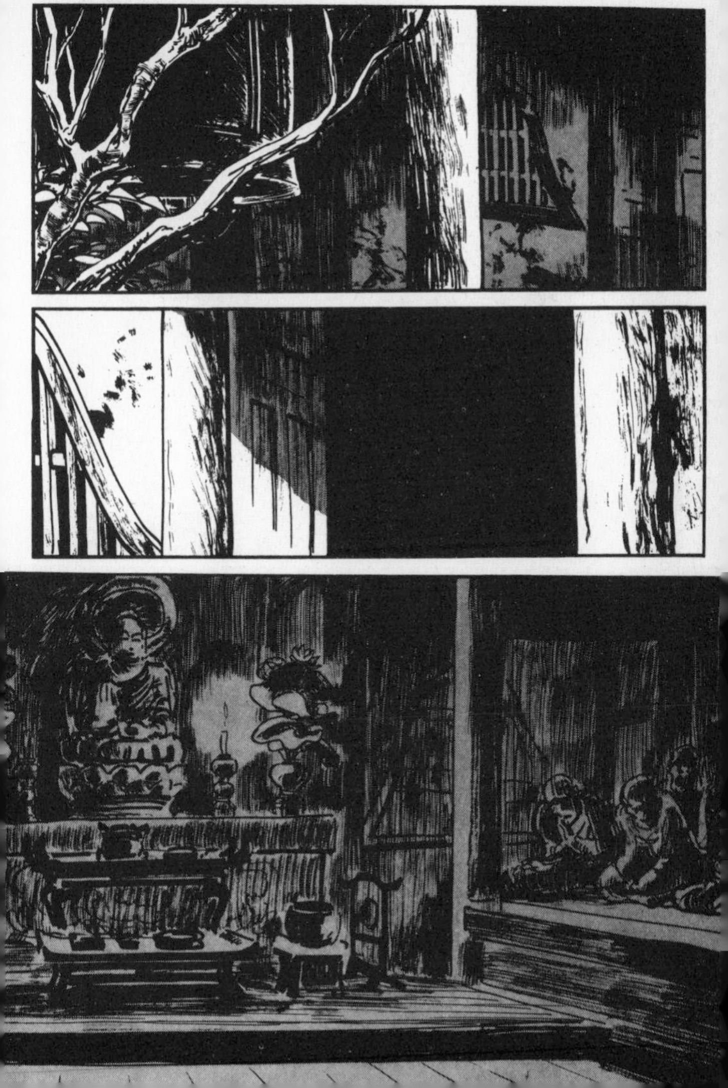

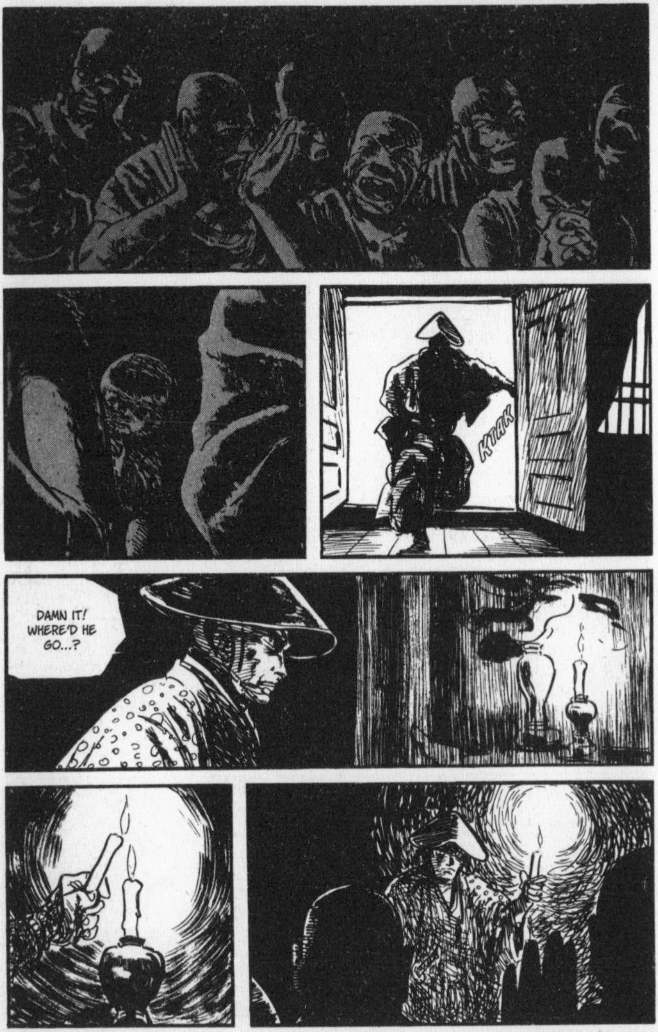
KTAK
DAMN IT! WHERE'D HE GO...?

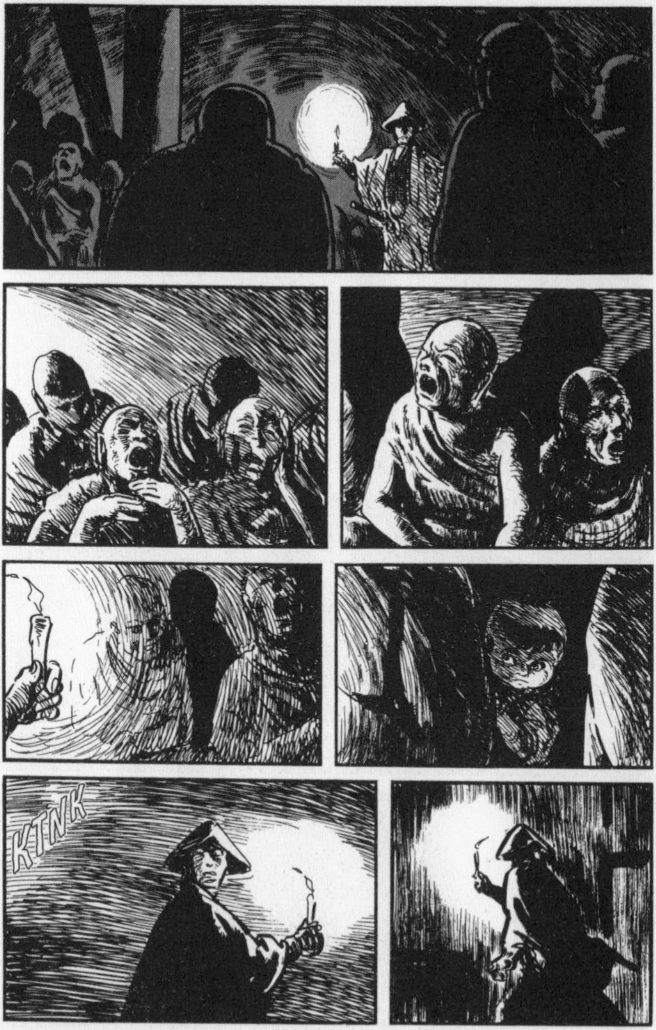
KTNK

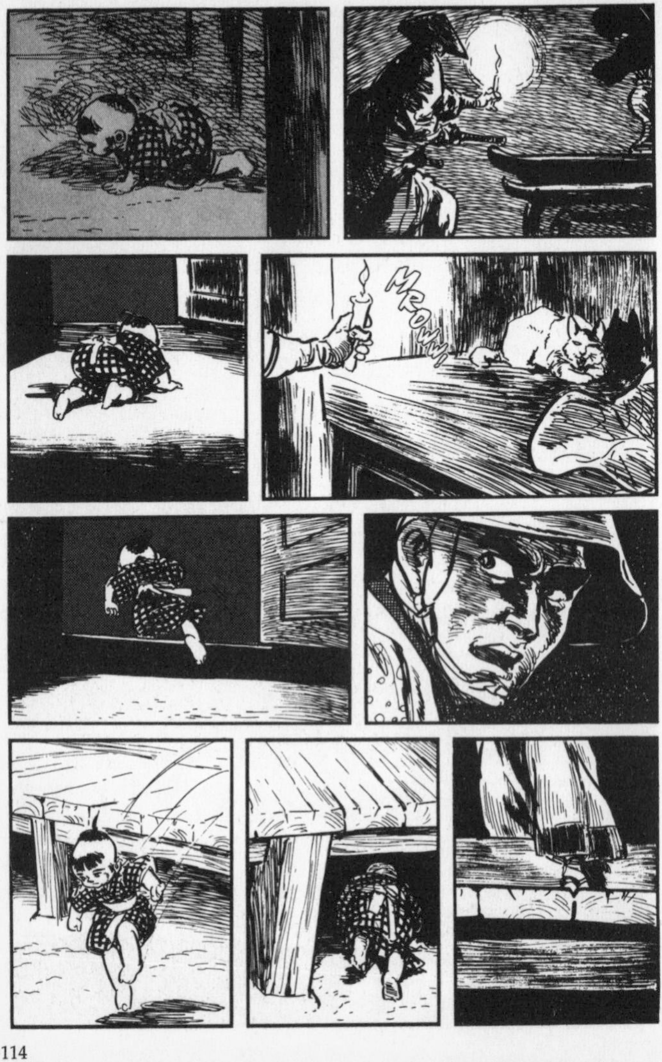
MROWW

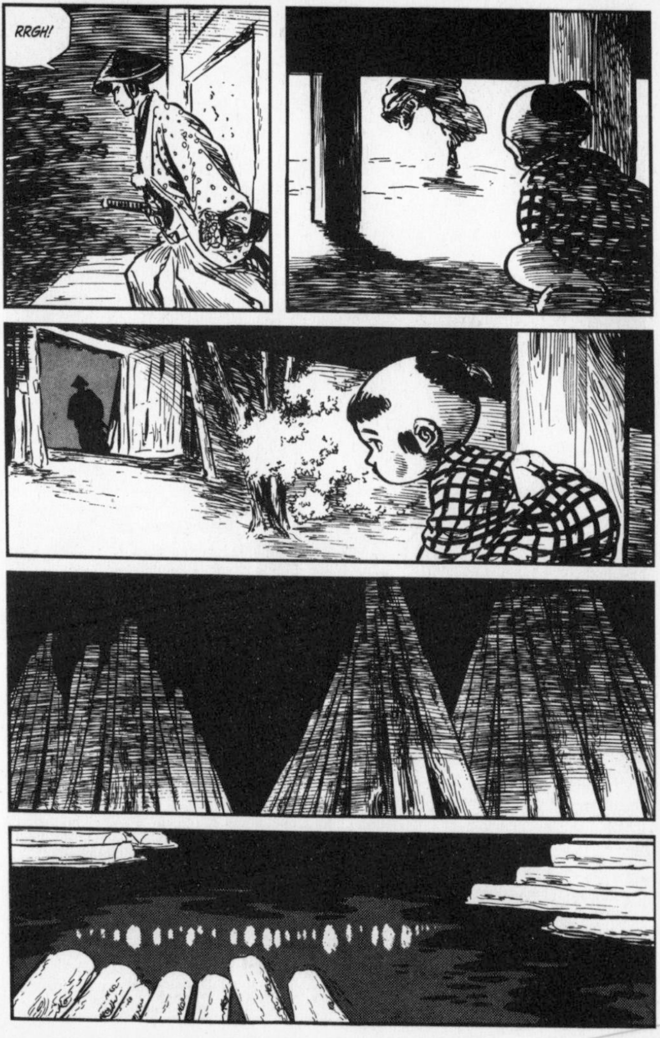
RRGH!

HOW COULD THE KILLER HAVE GOTTEN THROUGH ALL OUR SECURITY...?

AND WHERE IS THE WEAPON?!

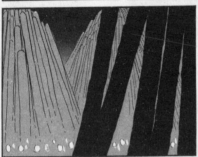

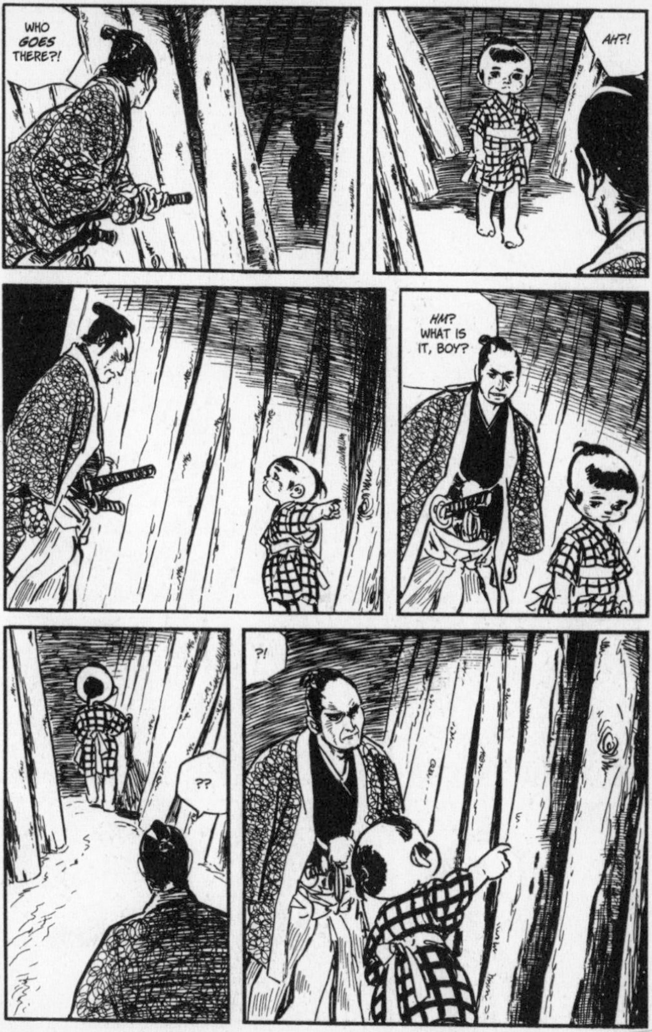
WHO GOES THERE?!
AH?!
HM? WHAT IS IT, BOY?
??
?!

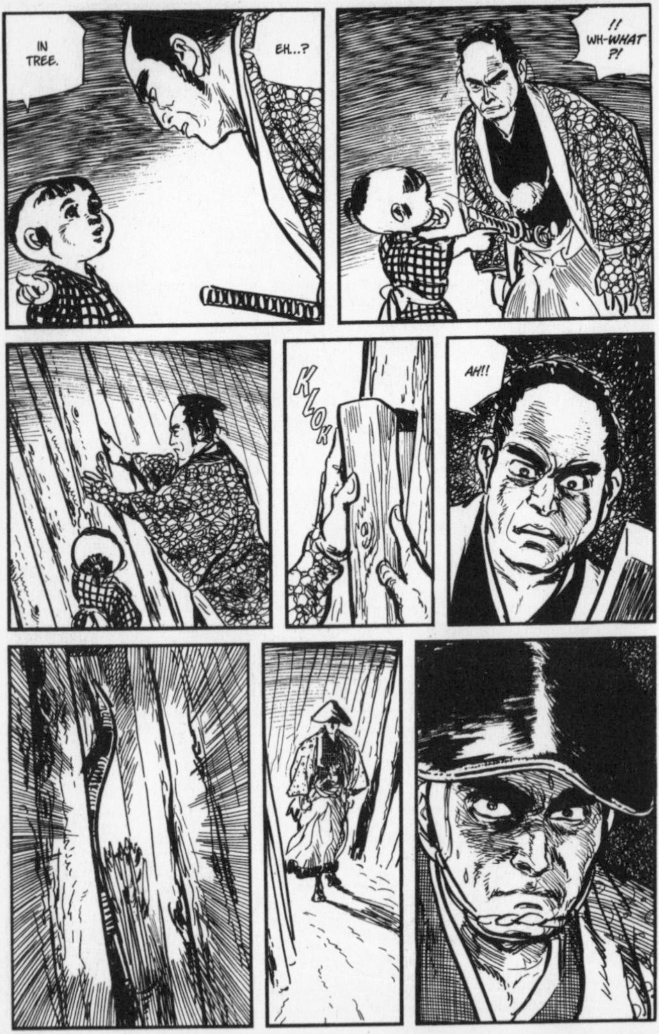
IN TREE.
EH...?
!! WH-WHAT ?!
KLOK
AH!!

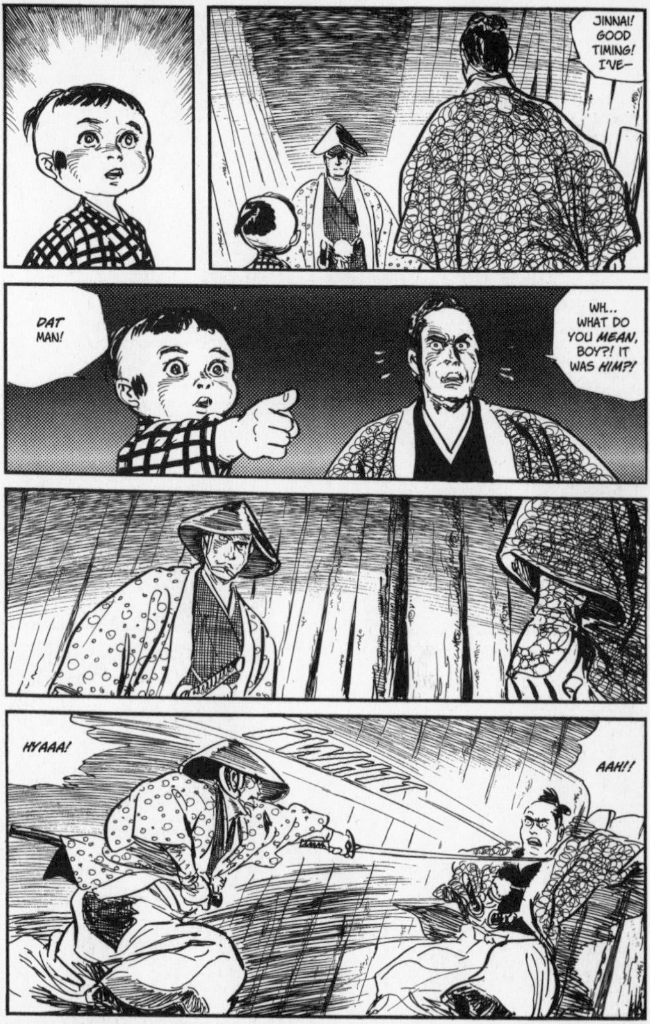
JINNAI! GOOD TIMING! I'VE—
DAT MAN!
WH.. WHAT DO YOU MEAN, BOY?! IT WAS HIM?!
HYAAA!
AAH!!

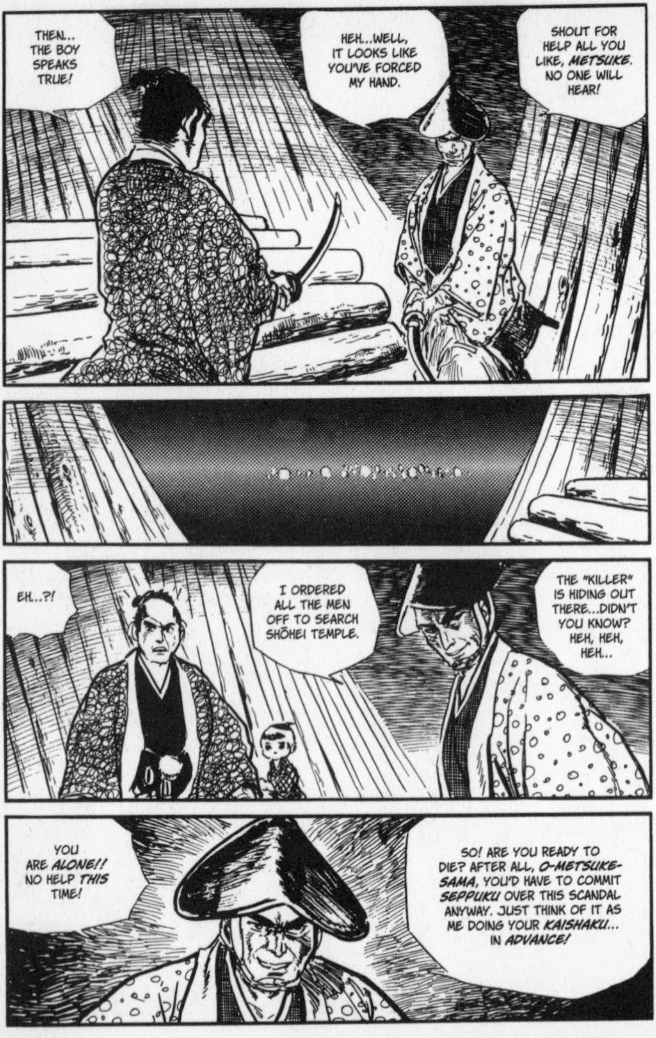
THEN... THE BOY SPEAKS TRUE!
HEH...WELL, IT LOOKS LIKE YOU'VE FORCED MY HAND.
SHOUT FOR HELP ALL YOU LIKE, *METSUKE*. NO ONE WILL HEAR!
EH...?!
I ORDERED ALL THE MEN OFF TO SEARCH SHŌHEI TEMPLE.
THE "KILLER" IS HIDING OUT THERE...DIDN'T YOU KNOW? HEH, HEH, HEH...
YOU ARE *ALONE!!* NO HELP *THIS* TIME!
SO! ARE YOU READY TO DIE? AFTER ALL, *O-METSUKE-SAMA*, YOU'D HAVE TO COMMIT *SEPPUKU* OVER THIS SCANDAL ANYWAY. JUST THINK OF IT AS ME DOING YOUR *KAISHAKU*... IN *ADVANCE!*

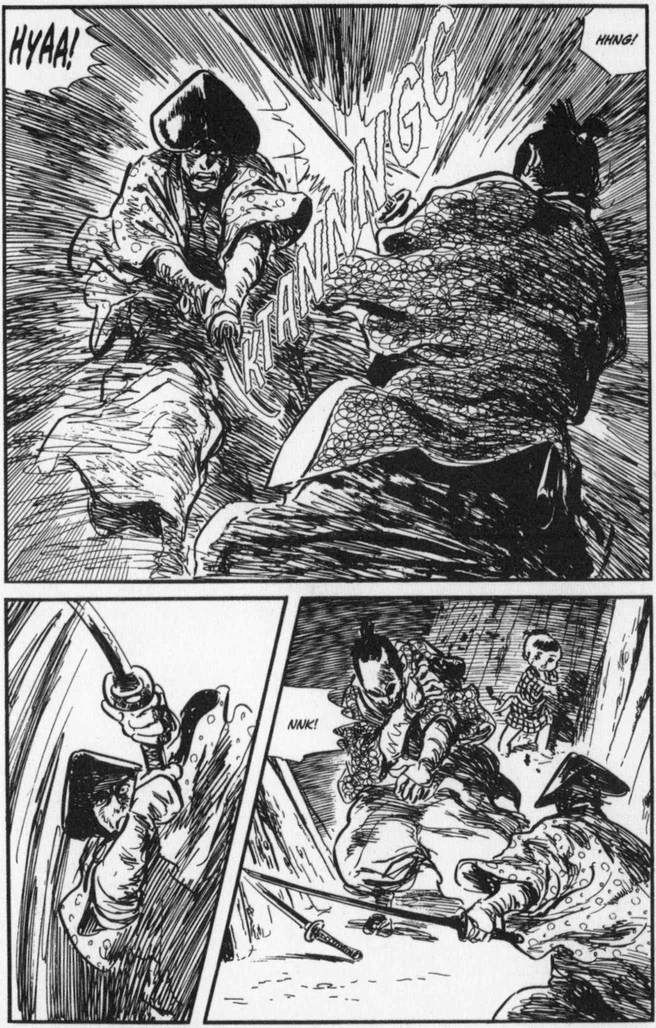
HYAA!
KTANNNGG
HHNG!
NNK!

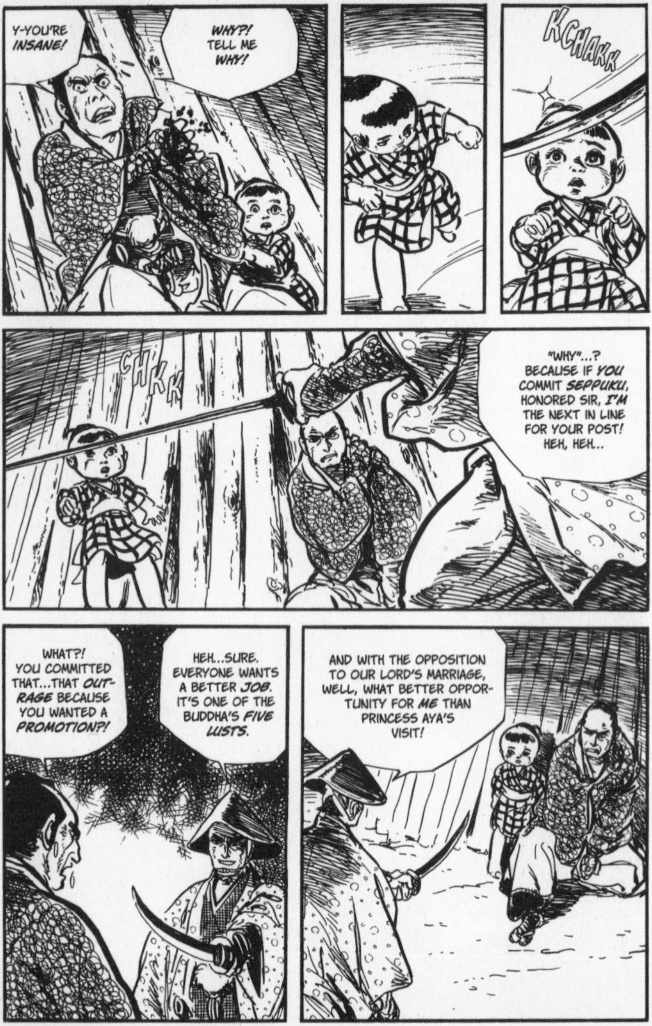

Y-YOU'RE INSANE!
WHY?! TELL ME WHY!
KCHAKK
CHKK
"WHY"...? BECAUSE IF YOU COMMIT SEPPUKU, HONORED SIR, I'M THE NEXT IN LINE FOR YOUR POST! HEH, HEH...
WHAT?! YOU COMMITTED THAT...THAT OUTRAGE BECAUSE YOU WANTED A PROMOTION?!
HEH...SURE. EVERYONE WANTS A BETTER JOB. IT'S ONE OF THE BUDDHA'S FIVE LUSTS.
AND WITH THE OPPOSITION TO OUR LORD'S MARRIAGE, WELL, WHAT BETTER OPPORTUNITY FOR ME THAN PRINCESS AYA'S VISIT!

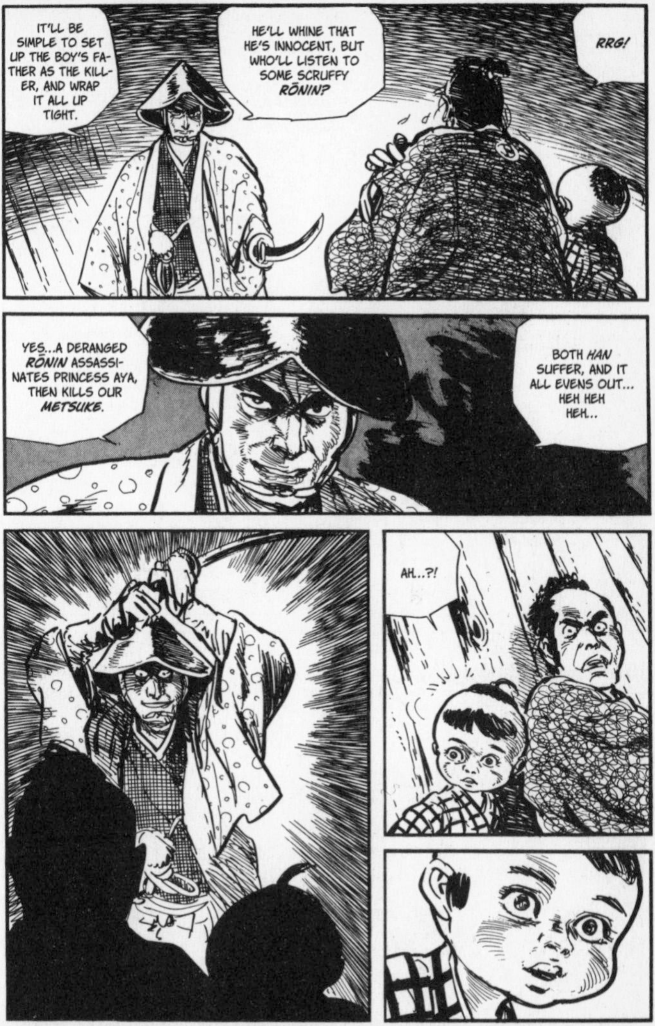
IT'LL BE SIMPLE TO SET UP THE BOY'S FATHER AS THE KILLER, AND WRAP IT ALL UP TIGHT.
HE'LL WHINE THAT HE'S INNOCENT, BUT WHO'LL LISTEN TO SOME SCRUFFY *RŌNIN?*
RRG!
YES...A DERANGED *RŌNIN* ASSASSINATES PRINCESS AYA, THEN KILLS OUR *METSUKE*.
BOTH *HAN* SUFFER, AND IT ALL EVENS OUT... HEH HEH HEH...
AH..?!

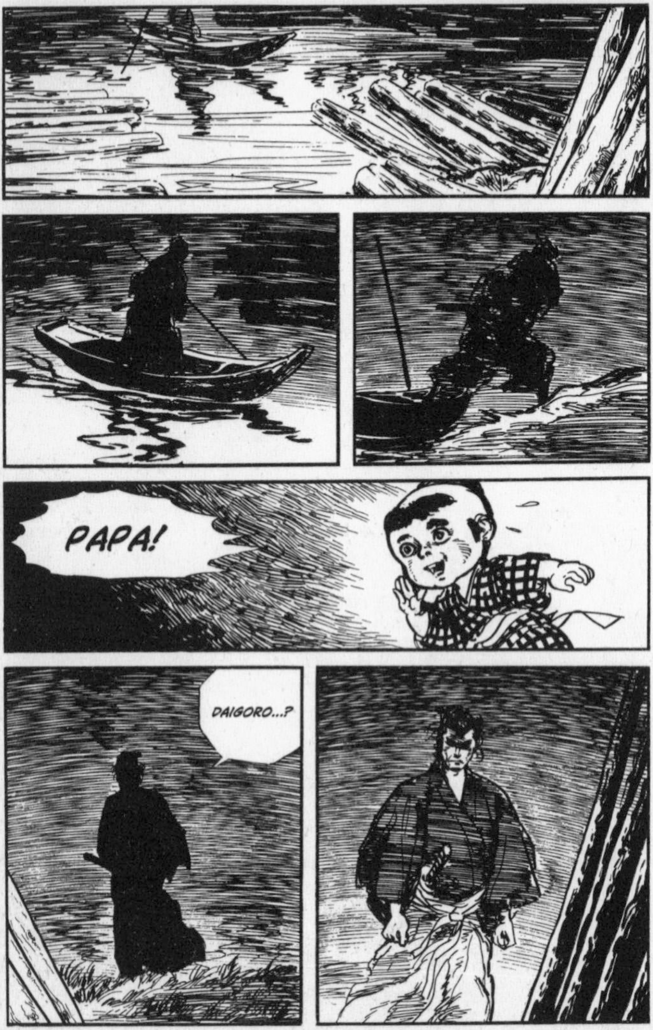
PAPA!
DAIGORO...?

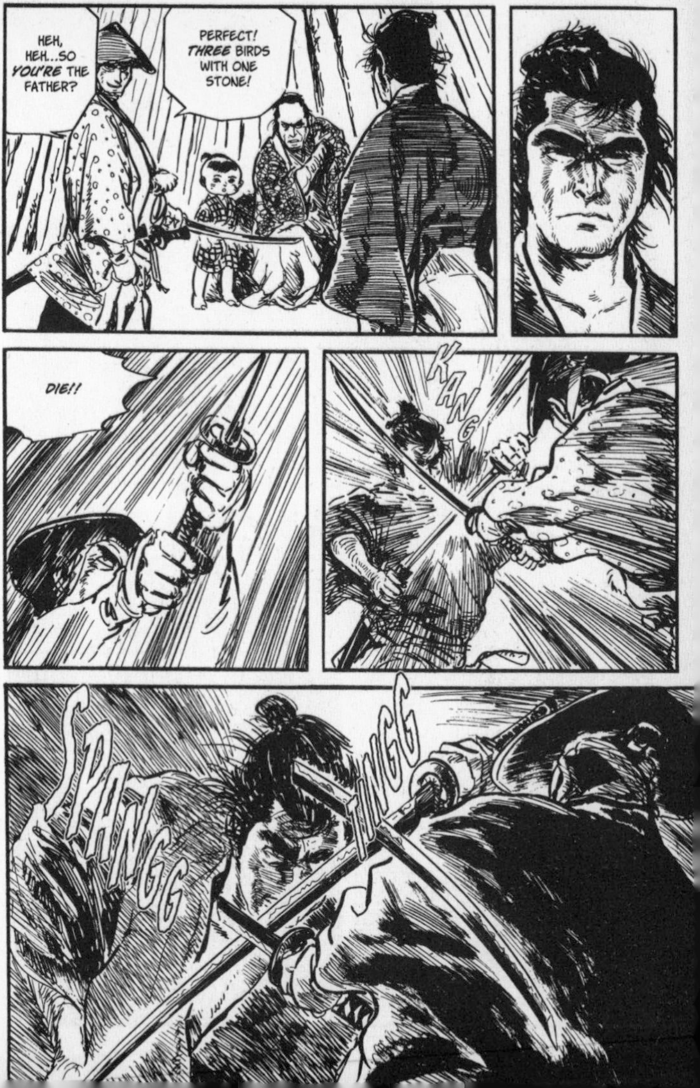
HEH, HEH...SO YOU'RE THE FATHER?
PERFECT! THREE BIRDS WITH ONE STONE!
DIE!!
KANG
SPANGG
TINGG

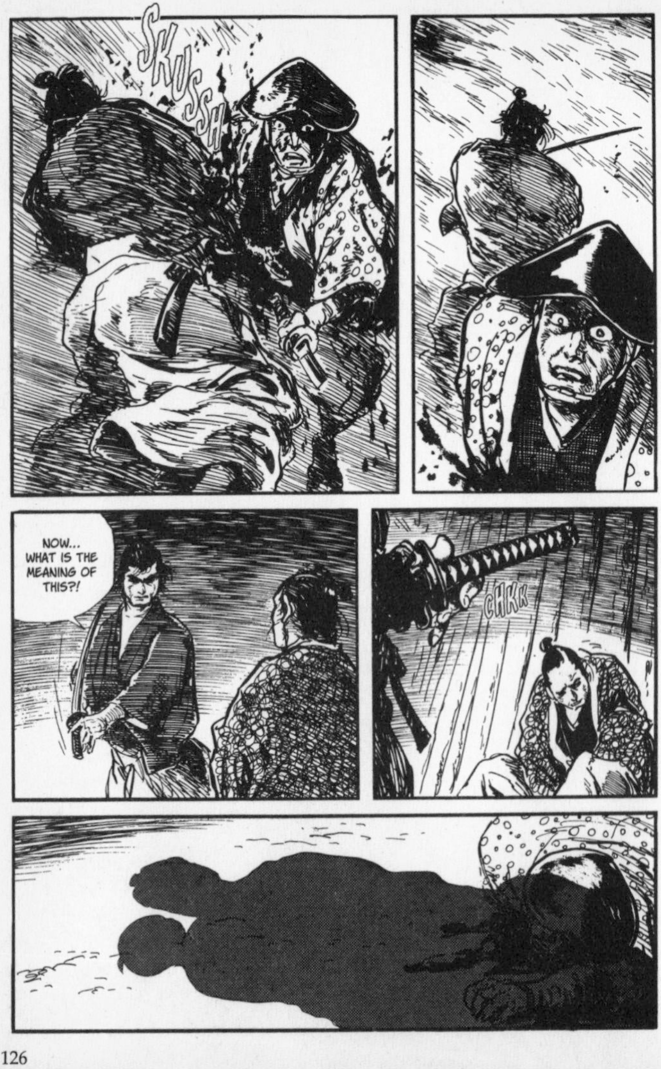
SKUSSH
NOW... WHAT IS THE MEANING OF THIS?!
CHKK

the thirty-sixth

Cloud Dragon, Wind Tiger

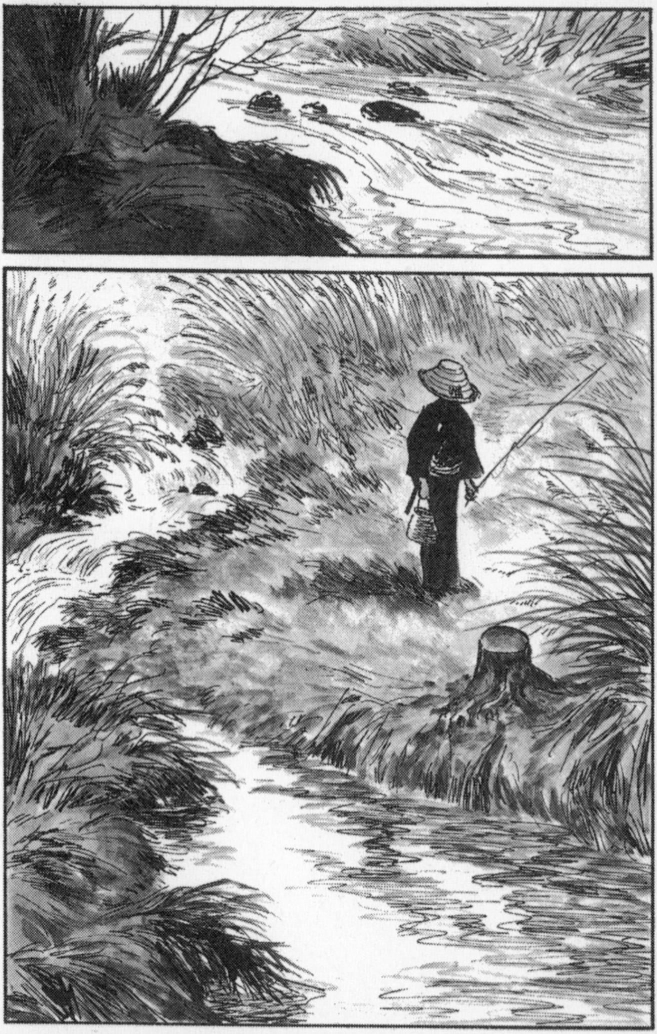

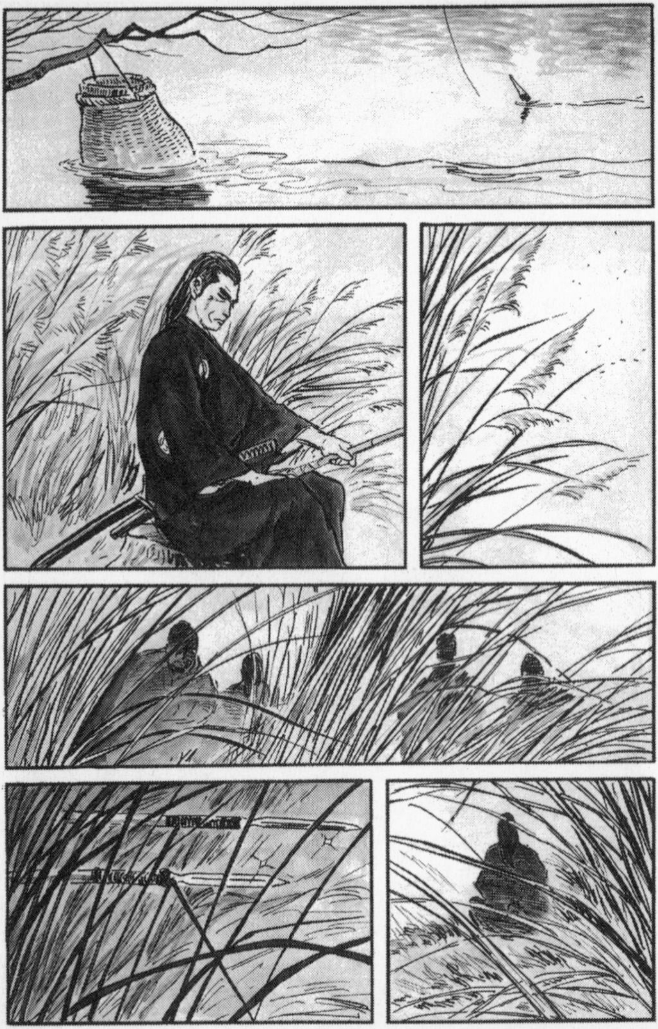

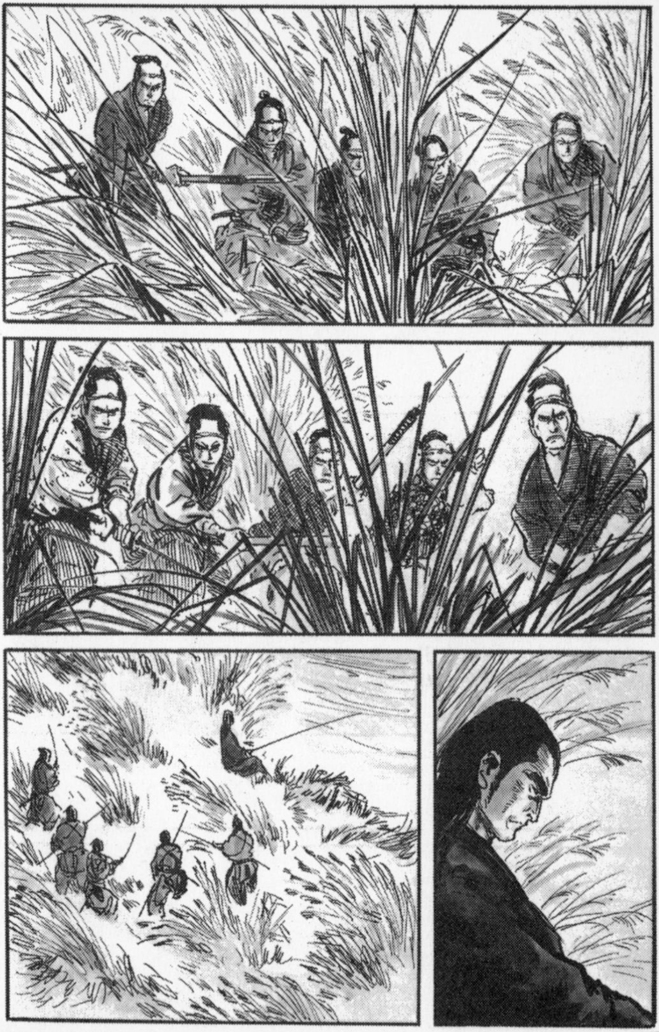

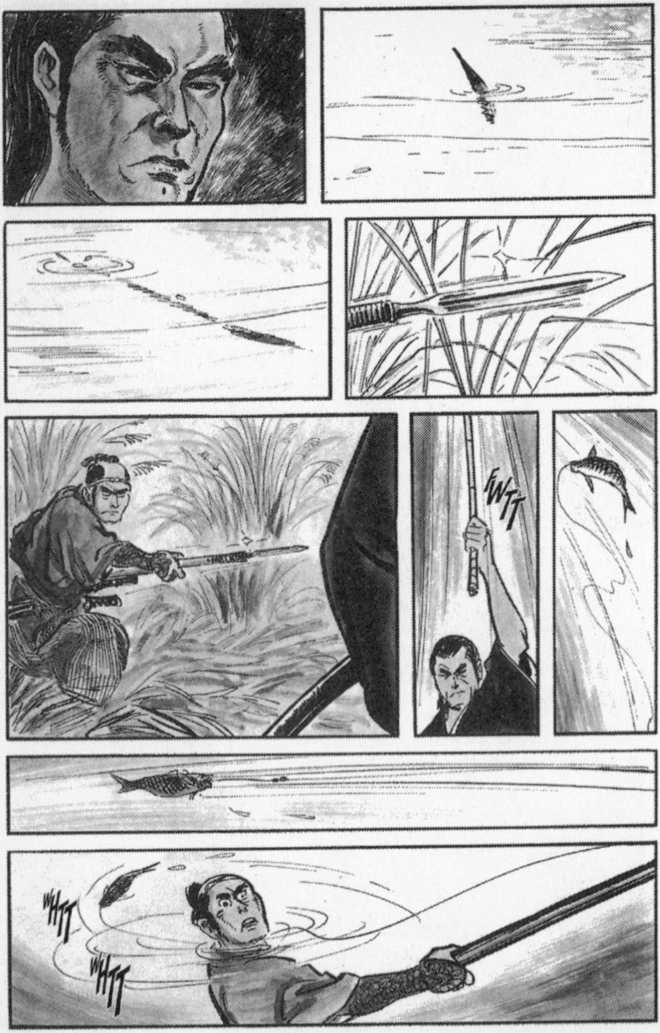
FWTT
WHTT
WHTT

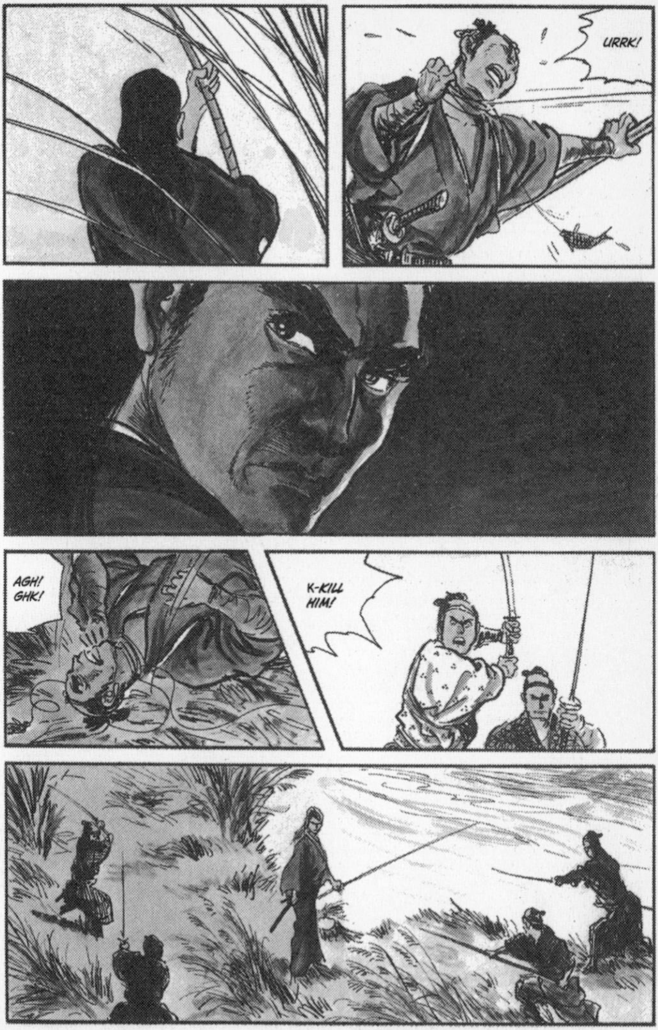
URRK!
AGH! GHK!
K-KILL HIM!

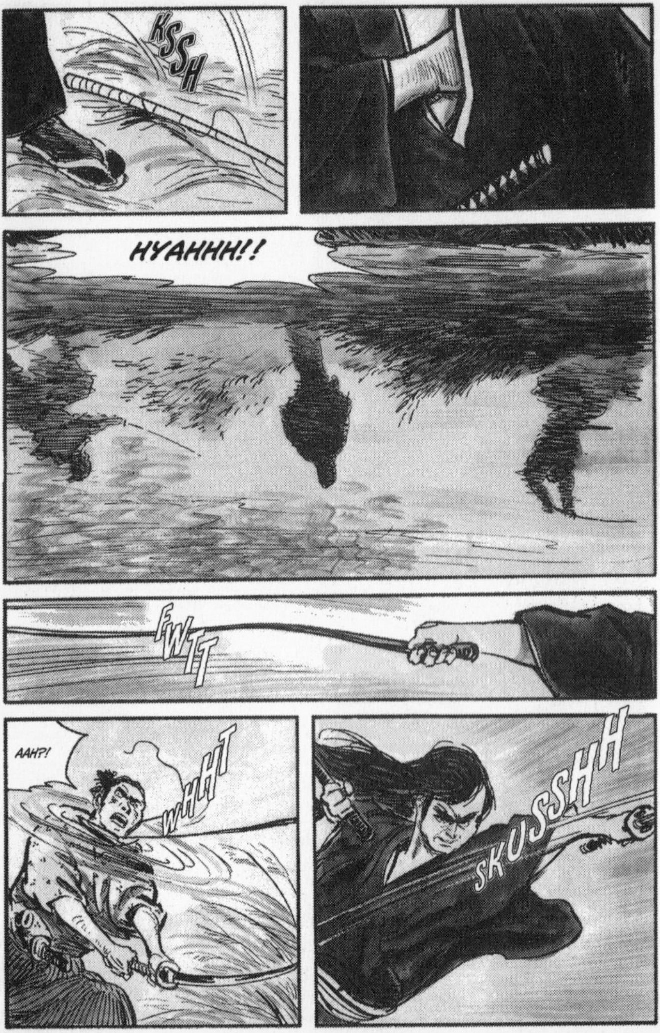
KSSH
HYAHHH!!
FWTT
AAH?!
WHHHT
SKUSSHH

NGGK!

GLLK!

WHSST

RYAA!

WHSS

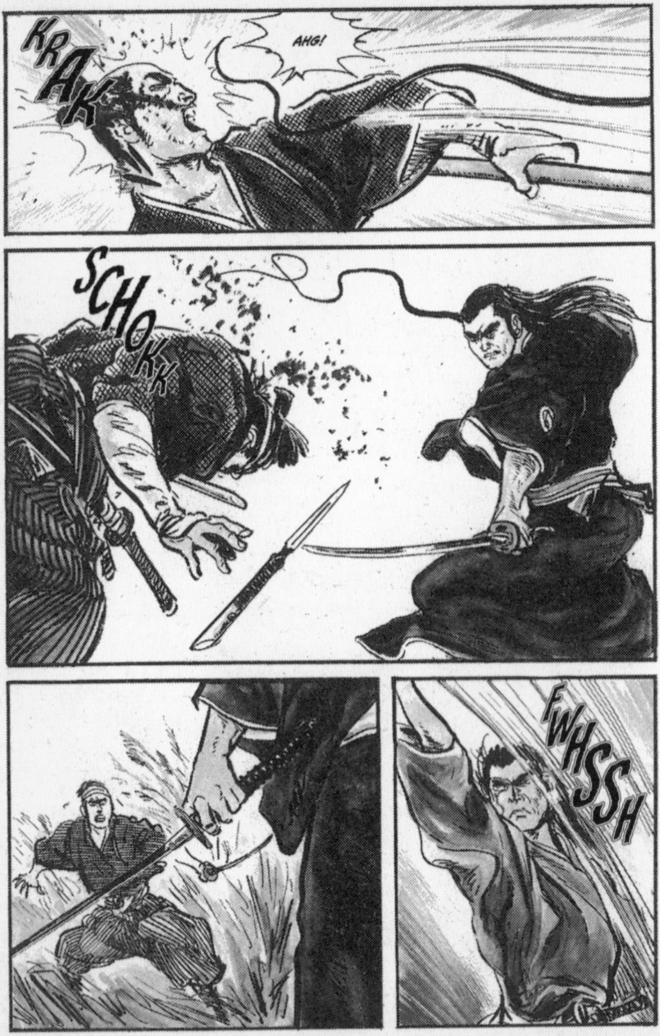
KRAK
AHG!
SCHOKK
FWHSSH

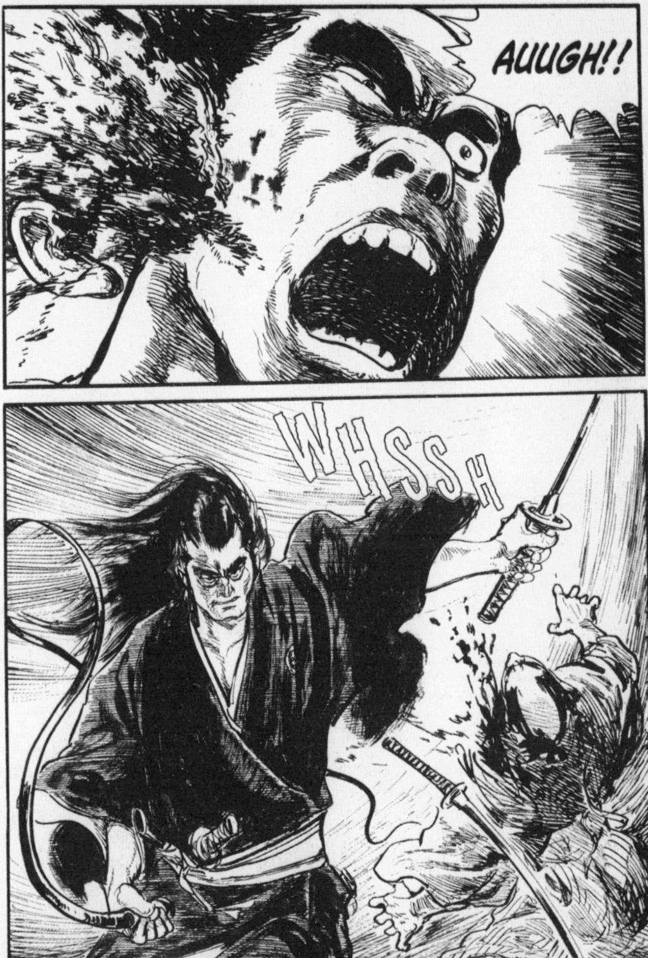
AUUGH!!
WHSSH

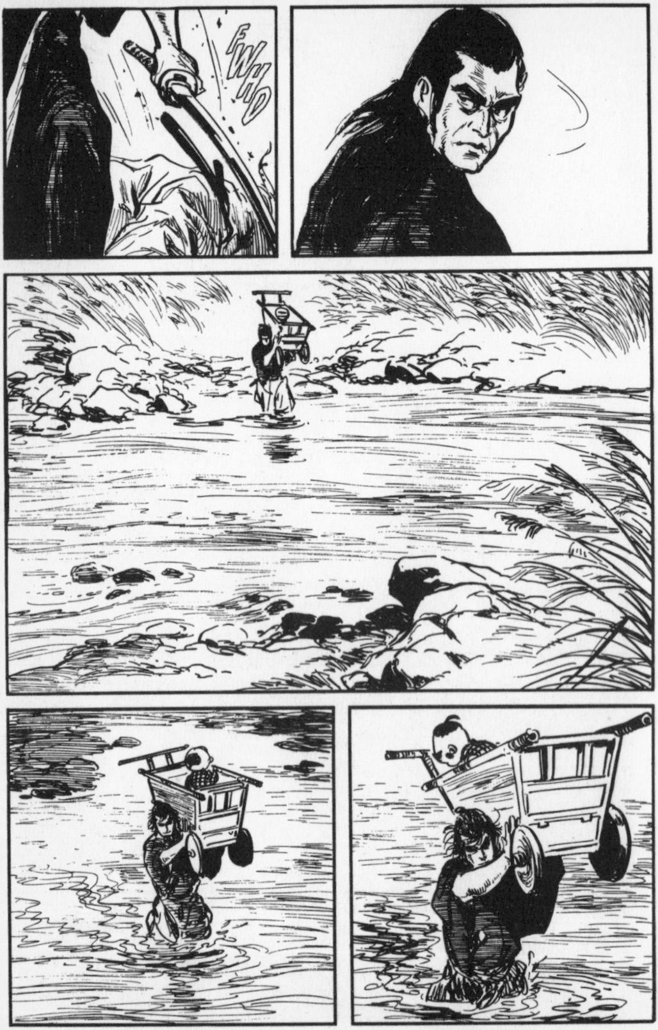
FWHD

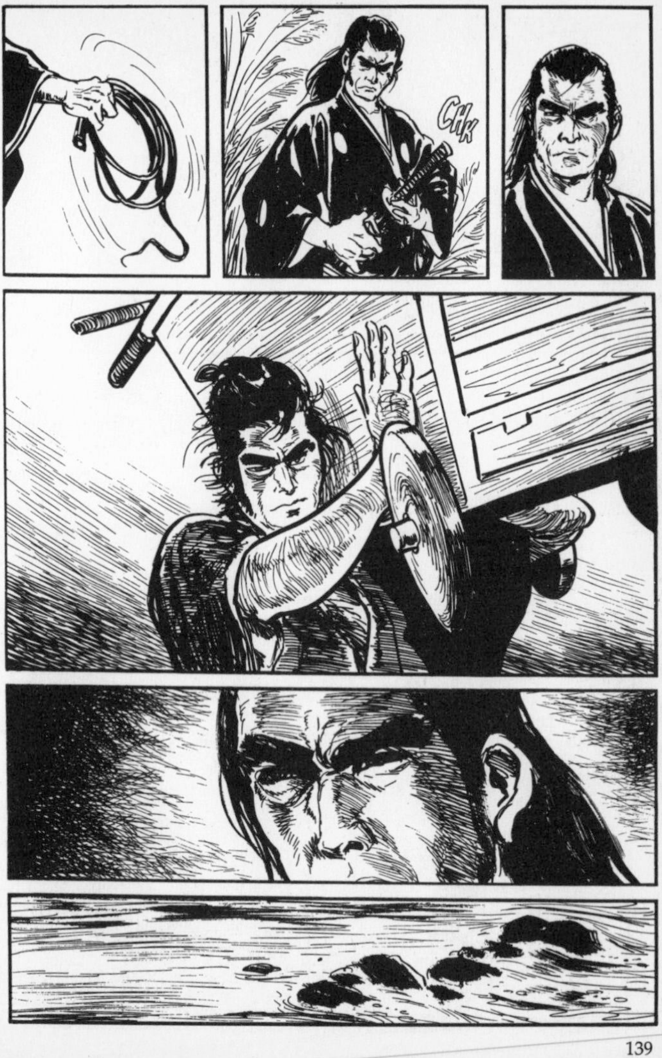
CHK

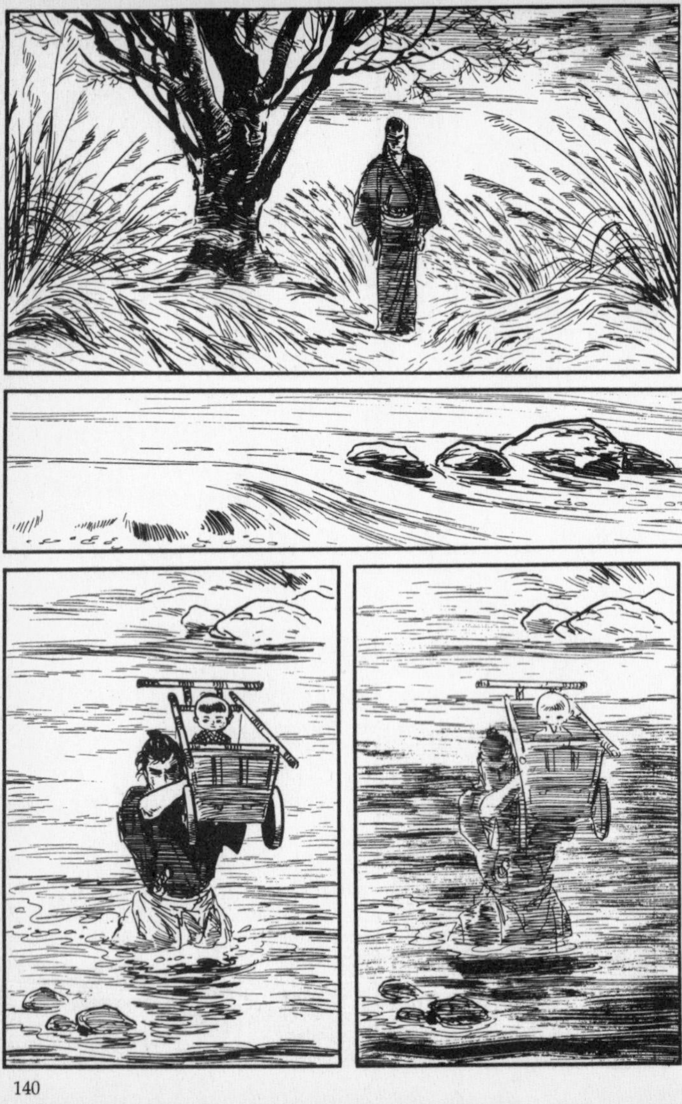

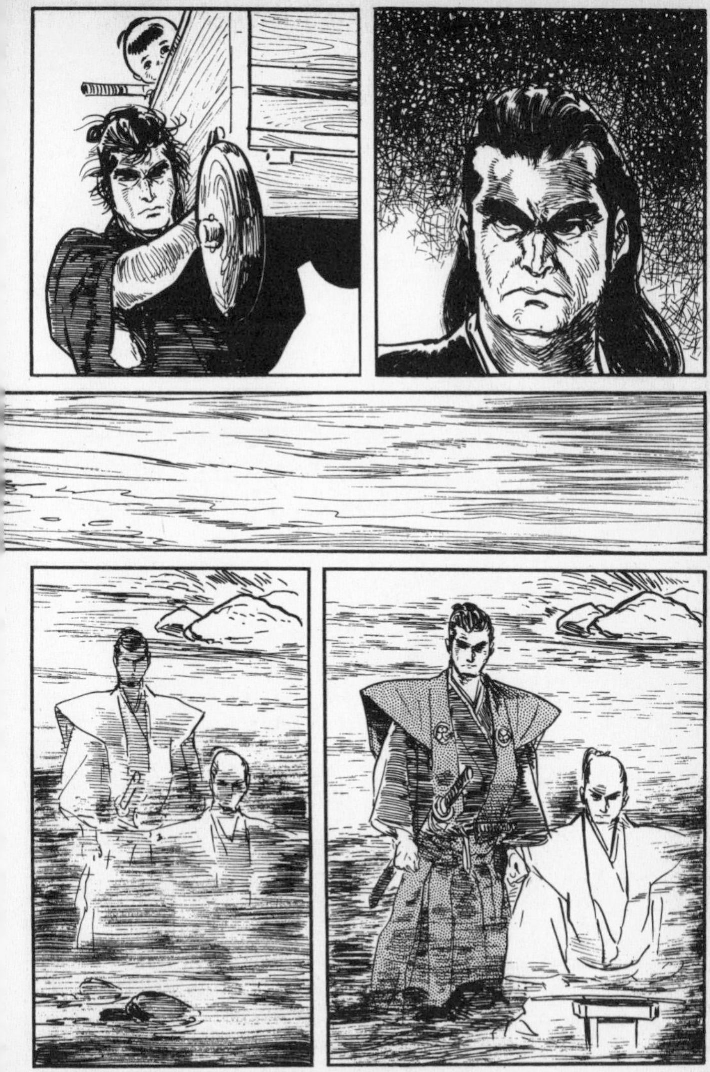

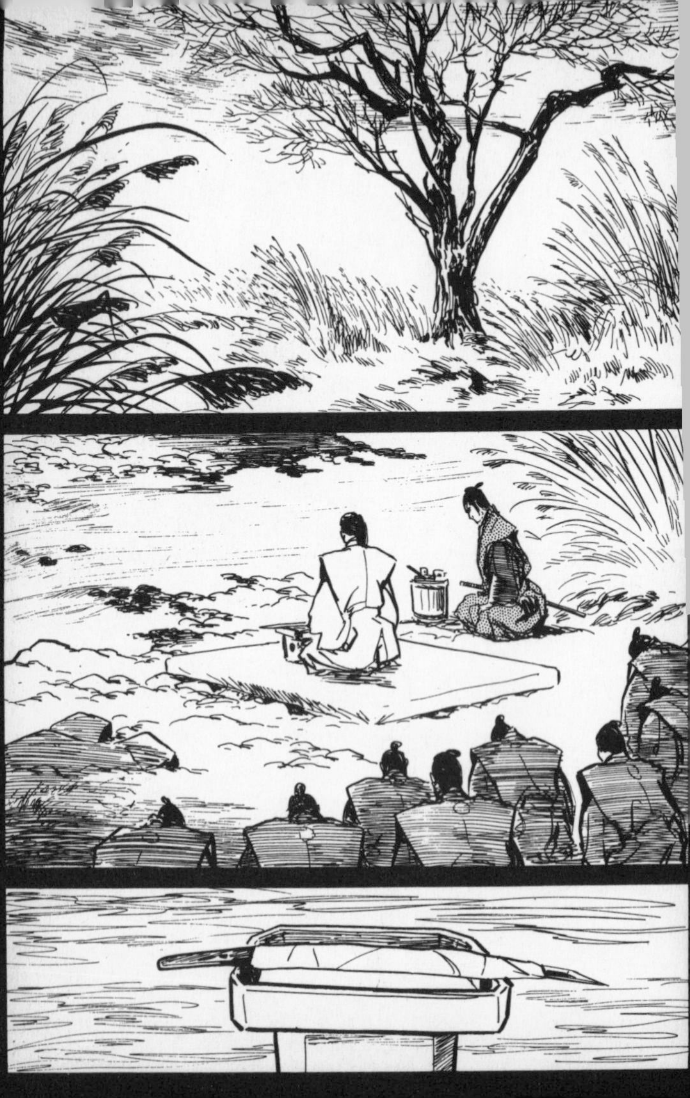

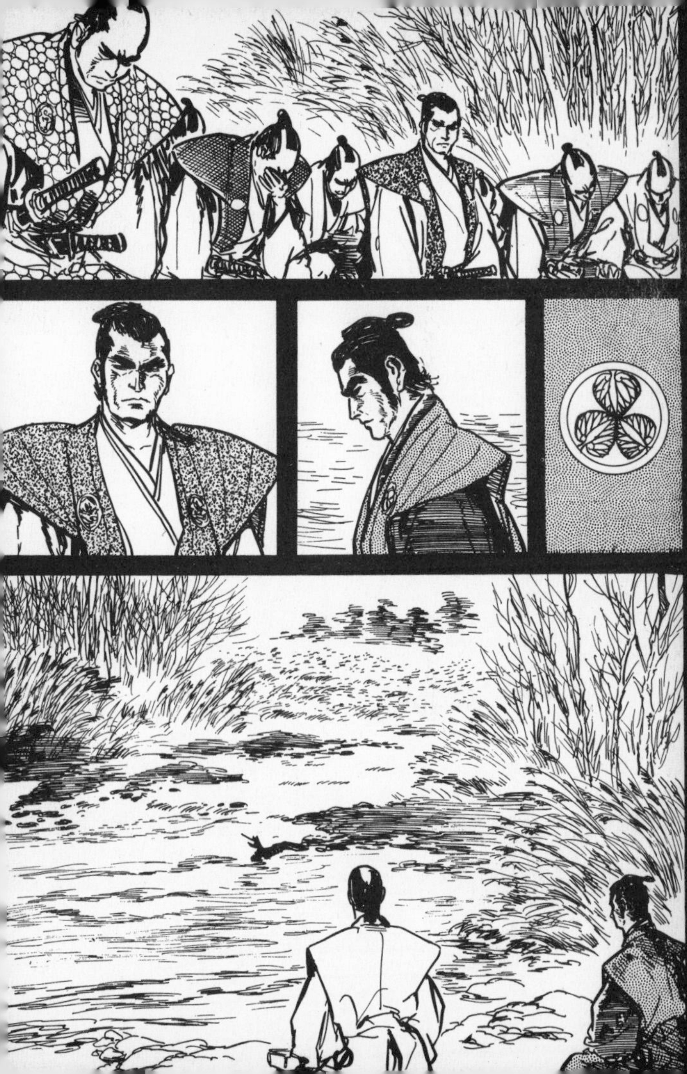

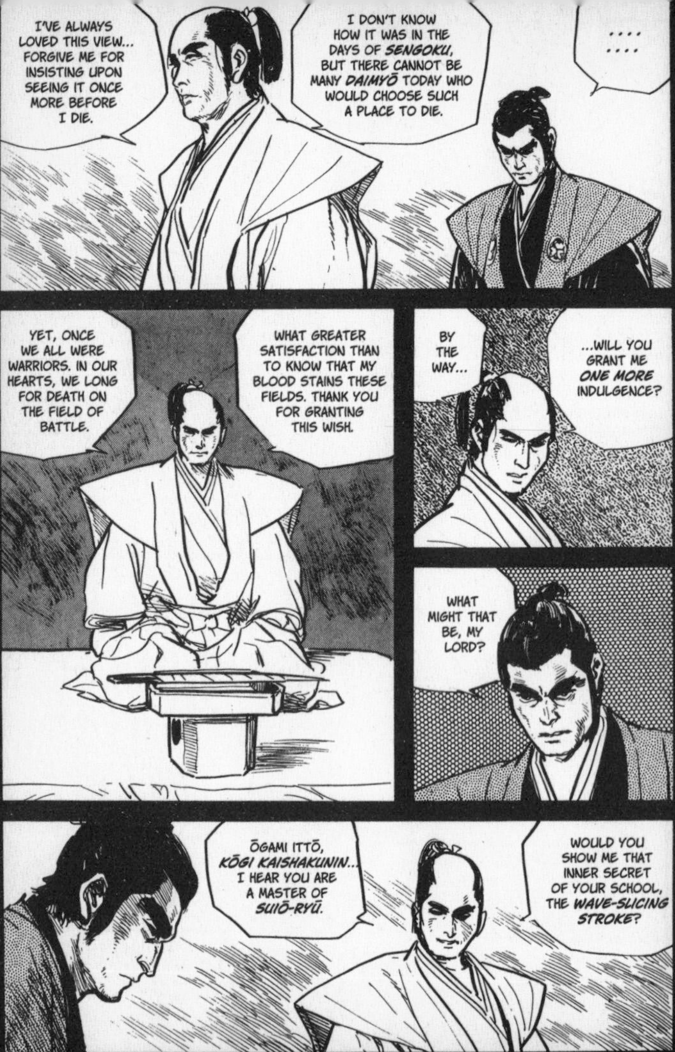
I'VE ALWAYS LOVED THIS VIEW... FORGIVE ME FOR INSISTING UPON SEEING IT ONCE MORE BEFORE I DIE.
I DON'T KNOW HOW IT WAS IN THE DAYS OF *SENGOKU*, BUT THERE CANNOT BE MANY *DAIMYŌ* TODAY WHO WOULD CHOOSE SUCH A PLACE TO DIE.
....
....
YET, ONCE WE ALL WERE WARRIORS. IN OUR HEARTS, WE LONG FOR DEATH ON THE FIELD OF BATTLE.
WHAT GREATER SATISFACTION THAN TO KNOW THAT MY BLOOD STAINS THESE FIELDS. THANK YOU FOR GRANTING THIS WISH.
BY THE WAY...
...WILL YOU GRANT ME *ONE MORE* INDULGENCE?
WHAT MIGHT THAT BE, MY LORD?
ŌGAMI ITTŌ, *KŌGI KAISHAKUNIN*... I HEAR YOU ARE A MASTER OF *SUIŌ-RYŪ*.
WOULD YOU SHOW ME THAT INNER SECRET OF YOUR SCHOOL, THE *WAVE-SLICING STROKE*?

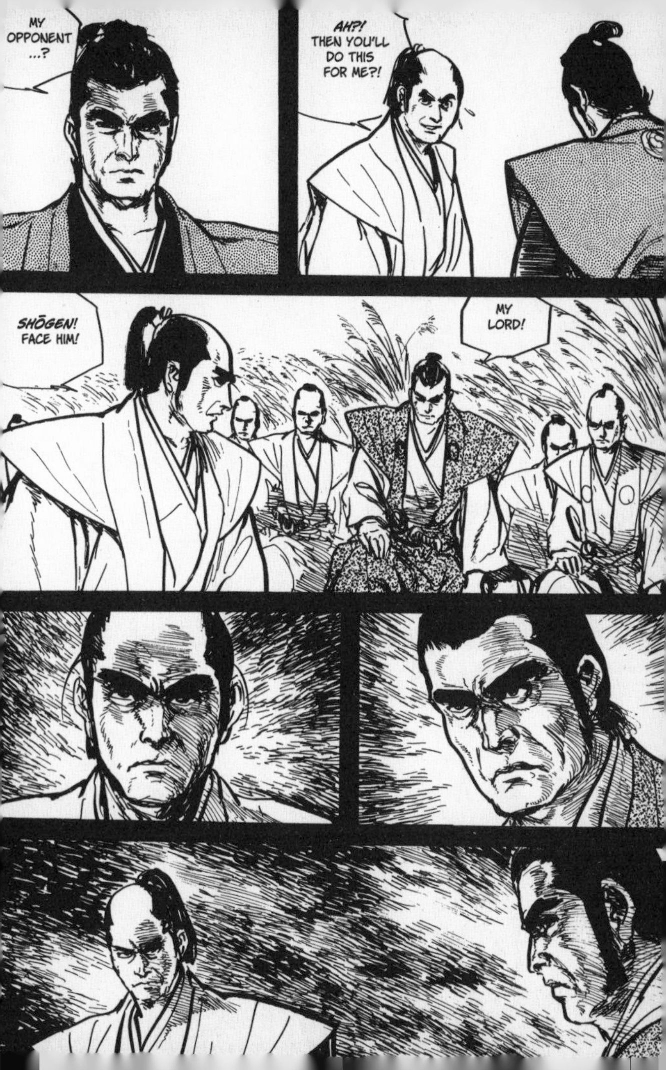
MY OPPONENT ...?
AH?! THEN YOU'LL DO THIS FOR ME?!
SHŌGEN! FACE HIM!
MY LORD!

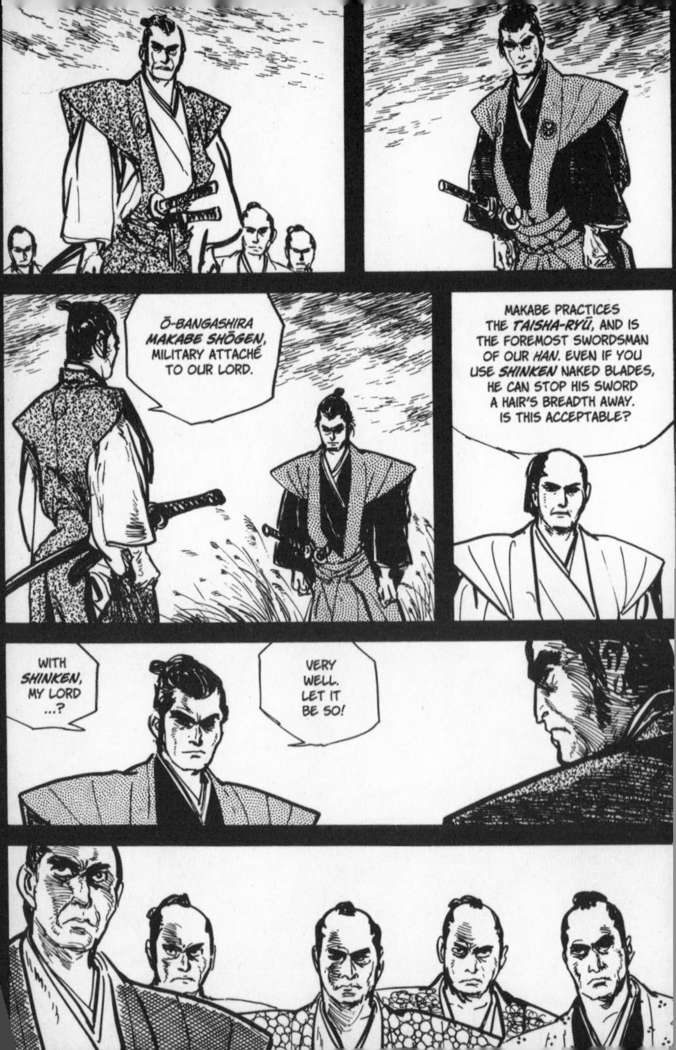
Ō-BANGASHIRA MAKABE SHŌGEN, MILITARY ATTACHÉ TO OUR LORD.
MAKABE PRACTICES THE TAISHA-RYŪ, AND IS THE FOREMOST SWORDSMAN OF OUR HAN. EVEN IF YOU USE SHINKEN NAKED BLADES, HE CAN STOP HIS SWORD A HAIR'S BREADTH AWAY. IS THIS ACCEPTABLE?
WITH SHINKEN, MY LORD ...?
VERY WELL. LET IT BE SO!

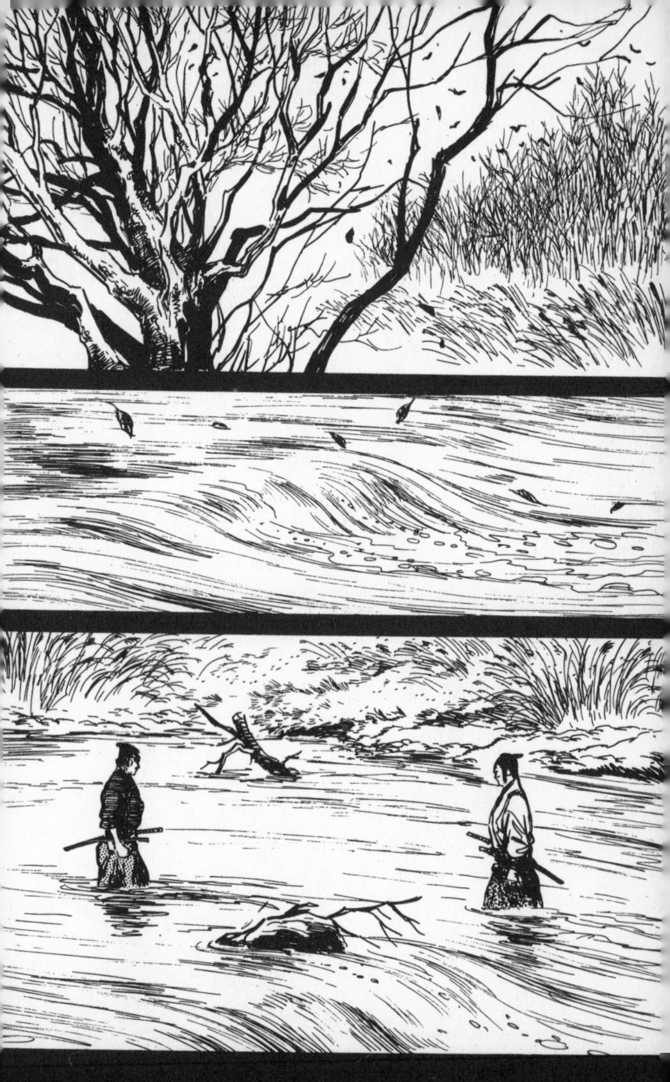

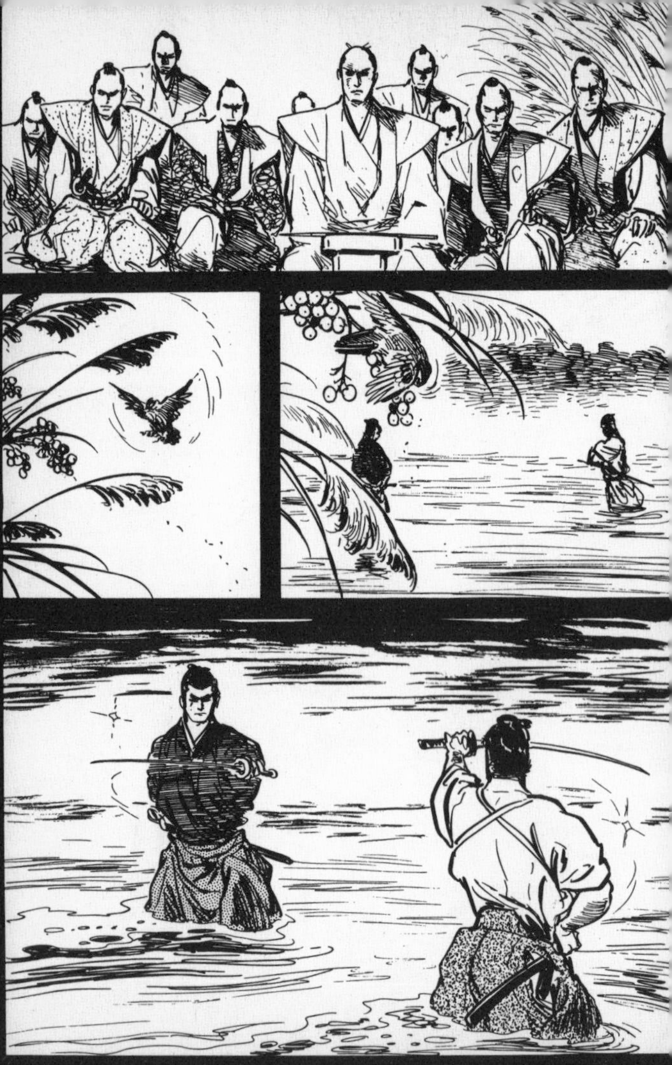

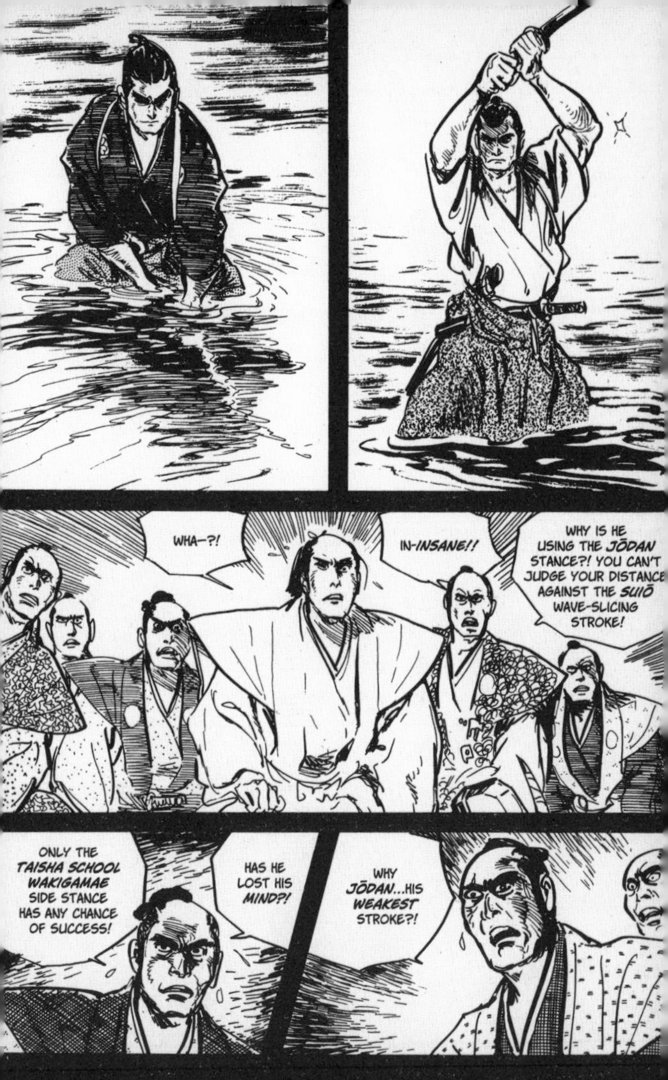
WHA-?!
IN-*INSANE!!*
WHY IS HE USING THE *JŌDAN* STANCE?! YOU CAN'T JUDGE YOUR DISTANCE AGAINST THE *SUIŌ* WAVE-SLICING STROKE!
ONLY THE *TAISHA SCHOOL WAKIGAMAE* SIDE STANCE HAS ANY CHANCE OF SUCCESS!
HAS HE LOST HIS *MIND?!*
WHY *JŌDAN*...HIS *WEAKEST* STROKE?!

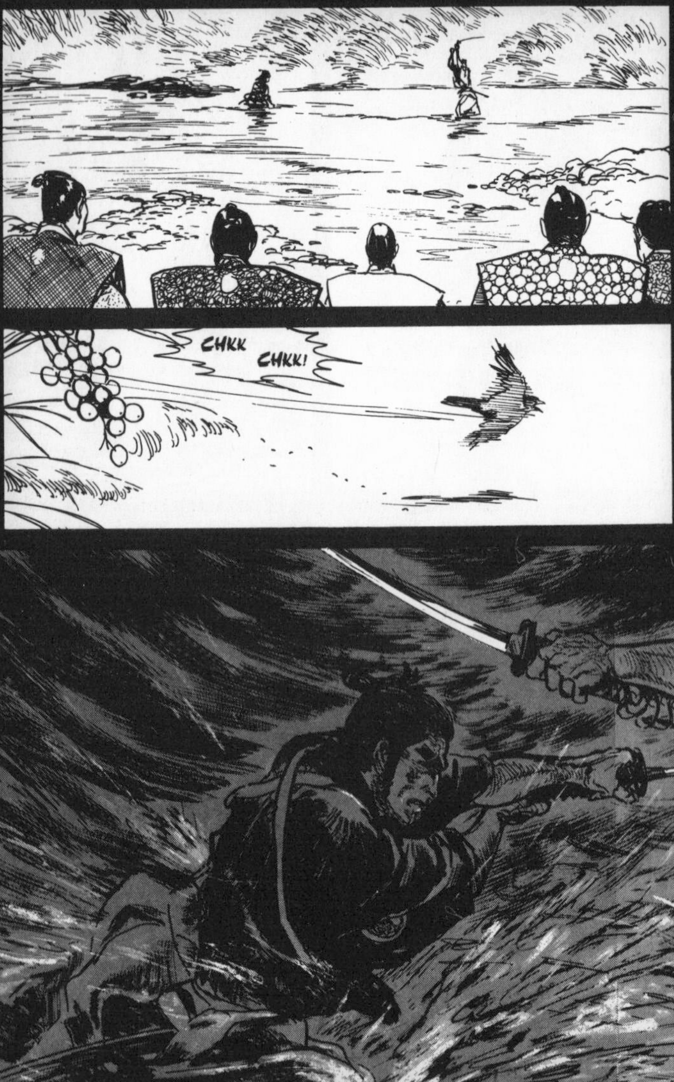
CHKK
CHKK!

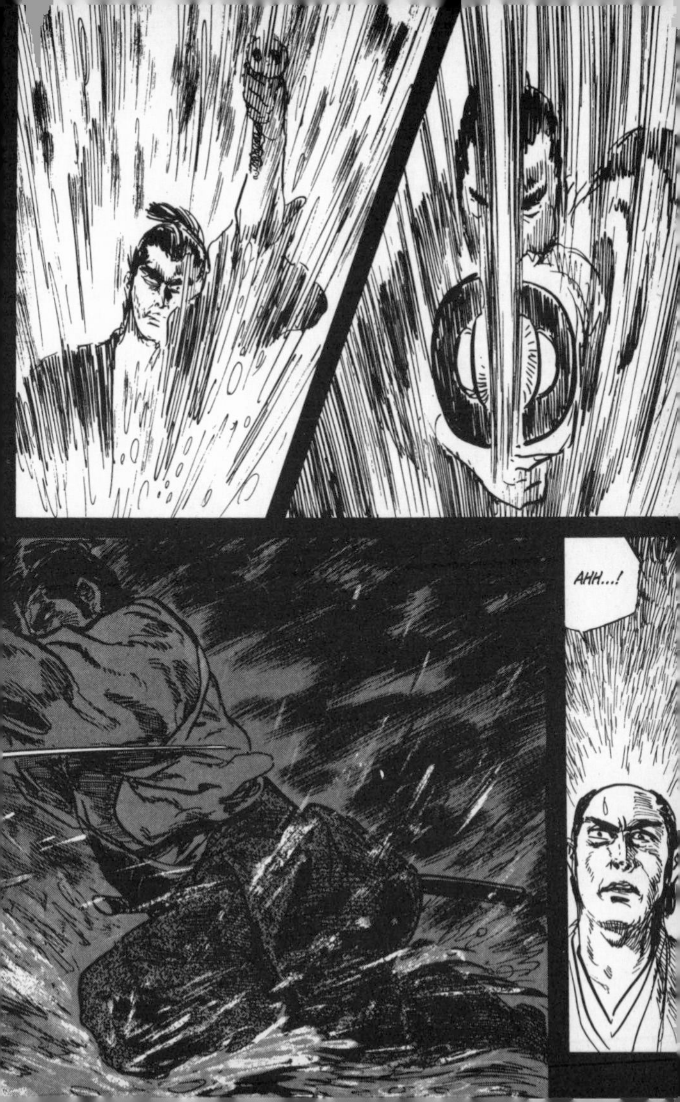
AHH...!

SLCCH

KCHOKK

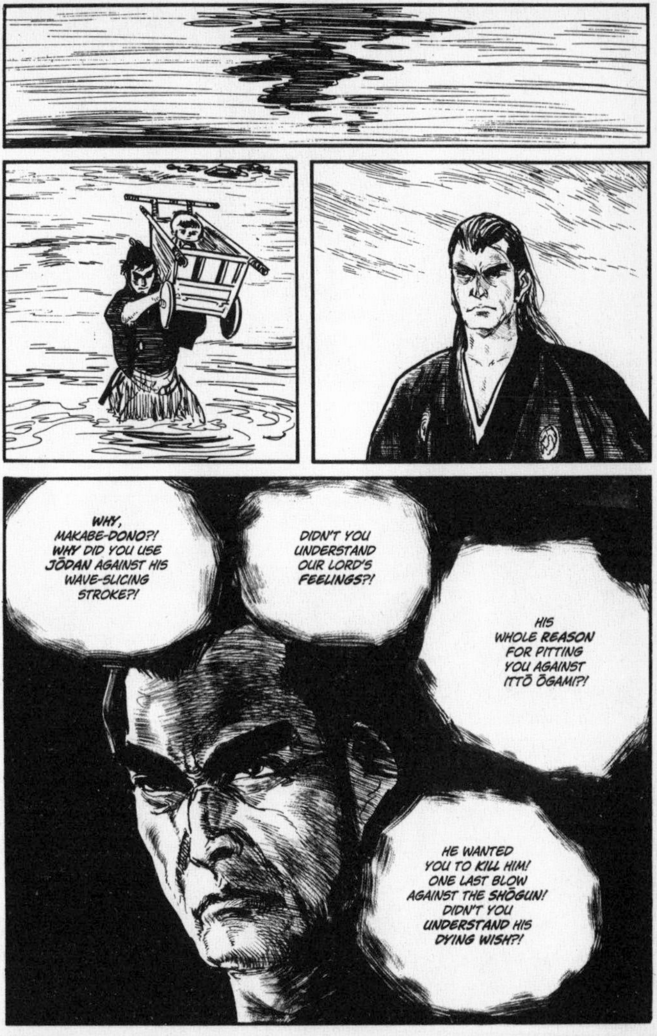
WHY, MAKABE-DONO?! WHY DID YOU USE JŌDAN AGAINST HIS WAVE-SLICING STROKE?!
DIDN'T YOU UNDERSTAND OUR LORD'S FEELINGS?!
HIS WHOLE REASON FOR PITTING YOU AGAINST ITTŌ ŌGAMI?!
HE WANTED YOU TO KILL HIM! ONE LAST BLOW AGAINST THE SHŌGUN! DIDN'T YOU UNDERSTAND HIS DYING WISH?!

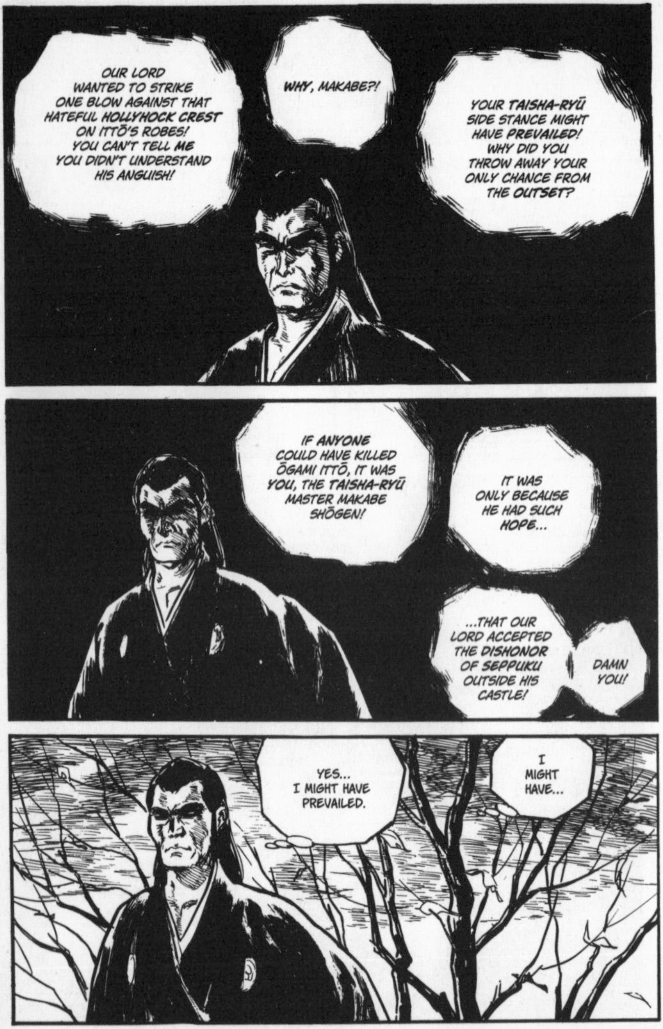
OUR LORD WANTED TO STRIKE ONE BLOW AGAINST THAT HATEFUL HOLLYHOCK CREST ON ITTŌ'S ROBES! YOU CAN'T TELL ME YOU DIDN'T UNDERSTAND HIS ANGUISH!
WHY, MAKABE?!
YOUR TAISHA-RYŪ SIDE STANCE MIGHT HAVE PREVAILED! WHY DID YOU THROW AWAY YOUR ONLY CHANCE FROM THE OUTSET?
IF ANYONE COULD HAVE KILLED ŌGAMI ITTŌ, IT WAS YOU, THE TAISHA-RYŪ MASTER MAKABE SHŌGEN!
IT WAS ONLY BECAUSE HE HAD SUCH HOPE...
...THAT OUR LORD ACCEPTED THE DISHONOR OF SEPPUKU OUTSIDE HIS CASTLE!
DAMN YOU!
YES... I MIGHT HAVE PREVAILED.
I MIGHT HAVE...

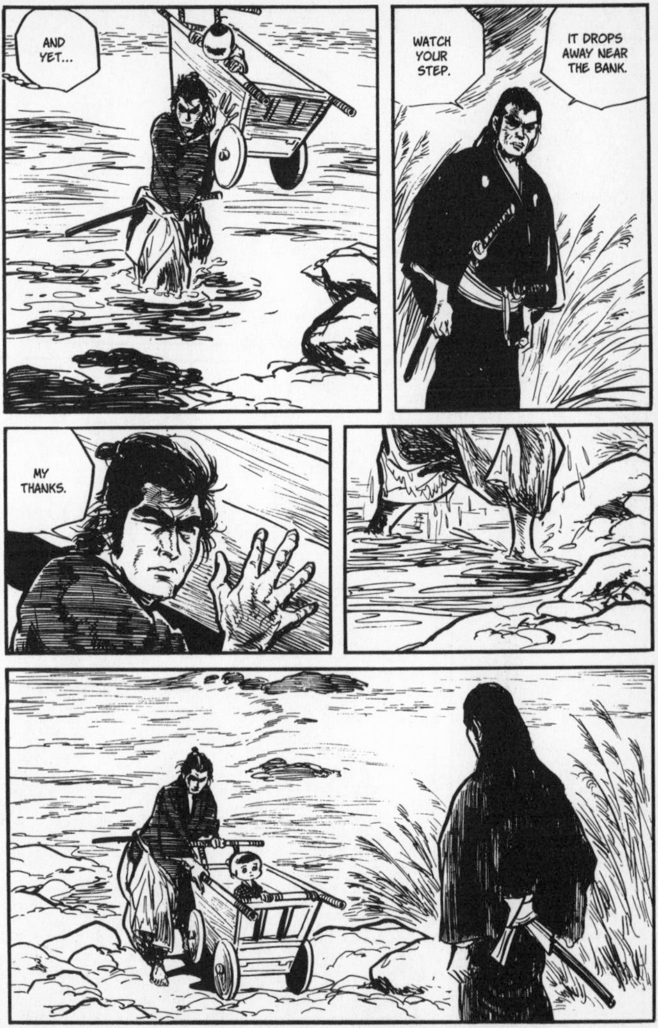
AND YET...
WATCH YOUR STEP.
IT DROPS AWAY NEAR THE BANK.
MY THANKS.

NO DOUBT YOU REMEMBER THESE RAPIDS... IT'S ONLY BEEN FOUR YEARS.

. . . .
. . . .

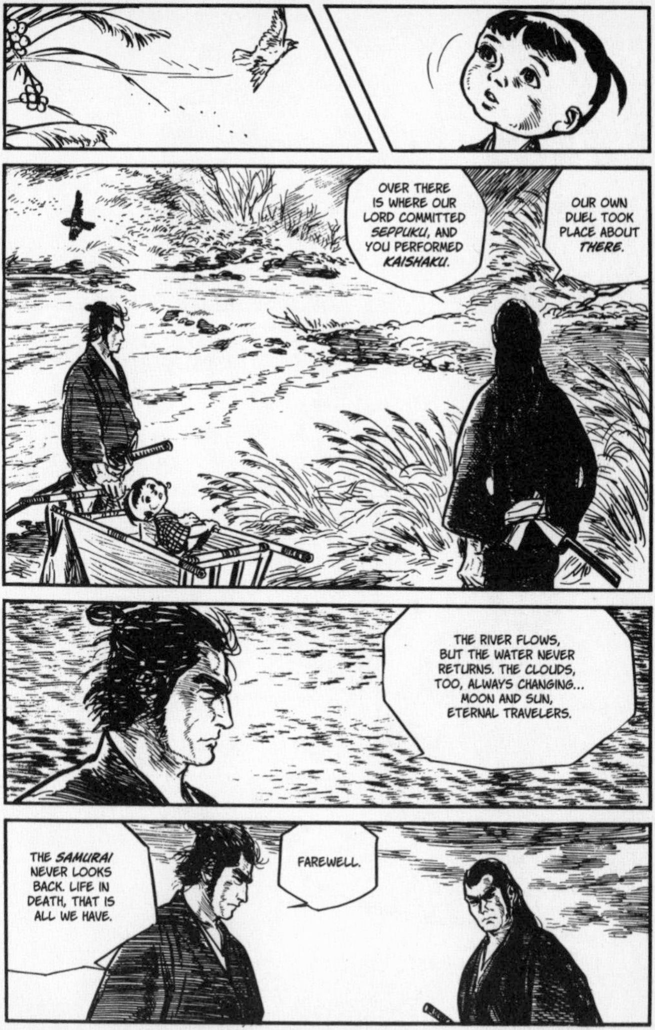
OVER THERE IS WHERE OUR LORD COMMITTED *SEPPUKU*, AND YOU PERFORMED *KAISHAKU*.
OUR OWN DUEL TOOK PLACE ABOUT *THERE*.
THE RIVER FLOWS, BUT THE WATER NEVER RETURNS. THE CLOUDS, TOO, ALWAYS CHANGING... MOON AND SUN, ETERNAL TRAVELERS.
THE *SAMURAI* NEVER LOOKS BACK. LIFE IN DEATH, THAT IS ALL WE HAVE.
FAREWELL.

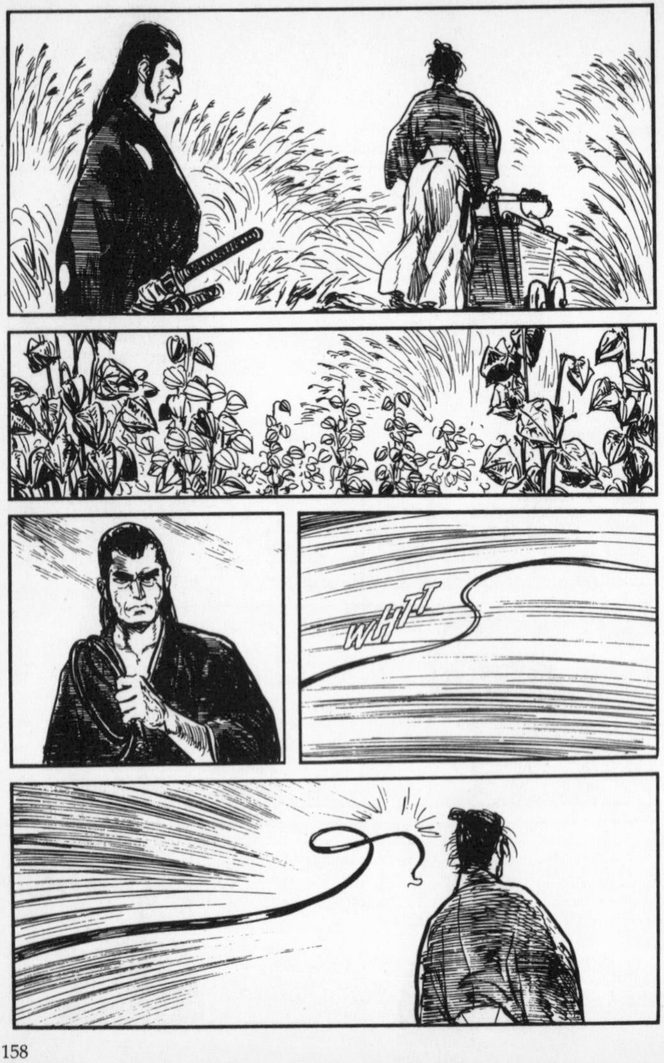
WHTT

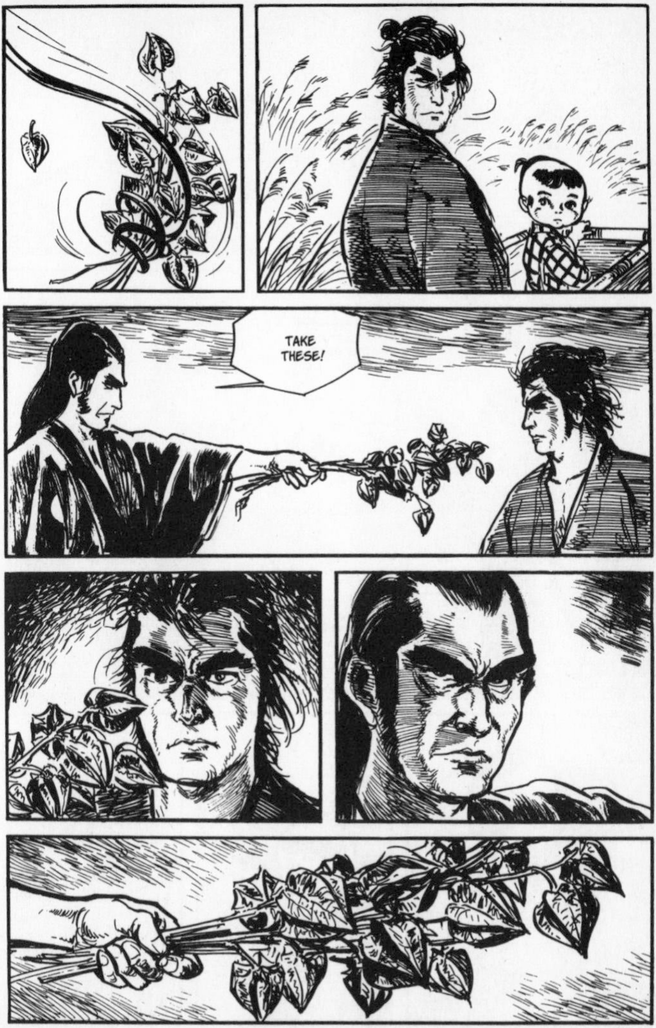
TAKE THESE!

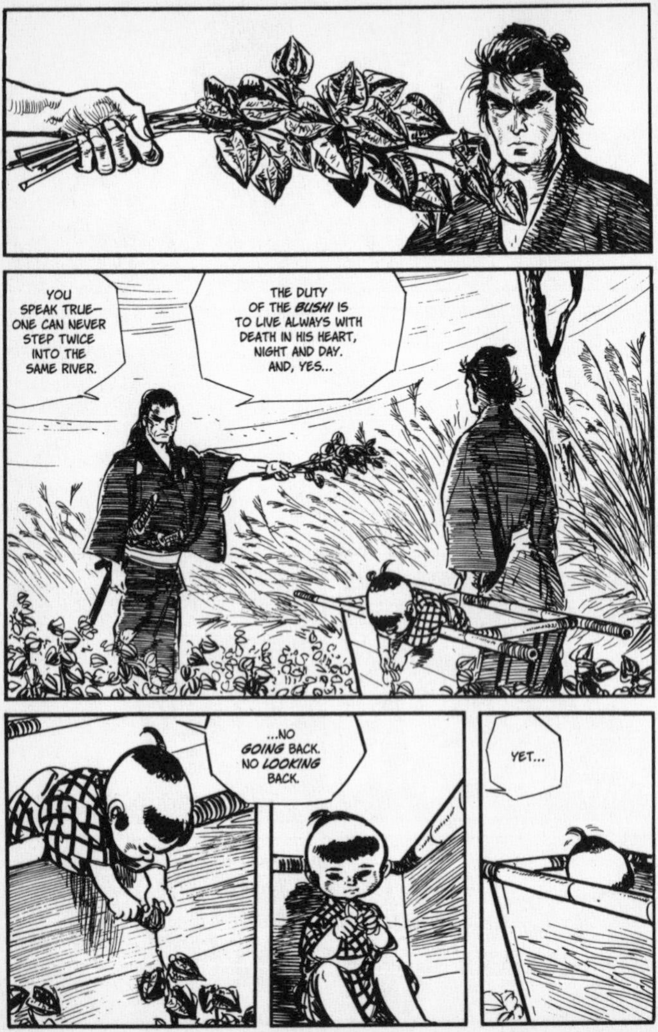
YOU SPEAK TRUE— ONE CAN NEVER STEP TWICE INTO THE SAME RIVER.
THE DUTY OF THE BUSHI IS TO LIVE ALWAYS WITH DEATH IN HIS HEART, NIGHT AND DAY. AND, YES...
...NO GOING BACK. NO LOOKING BACK.
YET...

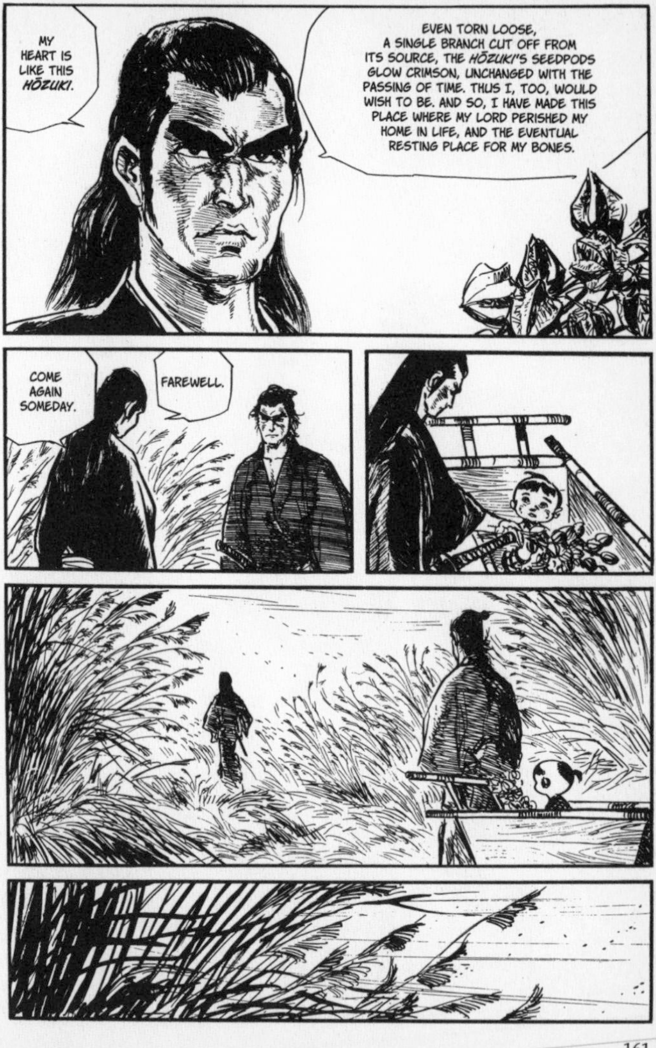
MY HEART IS LIKE THIS *HŌZUKI*.
EVEN TORN LOOSE, A SINGLE BRANCH CUT OFF FROM ITS SOURCE, THE *HŌZUKI*'S SEEDPODS GLOW CRIMSON, UNCHANGED WITH THE PASSING OF TIME. THUS I, TOO, WOULD WISH TO BE. AND SO, I HAVE MADE THIS PLACE WHERE MY LORD PERISHED MY HOME IN LIFE, AND THE EVENTUAL RESTING PLACE FOR MY BONES.
COME AGAIN SOMEDAY.
FAREWELL.

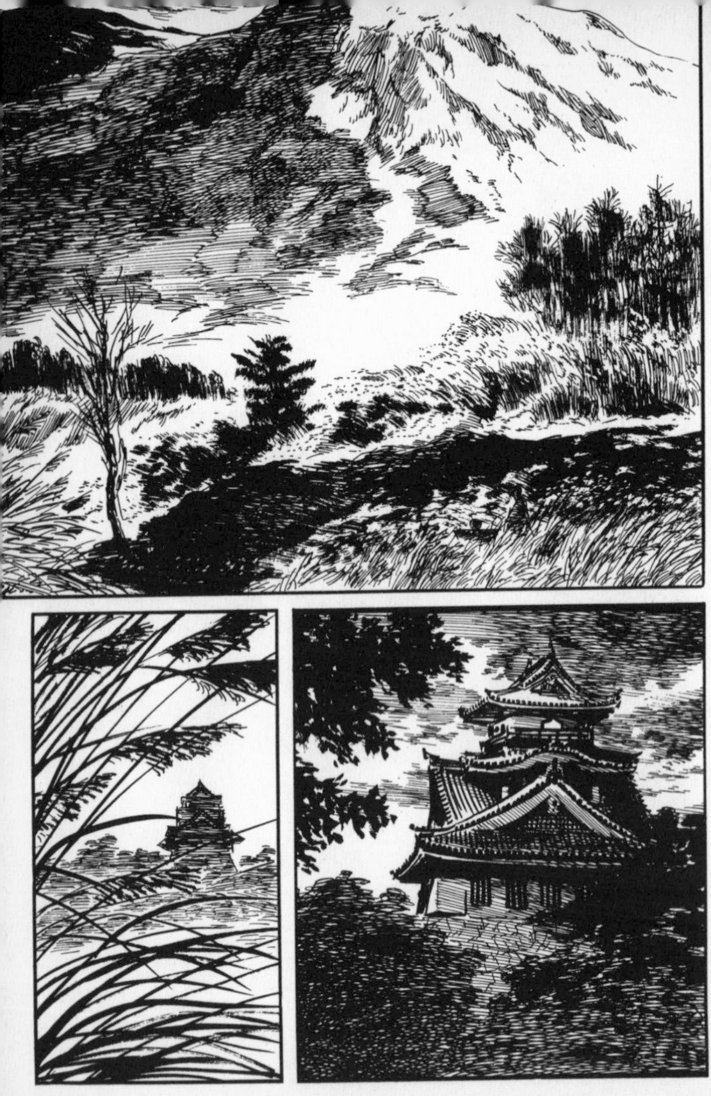

I NEED YOU TO KILL A SINGLE MAN... A *RŌNIN*.

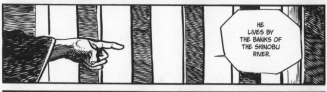

HE LIVES BY THE BANKS OF THE SHINOBU RIVER.

NORMALLY I'D JUST SEND OUT MY MEN TO DISPOSE OF HIM, BUT...IT'S NOT SO SIMPLE.

HE'S A LOYAL RETAINER OF THE FORMER *DAIMYŌ* ARIMA, DISBARRED FOUR YEARS AGO, AND A MASTER OF *TAISHA-RYŪ* SWORDSMANSHIP. FORMERLY *MAKABE SHŌGEN*, NOW HE GOES BY THE NAME *HŌZUKI*.

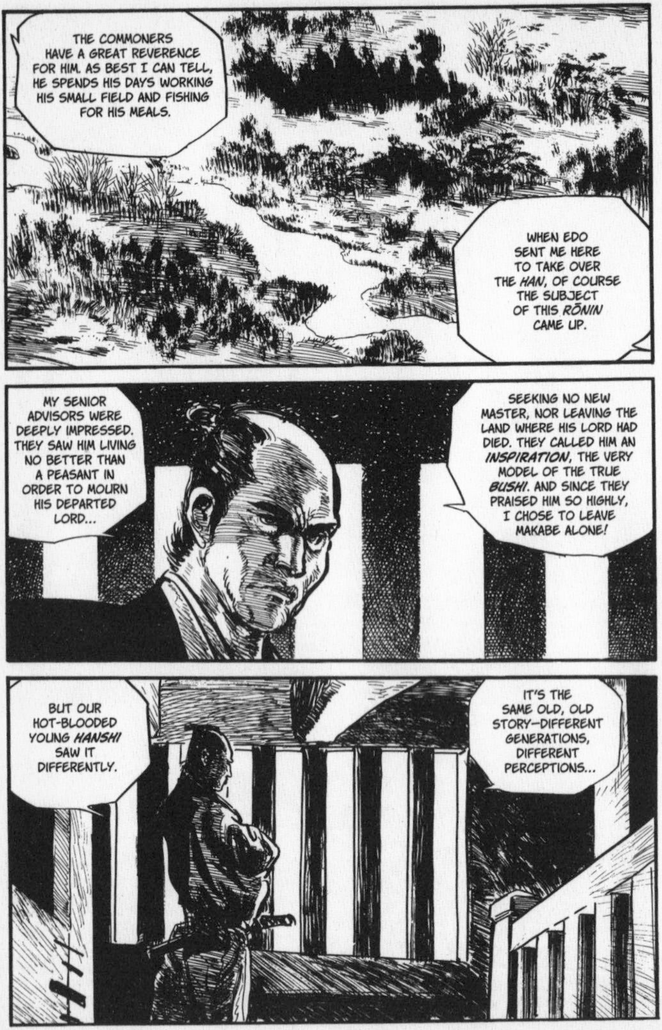
THE COMMONERS HAVE A GREAT REVERENCE FOR HIM. AS BEST I CAN TELL, HE SPENDS HIS DAYS WORKING HIS SMALL FIELD AND FISHING FOR HIS MEALS.
WHEN EDO SENT ME HERE TO TAKE OVER THE *HAN*, OF COURSE THE SUBJECT OF THIS *RŌNIN* CAME UP.
MY SENIOR ADVISORS WERE DEEPLY IMPRESSED. THEY SAW HIM LIVING NO BETTER THAN A PEASANT IN ORDER TO MOURN HIS DEPARTED LORD...
SEEKING NO NEW MASTER, NOR LEAVING THE LAND WHERE HIS LORD HAD DIED. THEY CALLED HIM AN ***INSPIRATION***, THE VERY MODEL OF THE TRUE ***BUSHI***. AND SINCE THEY PRAISED HIM SO HIGHLY, I CHOSE TO LEAVE MAKABE ALONE!
BUT OUR HOT-BLOODED YOUNG ***HANSHI*** SAW IT DIFFERENTLY.
IT'S THE SAME OLD, OLD STORY—DIFFERENT GENERATIONS, DIFFERENT PERCEPTIONS...

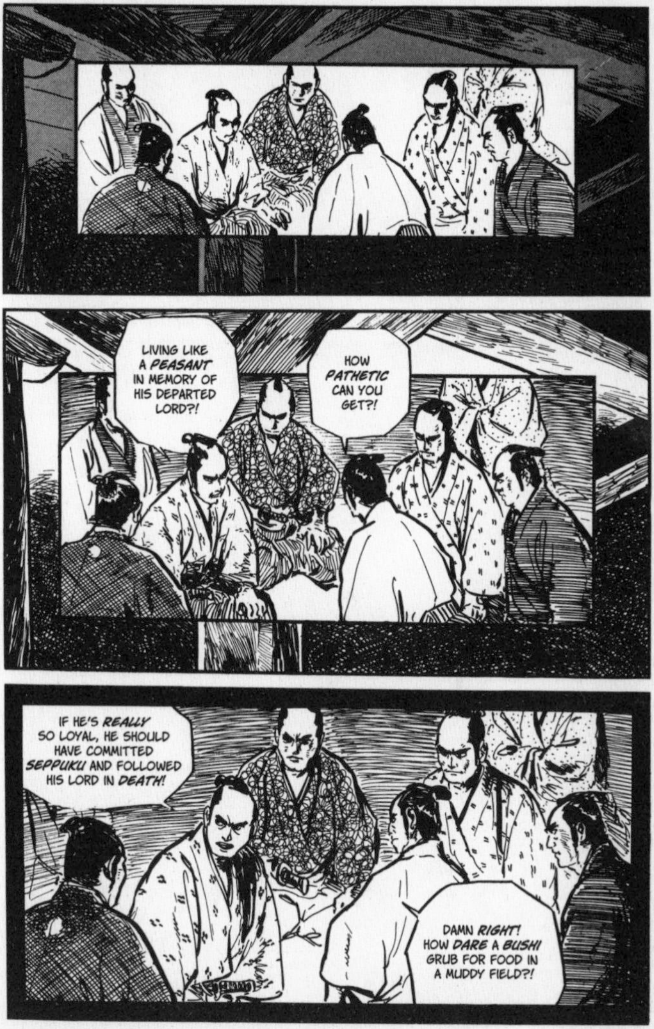
LIVING LIKE A PEASANT IN MEMORY OF HIS DEPARTED LORD?!
HOW PATHETIC CAN YOU GET?!
IF HE'S REALLY SO LOYAL, HE SHOULD HAVE COMMITTED SEPPUKU AND FOLLOWED HIS LORD IN DEATH!
DAMN RIGHT! HOW DARE A BUSHI GRUB FOR FOOD IN A MUDDY FIELD?!

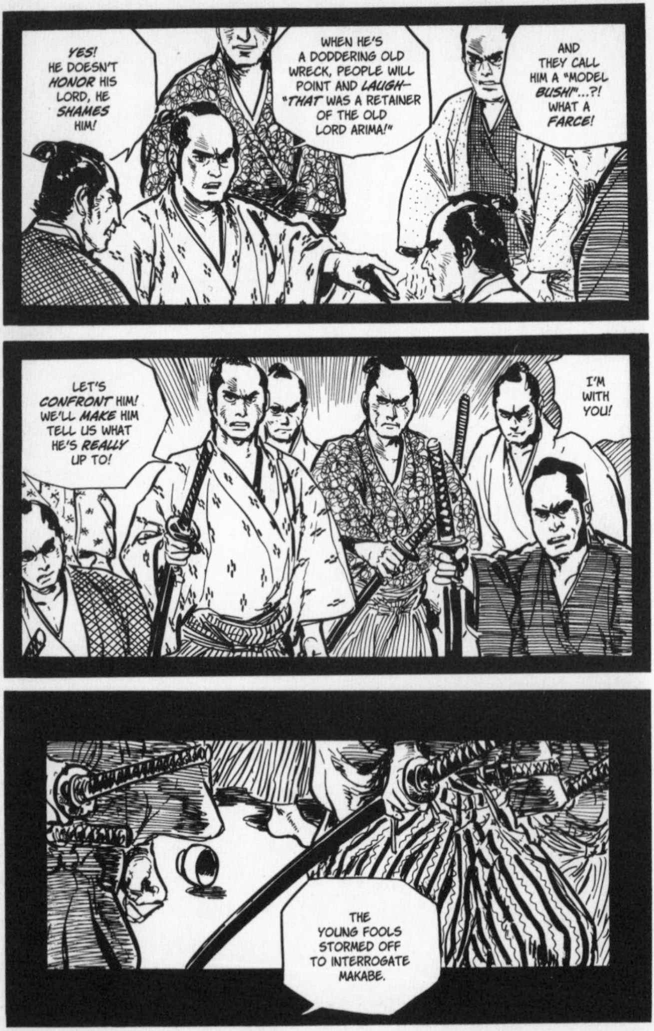
YES! HE DOESN'T HONOR HIS LORD, HE SHAMES HIM!
WHEN HE'S A DODDERING OLD WRECK, PEOPLE WILL POINT AND LAUGH— "THAT WAS A RETAINER OF THE OLD LORD ARIMA!"
AND THEY CALL HIM A "MODEL BUSHI"...?! WHAT A FARCE!
LET'S CONFRONT HIM! WE'LL MAKE HIM TELL US WHAT HE'S REALLY UP TO!
I'M WITH YOU!
THE YOUNG FOOLS STORMED OFF TO INTERROGATE MAKABE.

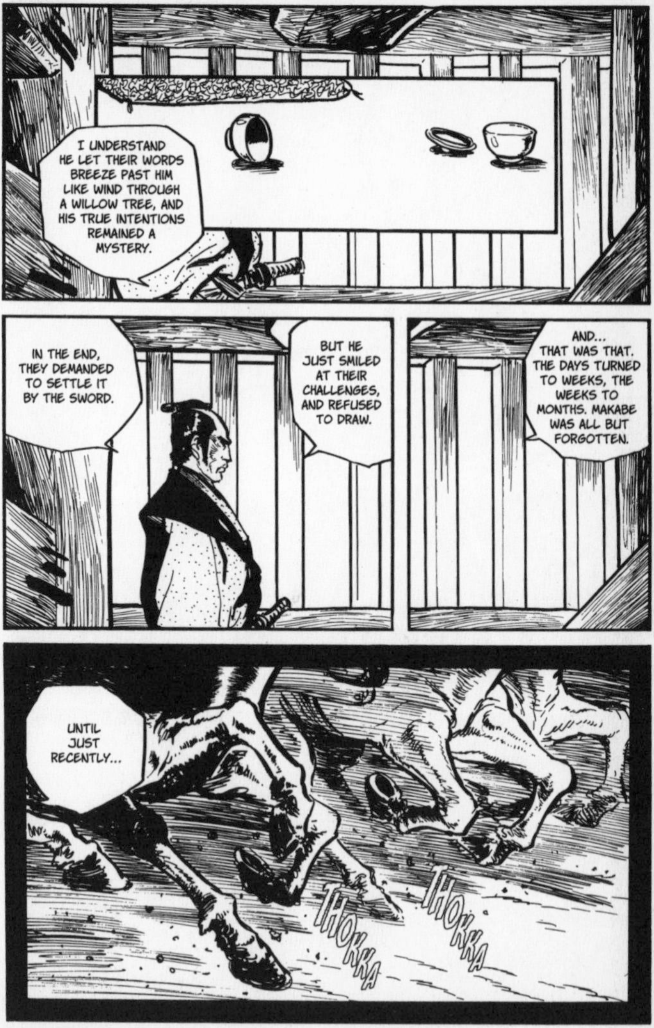
I UNDERSTAND HE LET THEIR WORDS BREEZE PAST HIM LIKE WIND THROUGH A WILLOW TREE, AND HIS TRUE INTENTIONS REMAINED A MYSTERY.
IN THE END, THEY DEMANDED TO SETTLE IT BY THE SWORD.
BUT HE JUST SMILED AT THEIR CHALLENGES, AND REFUSED TO DRAW.
AND... THAT WAS THAT. THE DAYS TURNED TO WEEKS, THE WEEKS TO MONTHS. MAKABE WAS ALL BUT FORGOTTEN.
UNTIL JUST RECENTLY...
THOKKA
THOKKA

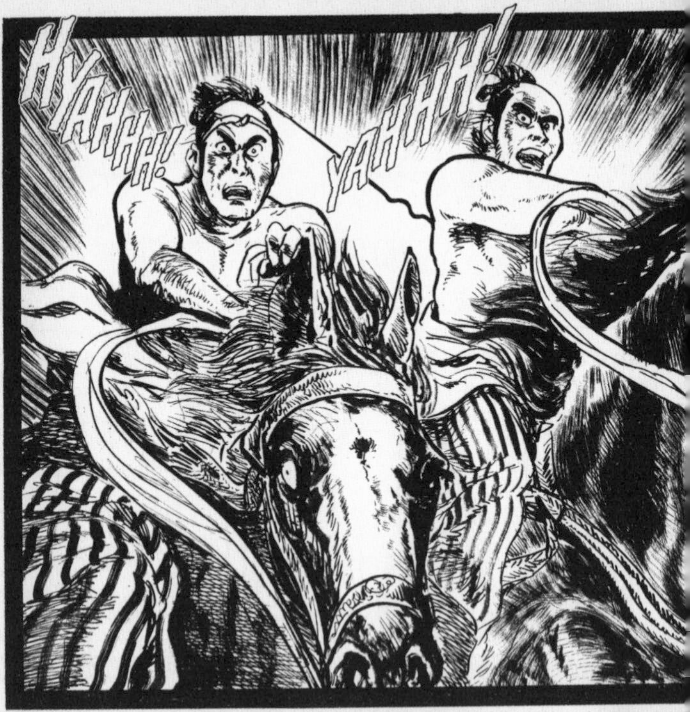
HYAHHH!
YAHHHH!
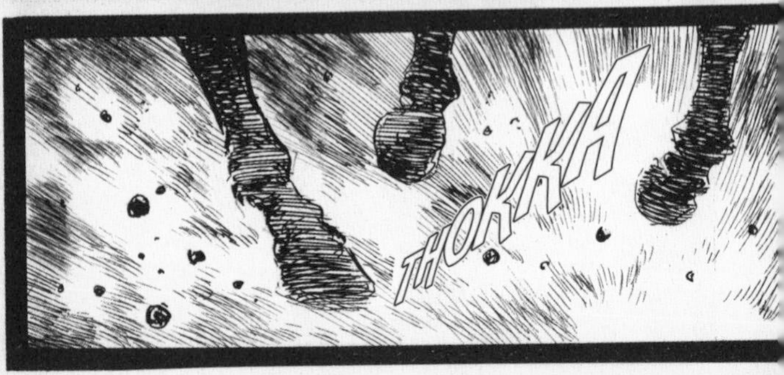
THOKKA

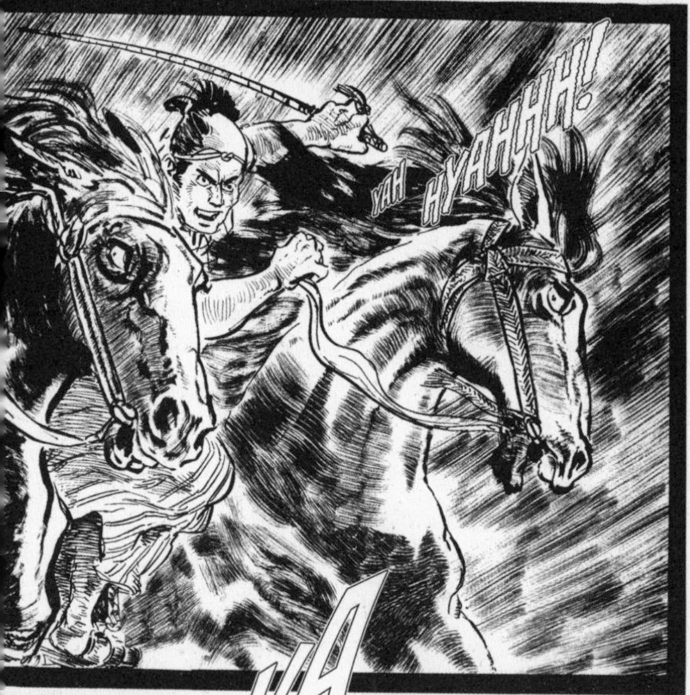
YAH HYAHHH!
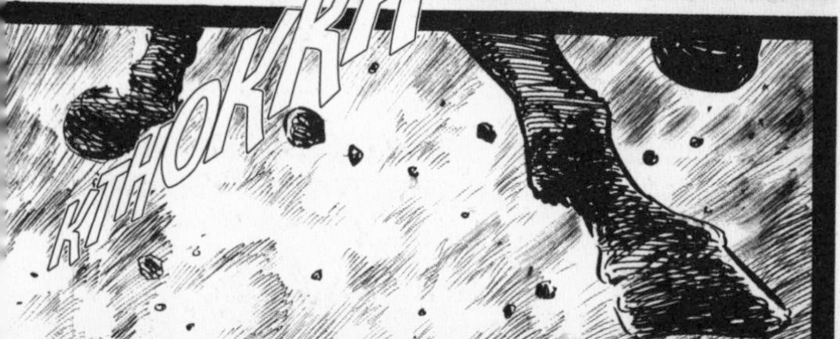
KITHOKKA

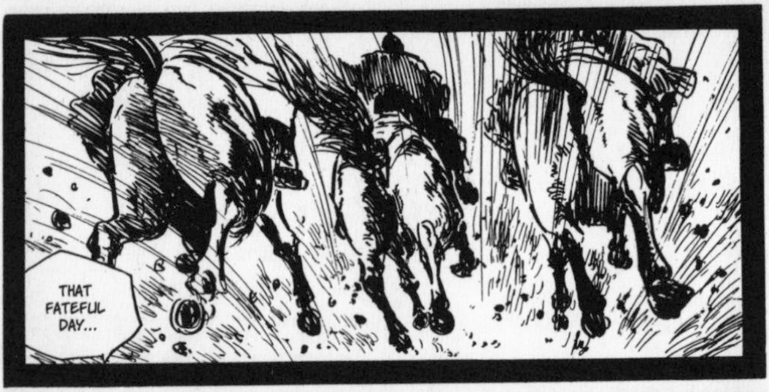
THAT FATEFUL DAY...

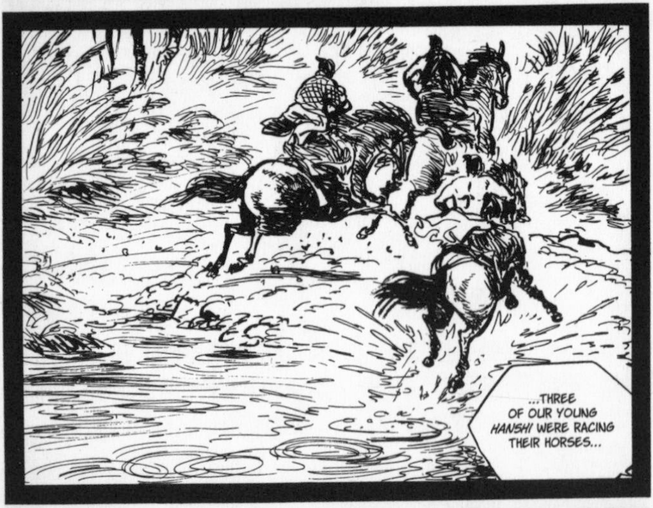
...THREE OF OUR YOUNG *HANSHI* WERE RACING THEIR HORSES...

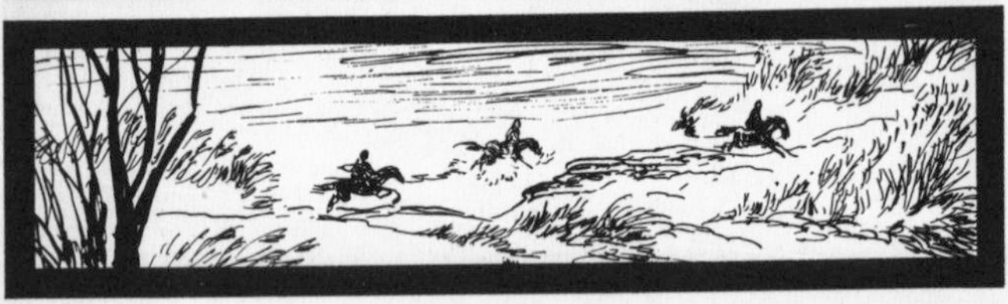

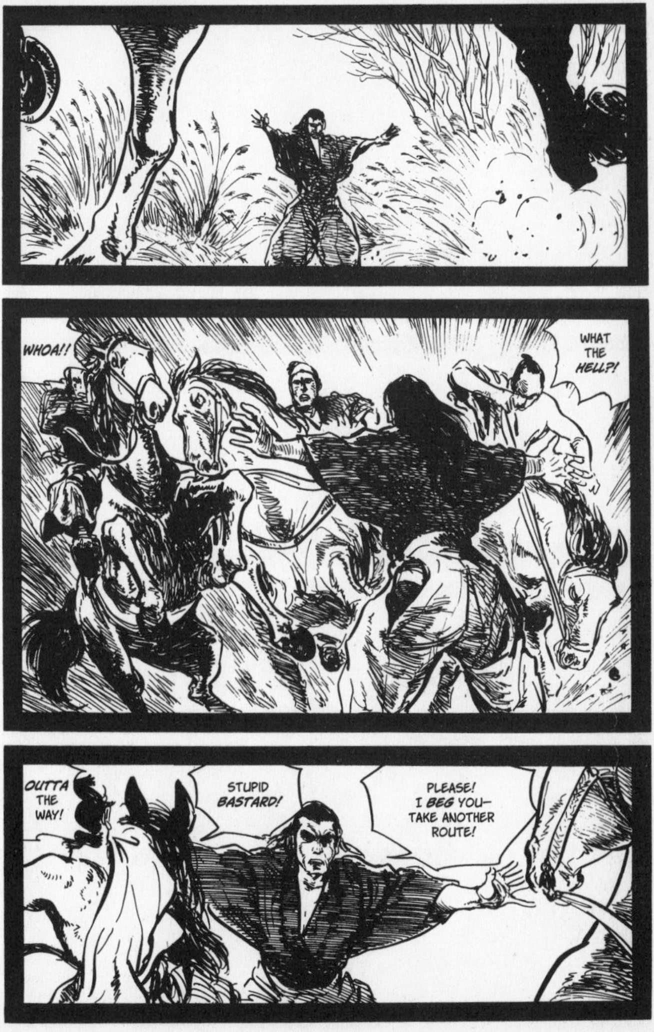
WHOA!!
WHAT THE HELL?!
OUTTA THE WAY!
STUPID BASTARD!
PLEASE! I BEG YOU— TAKE ANOTHER ROUTE!

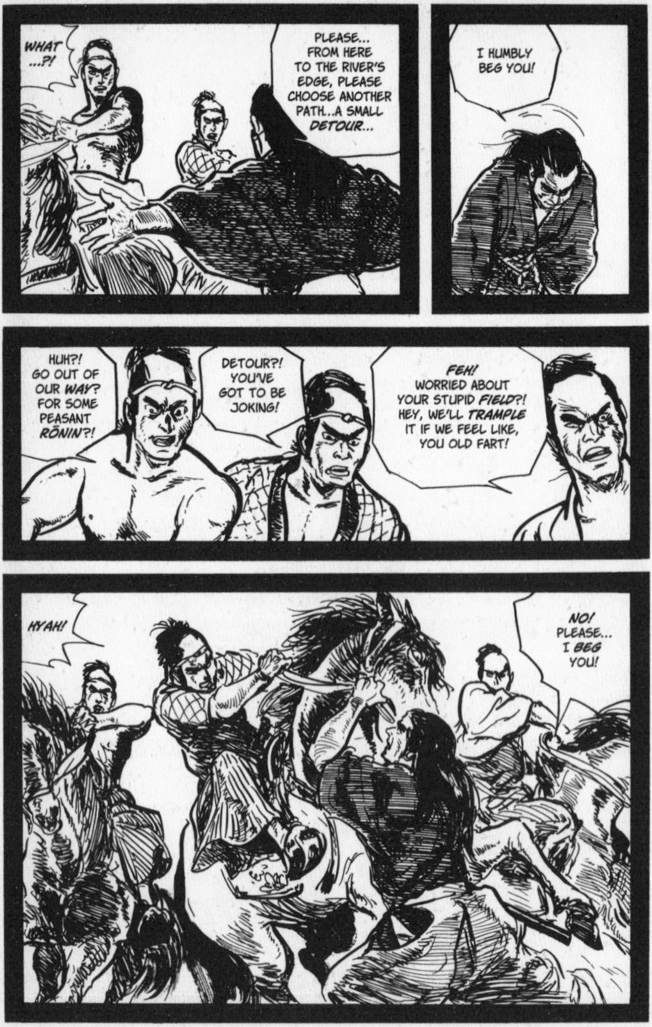
WHAT ...?!
PLEASE... FROM HERE TO THE RIVER'S EDGE, PLEASE CHOOSE ANOTHER PATH...A SMALL DETOUR...
I HUMBLY BEG YOU!
HUH?! GO OUT OF OUR WAY? FOR SOME PEASANT RŌNIN?!
DETOUR?! YOU'VE GOT TO BE JOKING!
FEH! WORRIED ABOUT YOUR STUPID FIELD?! HEY, WE'LL TRAMPLE IT IF WE FEEL LIKE, YOU OLD FART!
HYAH!
NO! PLEASE... I BEG YOU!

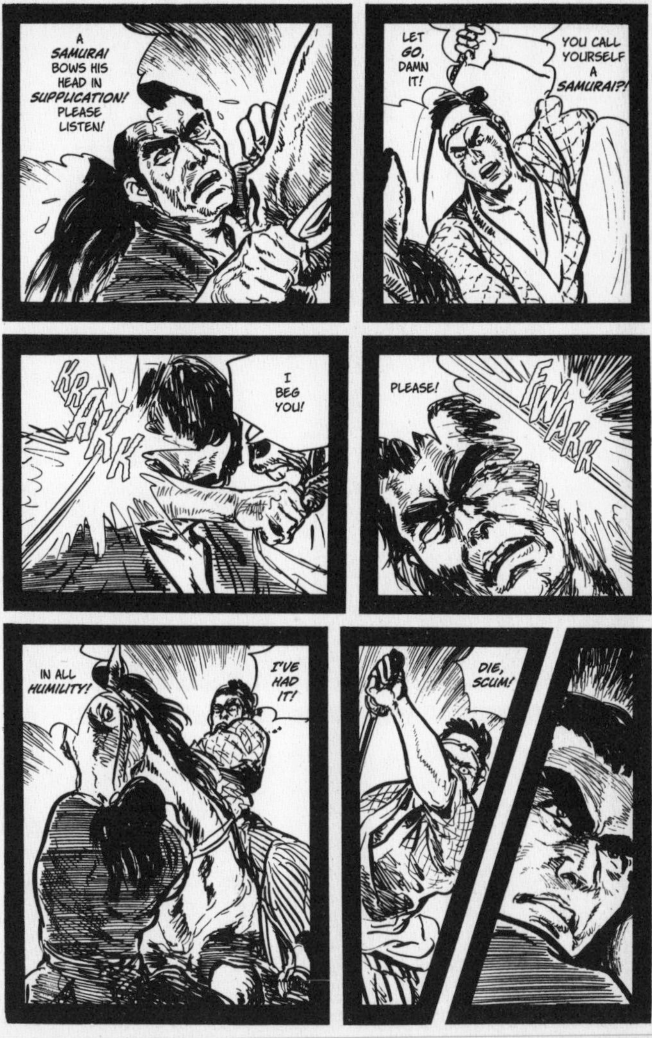
A SAMURAI BOWS HIS HEAD IN SUPPLICATION! PLEASE LISTEN!
LET GO, DAMN IT!
YOU CALL YOURSELF A SAMURAI?!
KRAKK
I BEG YOU!
PLEASE!
FWAKK
IN ALL HUMILITY!
I'VE HAD IT!
DIE, SCUM!

FSSHK
SKUSHH
NGHHK!
FWHOO
HYAH!
S-SON OF A BITCH!

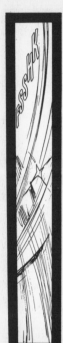

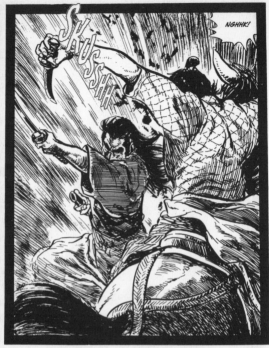

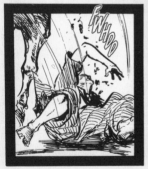

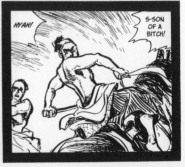

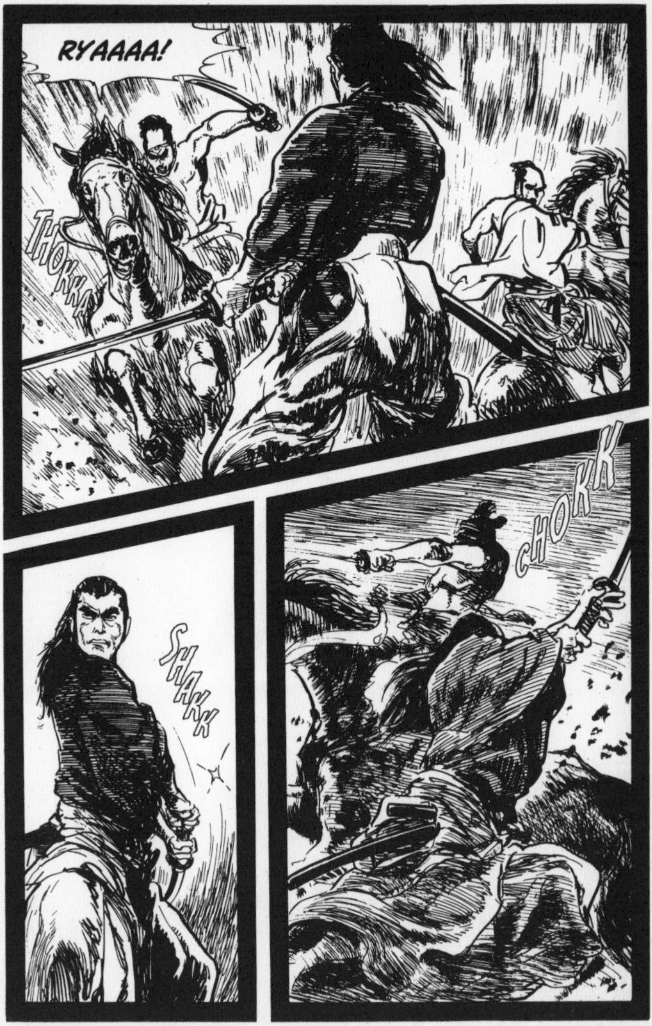
RYAAAA!
THOKKA
SHAKK
CHOKK

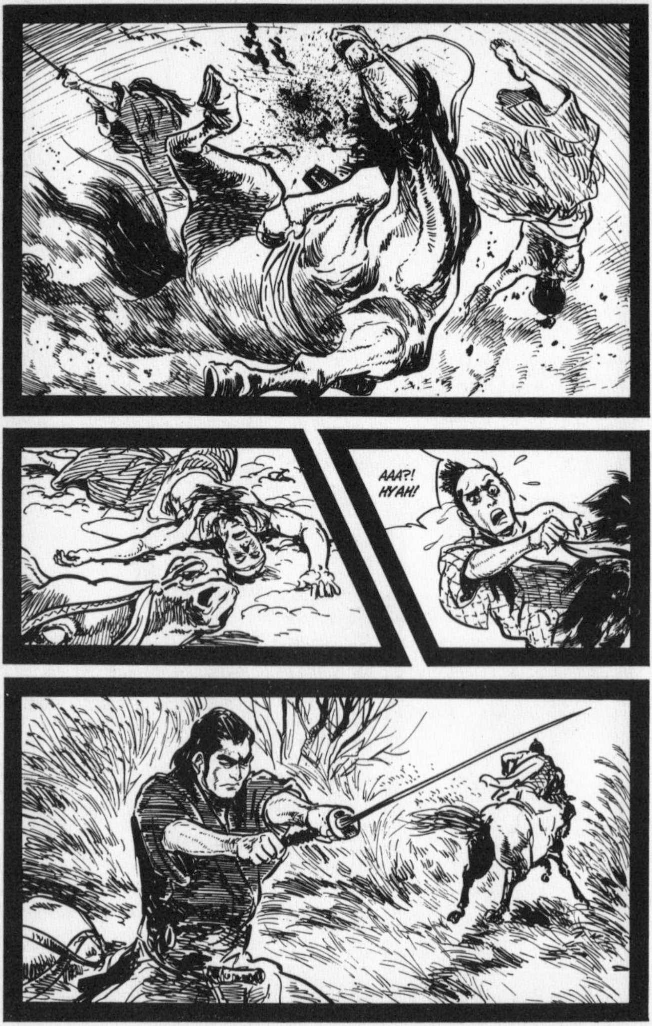
AAA?!
HYAH!

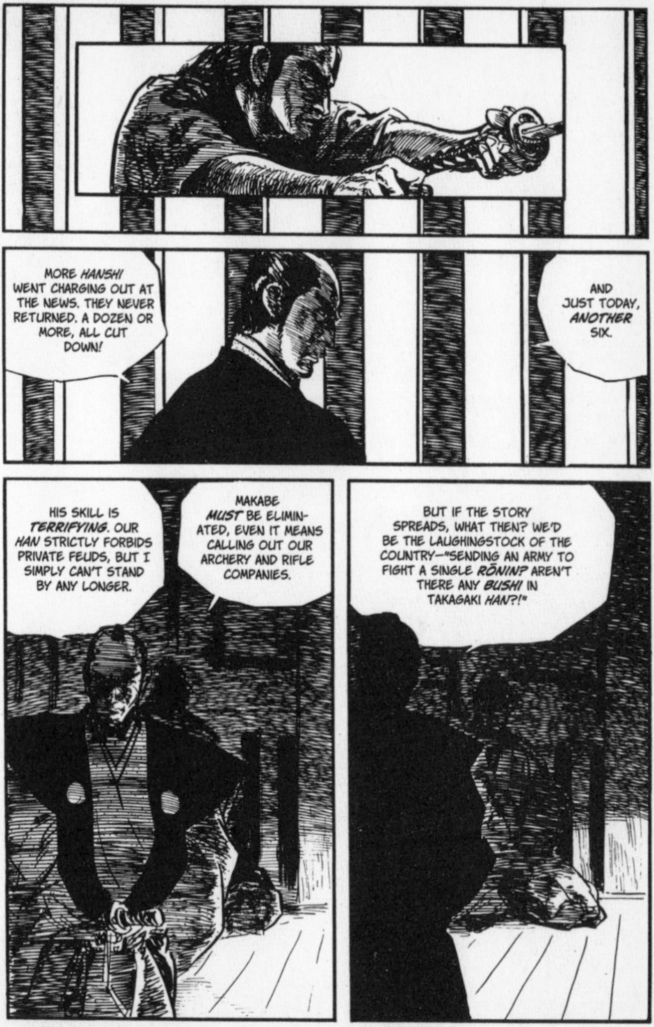
MORE HANSHI WENT CHARGING OUT AT THE NEWS. THEY NEVER RETURNED. A DOZEN OR MORE, ALL CUT DOWN!
AND JUST TODAY, ANOTHER SIX.
HIS SKILL IS TERRIFYING. OUR HAN STRICTLY FORBIDS PRIVATE FEUDS, BUT I SIMPLY CAN'T STAND BY ANY LONGER.
MAKABE MUST BE ELIMIN-ATED, EVEN IT MEANS CALLING OUT OUR ARCHERY AND RIFLE COMPANIES.
BUT IF THE STORY SPREADS, WHAT THEN? WE'D BE THE LAUGHINGSTOCK OF THE COUNTRY—"SENDING AN ARMY TO FIGHT A SINGLE RŌNIN? AREN'T THERE ANY BUSHI IN TAKAGAKI HAN?!"

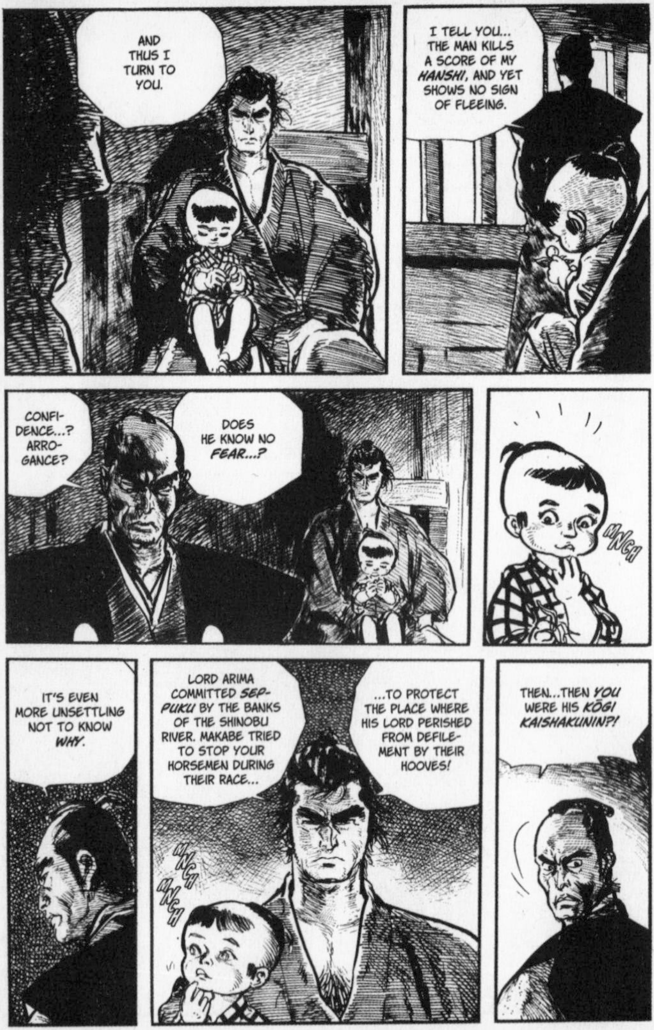
AND THUS I TURN TO YOU.
I TELL YOU... THE MAN KILLS A SCORE OF MY *HANSHI*, AND YET SHOWS NO SIGN OF FLEEING.
CONFIDENCE...? ARROGANCE?
DOES HE KNOW NO *FEAR...?*
MNCH
IT'S EVEN MORE UNSETTLING NOT TO KNOW *WHY*.
LORD ARIMA COMMITTED *SEPPUKU* BY THE BANKS OF THE SHINOBU RIVER. MAKABE TRIED TO STOP YOUR HORSEMEN DURING THEIR RACE...
MNCH
MNCH
...TO PROTECT THE PLACE WHERE HIS LORD PERISHED FROM DEFILEMENT BY THEIR HOOVES!
THEN...THEN *YOU* WERE HIS *KŌGI KAISHAKUNIN?!*

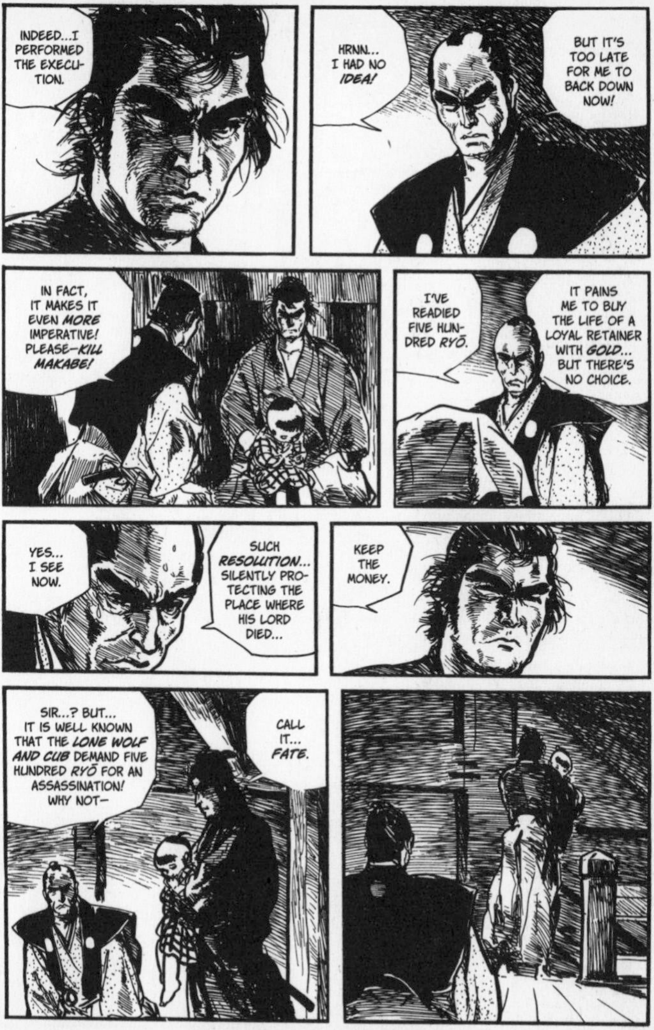
INDEED...I PERFORMED THE EXECUTION.
HRNN... I HAD NO *IDEA!*
BUT IT'S TOO LATE FOR ME TO BACK DOWN NOW!
IN FACT, IT MAKES IT EVEN *MORE* IMPERATIVE! PLEASE—*KILL MAKABE!*
I'VE READIED FIVE HUNDRED *RYŌ*.
IT PAINS ME TO BUY THE LIFE OF A LOYAL RETAINER WITH *GOLD*... BUT THERE'S NO CHOICE.
YES... I SEE NOW.
SUCH *RESOLUTION*... SILENTLY PROTECTING THE PLACE WHERE HIS LORD DIED...
KEEP THE MONEY.
SIR...? BUT... IT IS WELL KNOWN THAT THE *LONE WOLF AND CUB* DEMAND FIVE HUNDRED *RYŌ* FOR AN ASSASSINATION! WHY NOT—
CALL IT... *FATE*.

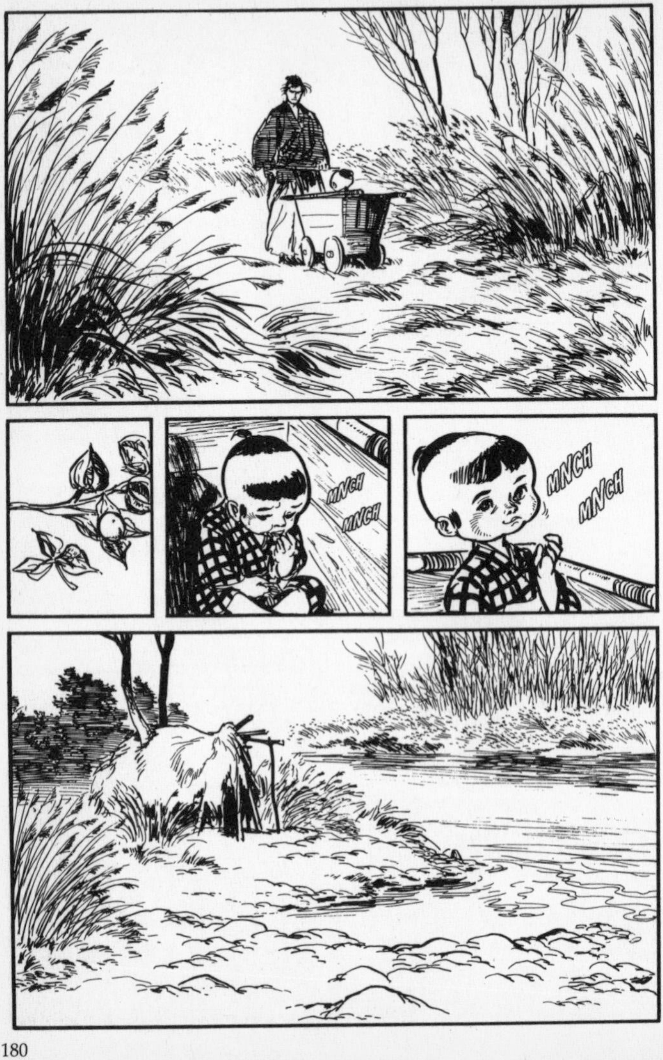
MNCH
MNCH
MNCH
MNCH

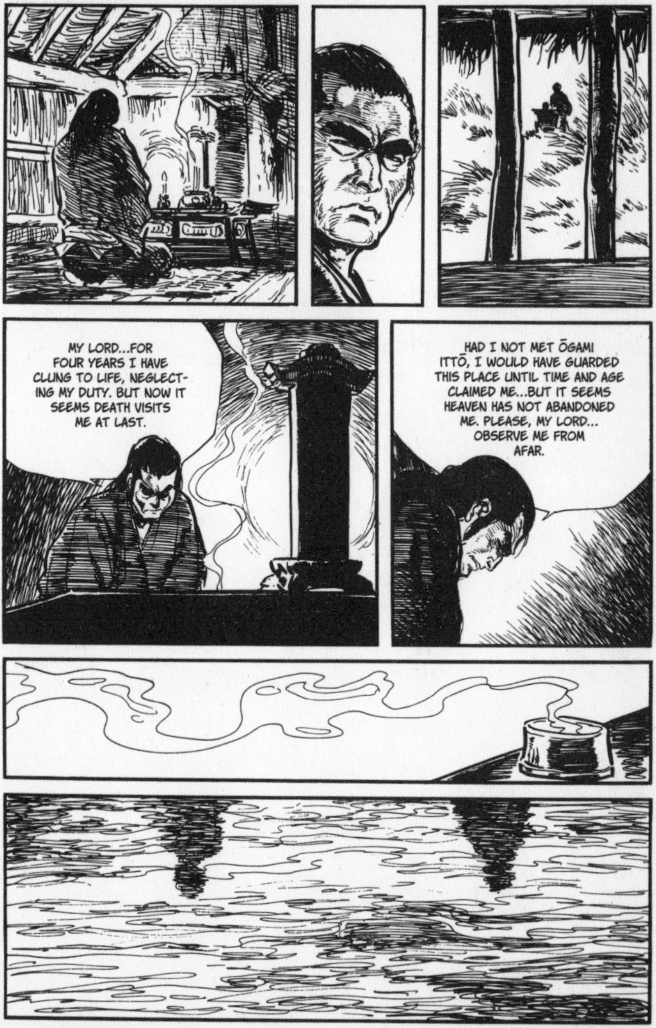
MY LORD...FOR FOUR YEARS I HAVE CLUNG TO LIFE, NEGLECTING MY DUTY. BUT NOW IT SEEMS DEATH VISITS ME AT LAST.
HAD I NOT MET ŌGAMI ITTŌ, I WOULD HAVE GUARDED THIS PLACE UNTIL TIME AND AGE CLAIMED ME...BUT IT SEEMS HEAVEN HAS NOT ABANDONED ME. PLEASE, MY LORD... OBSERVE ME FROM AFAR.

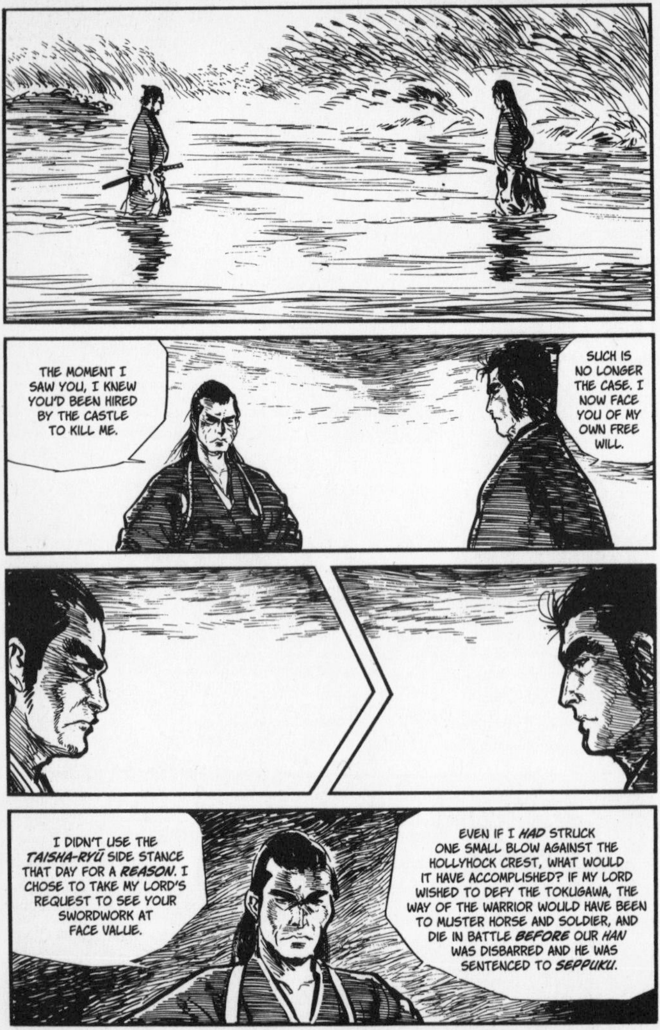

THE MOMENT I SAW YOU, I KNEW YOU'D BEEN HIRED BY THE CASTLE TO KILL ME.
SUCH IS NO LONGER THE CASE. I NOW FACE YOU OF MY OWN FREE WILL.
I DIDN'T USE THE TAISHA-RYŪ SIDE STANCE THAT DAY FOR A REASON. I CHOSE TO TAKE MY LORD'S REQUEST TO SEE YOUR SWORDWORK AT FACE VALUE.
EVEN IF I HAD STRUCK ONE SMALL BLOW AGAINST THE HOLLYHOCK CREST, WHAT WOULD IT HAVE ACCOMPLISHED? IF MY LORD WISHED TO DEFY THE TOKUGAWA, THE WAY OF THE WARRIOR WOULD HAVE BEEN TO MUSTER HORSE AND SOLDIER, AND DIE IN BATTLE BEFORE OUR HAN WAS DISBARRED AND HE WAS SENTENCED TO SEPPUKU.

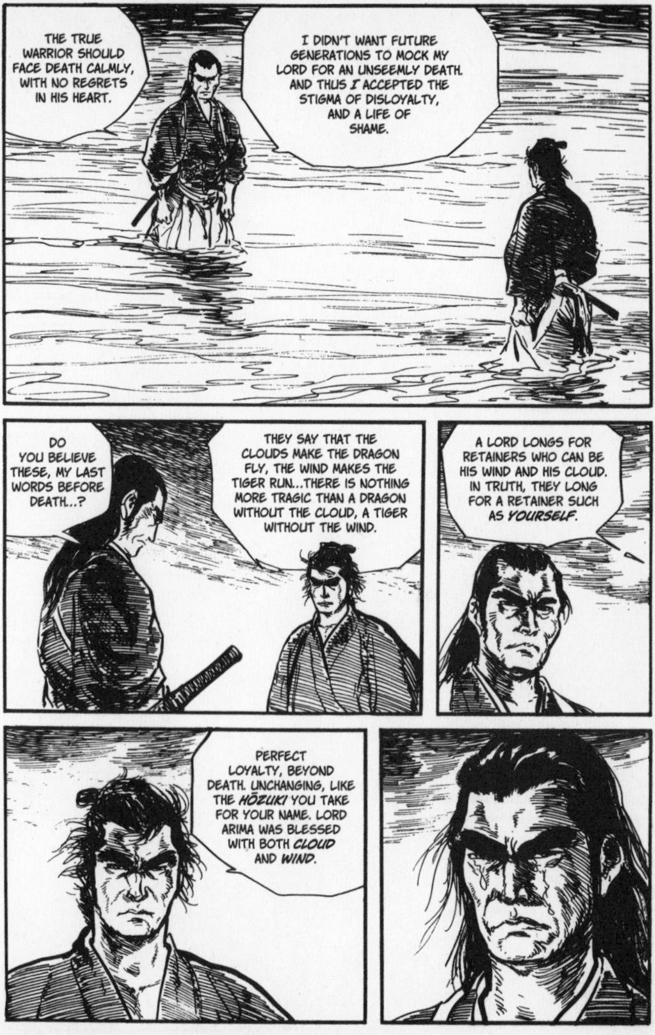
THE TRUE WARRIOR SHOULD FACE DEATH CALMLY, WITH NO REGRETS IN HIS HEART.
I DIDN'T WANT FUTURE GENERATIONS TO MOCK MY LORD FOR AN UNSEEMLY DEATH. AND THUS *I* ACCEPTED THE STIGMA OF DISLOYALTY, AND A LIFE OF SHAME.
DO YOU BELIEVE THESE, MY LAST WORDS BEFORE DEATH...?
THEY SAY THAT THE CLOUDS MAKE THE DRAGON FLY, THE WIND MAKES THE TIGER RUN...THERE IS NOTHING MORE TRAGIC THAN A DRAGON WITHOUT THE CLOUD, A TIGER WITHOUT THE WIND.
A LORD LONGS FOR RETAINERS WHO CAN BE HIS WIND AND HIS CLOUD. IN TRUTH, THEY LONG FOR A RETAINER SUCH AS *YOURSELF*.
PERFECT LOYALTY, BEYOND DEATH. UNCHANGING, LIKE THE *HŌZUKI* YOU TAKE FOR YOUR NAME. LORD ARIMA WAS BLESSED WITH BOTH *CLOUD* AND *WIND*.

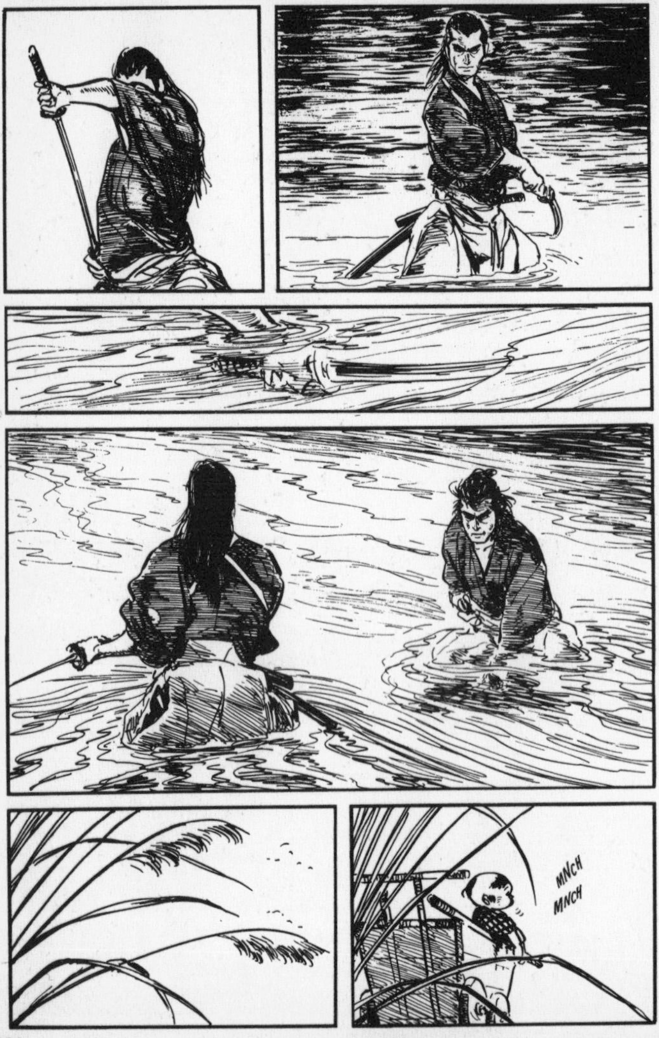
MNCH
MNCH

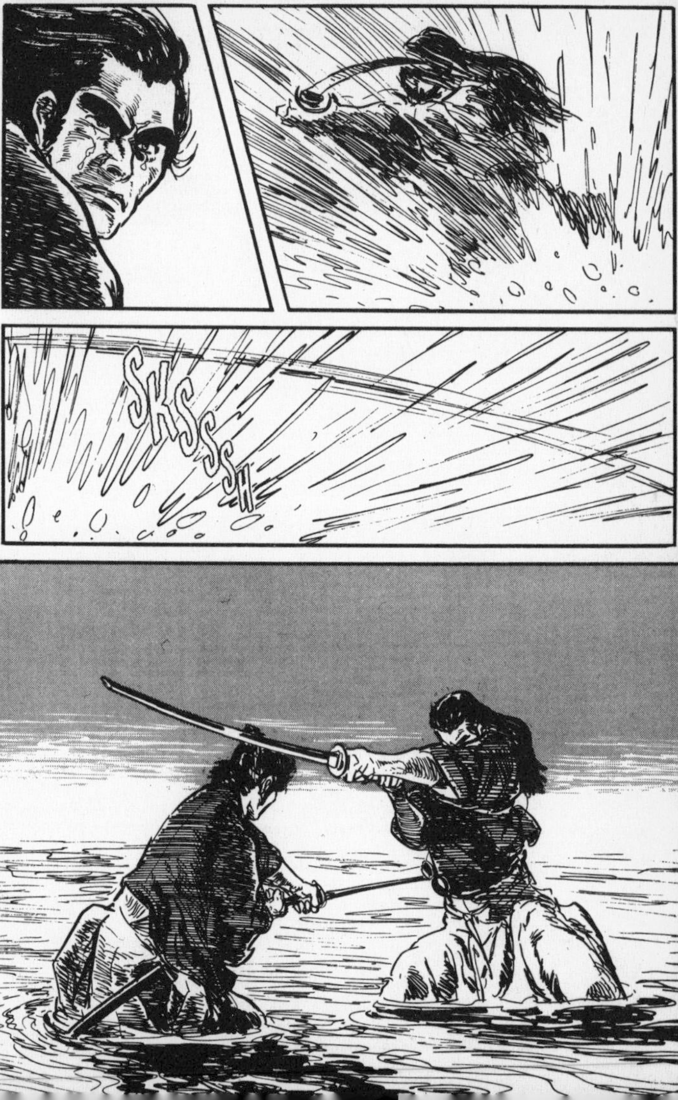
SKSSSH

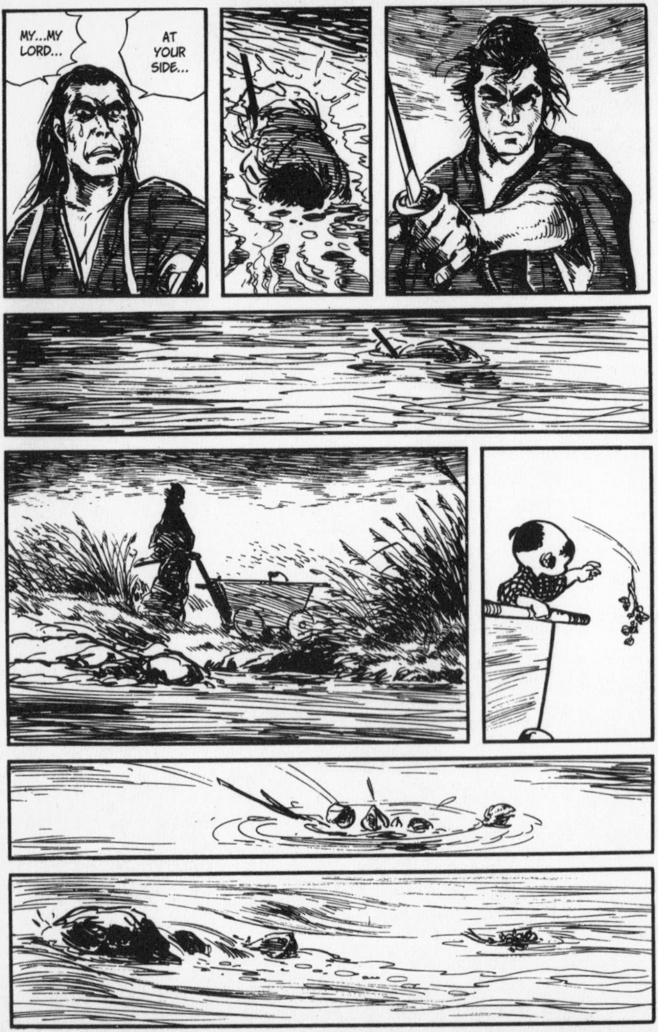
MY...MY LORD...
AT YOUR SIDE...

the thirty-seventh

Inn of
the Last
Chrysanthemum

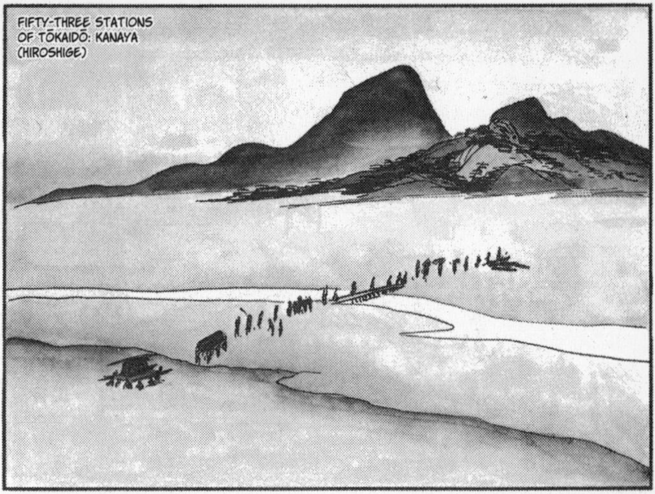
FIFTY-THREE STATIONS
OF TŌKAIDŌ: KANAYA
(HIROSHIGE)

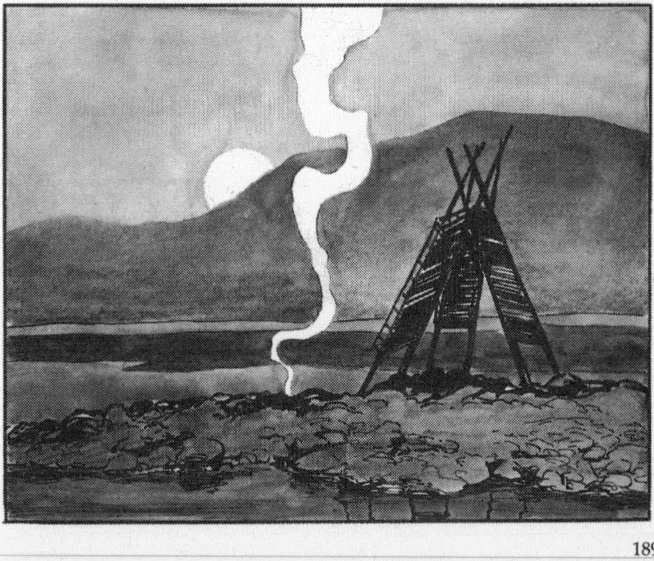

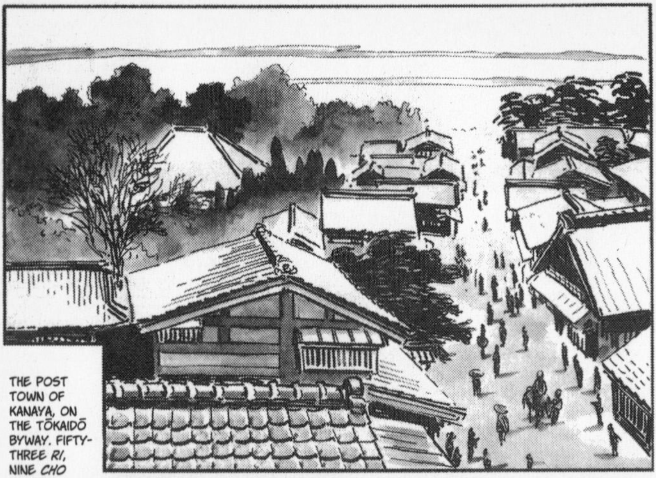

THE POST TOWN OF KANAYA, ON THE TŌKAIDŌ BYWAY. FIFTY-THREE *RI*, NINE *CHO* TO EDO; SEVENTY-TWO *RI*, ELEVEN *CHO* TO KYOTO.

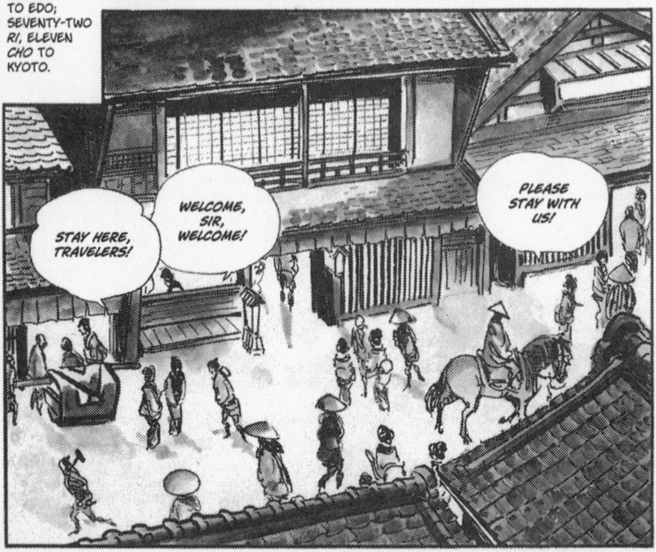
STAY HERE, TRAVELERS!
WELCOME, SIR, WELCOME!
PLEASE STAY WITH US!

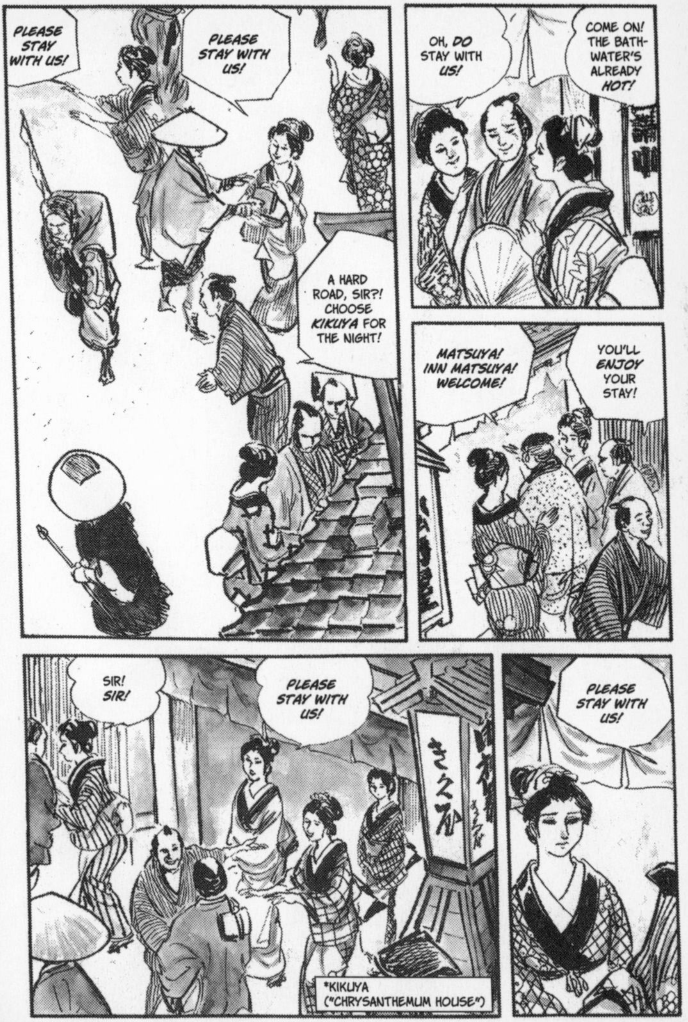
PLEASE STAY WITH US!
PLEASE STAY WITH US!
A HARD ROAD, SIR?! CHOOSE KIKUYA FOR THE NIGHT!
OH, DO STAY WITH US!
COME ON! THE BATH-WATER'S ALREADY HOT!
MATSUYA! INN MATSUYA! WELCOME!
YOU'LL ENJOY YOUR STAY!
SIR! SIR!
PLEASE STAY WITH US!
*KIKUYA ("CHRYSANTHEMUM HOUSE")
PLEASE STAY WITH US!

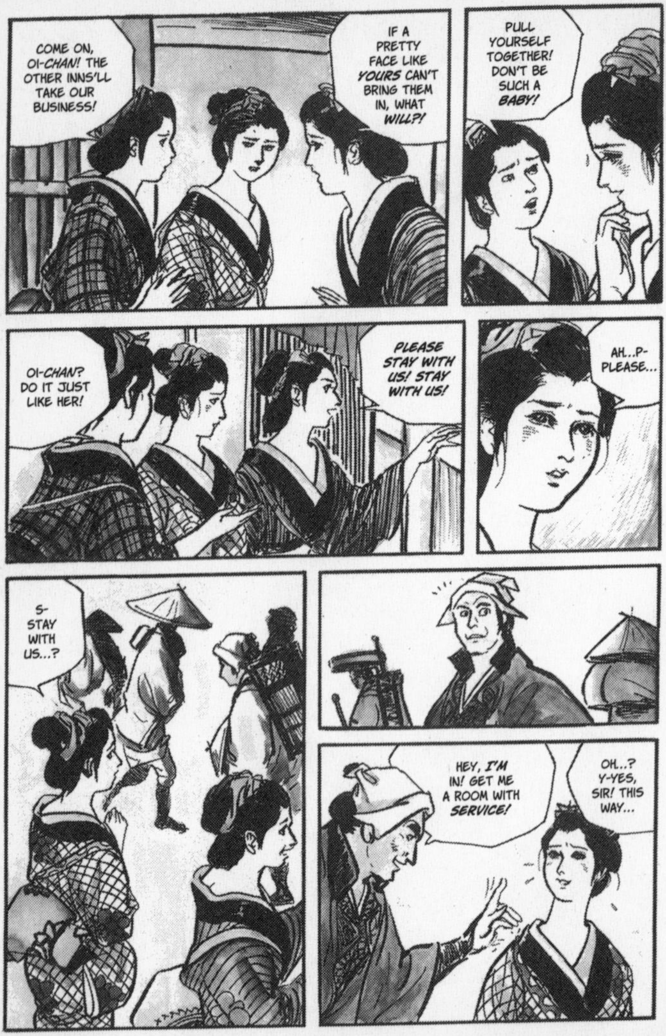
COME ON, OI-CHAN! THE OTHER INNS'LL TAKE OUR BUSINESS!
IF A PRETTY FACE LIKE YOURS CAN'T BRING THEM IN, WHAT WILL?!
PULL YOURSELF TOGETHER! DON'T BE SUCH A BABY!
OI-CHAN? DO IT JUST LIKE HER!
PLEASE STAY WITH US! STAY WITH US!
AH..P-PLEASE...
S-STAY WITH US...?
HEY, I'M IN! GET ME A ROOM WITH SERVICE!
OH..? Y-YES, SIR! THIS WAY...

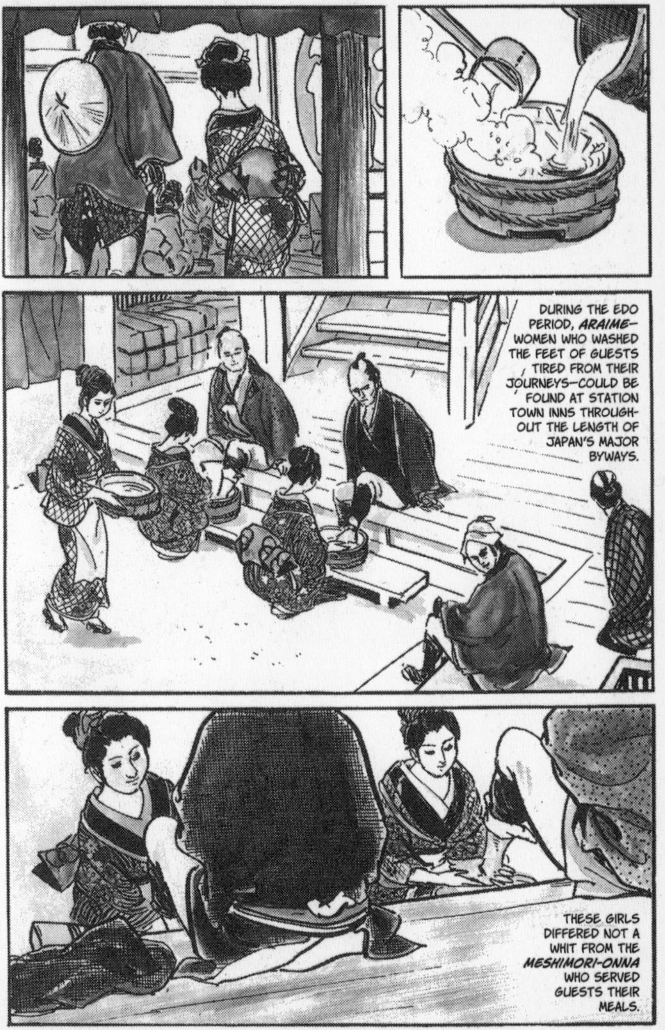
DURING THE EDO PERIOD, *ARAIME*—WOMEN WHO WASHED THE FEET OF GUESTS, TIRED FROM THEIR JOURNEYS—COULD BE FOUND AT STATION TOWN INNS THROUGHOUT THE LENGTH OF JAPAN'S MAJOR BYWAYS.
THESE GIRLS DIFFERED NOT A WHIT FROM THE *MESHIMORI-ONNA* WHO SERVED GUESTS THEIR MEALS.

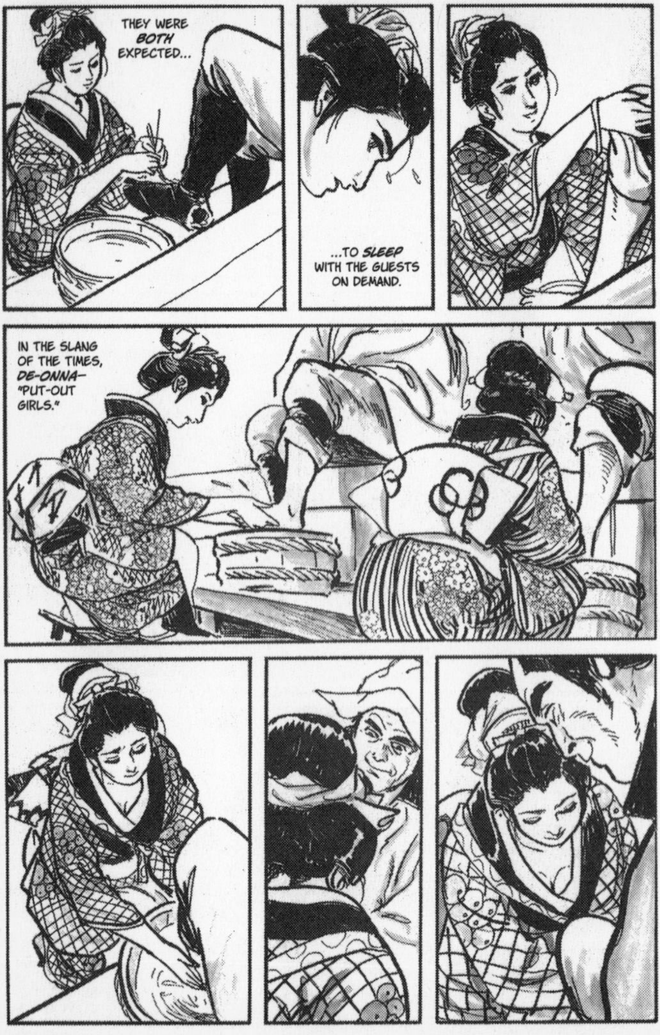
THEY WERE *BOTH* EXPECTED...
...TO *SLEEP* WITH THE GUESTS ON DEMAND.
IN THE SLANG OF THE TIMES, *DE-ONNA*— "PUT-OUT GIRLS."

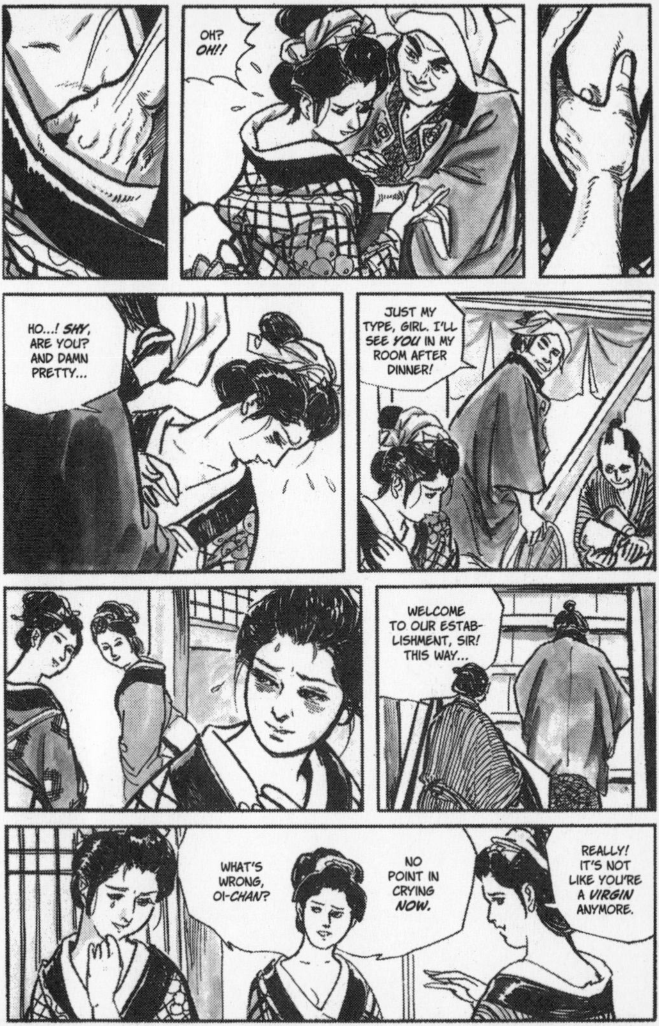
OH?
OH!!
HO...! SHY, ARE YOU? AND DAMN PRETTY...
JUST MY TYPE, GIRL. I'LL SEE YOU IN MY ROOM AFTER DINNER!
WELCOME TO OUR ESTAB-LISHMENT, SIR! THIS WAY...
WHAT'S WRONG, OI-CHAN?
NO POINT IN CRYING NOW.
REALLY! IT'S NOT LIKE YOU'RE A VIRGIN ANYMORE.

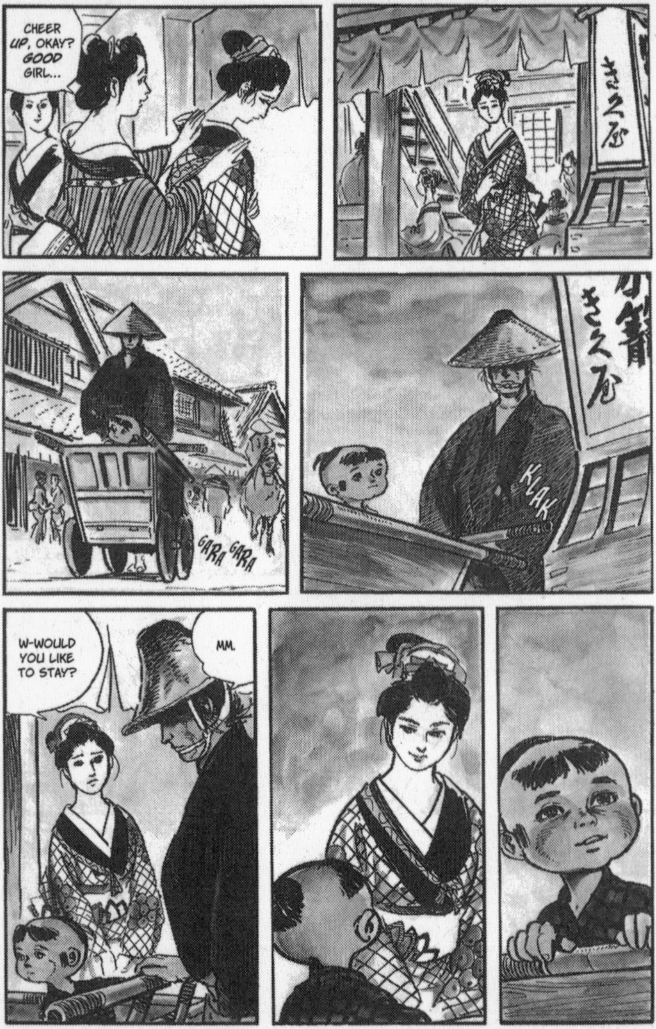
CHEER UP, OKAY? GOOD GIRL...
GARA GARA
KLAK
W-WOULD YOU LIKE TO STAY?
MM.

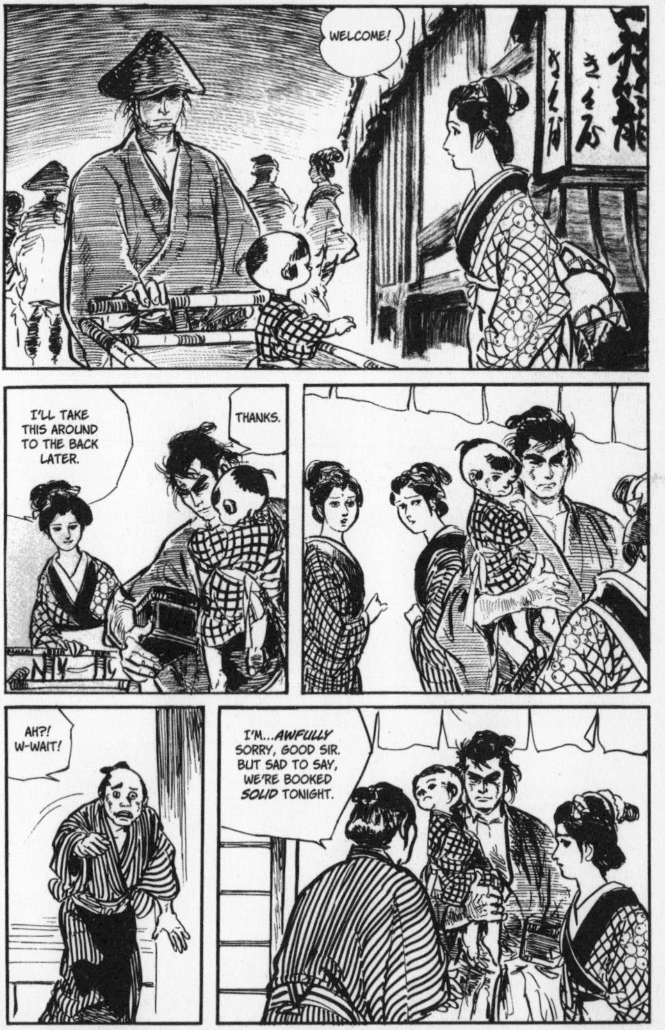
WELCOME!
I'LL TAKE THIS AROUND TO THE BACK LATER.
THANKS.
AH?! W-WAIT!
I'M...AWFULLY SORRY, GOOD SIR. BUT SAD TO SAY, WE'RE BOOKED SOLID TONIGHT.

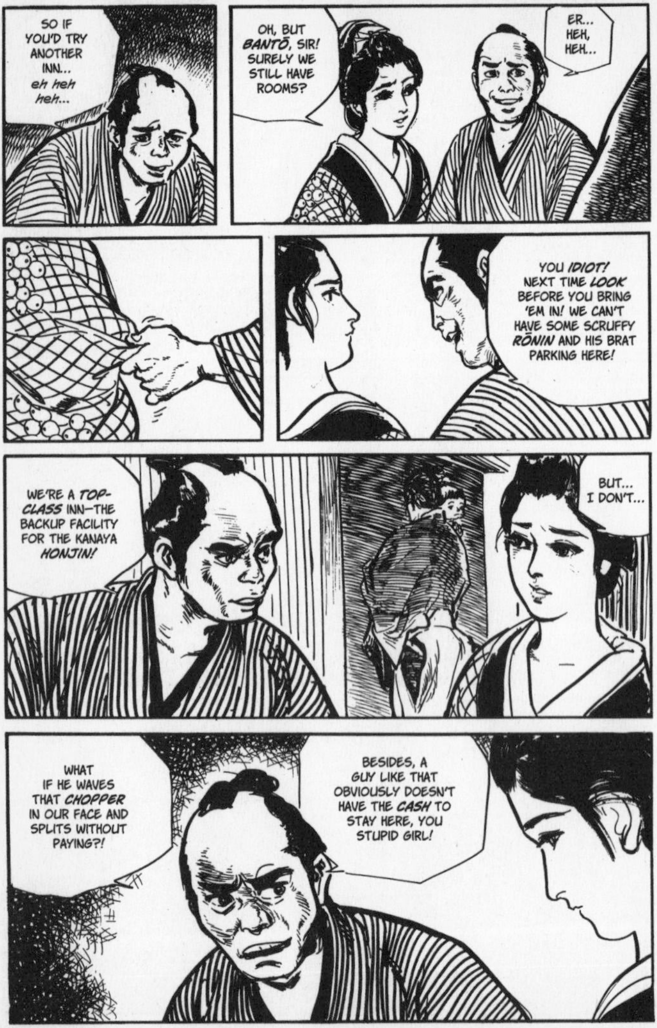
SO IF YOU'D TRY ANOTHER INN... eh heh heh...
OH, BUT BANTŌ, SIR! SURELY WE STILL HAVE ROOMS?
ER... HEH, HEH...
YOU IDIOT! NEXT TIME LOOK BEFORE YOU BRING 'EM IN! WE CAN'T HAVE SOME SCRUFFY RŌNIN AND HIS BRAT PARKING HERE!
WE'RE A TOP-CLASS INN—THE BACKUP FACILITY FOR THE KANAYA HONJIN!
BUT... I DON'T...
WHAT IF HE WAVES THAT CHOPPER IN OUR FACE AND SPLITS WITHOUT PAYING?!
BESIDES, A GUY LIKE THAT OBVIOUSLY DOESN'T HAVE THE CASH TO STAY HERE, YOU STUPID GIRL!

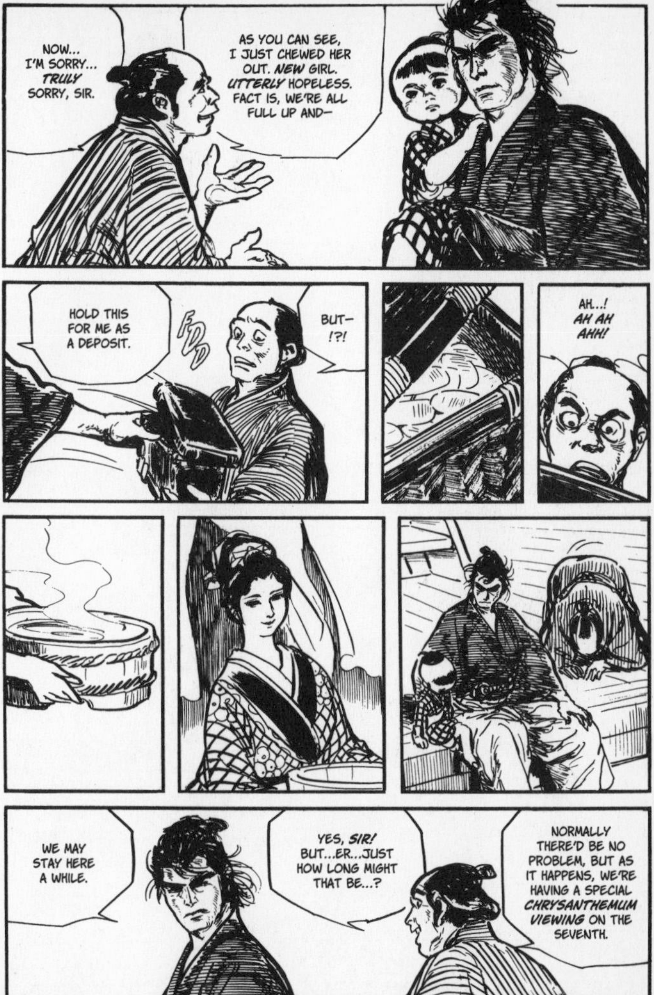
NOW... I'M SORRY... TRULY SORRY, SIR.
AS YOU CAN SEE, I JUST CHEWED HER OUT. NEW GIRL. UTTERLY HOPELESS. FACT IS, WE'RE ALL FULL UP AND—
HOLD THIS FOR ME AS A DEPOSIT.
FDD
BUT— !?!
AH...! AH AH AHH!
WE MAY STAY HERE A WHILE.
YES, SIR! BUT...ER...JUST HOW LONG MIGHT THAT BE...?
NORMALLY THERE'D BE NO PROBLEM, BUT AS IT HAPPENS, WE'RE HAVING A SPECIAL CHRYSANTHEMUM VIEWING ON THE SEVENTH.

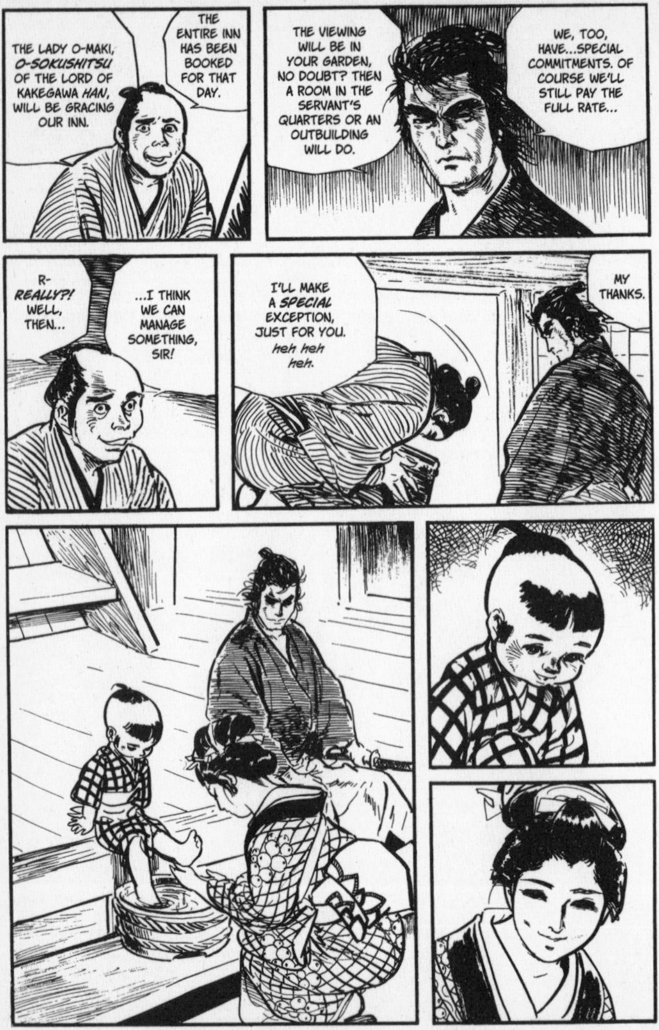
THE LADY O-MAKI, *O-SOKUSHITSU* OF THE LORD OF KAKEGAWA *HAN*, WILL BE GRACING OUR INN.
THE ENTIRE INN HAS BEEN BOOKED FOR THAT DAY.
THE VIEWING WILL BE IN YOUR GARDEN, NO DOUBT? THEN A ROOM IN THE SERVANT'S QUARTERS OR AN OUTBUILDING WILL DO.
WE, TOO, HAVE...SPECIAL COMMITMENTS. OF COURSE WE'LL STILL PAY THE FULL RATE...
R- *REALLY?!* WELL, THEN...
...I THINK WE CAN MANAGE SOMETHING, SIR!
I'LL MAKE A *SPECIAL* EXCEPTION, JUST FOR YOU. *heh heh heh.*
MY THANKS.

ER...*THIS*
GIRL'S ALREADY
SPOKEN FOR,
SIR...

...BUT IF YOU'D
LIKE A SPOT OF...
FUN, JUST SAY
THE WORD.

WE CAN
KEEP YOUR BOY
AMUSED FOR A
HOUR OR TWO
WHILE YOU—

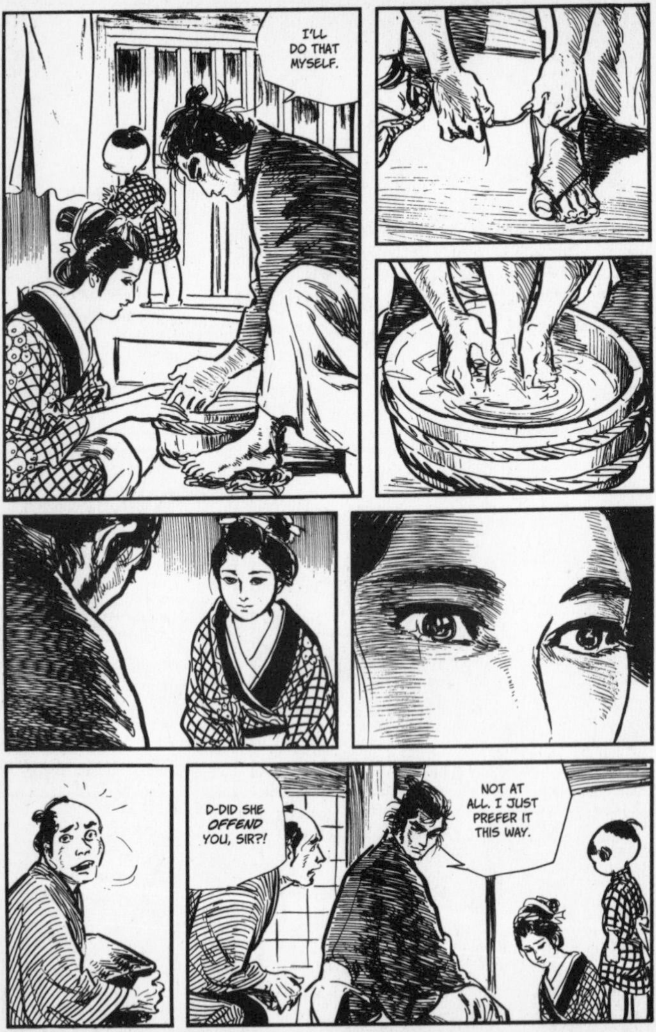
I'LL DO THAT MYSELF.
D-DID SHE OFFEND YOU, SIR?!
NOT AT ALL. I JUST PREFER IT THIS WAY.

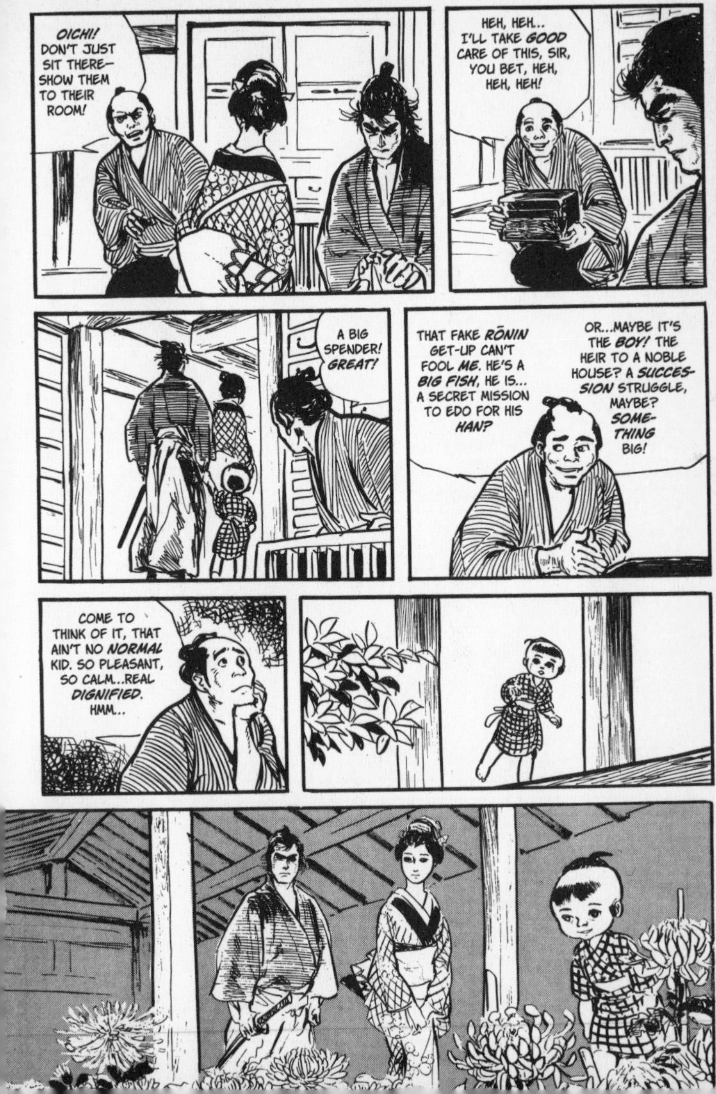

OICHI! DON'T JUST SIT THERE— SHOW THEM TO THEIR ROOM!
HEH, HEH... I'LL TAKE GOOD CARE OF THIS, SIR, YOU BET, HEH, HEH, HEH!
A BIG SPENDER! GREAT!
THAT FAKE RŌNIN GET-UP CAN'T FOOL ME. HE'S A BIG FISH, HE IS... A SECRET MISSION TO EDO FOR HIS HAN?
OR...MAYBE IT'S THE BOY! THE HEIR TO A NOBLE HOUSE? A SUCCES-SION STRUGGLE, MAYBE? SOME-THING BIG!
COME TO THINK OF IT, THAT AIN'T NO NORMAL KID. SO PLEASANT, SO CALM...REAL DIGNIFIED. HMM...

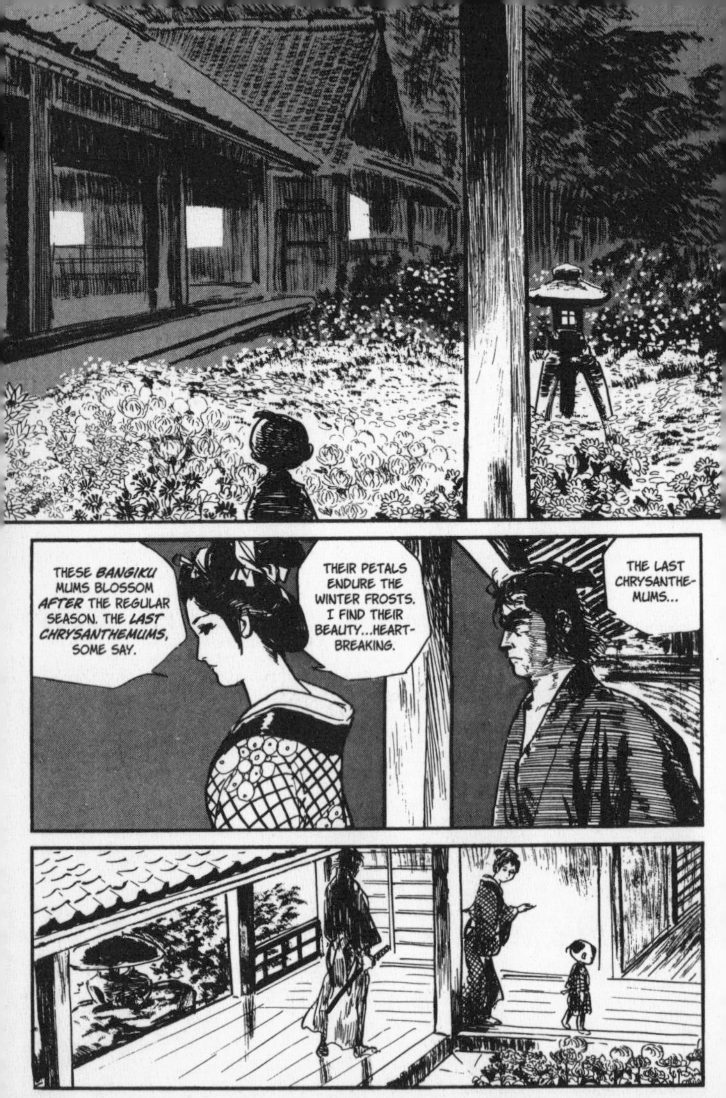

THESE BANGIKU MUMS BLOSSOM AFTER THE REGULAR SEASON. THE LAST CHRYSANTHEMUMS, SOME SAY.
THEIR PETALS ENDURE THE WINTER FROSTS. I FIND THEIR BEAUTY...HEART-BREAKING.
THE LAST CHRYSANTHE-MUMS...

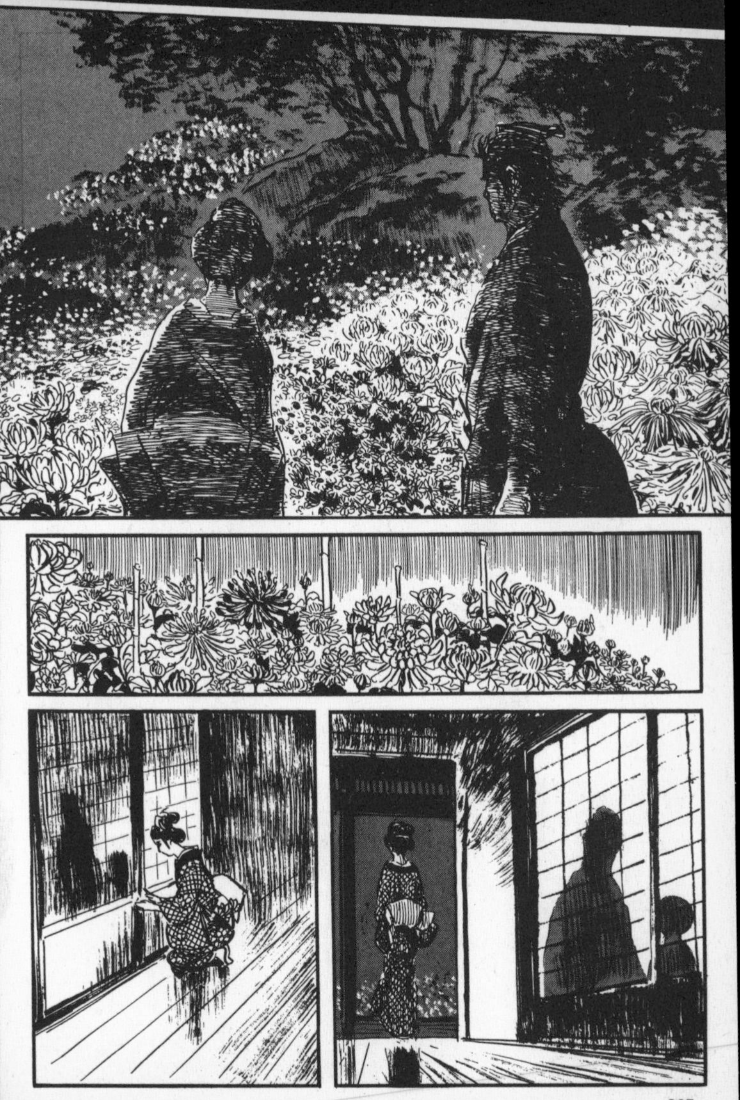

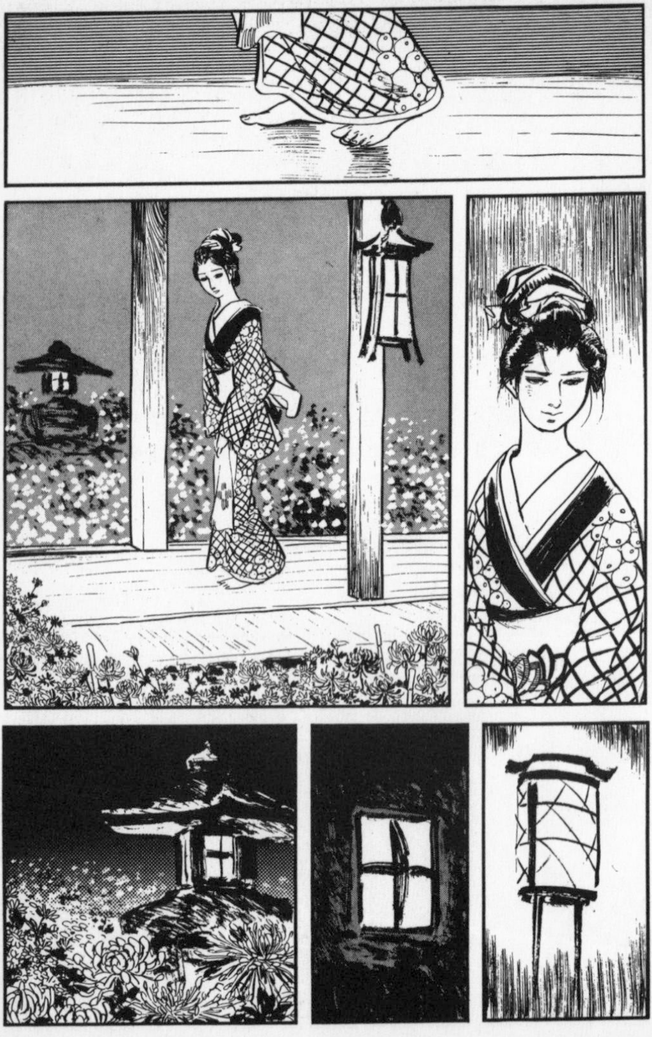

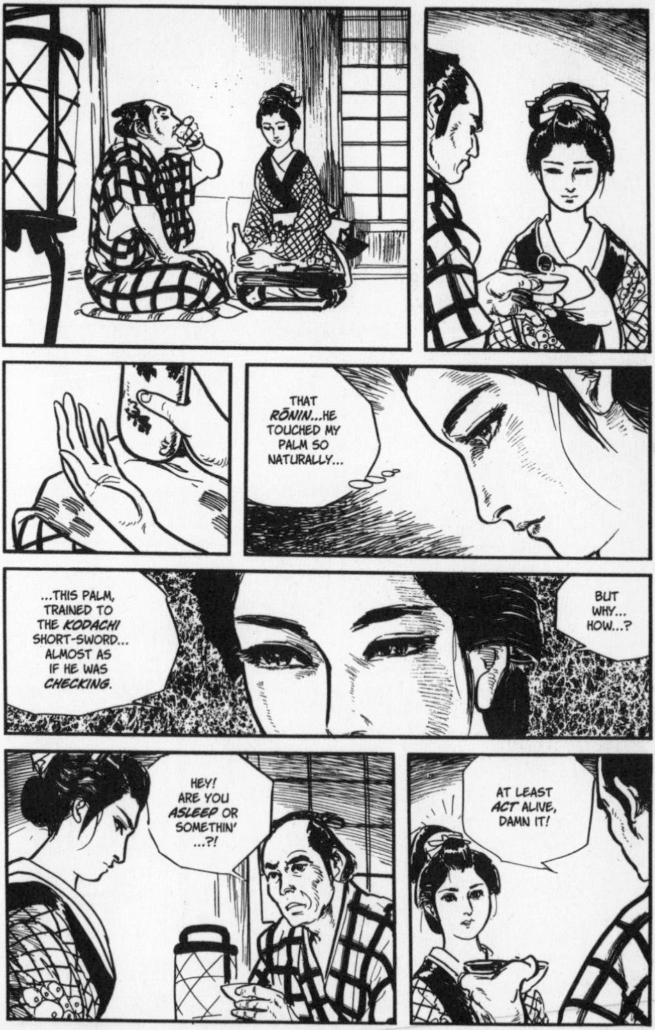
THAT RŌNIN...HE TOUCHED MY PALM SO NATURALLY...
...THIS PALM, TRAINED TO THE KODACHI SHORT-SWORD... ALMOST AS IF HE WAS CHECKING.
BUT WHY... HOW...?
HEY! ARE YOU ASLEEP OR SOMETHIN' ...?!
AT LEAST ACT ALIVE, DAMN IT!

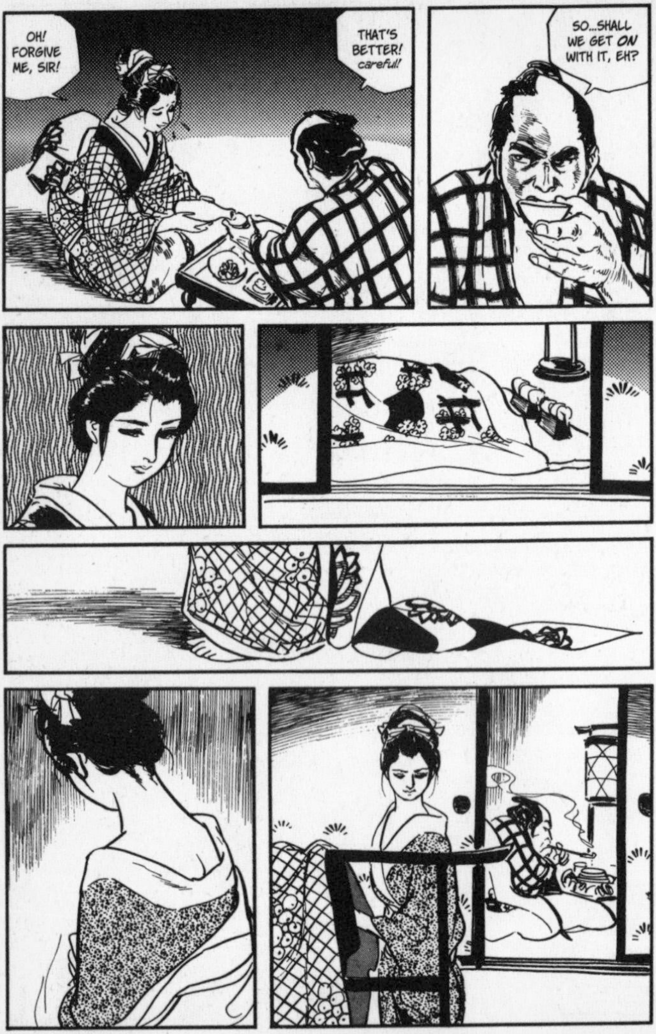
OH! FORGIVE ME, SIR!
THAT'S BETTER! careful!
SO...SHALL WE GET ON WITH IT, EH?

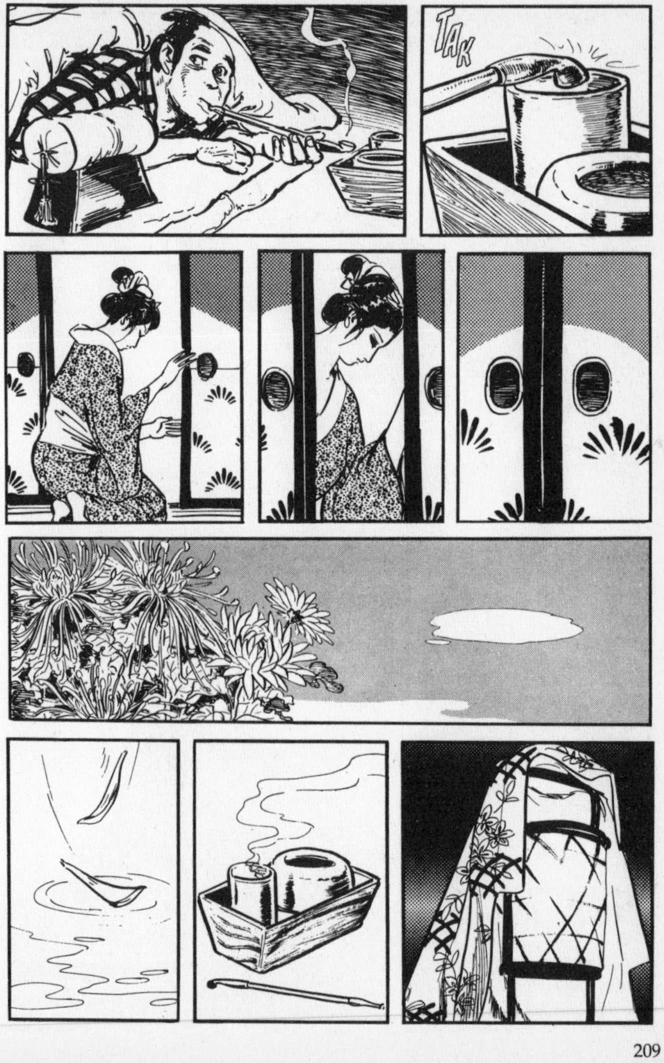
TAK

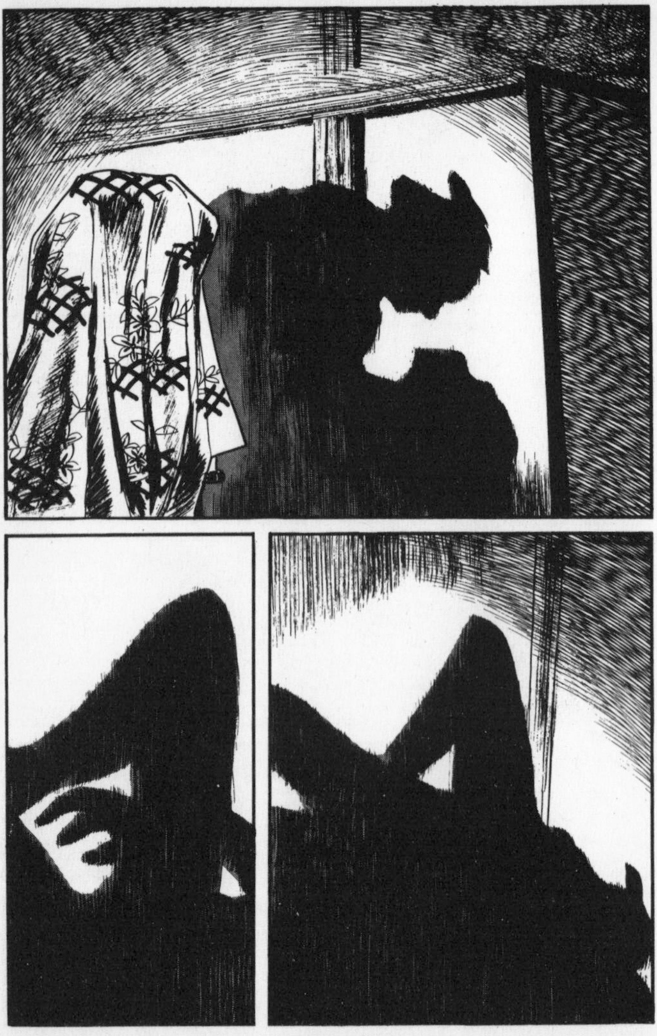

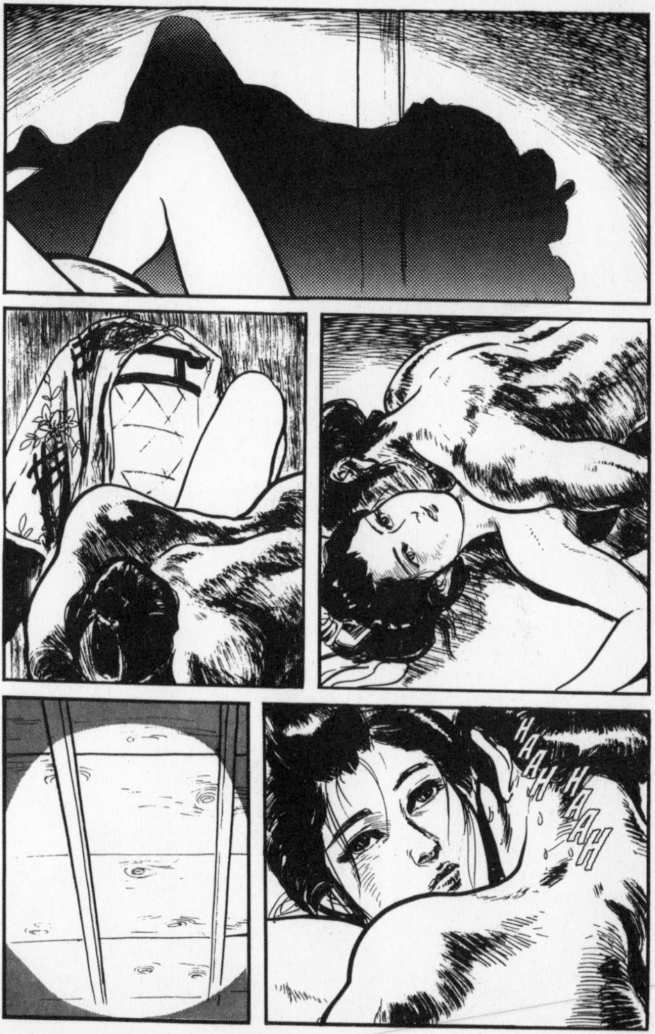
HAAH
HAAAH

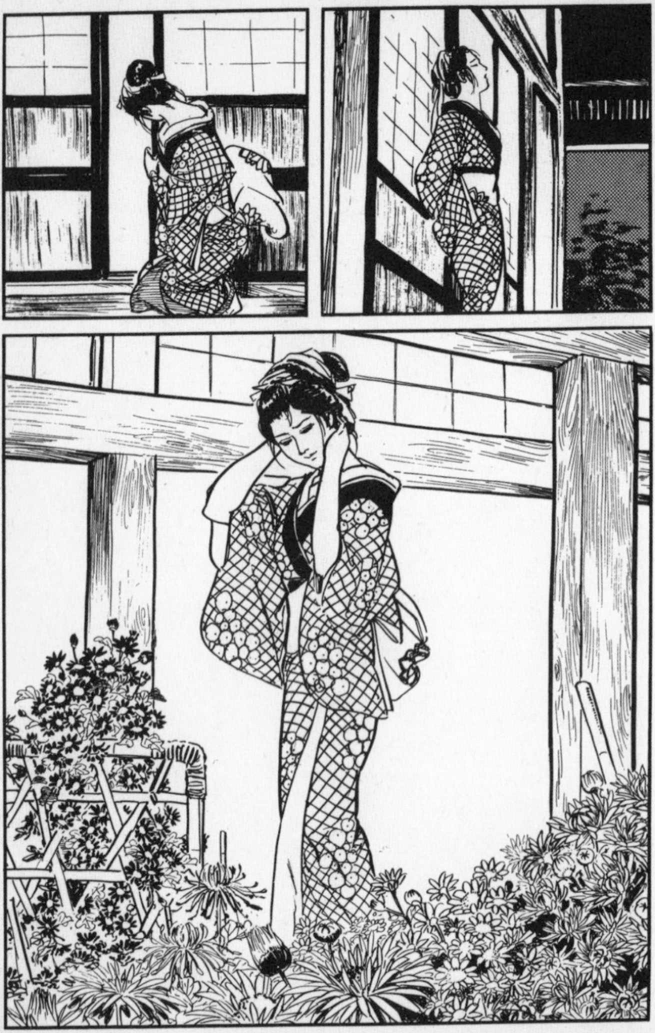

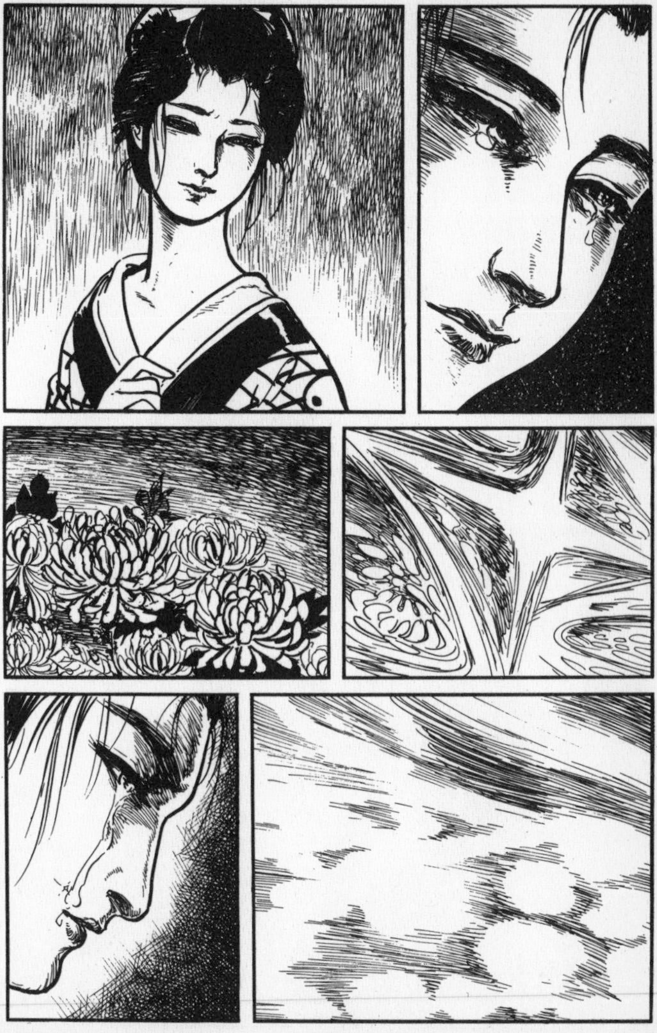

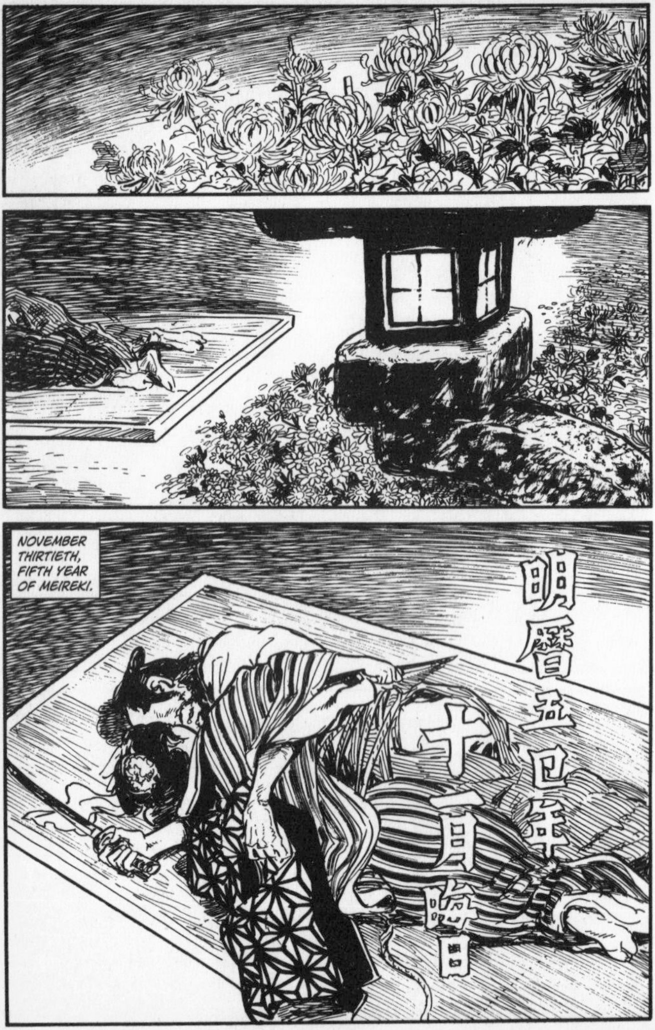

NOVEMBER THIRTIETH, FIFTH YEAR OF MEIREKI.
明暦五巳年
十一月晦日

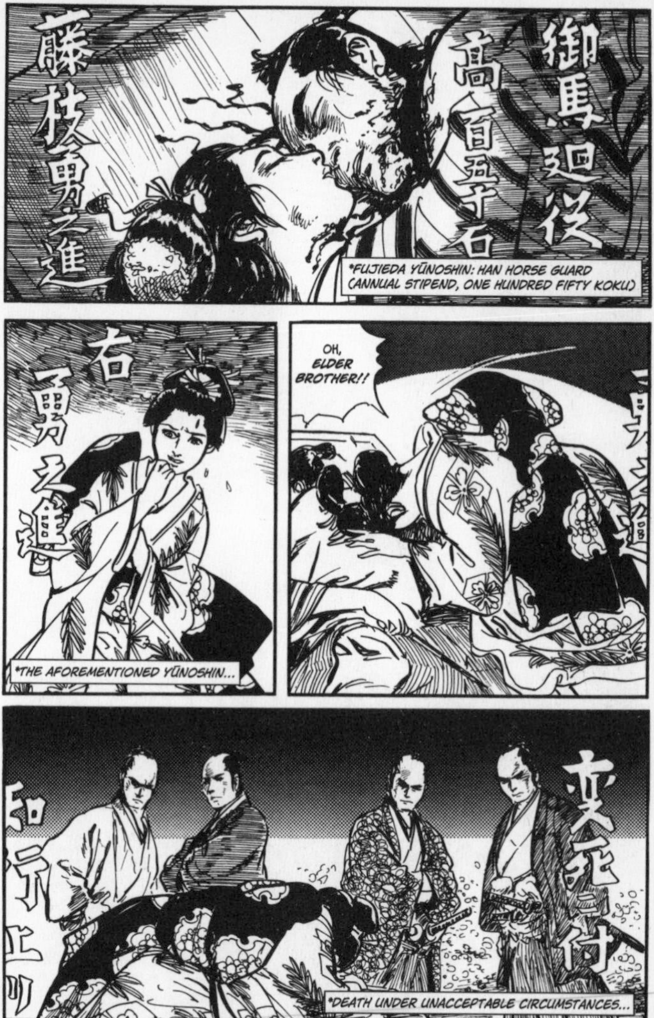
御馬廻役
高百五十石
藤枝勇之進
*FUJIEDA YŪNOSHIN: HAN HORSE GUARD (ANNUAL STIPEND, ONE HUNDRED FIFTY KOKU)
右勇之進
*THE AFOREMENTIONED YŪNOSHIN...
OH, ELDER BROTHER!!
変死ニ付
*DEATH UNDER UNACCEPTABLE CIRCUMSTANCES...

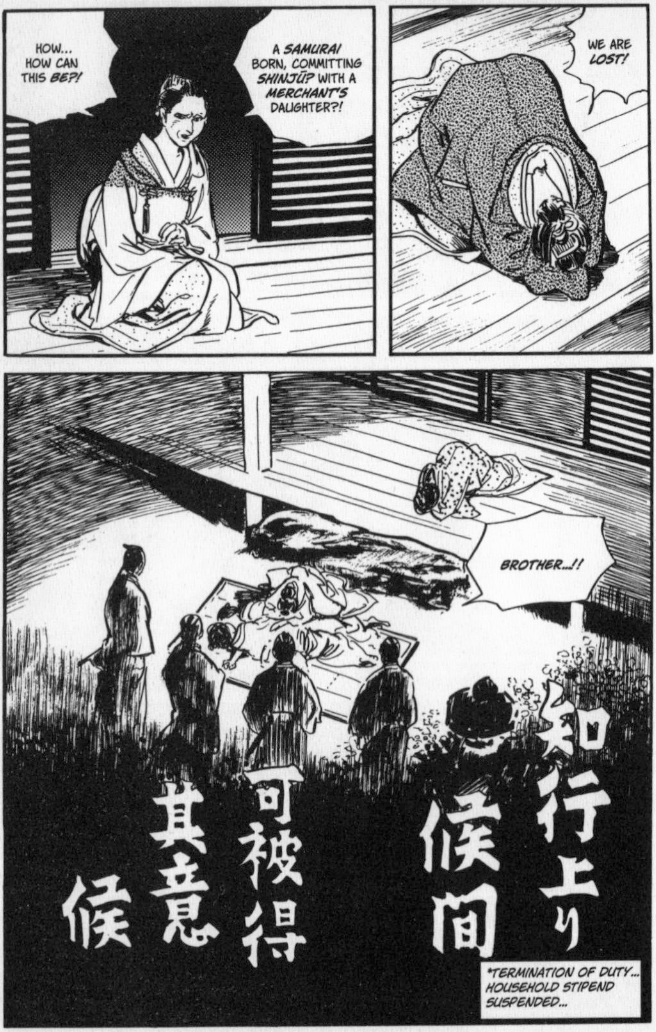
HOW... HOW CAN THIS BE?!
A SAMURAI BORN, COMMITTING SHINJŪ? WITH A MERCHANT'S DAUGHTER?!
WE ARE LOST!
BROTHER...!!
知行上り候間可被得其意候
*TERMINATION OF DUTY... HOUSEHOLD STIPEND SUSPENDED...

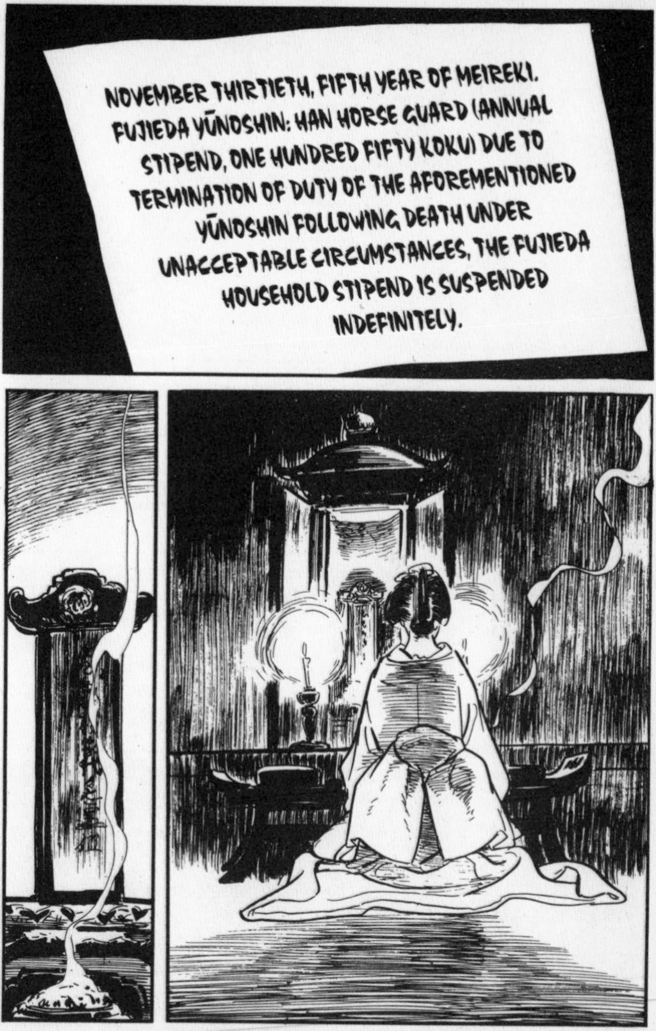
NOVEMBER THIRTIETH, FIFTH YEAR OF MEIREKI. FUJIEDA YŪNOSHIN: HAN HORSE GUARD (ANNUAL STIPEND, ONE HUNDRED FIFTY KOKU) DUE TO TERMINATION OF DUTY OF THE AFOREMENTIONED YŪNOSHIN FOLLOWING DEATH UNDER UNACCEPTABLE CIRCUMSTANCES, THE FUJIEDA HOUSEHOLD STIPEND IS SUSPENDED INDEFINITELY.

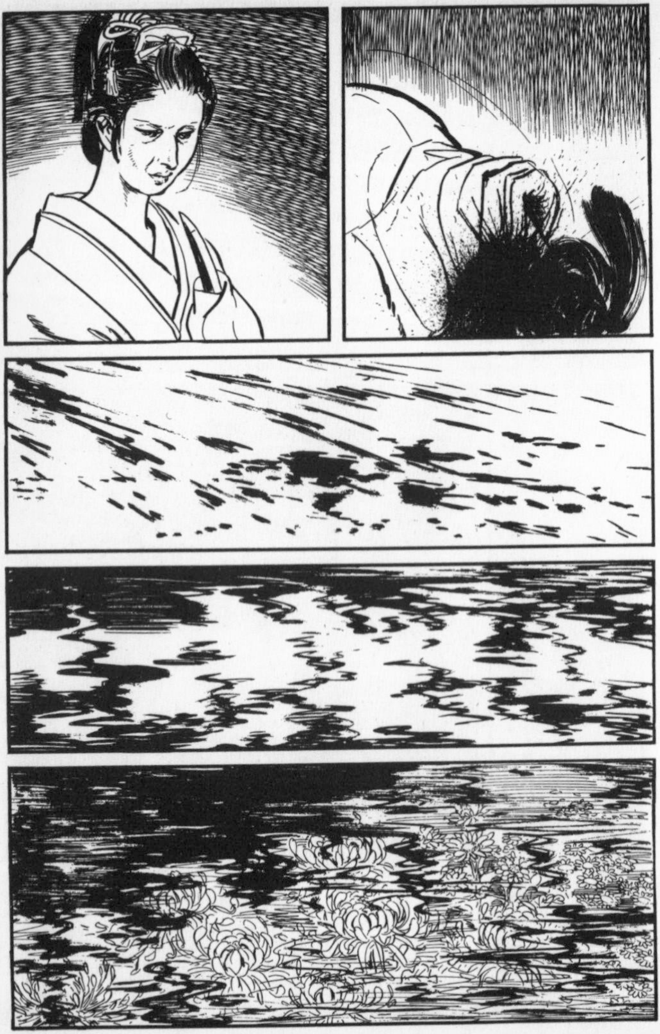

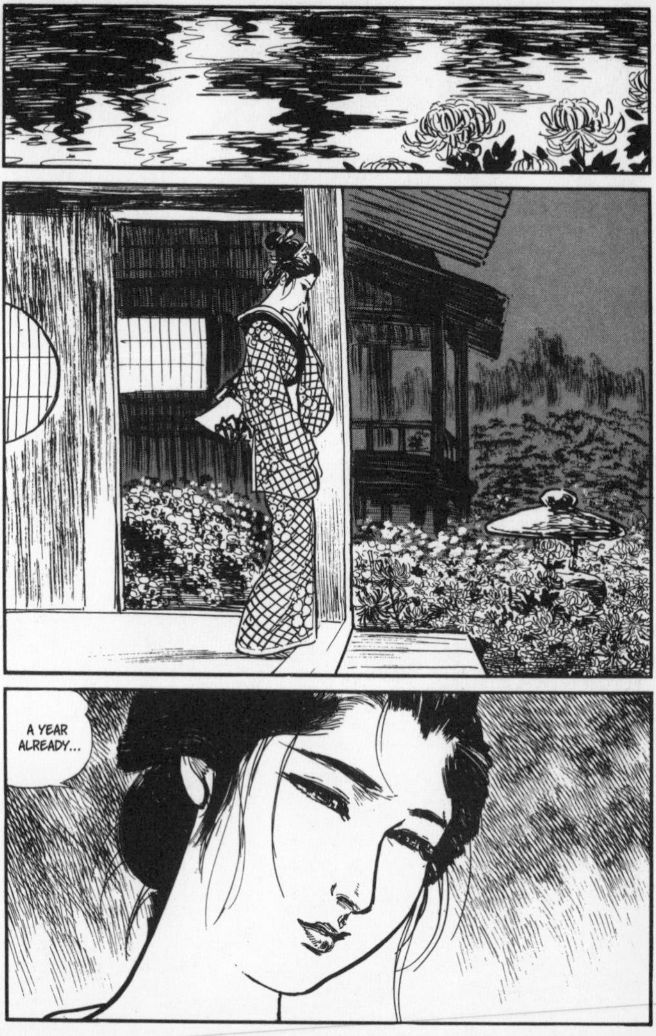
A YEAR ALREADY...

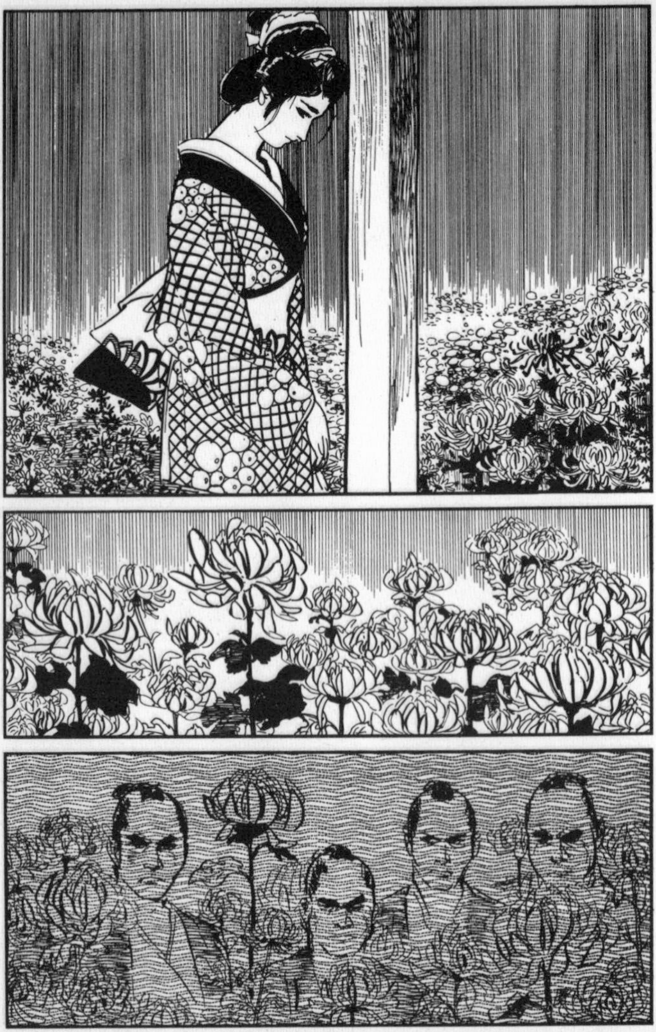

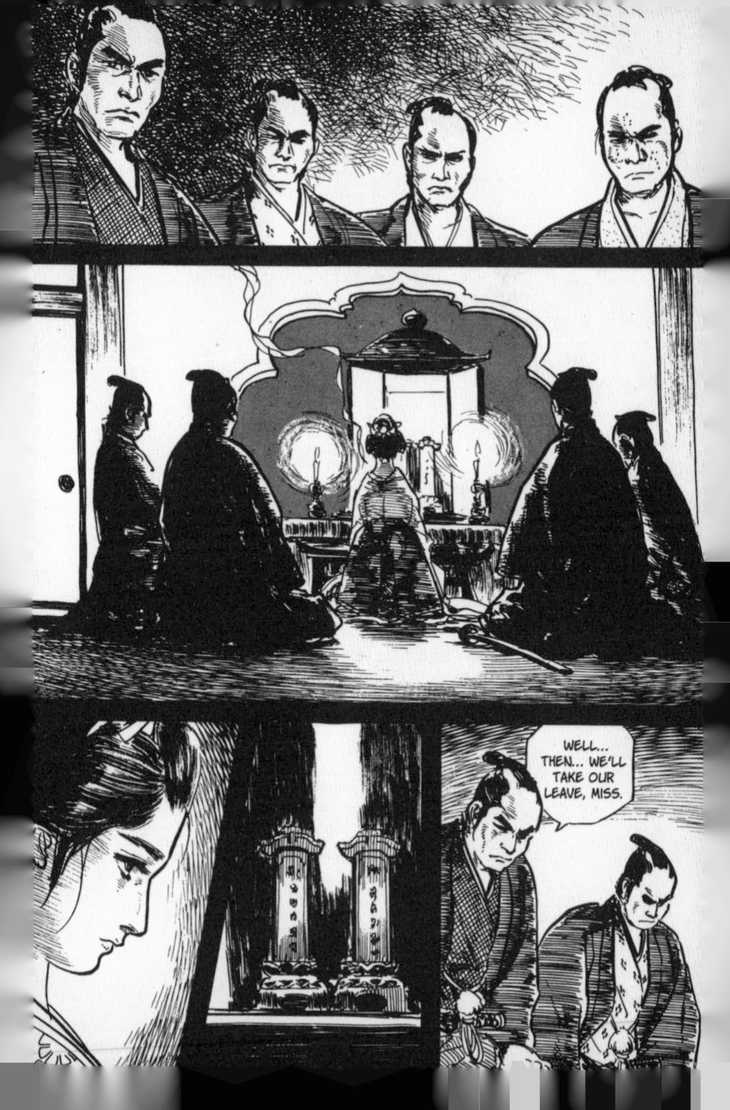
WELL... THEN... WE'LL TAKE OUR LEAVE, MISS.

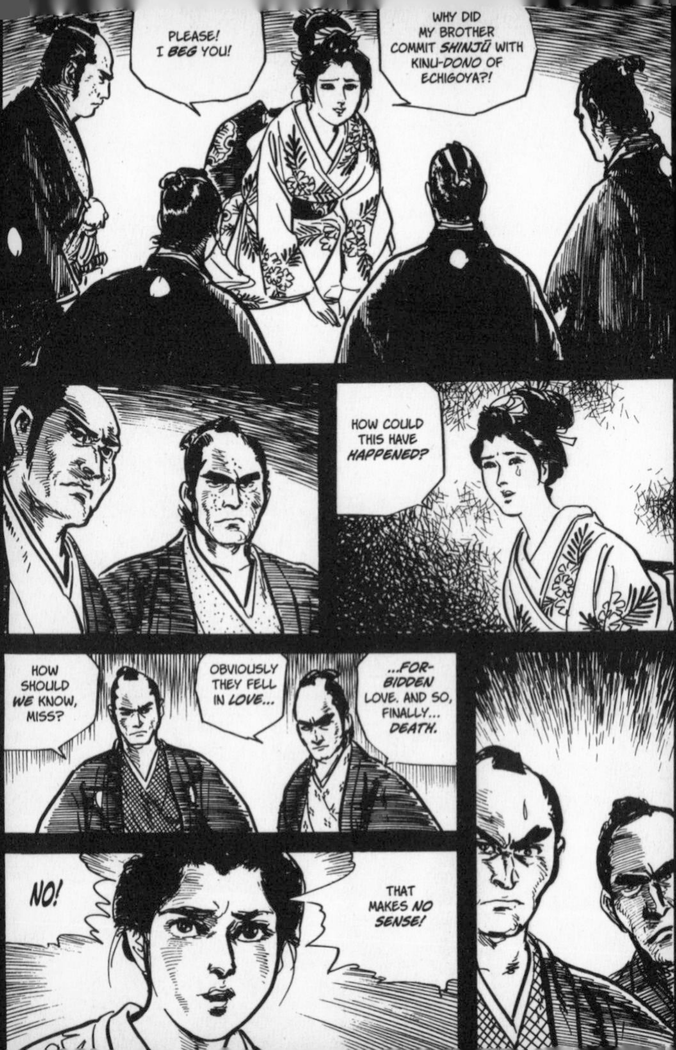
PLEASE! I BEG YOU!
WHY DID MY BROTHER COMMIT SHINJŪ WITH KINU-DONO OF ECHIGOYA?!
HOW COULD THIS HAVE HAPPENED?
HOW SHOULD WE KNOW, MISS?
OBVIOUSLY THEY FELL IN LOVE...
...FOR-BIDDEN LOVE. AND SO, FINALLY... DEATH.
NO!
THAT MAKES NO SENSE!

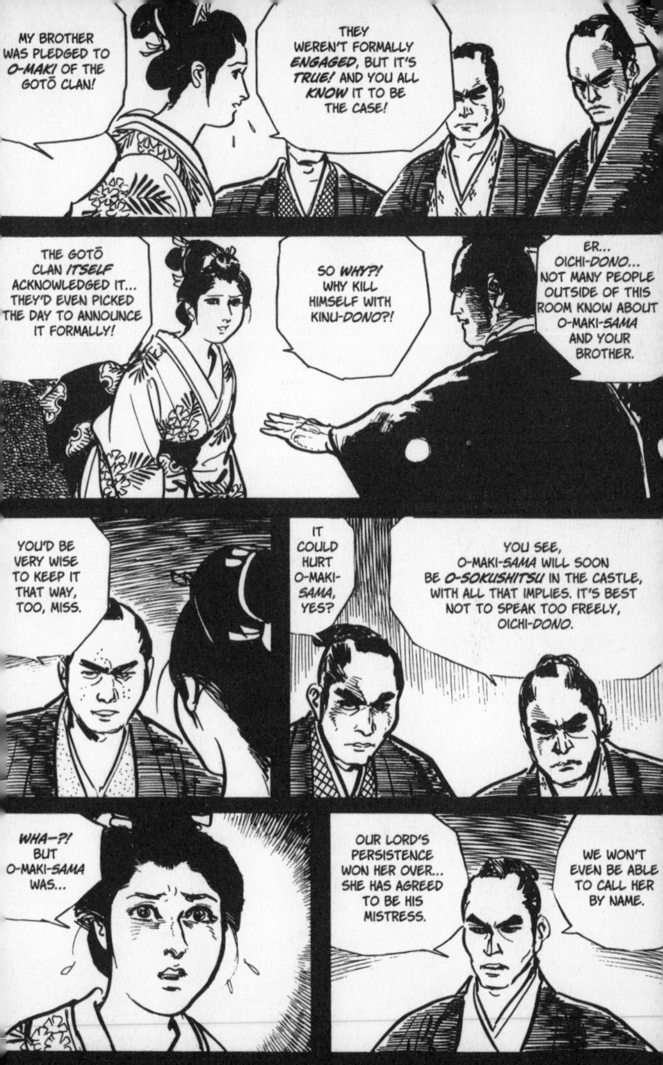
MY BROTHER WAS PLEDGED TO O-MAKI OF THE GOTŌ CLAN!
THEY WEREN'T FORMALLY ENGAGED, BUT IT'S TRUE! AND YOU ALL KNOW IT TO BE THE CASE!
THE GOTŌ CLAN ITSELF ACKNOWLEDGED IT... THEY'D EVEN PICKED THE DAY TO ANNOUNCE IT FORMALLY!
SO WHY?! WHY KILL HIMSELF WITH KINU-DONO?!
ER... OICHI-DONO... NOT MANY PEOPLE OUTSIDE OF THIS ROOM KNOW ABOUT O-MAKI-SAMA AND YOUR BROTHER.
YOU'D BE VERY WISE TO KEEP IT THAT WAY, TOO, MISS.
IT COULD HURT O-MAKI-SAMA, YES?
YOU SEE, O-MAKI-SAMA WILL SOON BE O-SOKUSHITSU IN THE CASTLE, WITH ALL THAT IMPLIES. IT'S BEST NOT TO SPEAK TOO FREELY, OICHI-DONO.
WHA-?! BUT O-MAKI-SAMA WAS...
OUR LORD'S PERSISTENCE WON HER OVER... SHE HAS AGREED TO BE HIS MISTRESS.
WE WON'T EVEN BE ABLE TO CALL HER BY NAME.

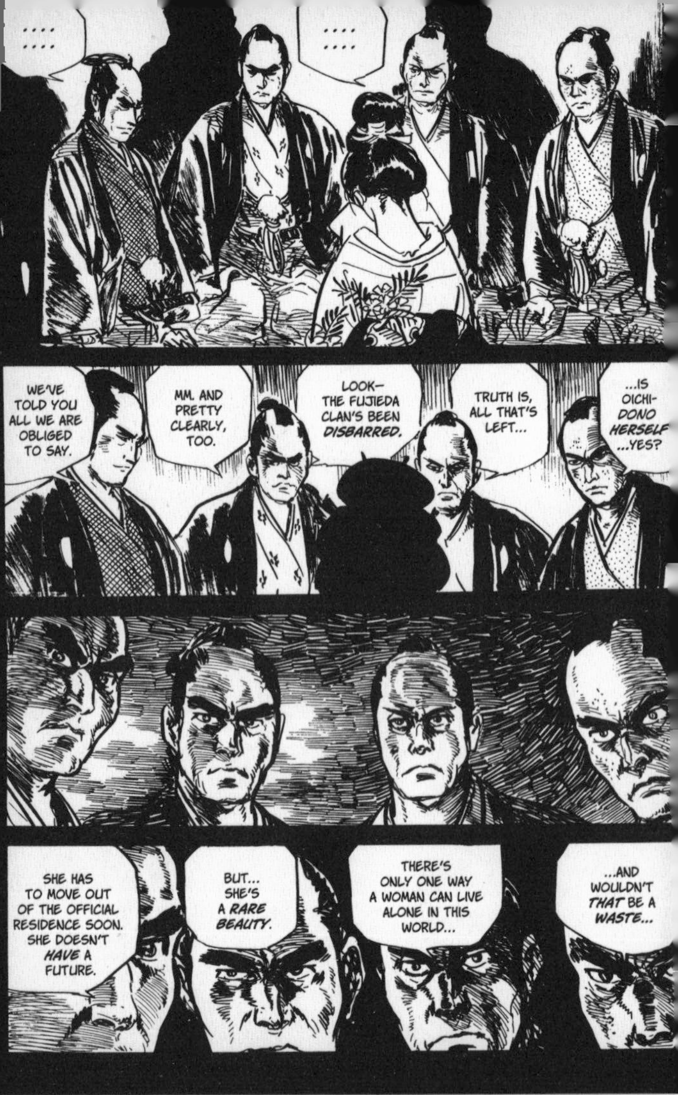
....
....
....
....
WE'VE TOLD YOU ALL WE ARE OBLIGED TO SAY.
MM. AND PRETTY CLEARLY, TOO.
LOOK— THE FUJIEDA CLAN'S BEEN *DISBARRED.*
TRUTH IS, ALL THAT'S LEFT...
...IS OICHI-DONO *HERSELF* ...YES?
SHE HAS TO MOVE OUT OF THE OFFICIAL RESIDENCE SOON. SHE DOESN'T *HAVE* A FUTURE.
BUT... SHE'S A *RARE BEAUTY.*
THERE'S ONLY ONE WAY A WOMAN CAN LIVE ALONE IN THIS WORLD...
...AND WOULDN'T *THAT* BE A *WASTE...*

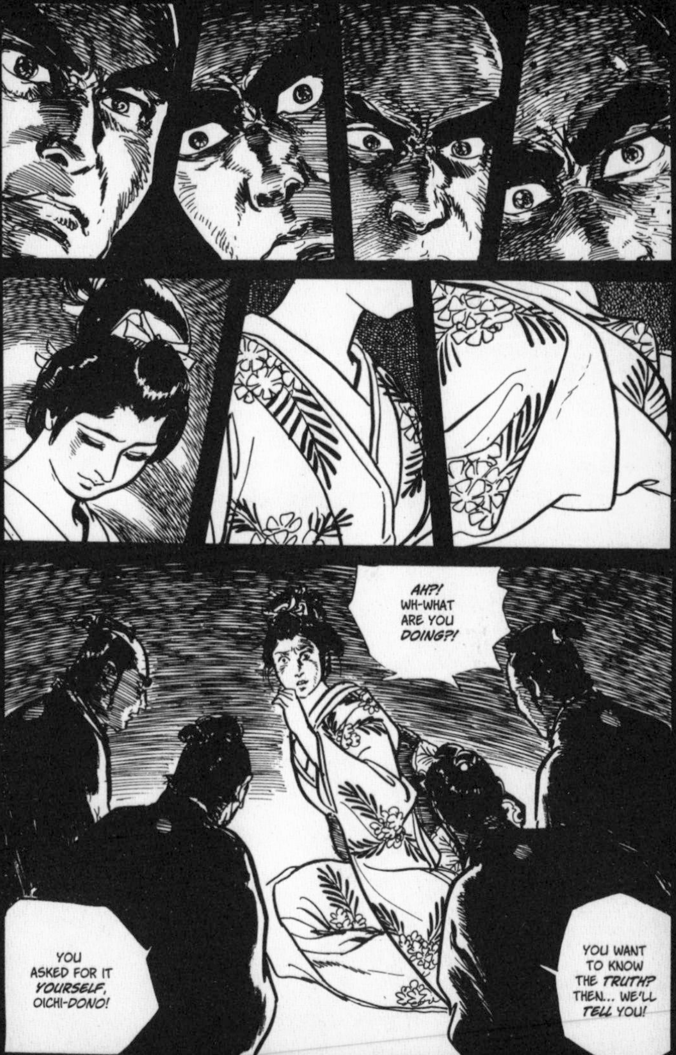
AH?! WH-WHAT ARE YOU DOING?!
YOU ASKED FOR IT YOURSELF, OICHI-DONO!
YOU WANT TO KNOW THE TRUTH? THEN... WE'LL TELL YOU!

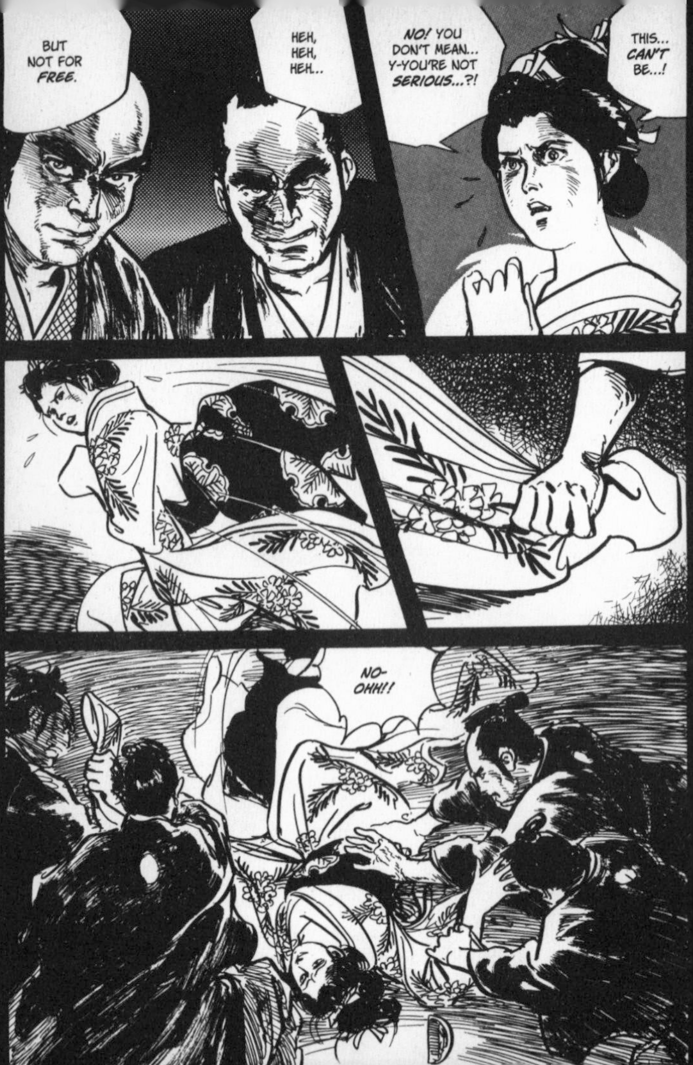

BUT NOT FOR FREE.
HEH, HEH, HEH...
NO! YOU DON'T MEAN... Y-YOU'RE NOT SERIOUS...?!
THIS... CAN'T BE...!
NO-OHH!!

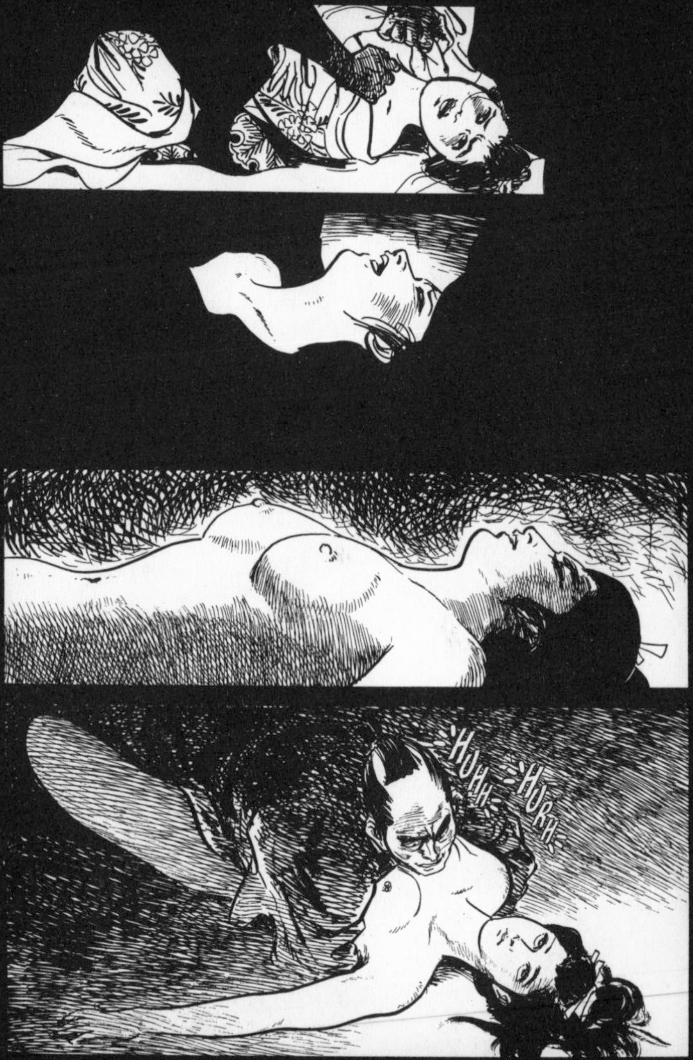
HUHH
HURH

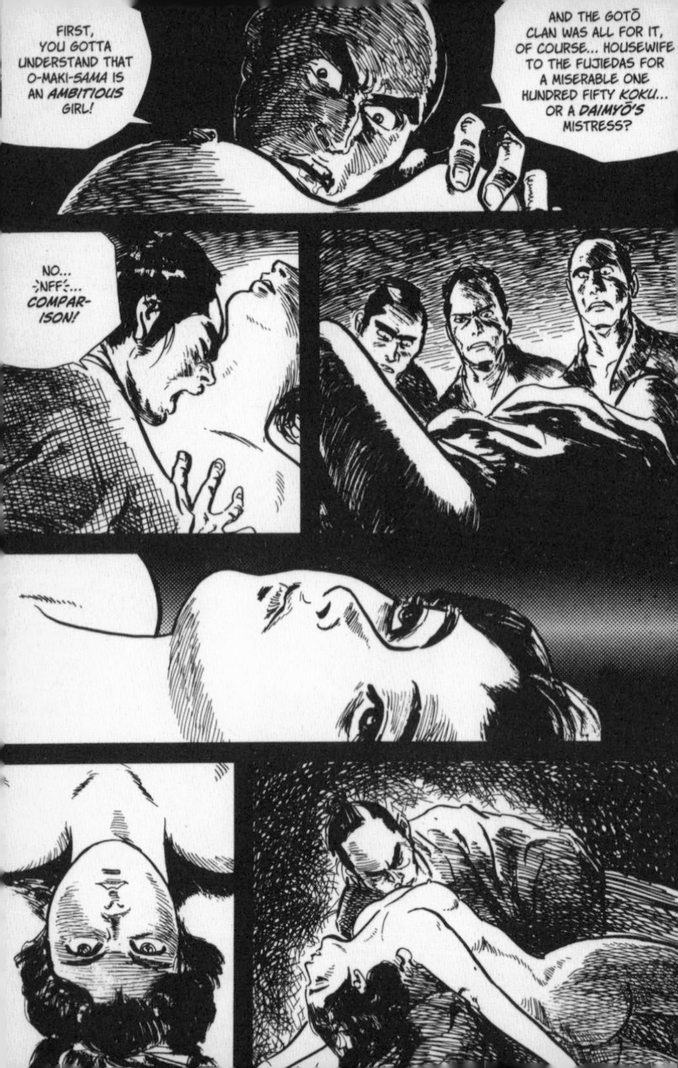
FIRST, YOU GOTTA UNDERSTAND THAT O-MAKI-*SAMA* IS AN *AMBITIOUS* GIRL!
AND THE GOTŌ CLAN WAS ALL FOR IT, OF COURSE... HOUSEWIFE TO THE FUJIEDAS FOR A MISERABLE ONE HUNDRED FIFTY *KOKU*... OR A *DAIMYŌ'S* MISTRESS?
NO... NFF... *COMPARISON!*

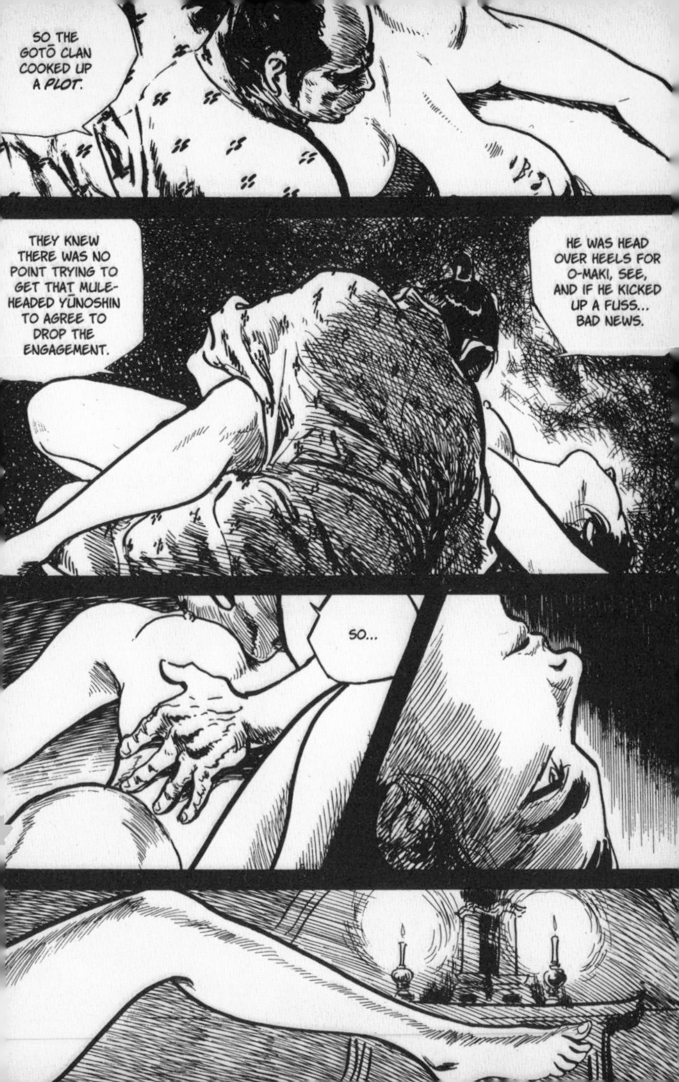
SO THE GOTŌ CLAN COOKED UP A *PLOT*.
HE WAS HEAD OVER HEELS FOR O-MAKI, SEE, AND IF HE KICKED UP A FUSS... BAD NEWS.
THEY KNEW THERE WAS NO POINT TRYING TO GET THAT MULE-HEADED YŪNOSHIN TO AGREE TO DROP THE ENGAGEMENT.
SO...

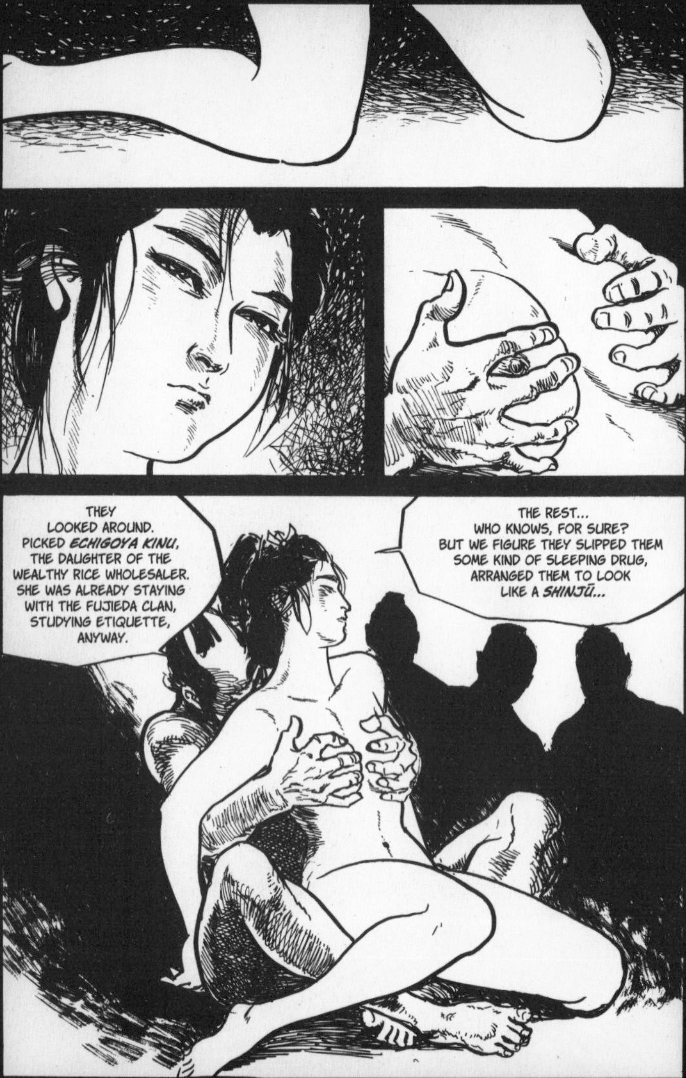
THEY LOOKED AROUND. PICKED *ECHIGOYA KINU*, THE DAUGHTER OF THE WEALTHY RICE WHOLESALER. SHE WAS ALREADY STAYING WITH THE FUJIEDA CLAN, STUDYING ETIQUETTE, ANYWAY.
THE REST... WHO KNOWS, FOR SURE? BUT WE FIGURE THEY SLIPPED THEM SOME KIND OF SLEEPING DRUG, ARRANGED THEM TO LOOK LIKE A *SHINJŪ*...

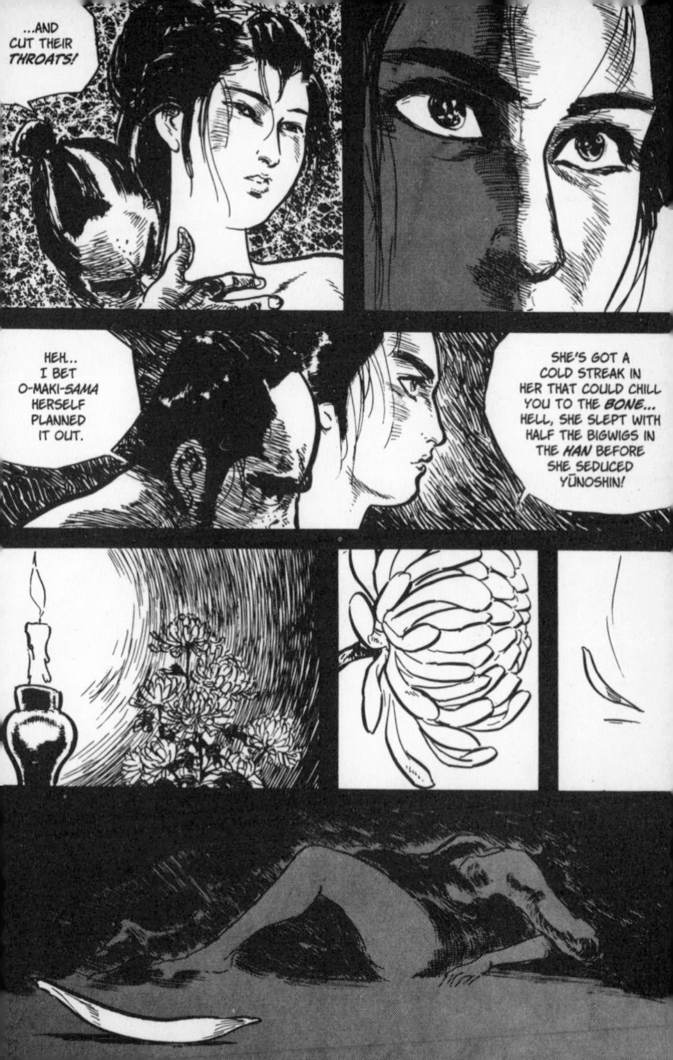
...AND CUT THEIR *THROATS!*
HEH... I BET O-MAKI-*SAMA* HERSELF PLANNED IT OUT.
SHE'S GOT A COLD STREAK IN HER THAT COULD CHILL YOU TO THE *BONE...* HELL, SHE SLEPT WITH HALF THE BIGWIGS IN THE *HAN* BEFORE SHE SEDUCED YŪNOSHIN!

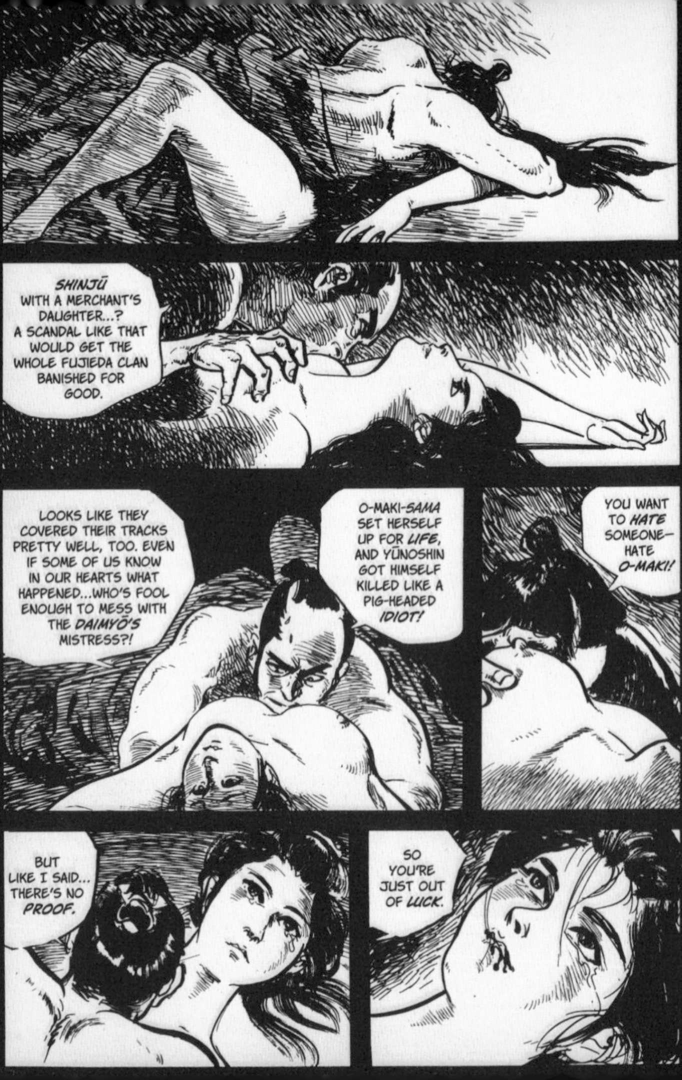
SHINJŪ WITH A MERCHANT'S DAUGHTER...? A SCANDAL LIKE THAT WOULD GET THE WHOLE FUJIEDA CLAN BANISHED FOR GOOD.
LOOKS LIKE THEY COVERED THEIR TRACKS PRETTY WELL, TOO. EVEN IF SOME OF US KNOW IN OUR HEARTS WHAT HAPPENED...WHO'S FOOL ENOUGH TO MESS WITH THE DAIMYŌ'S MISTRESS?!
O-MAKI-SAMA SET HERSELF UP FOR LIFE, AND YŪNOSHIN GOT HIMSELF KILLED LIKE A PIG-HEADED IDIOT!
YOU WANT TO HATE SOMEONE–HATE O-MAKI!
BUT LIKE I SAID... THERE'S NO PROOF.
SO YOU'RE JUST OUT OF LUCK.

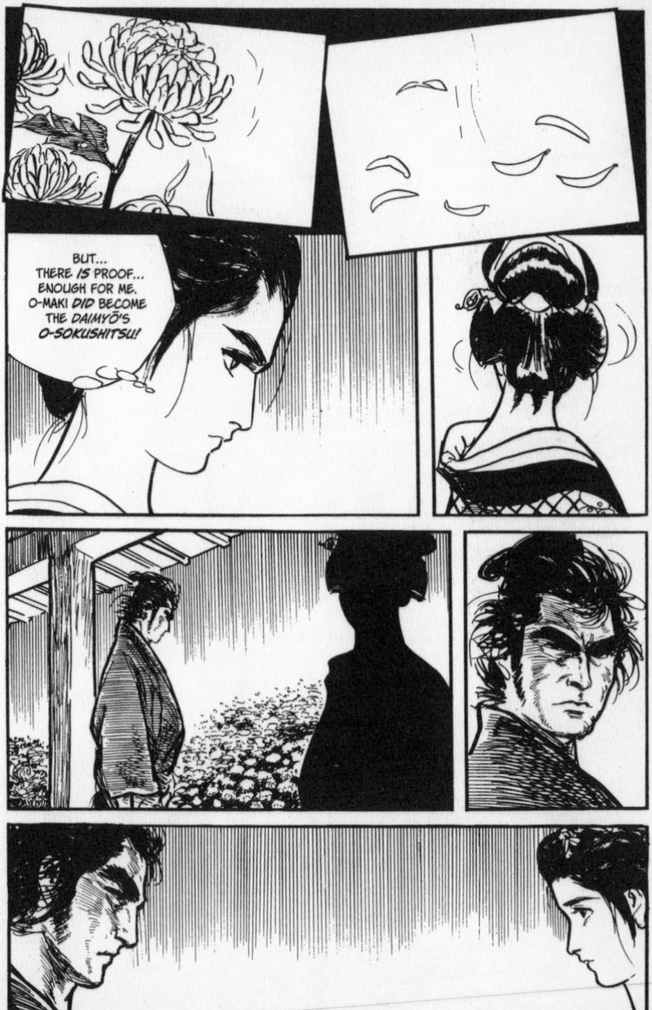
BUT... THERE *IS* PROOF... ENOUGH FOR ME. O-MAKI *DID* BECOME THE *DAIMYŌ'S* *O-SOKUSHITSU!*

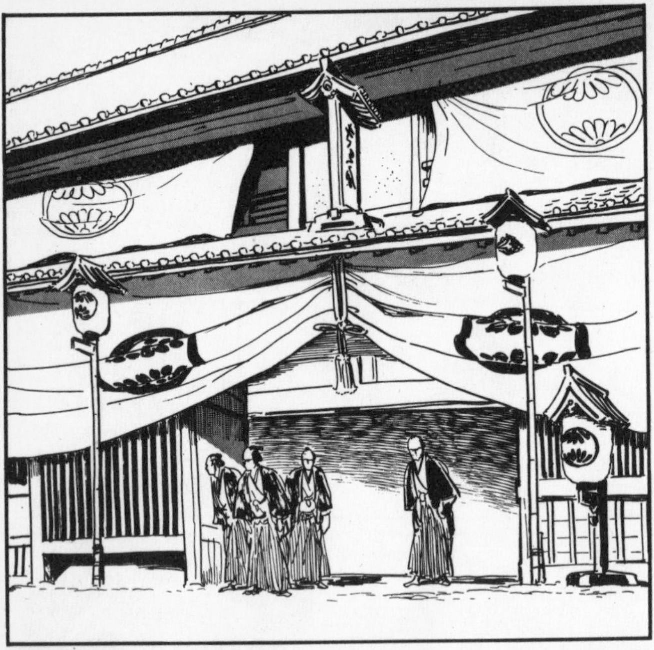

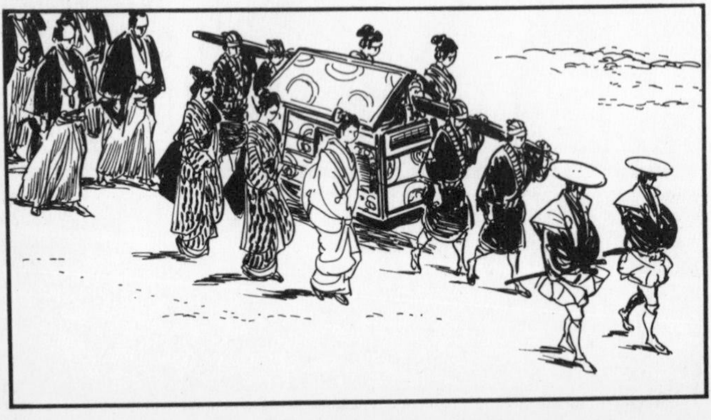

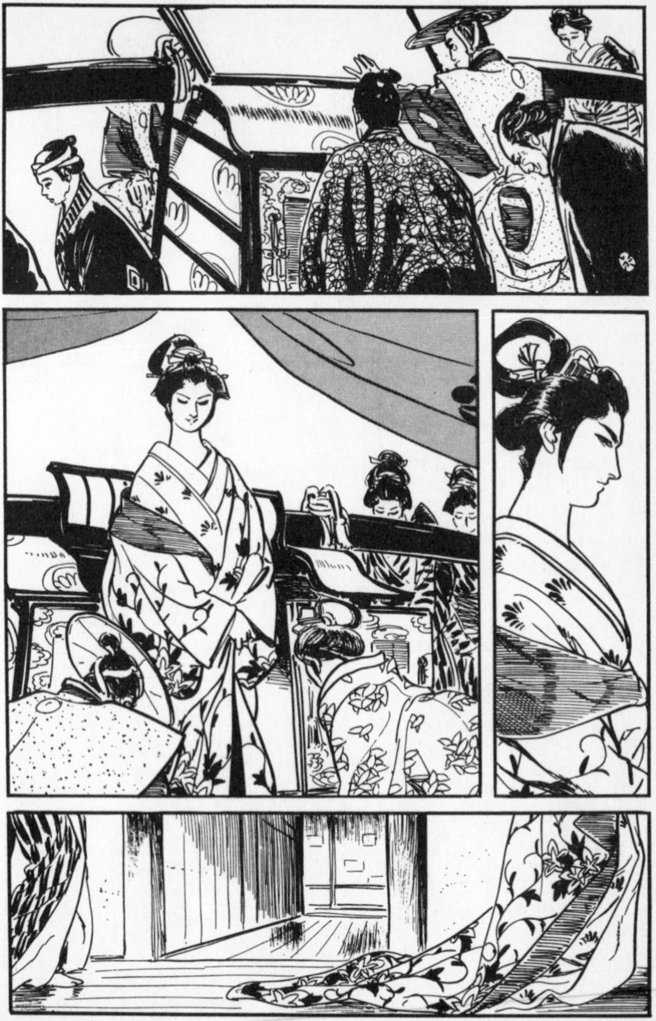

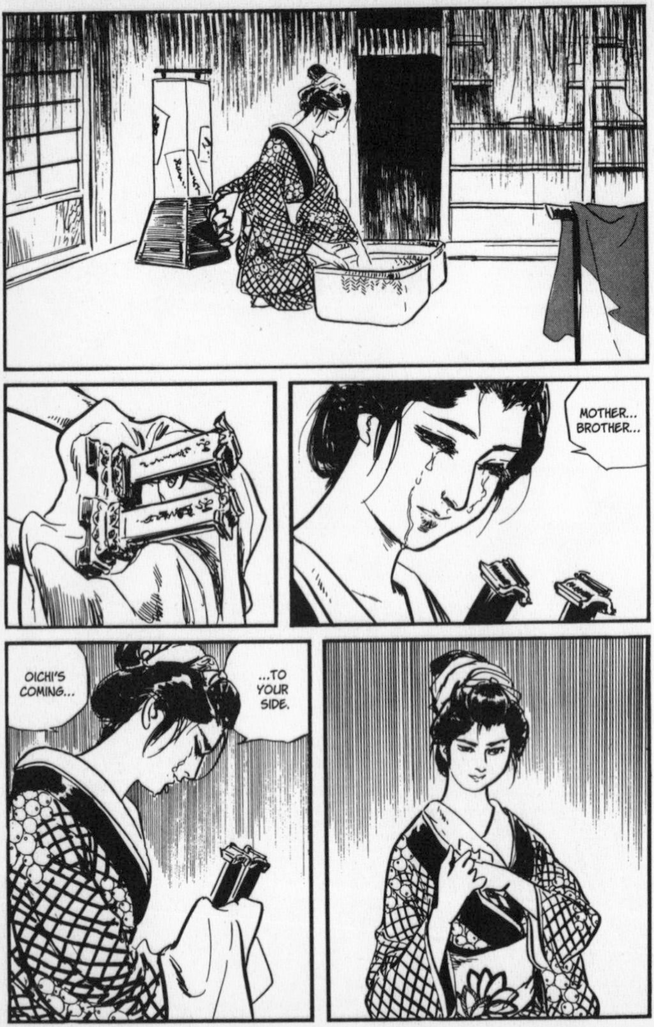
MOTHER... BROTHER...
OICHI'S COMING...
...TO YOUR SIDE.

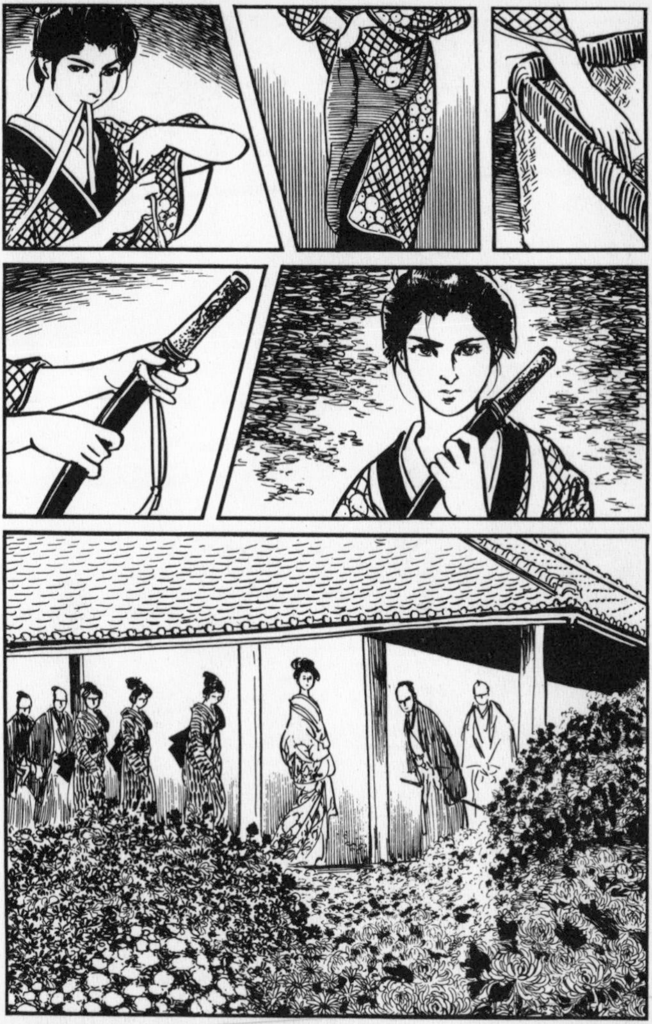

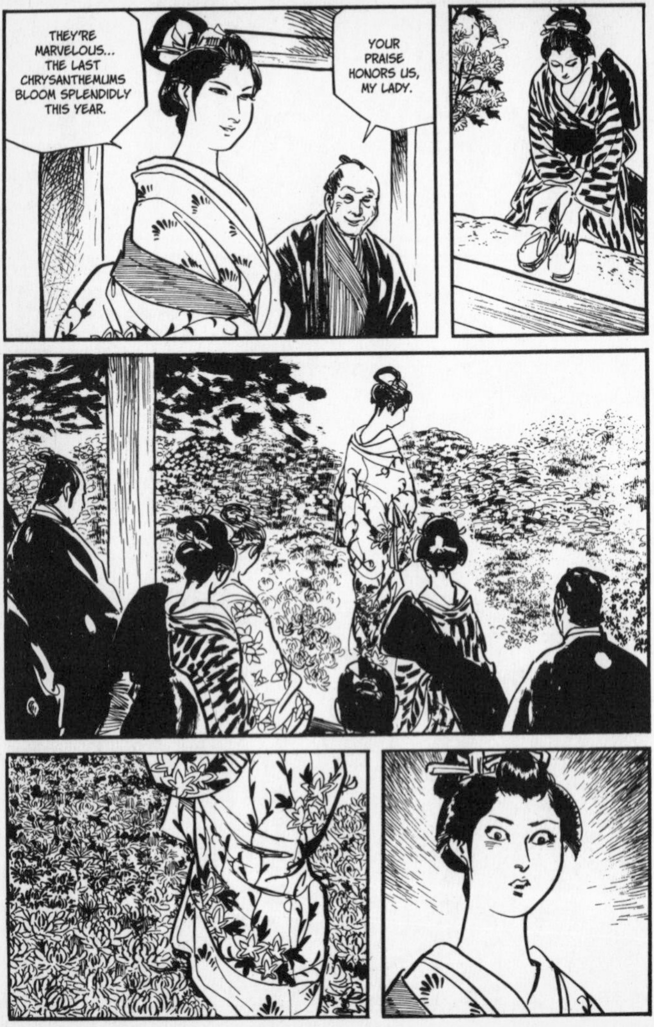
THEY'RE MARVELOUS... THE LAST CHRYSANTHEMUMS BLOOM SPLENDIDLY THIS YEAR.
YOUR PRAISE HONORS US, MY LADY.

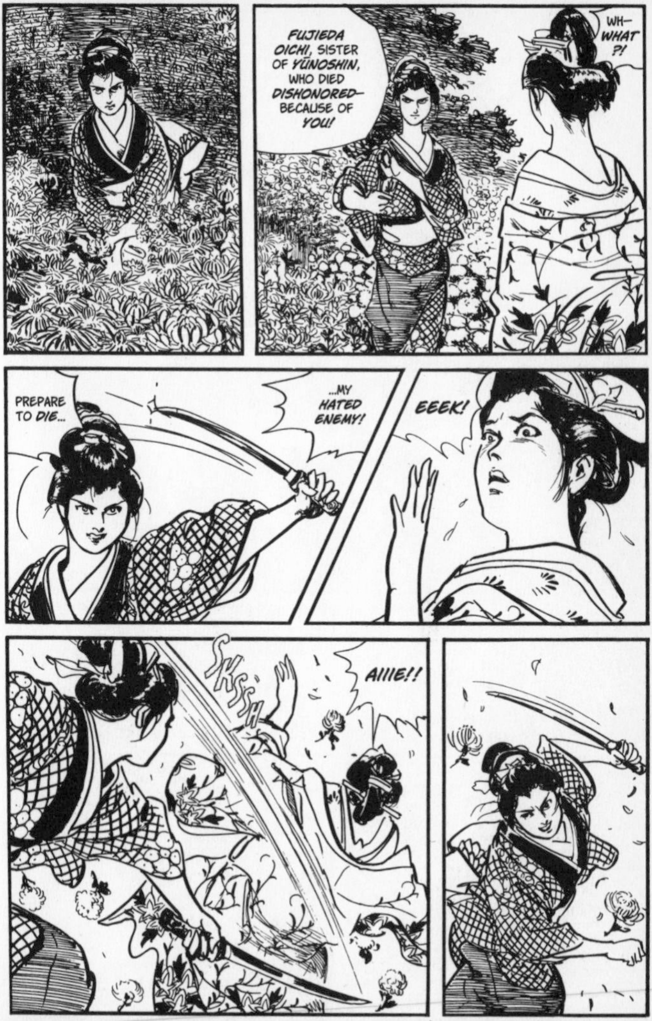
FUJIEDA OICHI, SISTER OF YŪNOSHIN, WHO DIED DISHONORED— BECAUSE OF YOU!
WH— WHAT ?!
PREPARE TO DIE...
...MY HATED ENEMY!
EEEK!
SKSSH
AIIIE!!

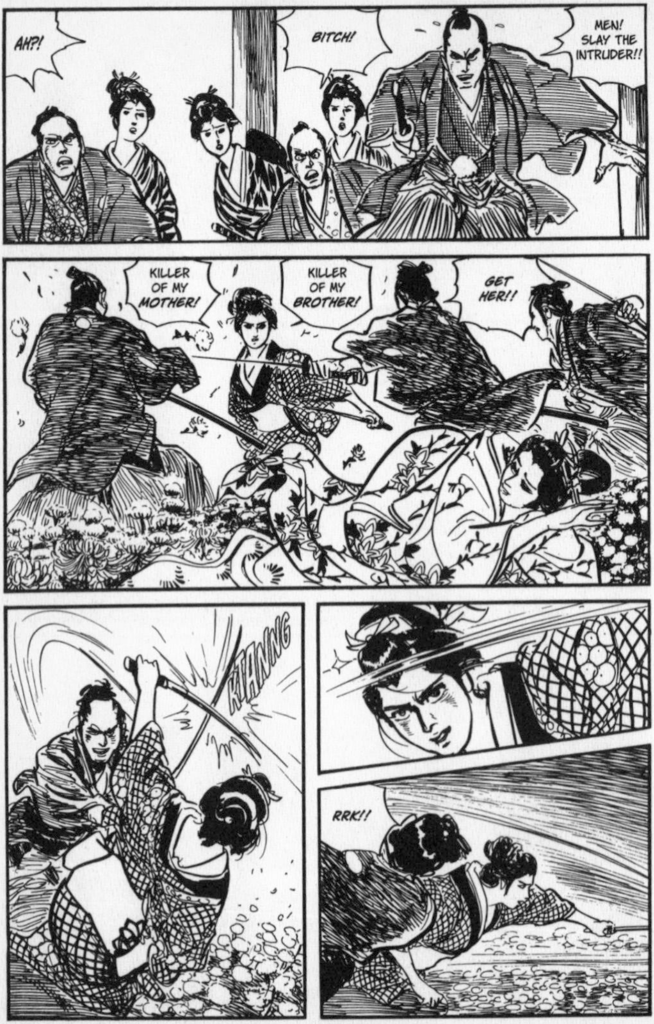
AH?!
BITCH!
MEN! SLAY THE INTRUDER!!
KILLER OF MY MOTHER!
KILLER OF MY BROTHER!
GET HER!!
KITANNG
RRK!!

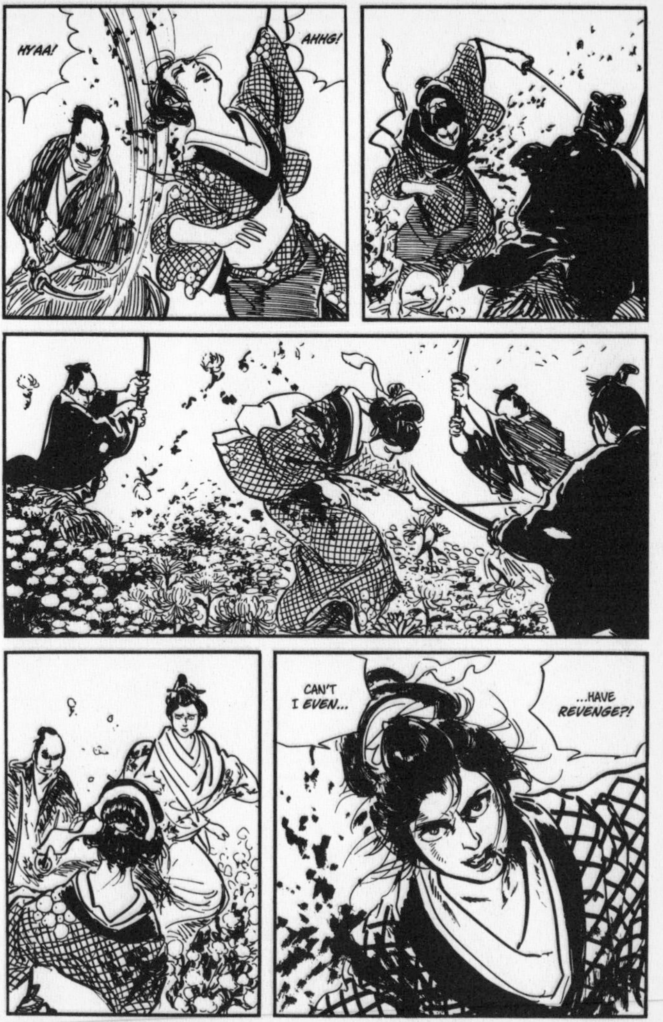
HYAA!
AHHG!
CAN'T I EVEN...
...HAVE REVENGE?!

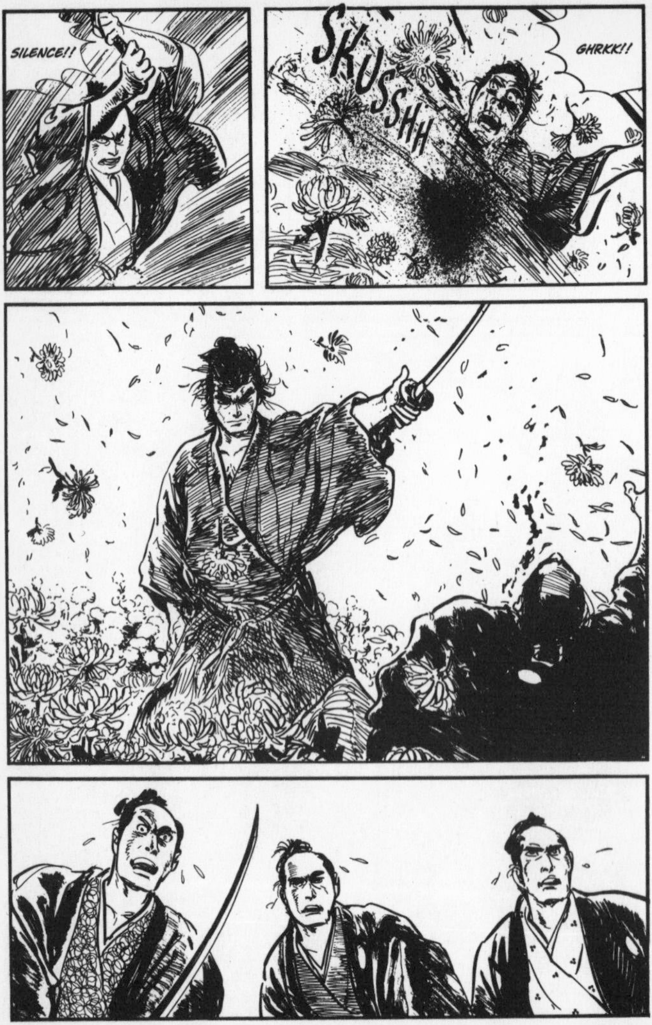
SILENCE!!
SKUSSHH
GHRKK!!

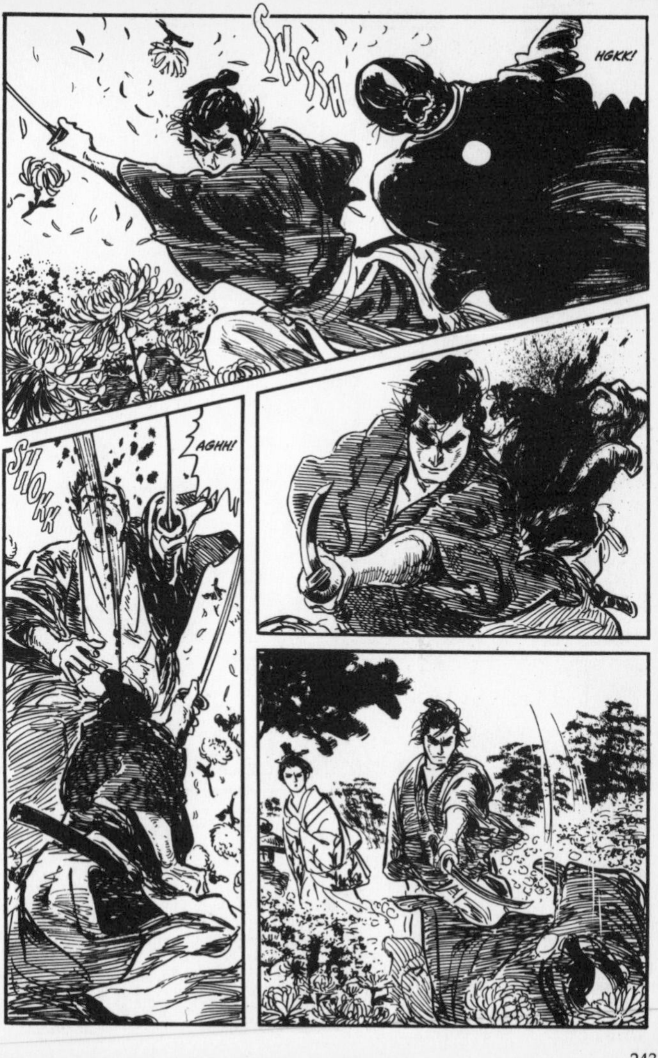
SHSSSH
HGKK!
SHOKK
AGHH!

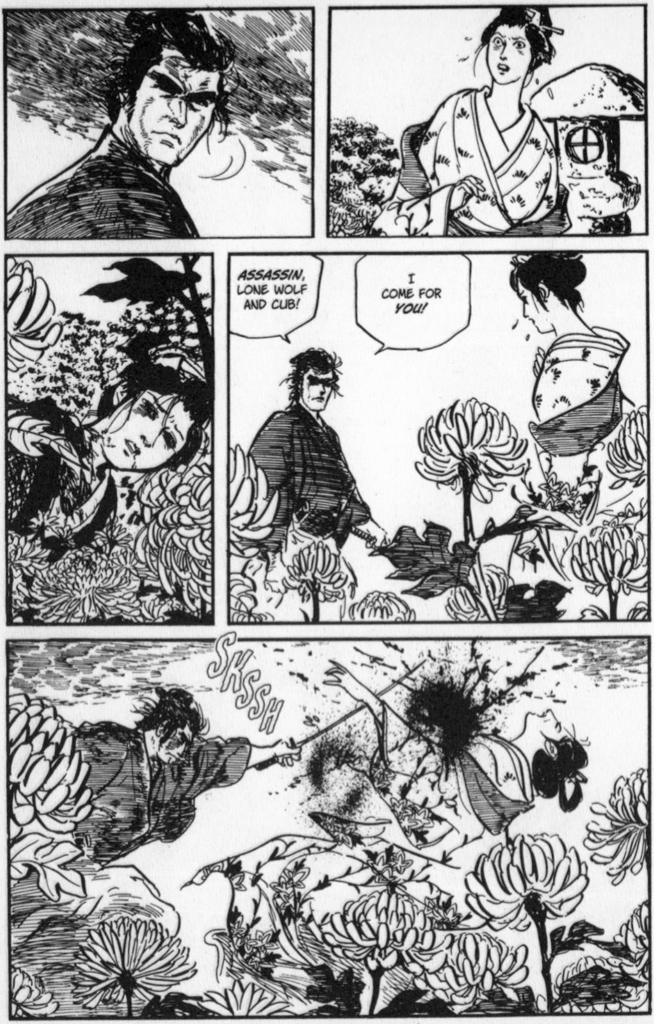

ASSASSIN, LONE WOLF AND CUB!
I COME FOR YOU!
SKSSH

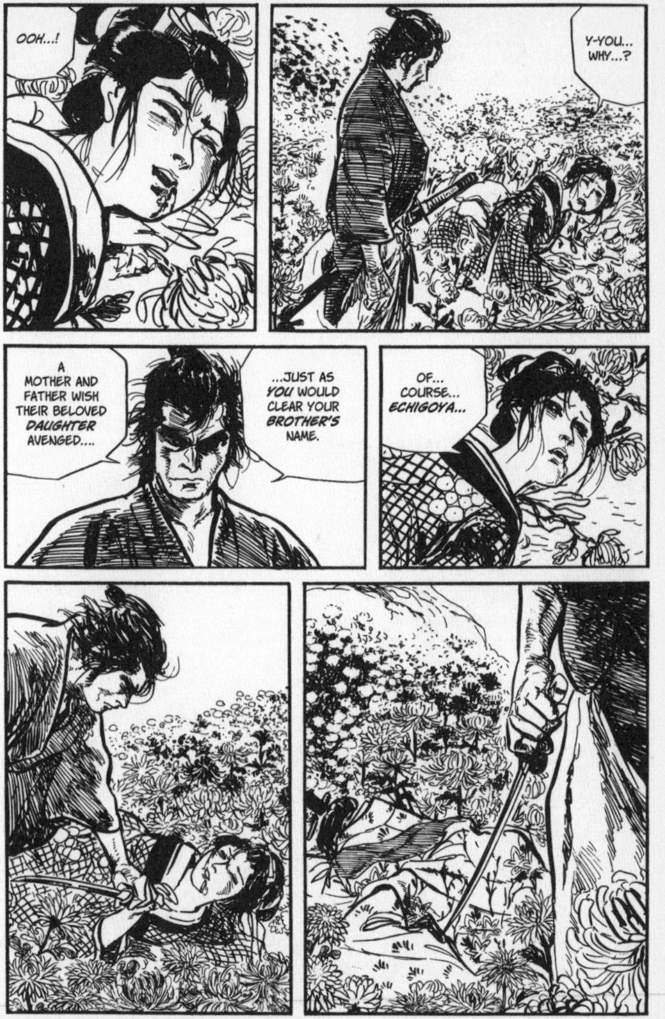
OOH...!
Y-YOU... WHY...?
A MOTHER AND FATHER WISH THEIR BELOVED *DAUGHTER* AVENGED....
...JUST AS *YOU* WOULD CLEAR YOUR *BROTHER'S* NAME.
OF... COURSE... *ECHIGOYA*...

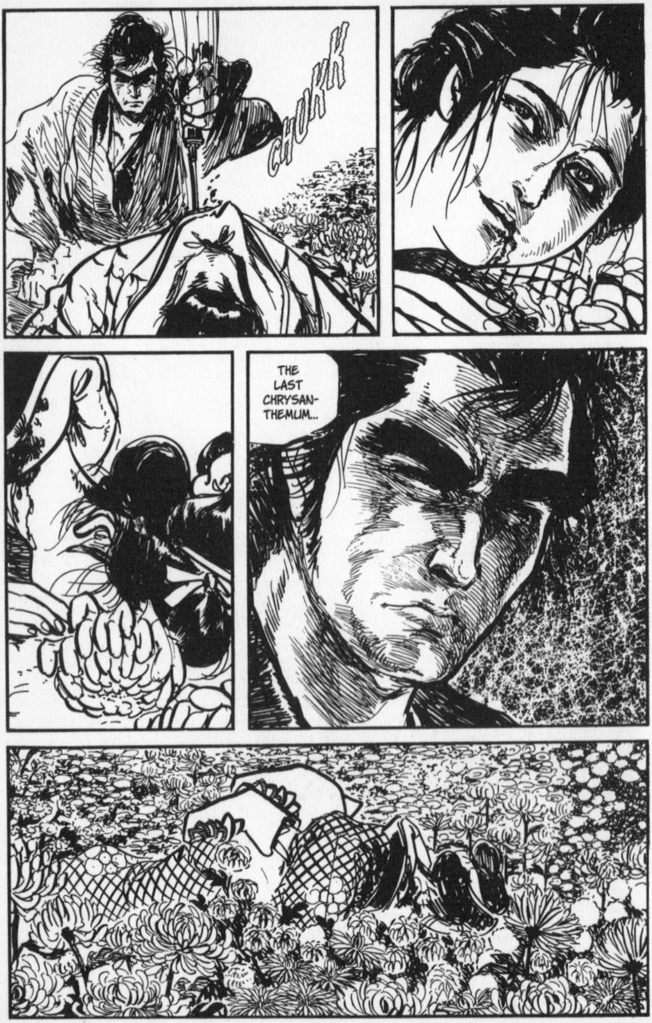
CHOKK
THE LAST CHRYSANTHEMUM...

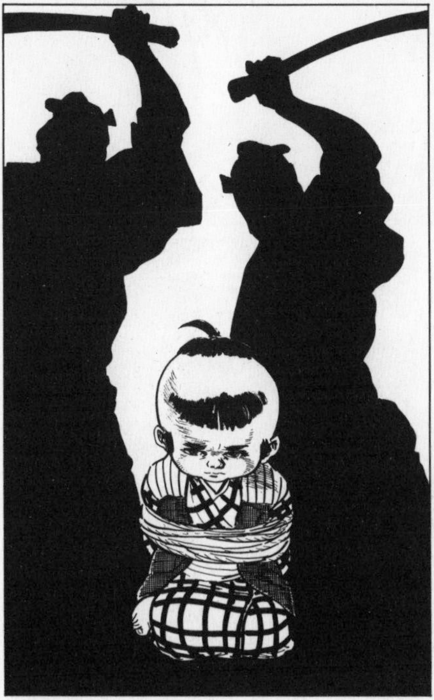

the thirty-eighth

Penal Code Article Seventy-nine

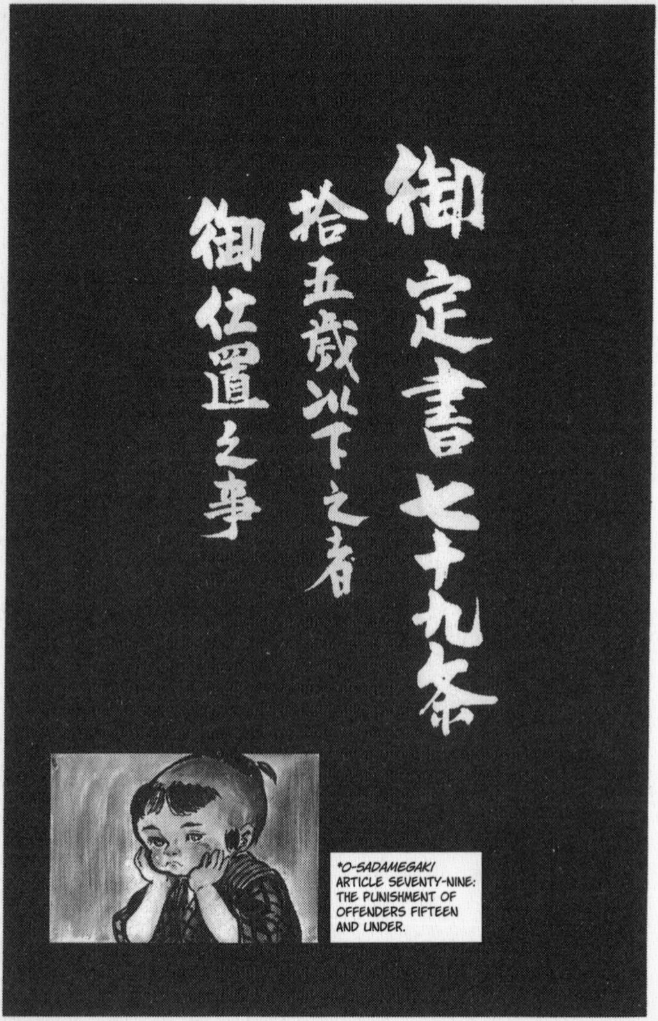
御定書七十九条
拾五歳以下之者
御仕置之事
*O-SADAMEGAKI ARTICLE SEVENTY-NINE: THE PUNISHMENT OF OFFENDERS FIFTEEN AND UNDER.

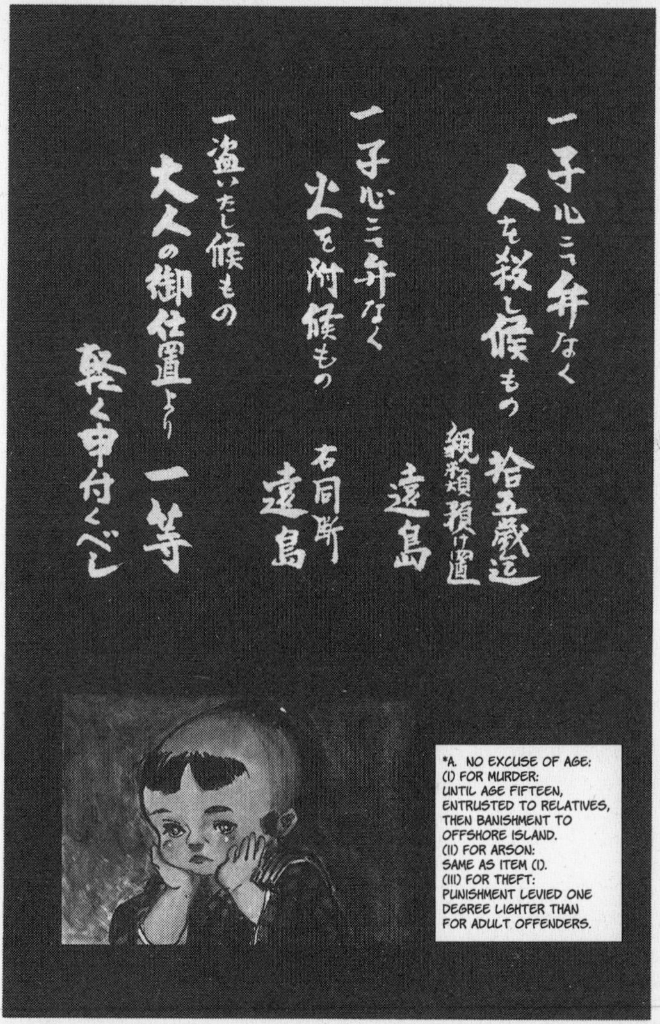
一子心ニて弁なく
人を殺し候もの
拾五歳迄
親類預け置
遠島
一子心ニて弁なく
火を附候もの
右同断
遠島
一盗いたし候もの
大人の御仕置より
一等
軽く申付くべし
*A. NO EXCUSE OF AGE:
(I) FOR MURDER:
UNTIL AGE FIFTEEN, ENTRUSTED TO RELATIVES, THEN BANISHMENT TO OFFSHORE ISLAND.
(II) FOR ARSON:
SAME AS ITEM (I).
(III) FOR THEFT:
PUNISHMENT LEVIED ONE DEGREE LIGHTER THAN FOR ADULT OFFENDERS.

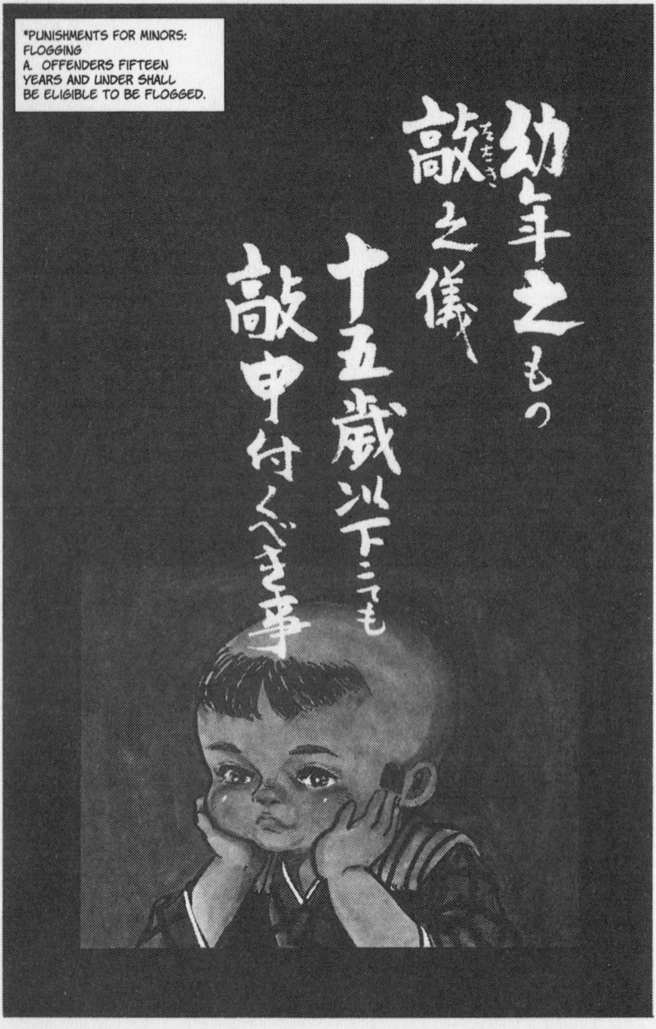
*PUNISHMENTS FOR MINORS:
FLOGGING
A. OFFENDERS FIFTEEN
YEARS AND UNDER SHALL
BE ELIGIBLE TO BE FLOGGED.
幼年之もの
敲之儀
十五歳以下ニても
敲申付くべき事

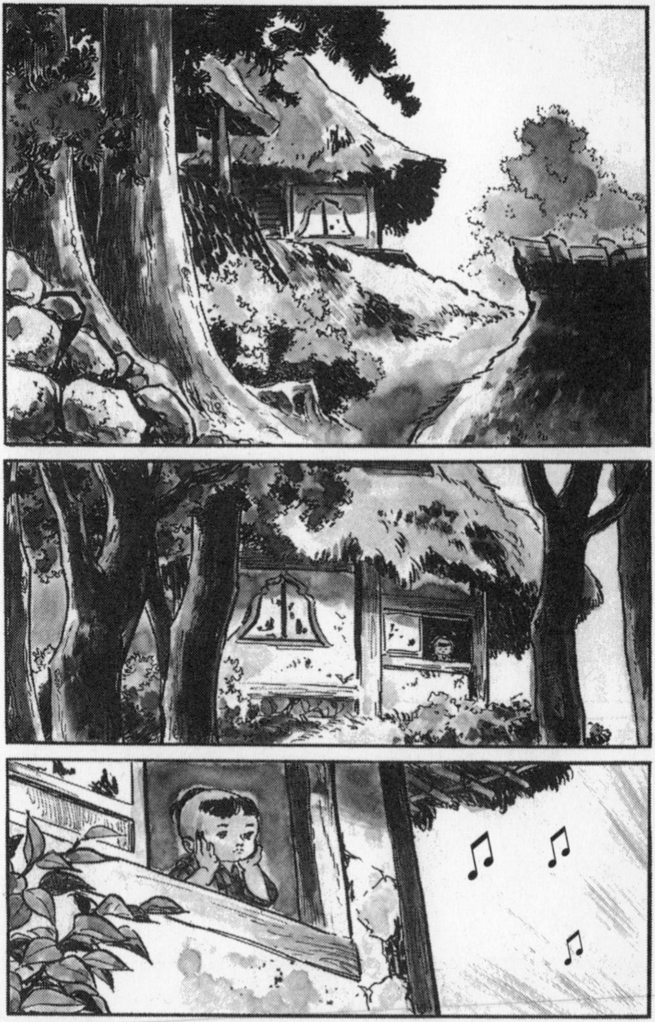

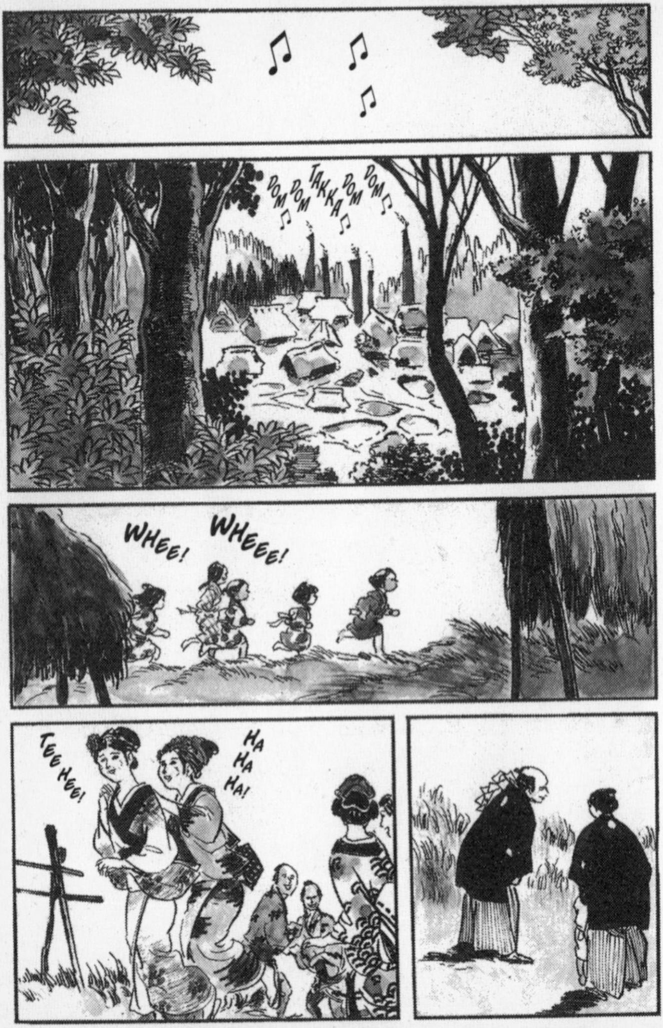
DOM DOM TAKKA DOM DOM
WHEE!
WHEEE!
TEE HEE!
HA HA HA!

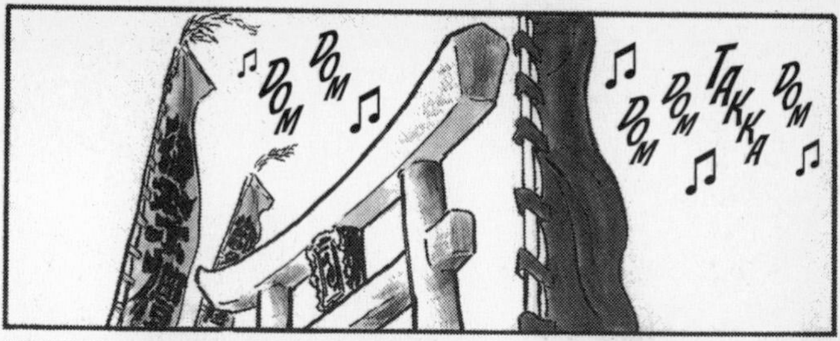
♫ DOM DOM ♫
♫ DOM DOM TAKKA DOM ♫ ♫
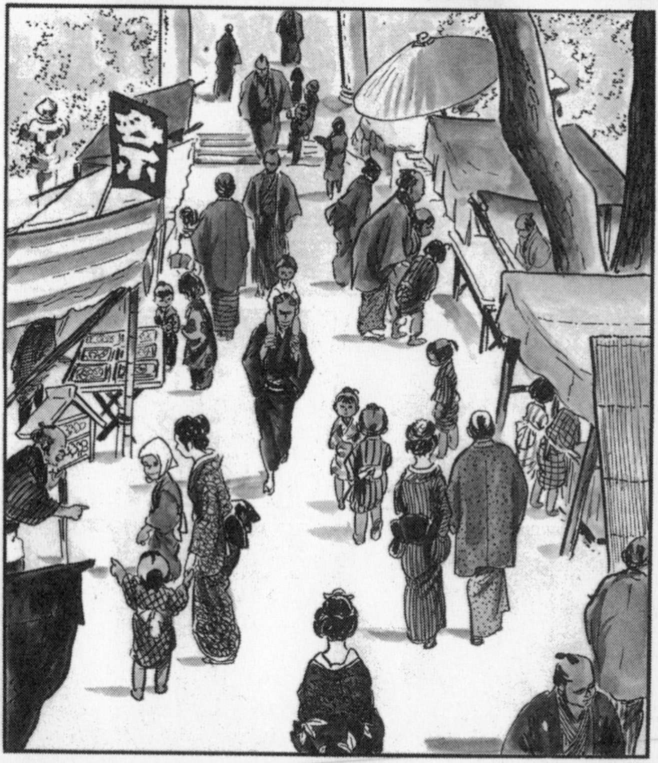

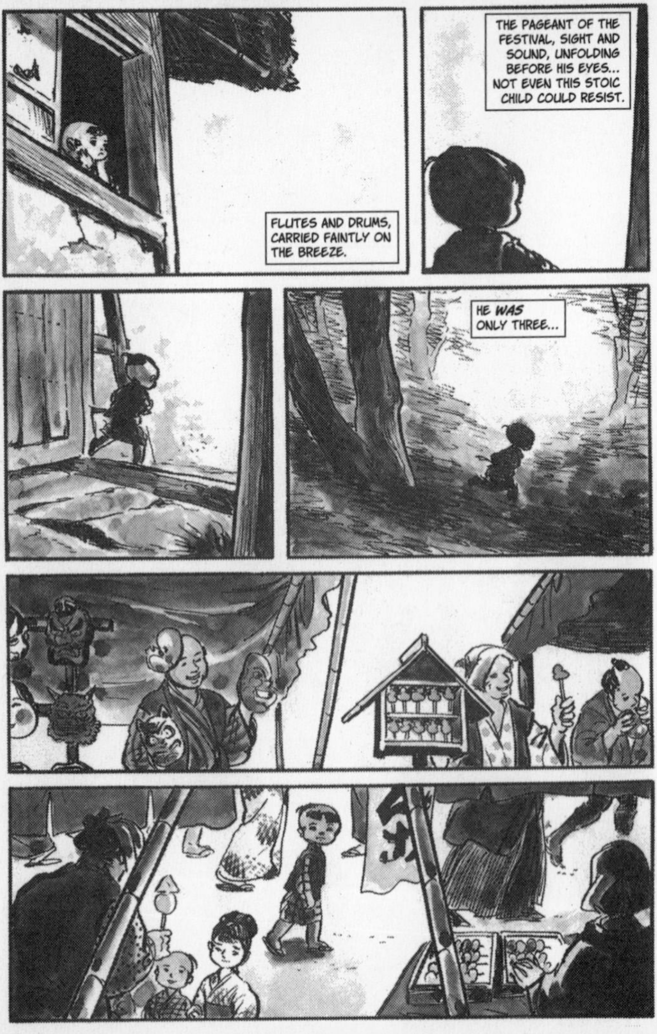
FLUTES AND DRUMS, CARRIED FAINTLY ON THE BREEZE.
THE PAGEANT OF THE FESTIVAL, SIGHT AND SOUND, UNFOLDING BEFORE HIS EYES... NOT EVEN THIS STOIC CHILD COULD RESIST.
HE WAS ONLY THREE...

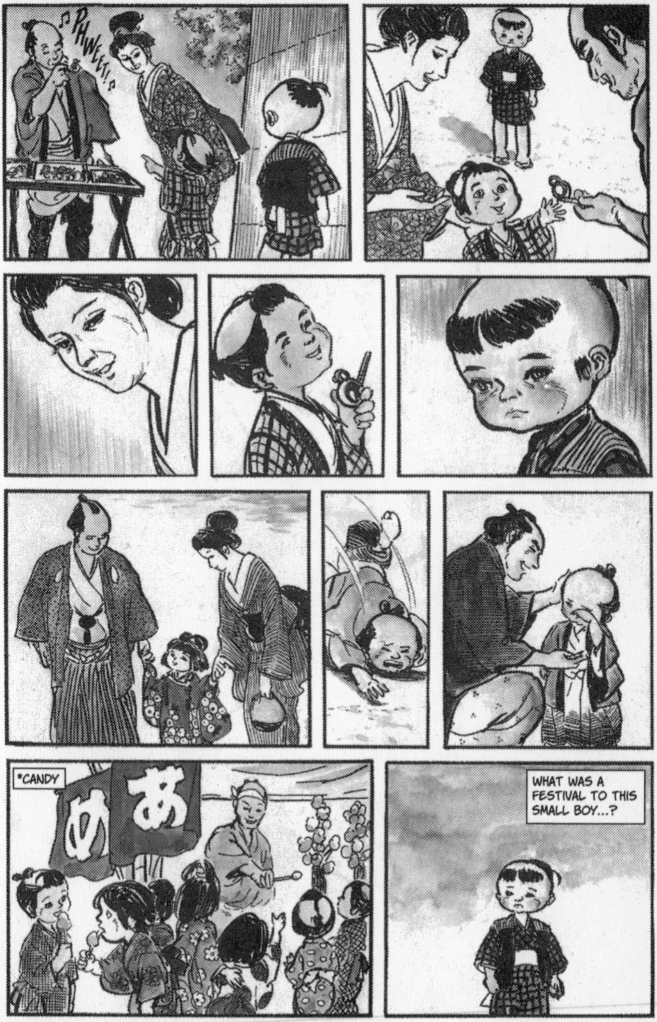
♪ PHWEET! ♪
*CANDY
め
あ
WHAT WAS A FESTIVAL TO THIS SMALL BOY...?

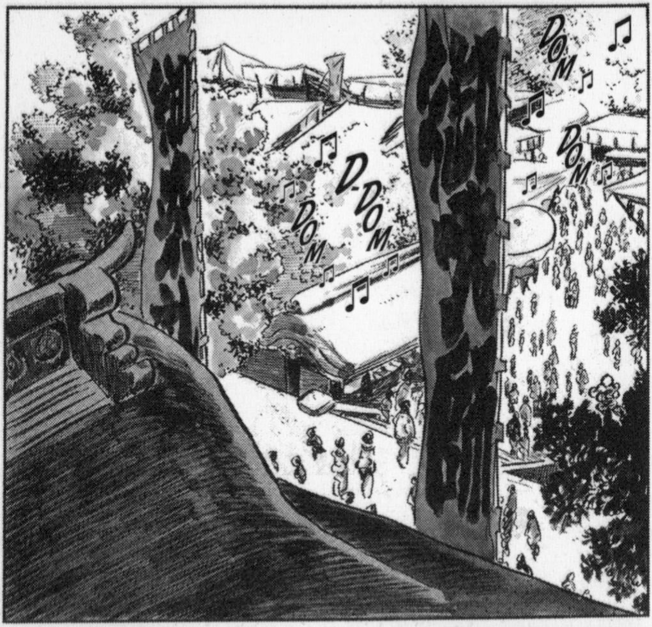
D-DOM
DOM
DOM
DOM

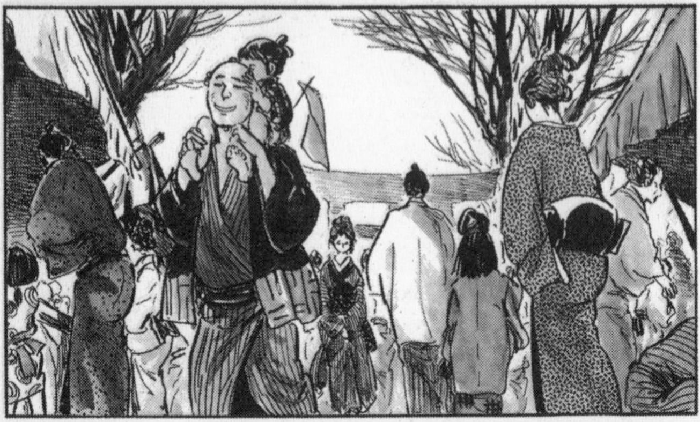

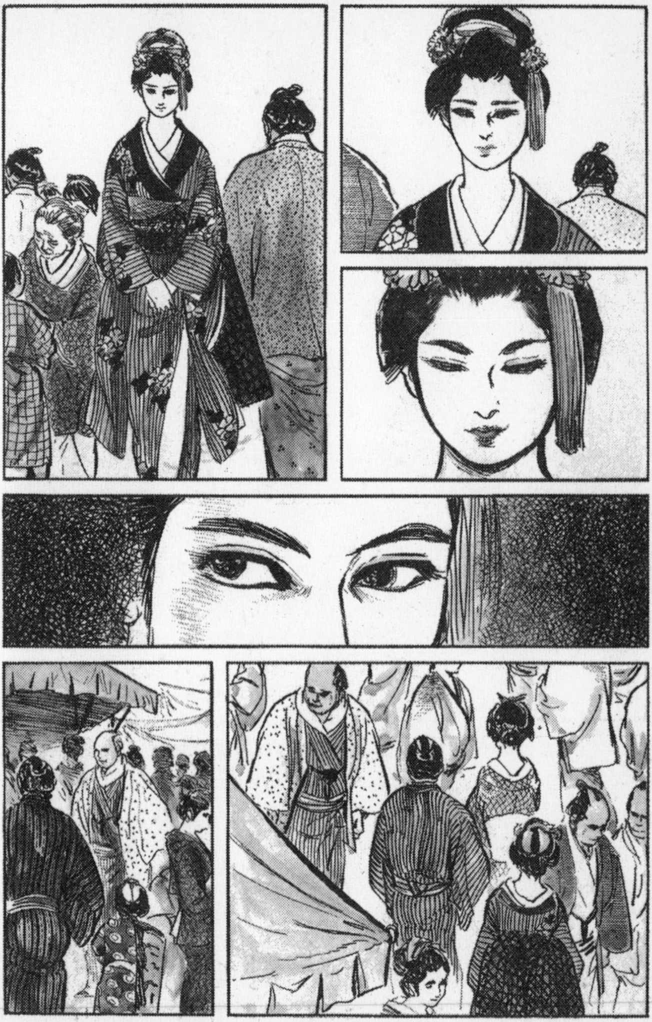

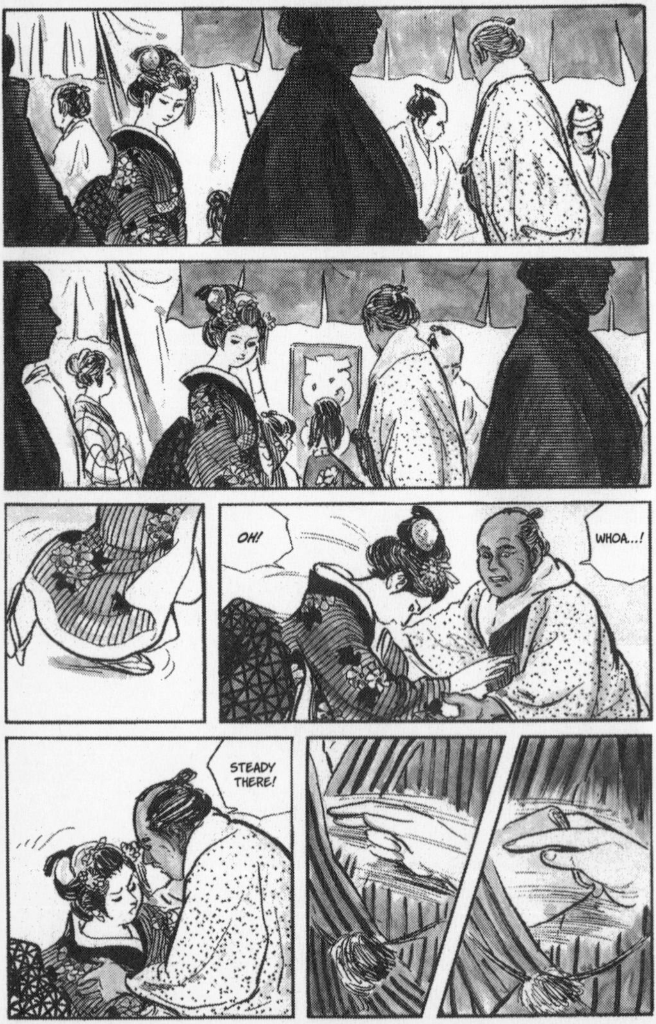

OH!
WHOA...!
STEADY THERE!

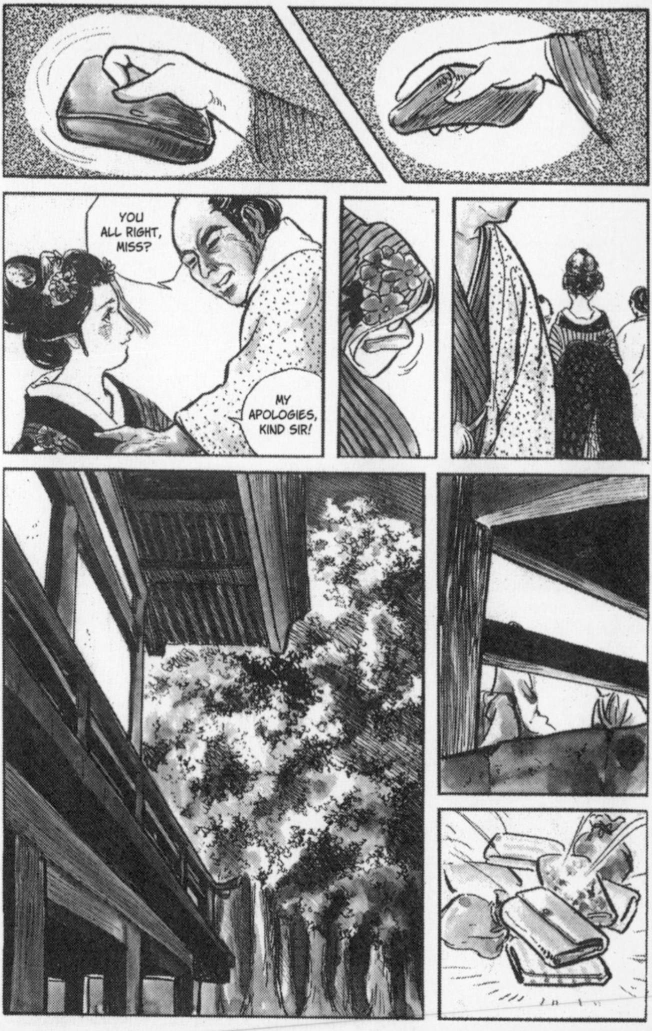
YOU ALL RIGHT, MISS?
MY APOLOGIES, KIND SIR!

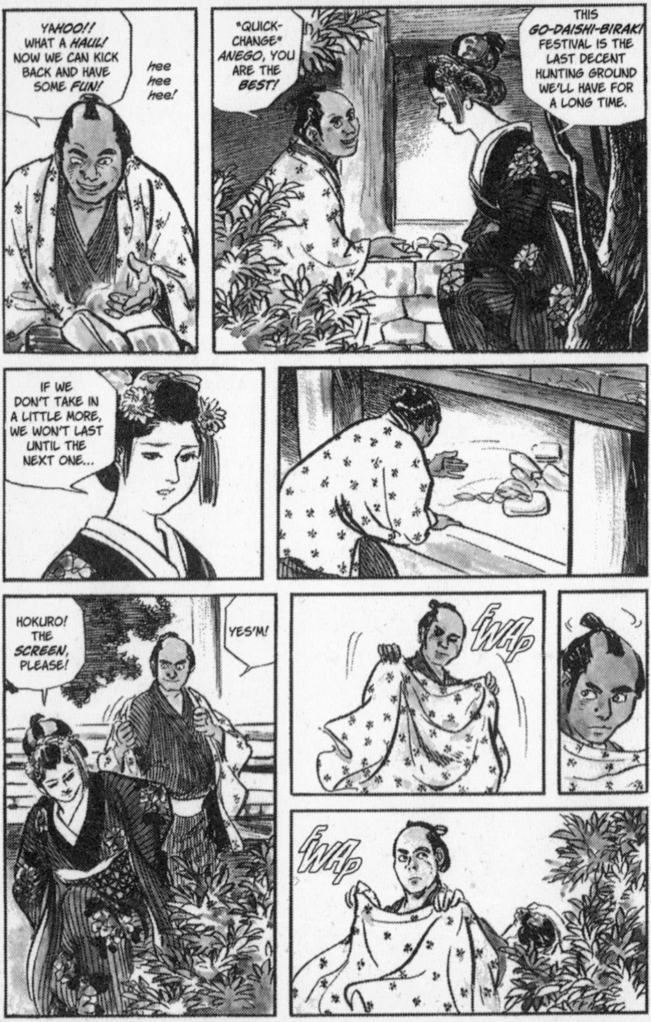
YAHOO!! WHAT A HAUL! NOW WE CAN KICK BACK AND HAVE SOME FUN!
hee hee hee!
"QUICK-CHANGE" ANEGO, YOU ARE THE BEST!
THIS GO-DAISHI-BIRAKI FESTIVAL IS THE LAST DECENT HUNTING GROUND WE'LL HAVE FOR A LONG TIME.
IF WE DON'T TAKE IN A LITTLE MORE, WE WON'T LAST UNTIL THE NEXT ONE...
HOKURO! THE SCREEN, PLEASE!
YES'M!
FWAP
FWAP

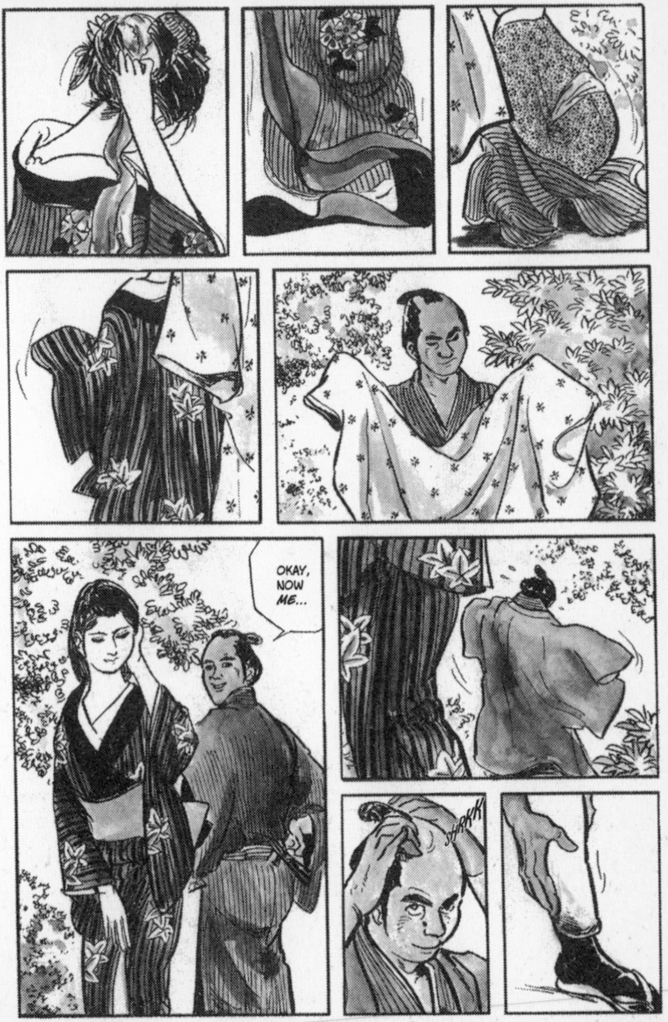
OKAY, NOW ME...
SHRKK

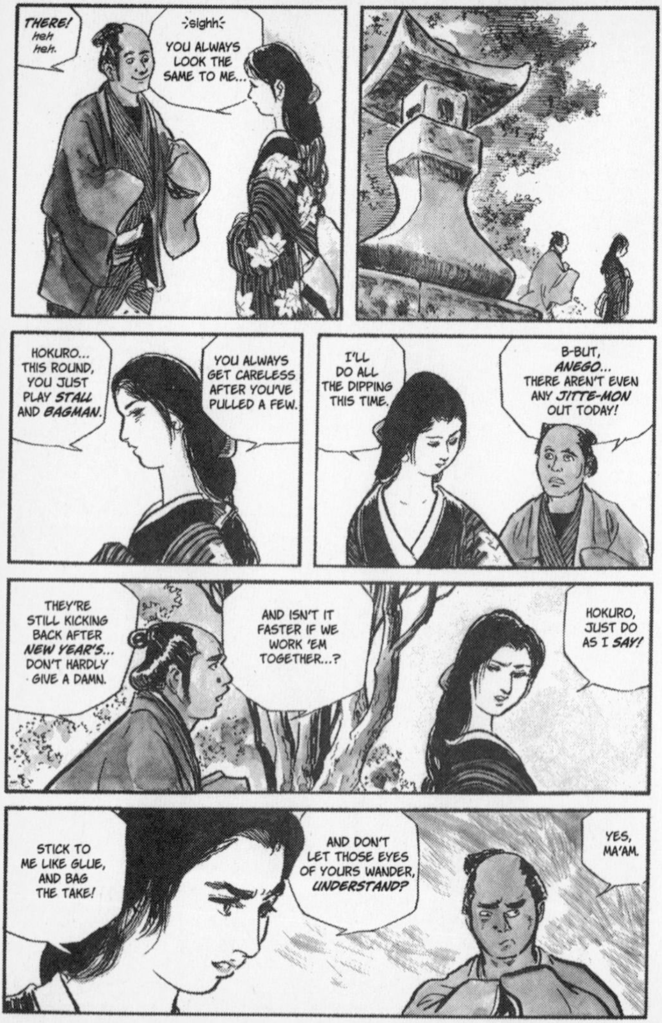
THERE! heh heh.
-sighh-
YOU ALWAYS LOOK THE SAME TO ME...
HOKURO... THIS ROUND, YOU JUST PLAY STALL AND BAGMAN.
YOU ALWAYS GET CARELESS AFTER YOU'VE PULLED A FEW.
I'LL DO ALL THE DIPPING THIS TIME.
B-BUT, ANEGO... THERE AREN'T EVEN ANY JITTE-MON OUT TODAY!
THEY'RE STILL KICKING BACK AFTER NEW YEAR'S... DON'T HARDLY GIVE A DAMN.
AND ISN'T IT FASTER IF WE WORK 'EM TOGETHER...?
HOKURO, JUST DO AS I SAY!
STICK TO ME LIKE GLUE, AND BAG THE TAKE!
AND DON'T LET THOSE EYES OF YOURS WANDER, UNDERSTAND?
YES, MA'AM.

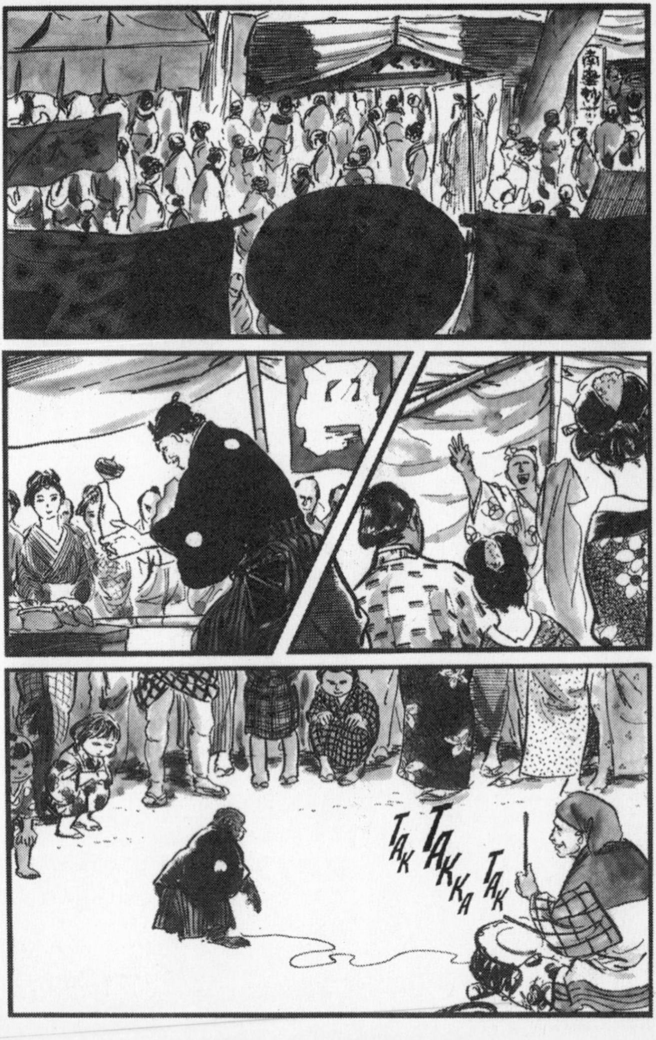
TAK
TAKKA
TAK

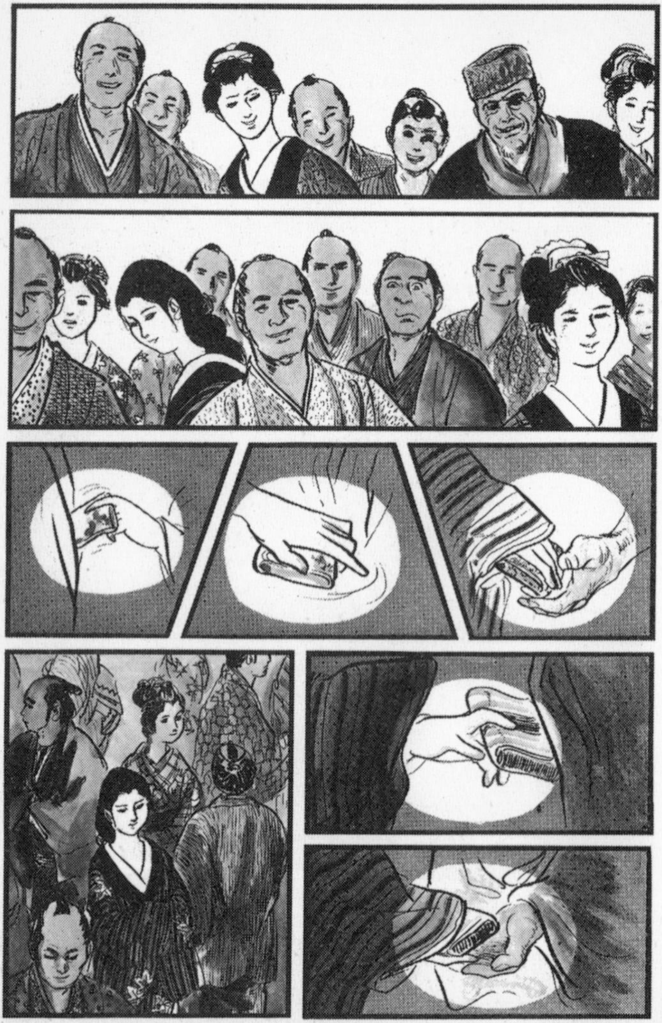

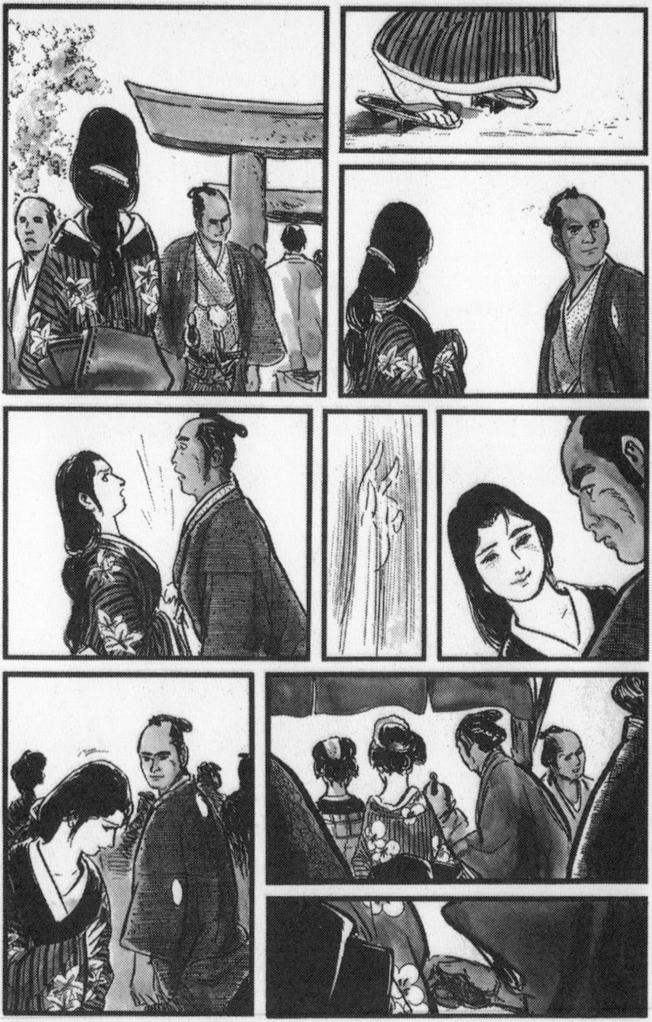

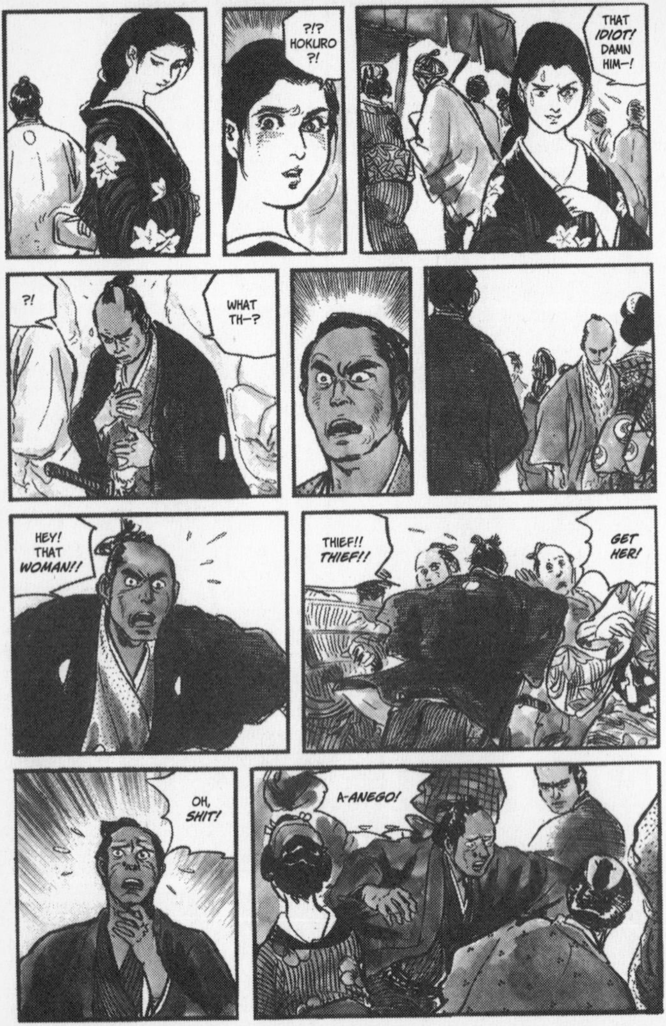
?!?
HOKURO
?!
THAT
IDIOT!
DAMN
HIM—!
?!
WHAT
TH—?
HEY!
THAT
WOMAN!!
THIEF!!
THIEF!!
GET
HER!
OH,
SHIT!
A-ANEGO!

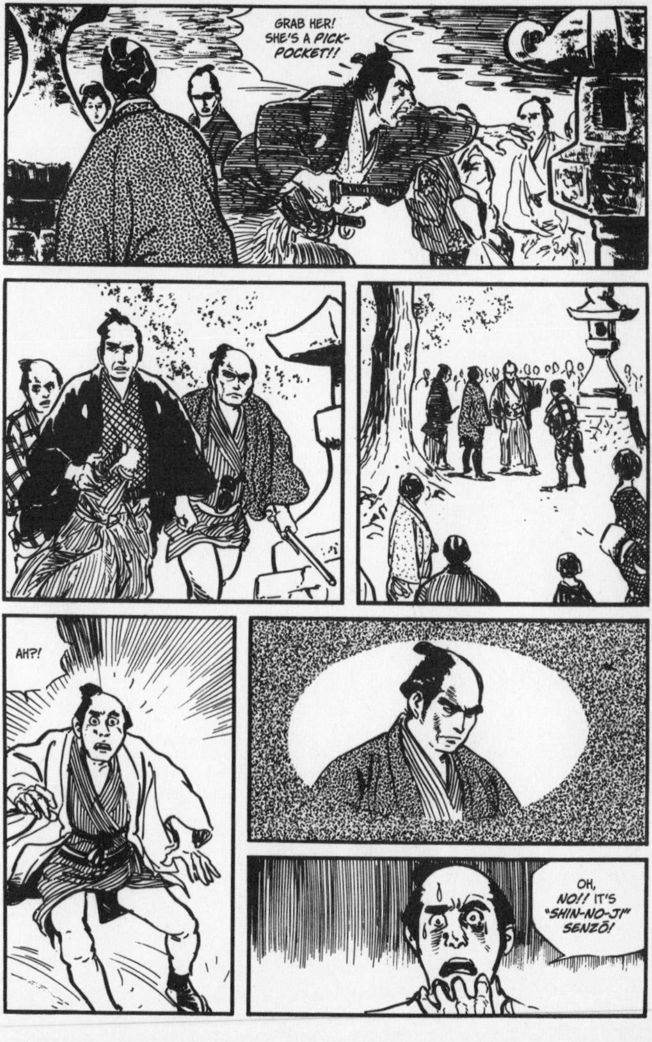
GRAB HER! SHE'S A PICK-POCKET!!
AH?!
OH, NO!! IT'S "SHIN-NO-JI" SENZŌ!

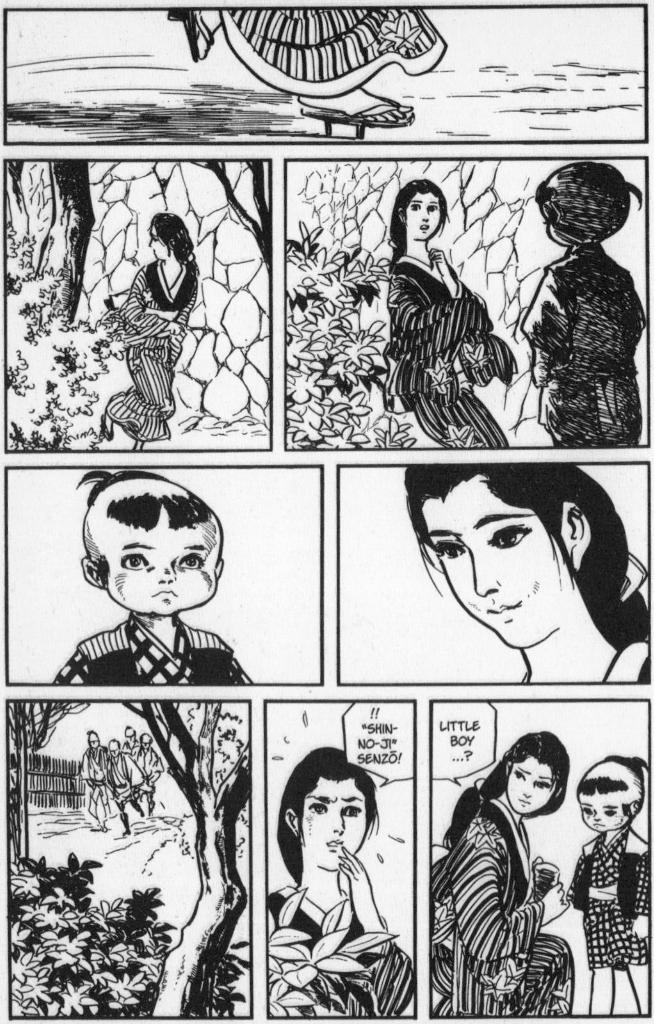
!!
"SHIN-NO-JI" SENZŌ!
LITTLE BOY ...?

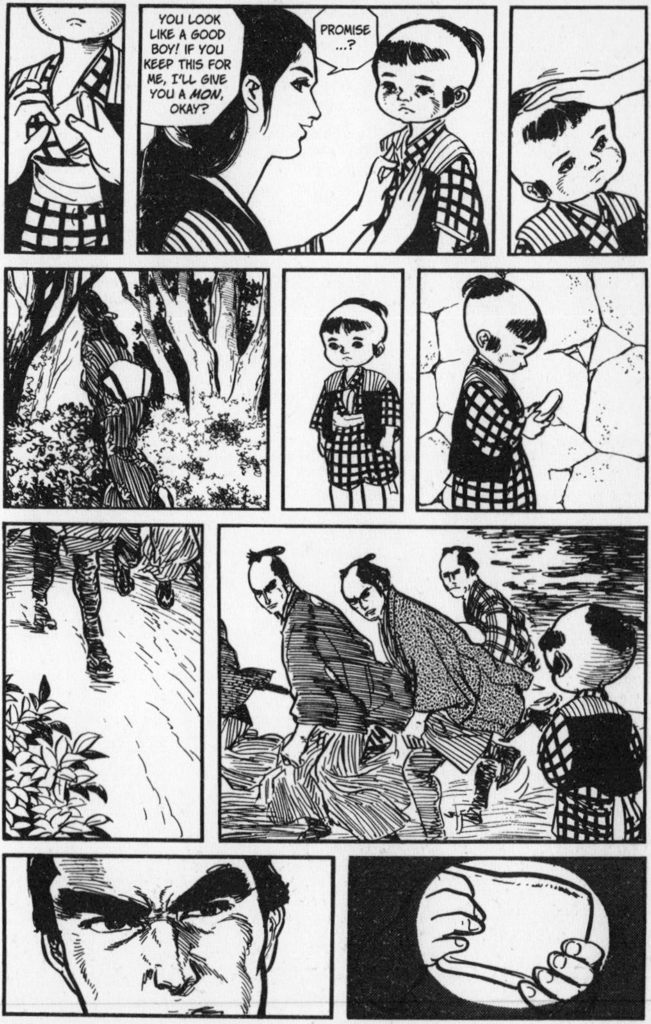
YOU LOOK LIKE A GOOD BOY! IF YOU KEEP THIS FOR ME, I'LL GIVE YOU A *MON*, OKAY?
PROMISE ...?

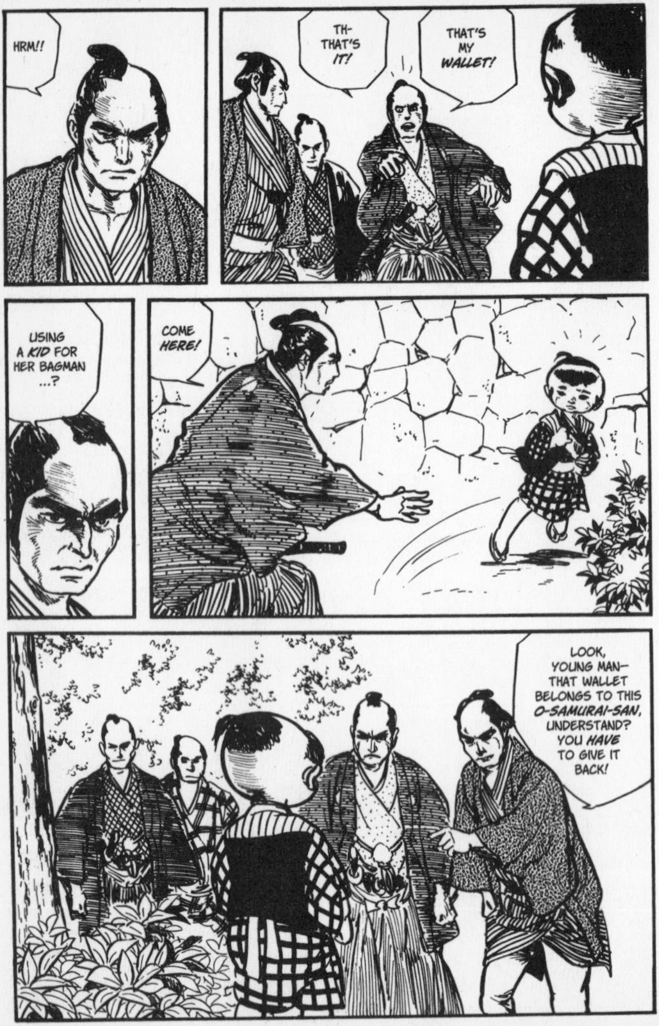
HRM!!
TH-THAT'S IT!
THAT'S MY WALLET!
USING A KID FOR HER BAGMAN ...?
COME HERE!
LOOK, YOUNG MAN— THAT WALLET BELONGS TO THIS O-SAMURAI-SAN, UNDERSTAND? YOU HAVE TO GIVE IT BACK!

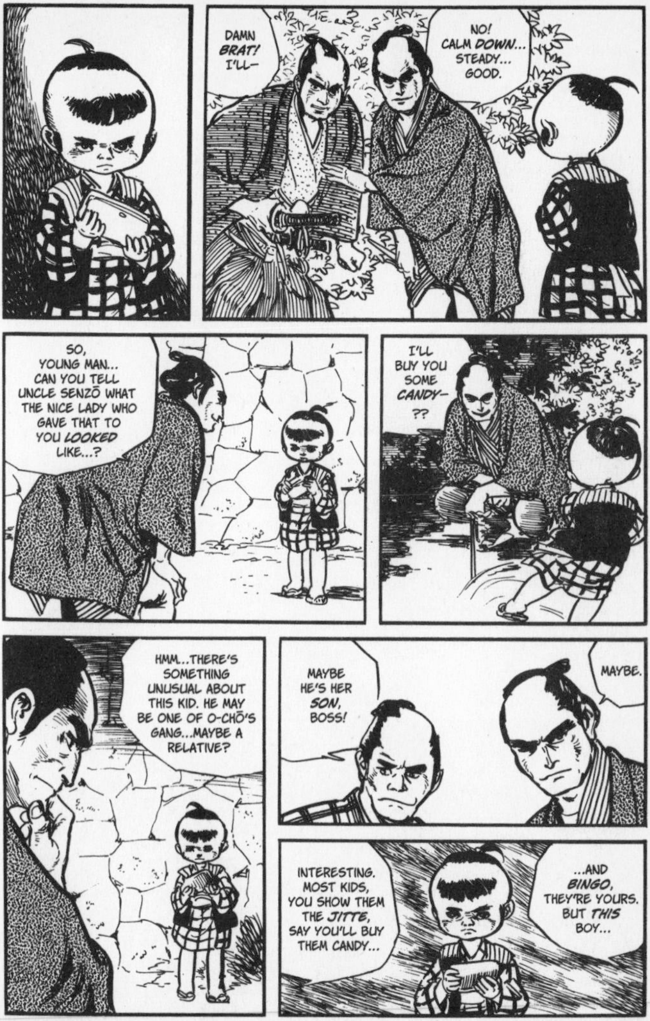
DAMN BRAT! I'LL—
NO! CALM DOWN... STEADY... GOOD.
SO, YOUNG MAN... CAN YOU TELL UNCLE SENZŌ WHAT THE NICE LADY WHO GAVE THAT TO YOU LOOKED LIKE...?
I'LL BUY YOU SOME CANDY—
??
HMM...THERE'S SOMETHING UNUSUAL ABOUT THIS KID. HE MAY BE ONE OF O-CHŌ'S GANG...MAYBE A RELATIVE?
MAYBE HE'S HER SON, BOSS!
MAYBE.
INTERESTING. MOST KIDS, YOU SHOW THEM THE JITTE, SAY YOU'LL BUY THEM CANDY...
...AND BINGO, THEY'RE YOURS. BUT THIS BOY...

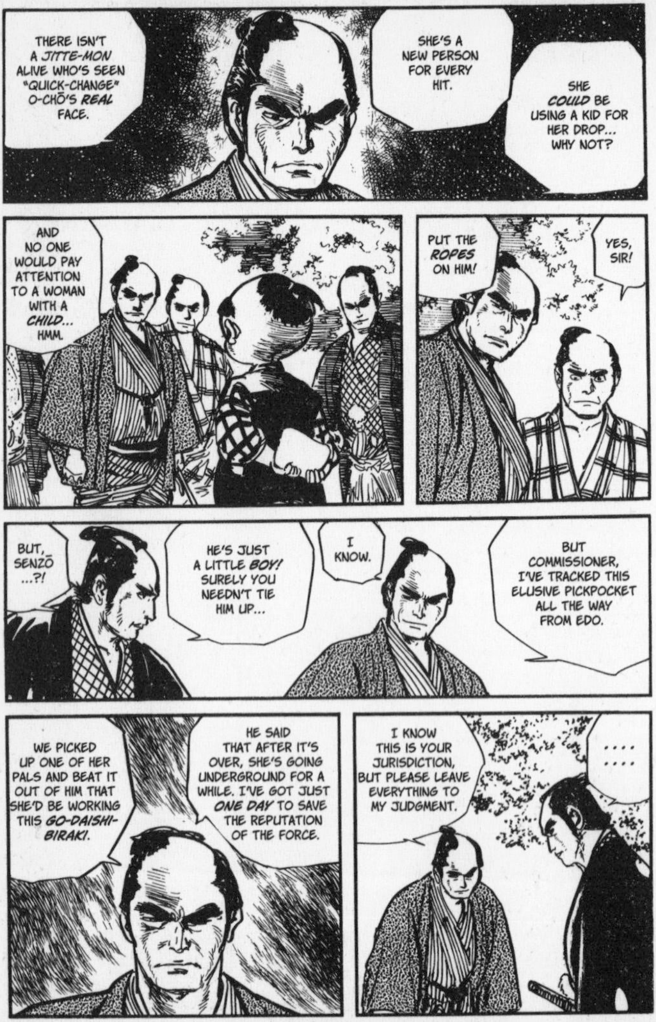
THERE ISN'T A *JITTE-MON* ALIVE WHO'S SEEN "QUICK-CHANGE" O-CHŌ'S *REAL* FACE.
SHE'S A NEW PERSON FOR EVERY HIT.
SHE *COULD* BE USING A KID FOR HER DROP... WHY NOT?
AND NO ONE WOULD PAY ATTENTION TO A WOMAN WITH A *CHILD*... HMM.
PUT THE *ROPES* ON HIM!
YES, SIR!
BUT, SENZŌ ...?!
HE'S JUST A LITTLE *BOY!* SURELY YOU NEEDN'T TIE HIM UP...
I KNOW.
BUT COMMISSIONER, I'VE TRACKED THIS ELUSIVE PICKPOCKET ALL THE WAY FROM EDO.
WE PICKED UP ONE OF HER PALS AND BEAT IT OUT OF HIM THAT SHE'D BE WORKING THIS *GO-DAISHI-BIRAKI*.
HE SAID THAT AFTER IT'S OVER, SHE'S GOING UNDERGROUND FOR A WHILE. I'VE GOT JUST *ONE DAY* TO SAVE THE REPUTATION OF THE FORCE.
I KNOW THIS IS YOUR JURISDICTION, BUT PLEASE LEAVE EVERYTHING TO MY JUDGMENT.
....
....

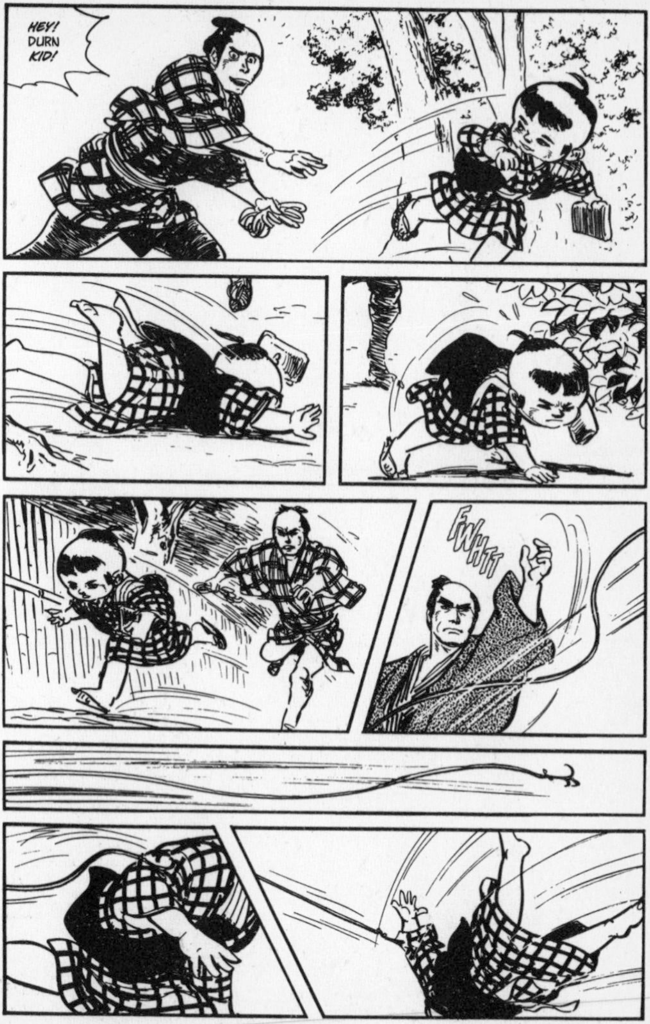
HEY!
DURN
KID!
FWHTT

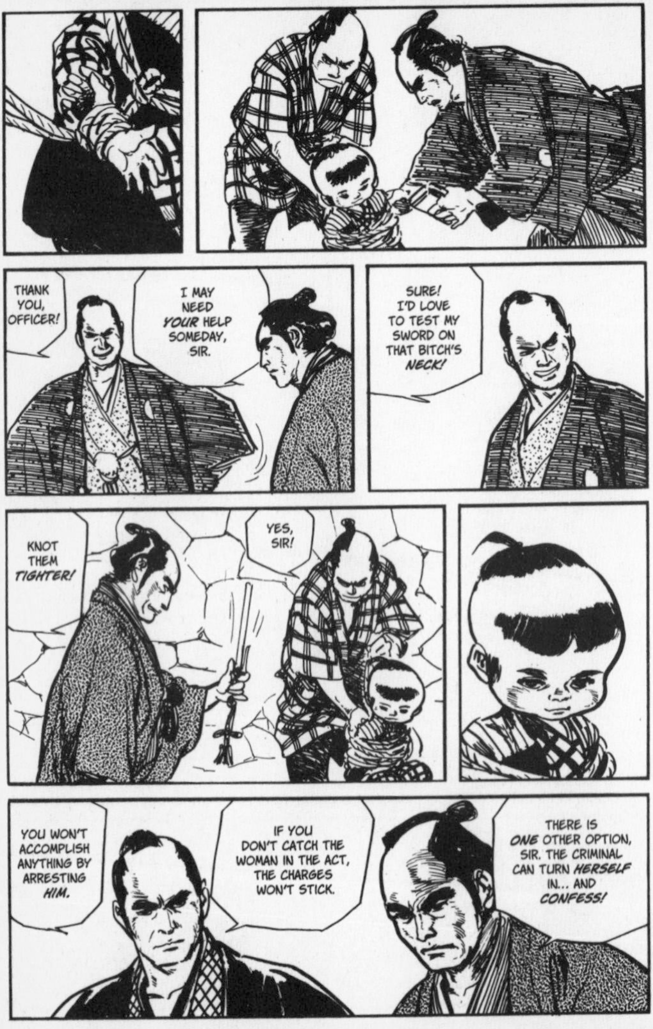
THANK YOU, OFFICER!
I MAY NEED YOUR HELP SOMEDAY, SIR.
SURE! I'D LOVE TO TEST MY SWORD ON THAT BITCH'S NECK!
KNOT THEM TIGHTER!
YES, SIR!
YOU WON'T ACCOMPLISH ANYTHING BY ARRESTING HIM.
IF YOU DON'T CATCH THE WOMAN IN THE ACT, THE CHARGES WON'T STICK.
THERE IS ONE OTHER OPTION, SIR. THE CRIMINAL CAN TURN HERSELF IN... AND CONFESS!

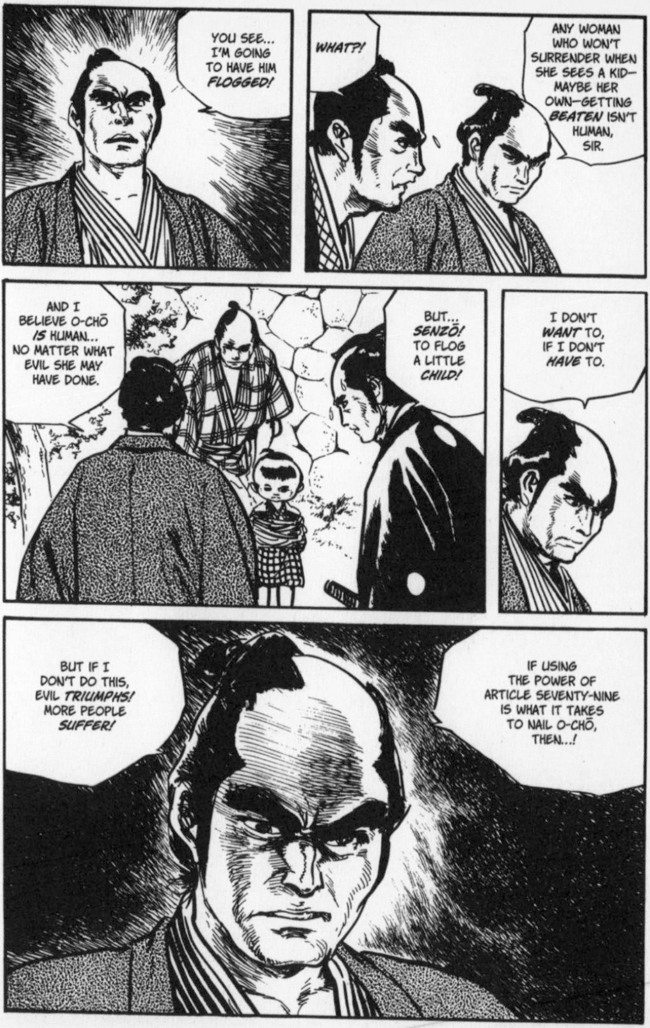
YOU SEE... I'M GOING TO HAVE HIM *FLOGGED!*
WHAT?!
ANY WOMAN WHO WON'T SURRENDER WHEN SHE SEES A KID—MAYBE HER OWN—GETTING *BEATEN* ISN'T HUMAN, SIR.
AND I BELIEVE O-CHŌ *IS* HUMAN... NO MATTER WHAT EVIL SHE MAY HAVE DONE.
BUT... *SENZŌ!* TO FLOG A LITTLE *CHILD!*
I DON'T *WANT* TO, IF I DON'T *HAVE* TO.
BUT IF I DON'T DO THIS, EVIL *TRIUMPHS!* MORE PEOPLE *SUFFER!*
IF USING THE POWER OF ARTICLE SEVENTY-NINE IS WHAT IT TAKES TO NAIL O-CHŌ, THEN...!

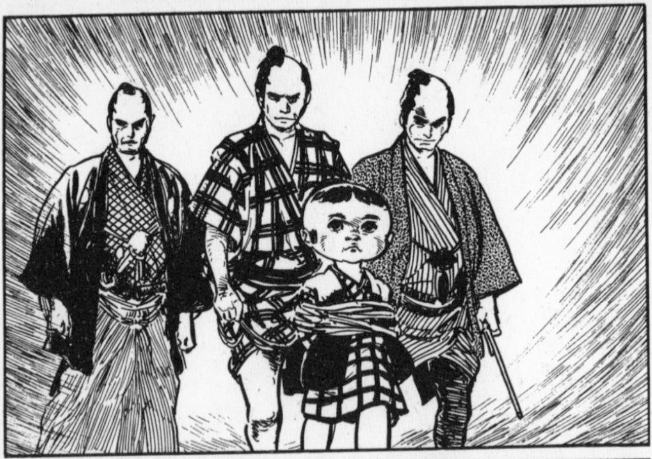
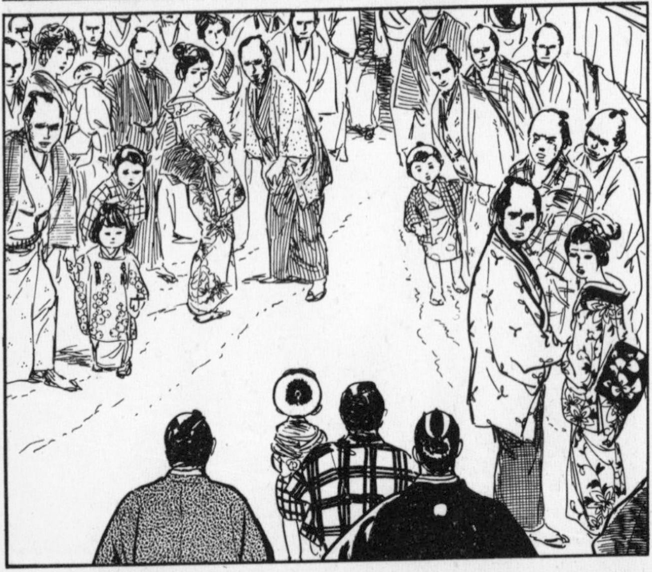

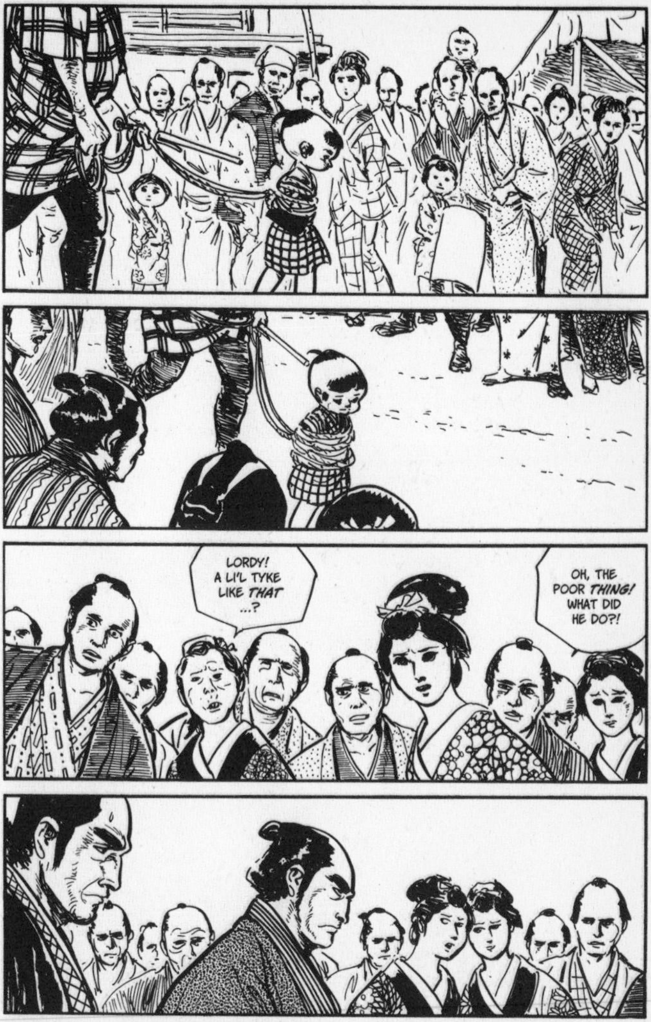
LORDY! A LI'L TYKE LIKE *THAT* ...?
OH, THE POOR *THING!* WHAT DID HE DO?!

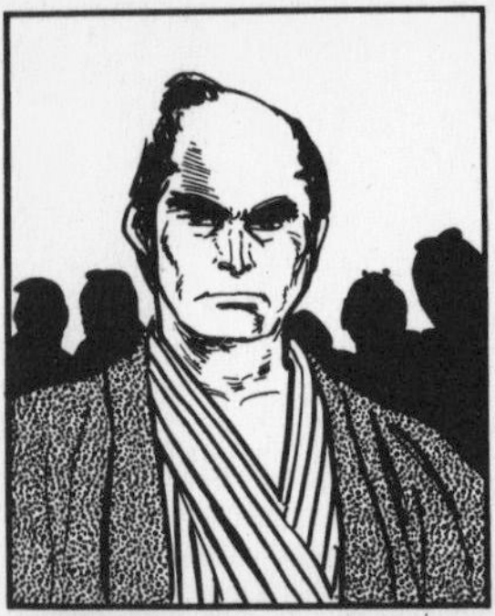

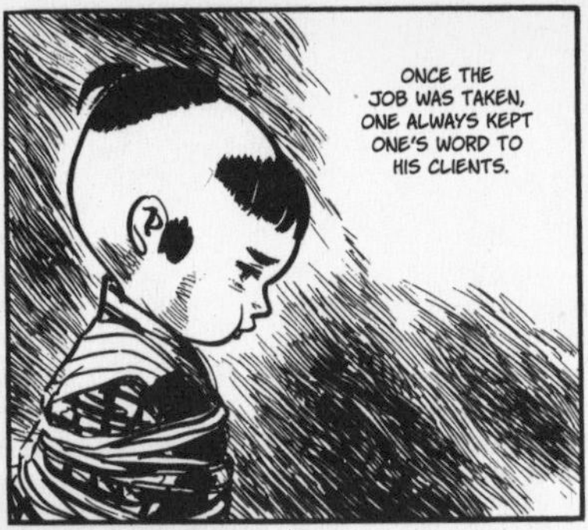
ONCE THE JOB WAS TAKEN, ONE ALWAYS KEPT ONE'S WORD TO HIS CLIENTS.

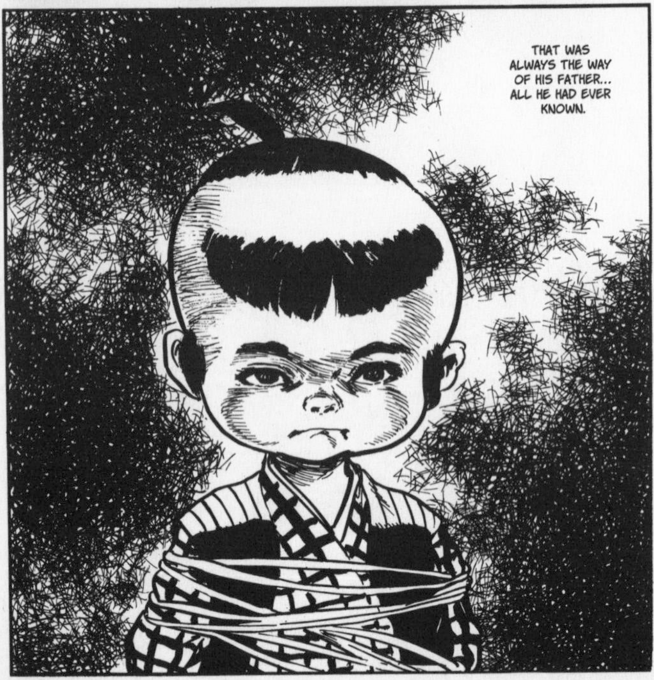
THAT WAS ALWAYS THE WAY OF HIS FATHER... ALL HE HAD EVER KNOWN.

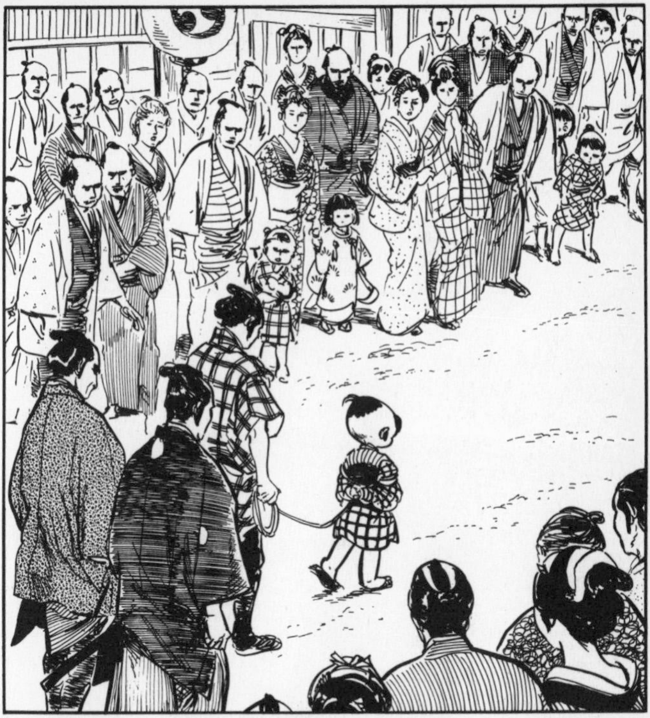

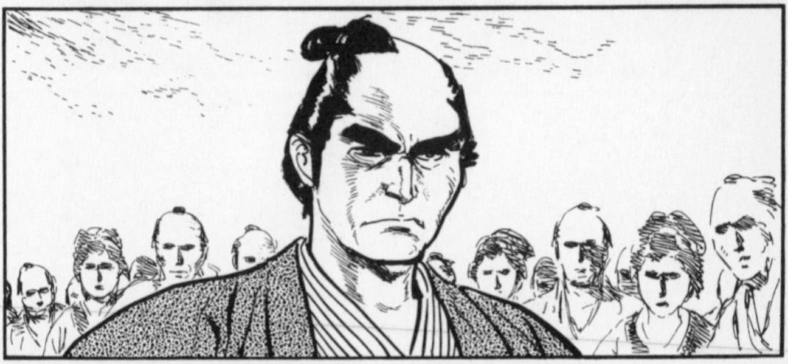

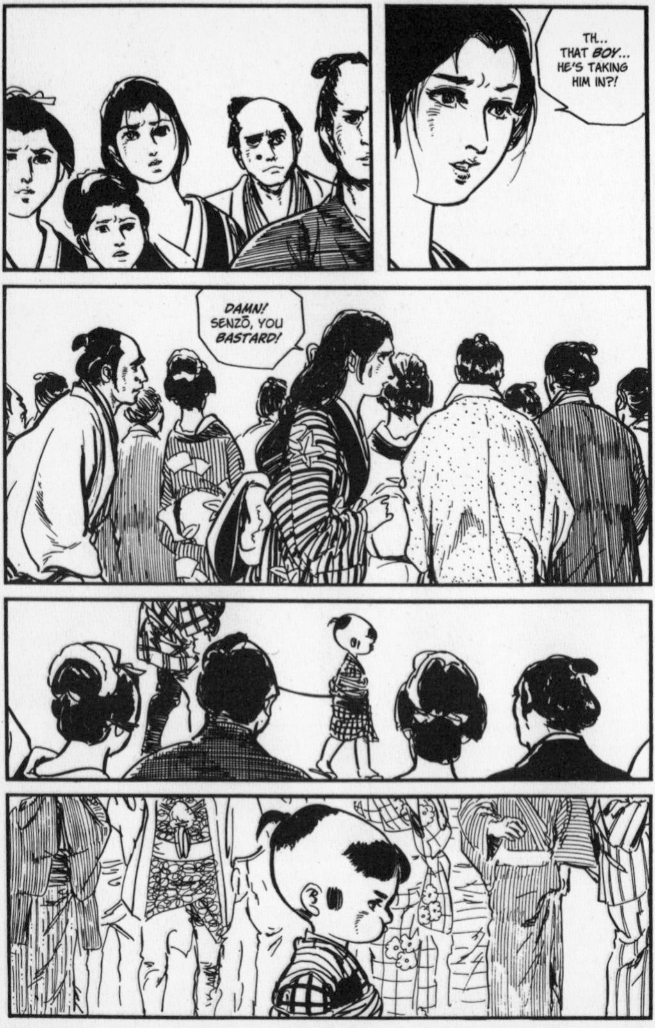
TH.. THAT *BOY*... HE'S TAKING HIM IN?!
DAMN! SENZŌ, YOU *BASTARD!*

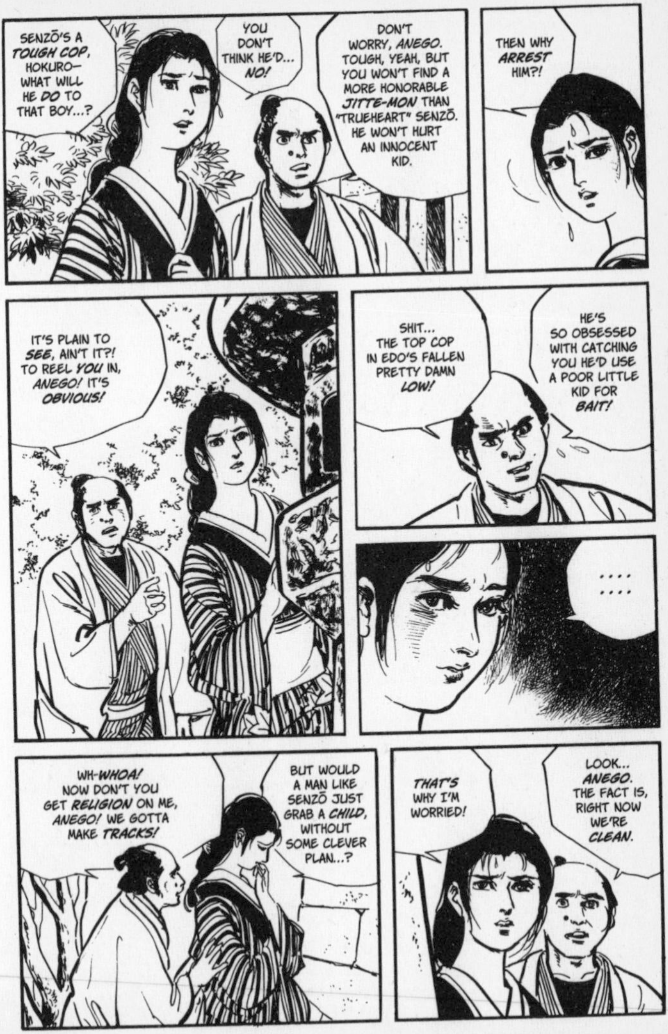
SENZŌ'S A TOUGH COP, HOKURO— WHAT WILL HE DO TO THAT BOY...?
YOU DON'T THINK HE'D... NO!
DON'T WORRY, ANEGO. TOUGH, YEAH, BUT YOU WON'T FIND A MORE HONORABLE JITTE-MON THAN "TRUEHEART" SENZŌ. HE WON'T HURT AN INNOCENT KID.
THEN WHY ARREST HIM?!
IT'S PLAIN TO SEE, AIN'T IT?! TO REEL YOU IN, ANEGO! IT'S OBVIOUS!
SHIT... THE TOP COP IN EDO'S FALLEN PRETTY DAMN LOW!
HE'S SO OBSESSED WITH CATCHING YOU HE'D USE A POOR LITTLE KID FOR BAIT!
....
....
WH-WHOA! NOW DON'T YOU GET RELIGION ON ME, ANEGO! WE GOTTA MAKE TRACKS!
BUT WOULD A MAN LIKE SENZŌ JUST GRAB A CHILD, WITHOUT SOME CLEVER PLAN...?
THAT'S WHY I'M WORRIED!
LOOK... ANEGO. THE FACT IS, RIGHT NOW WE'RE CLEAN.

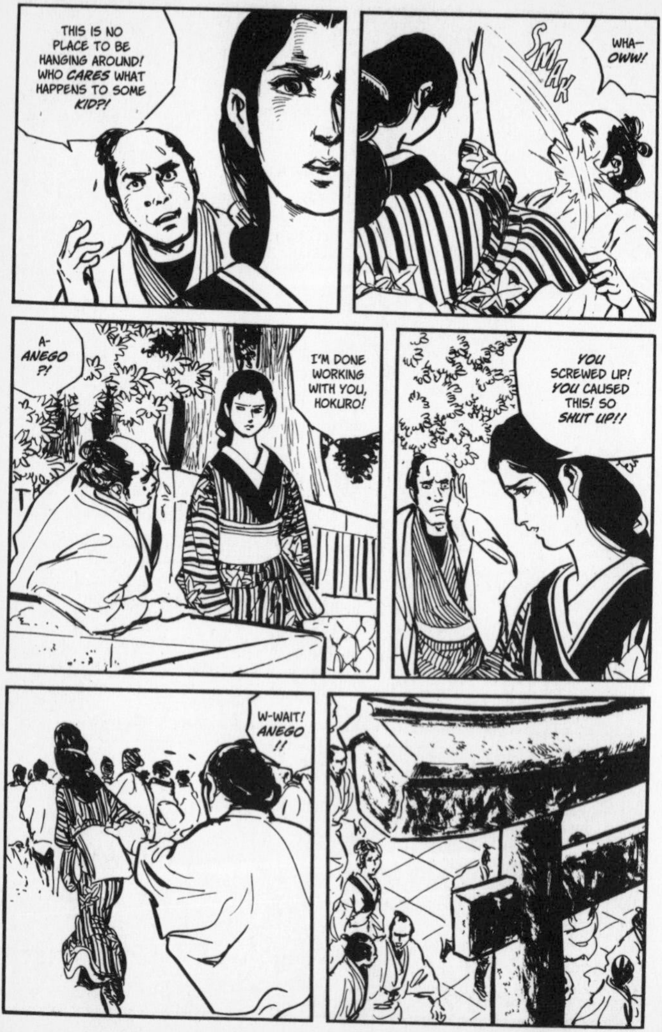
THIS IS NO PLACE TO BE HANGING AROUND! WHO CARES WHAT HAPPENS TO SOME KID?!
SMAK
WHA-OWW!
A- ANEGO ?!
I'M DONE WORKING WITH YOU, HOKURO!
YOU SCREWED UP! YOU CAUSED THIS! SO SHUT UP!!
W-WAIT! ANEGO !!

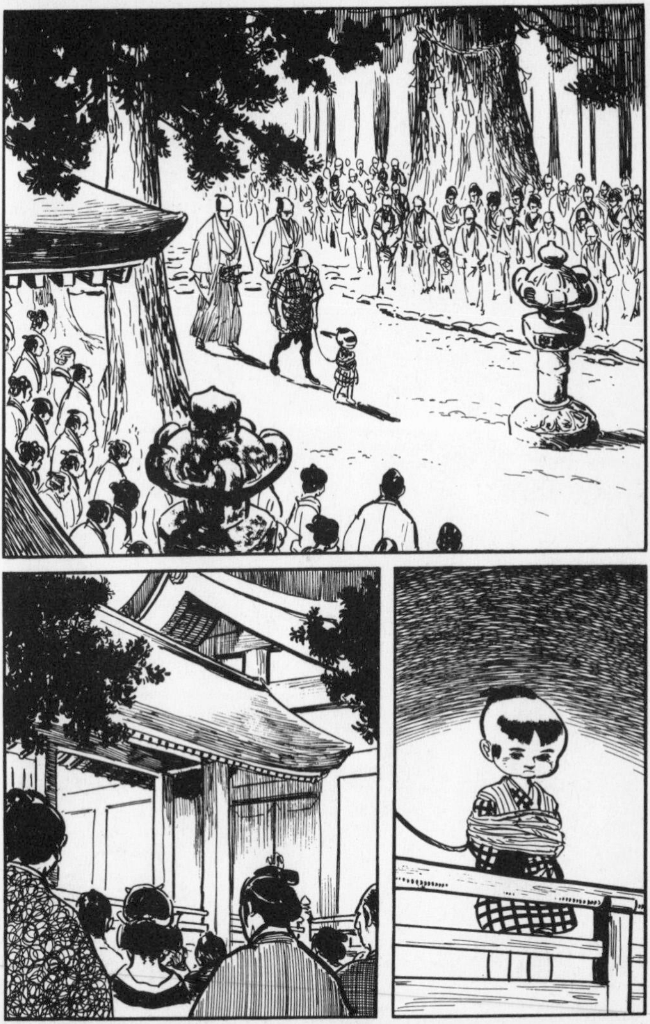

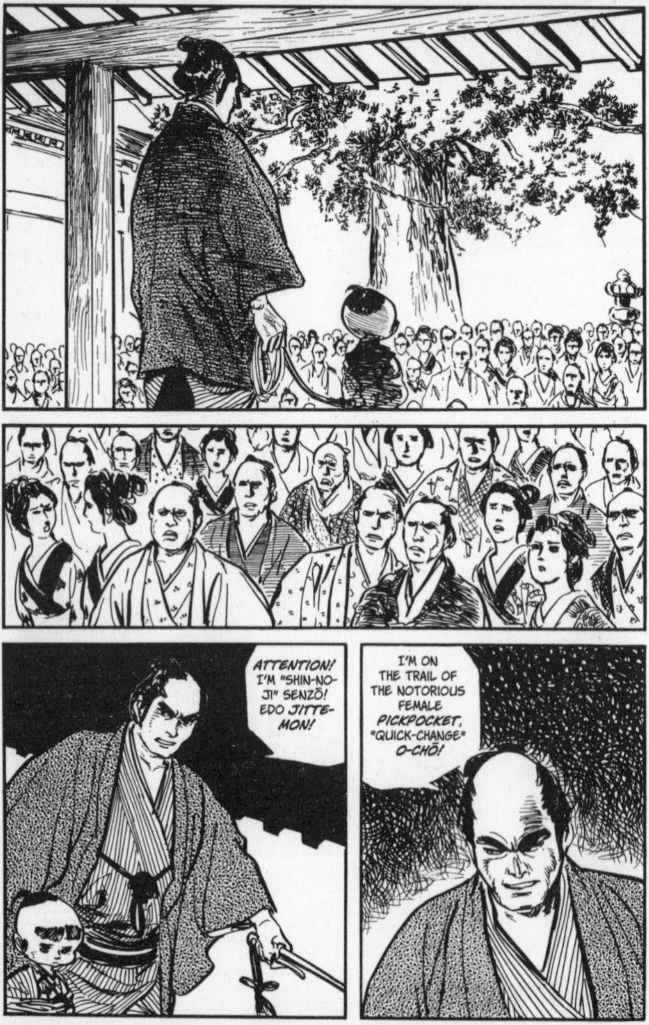
ATTENTION! I'M "SHIN-NO-JI" SENZŌ! EDO *JITTE-MON!*
I'M ON THE TRAIL OF THE NOTORIOUS FEMALE *PICKPOCKET*, "QUICK-CHANGE" *O-CHŌ!*

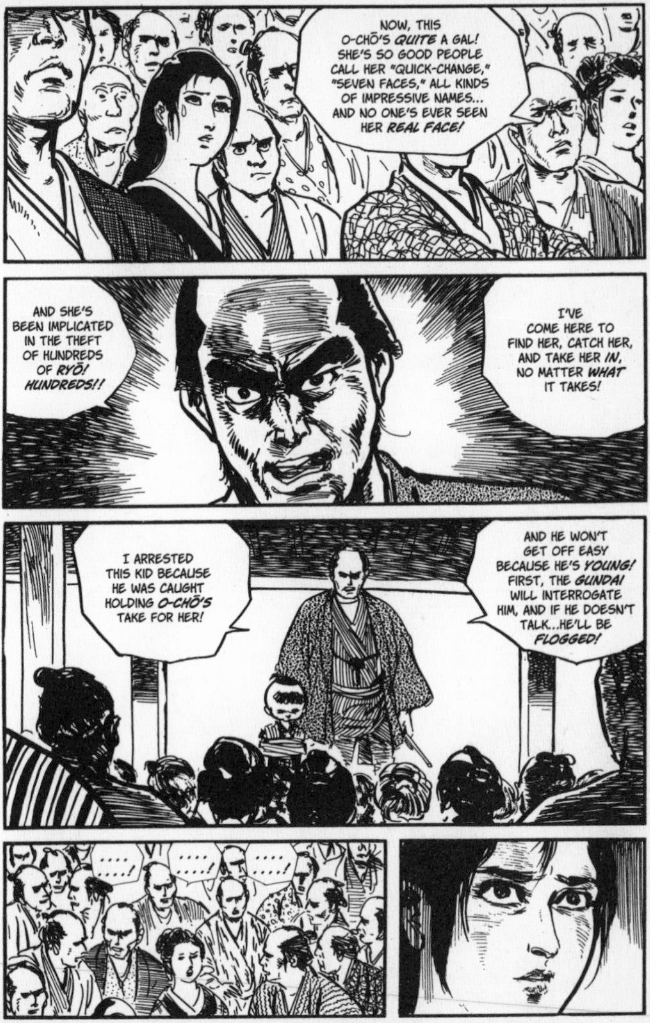
NOW, THIS O-CHŌ'S *QUITE* A GAL! SHE'S SO GOOD PEOPLE CALL HER "QUICK-CHANGE," "SEVEN FACES," ALL KINDS OF IMPRESSIVE NAMES... AND NO ONE'S EVER SEEN HER *REAL FACE!*
AND SHE'S BEEN IMPLICATED IN THE THEFT OF HUNDREDS OF *RYŌ! HUNDREDS!!*
I'VE COME HERE TO FIND HER, CATCH HER, AND TAKE HER *IN*, NO MATTER *WHAT* IT TAKES!
I ARRESTED THIS KID BECAUSE HE WAS CAUGHT HOLDING *O-CHŌ'S* TAKE FOR HER!
AND HE WON'T GET OFF EASY BECAUSE HE'S *YOUNG!* FIRST, THE *GUNDAI* WILL INTERROGATE HIM, AND IF HE DOESN'T TALK...HE'LL BE *FLOGGED!*
....!
....!
....!

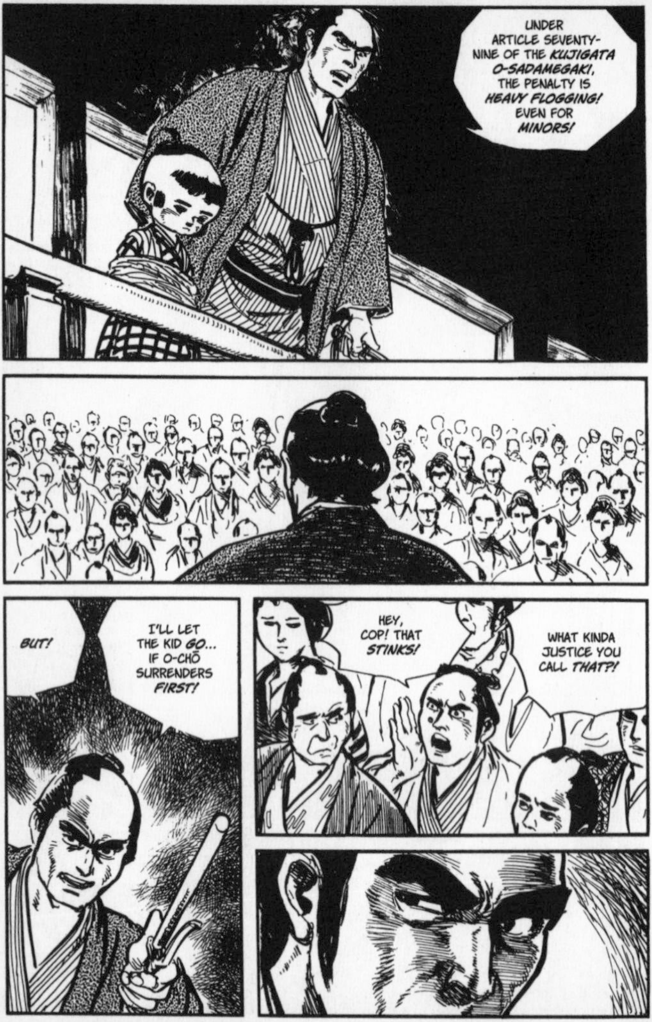
UNDER ARTICLE SEVENTY-NINE OF THE KUJIGATA O-SADAMEGAKI, THE PENALTY IS HEAVY FLOGGING! EVEN FOR MINORS!
BUT!
I'LL LET THE KID GO... IF O-CHŌ SURRENDERS FIRST!
HEY, COP! THAT STINKS!
WHAT KINDA JUSTICE YOU CALL THAT?!

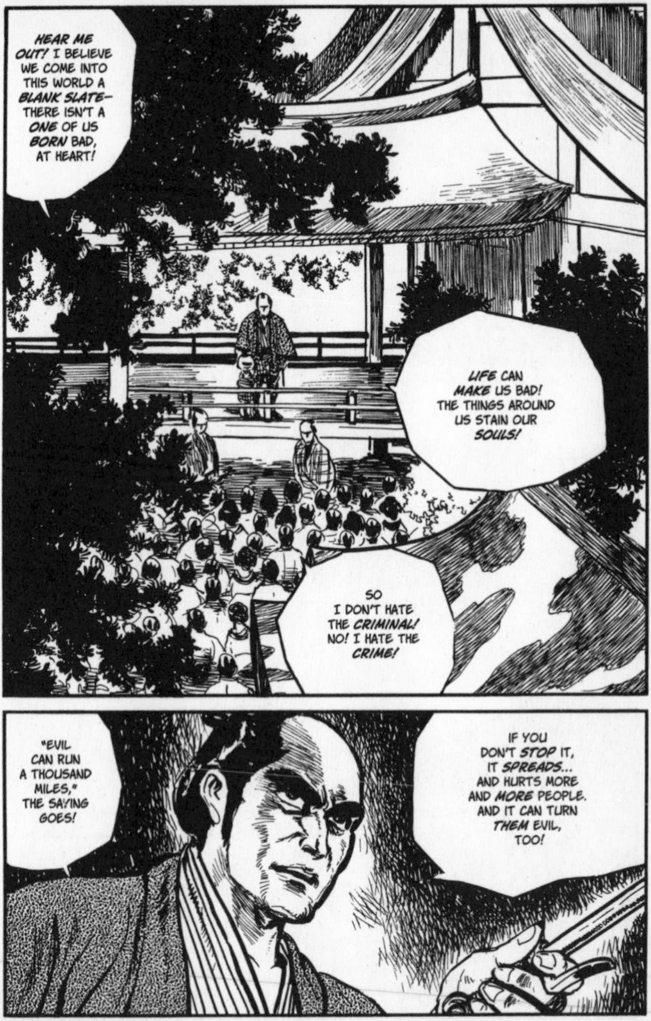
HEAR ME OUT! I BELIEVE WE COME INTO THIS WORLD A BLANK SLATE— THERE ISN'T A ONE OF US BORN BAD, AT HEART!
LIFE CAN MAKE US BAD! THE THINGS AROUND US STAIN OUR SOULS!
SO I DON'T HATE THE CRIMINAL! NO! I HATE THE CRIME!
"EVIL CAN RUN A THOUSAND MILES," THE SAYING GOES!
IF YOU DON'T STOP IT, IT SPREADS... AND HURTS MORE AND MORE PEOPLE. AND IT CAN TURN THEM EVIL, TOO!

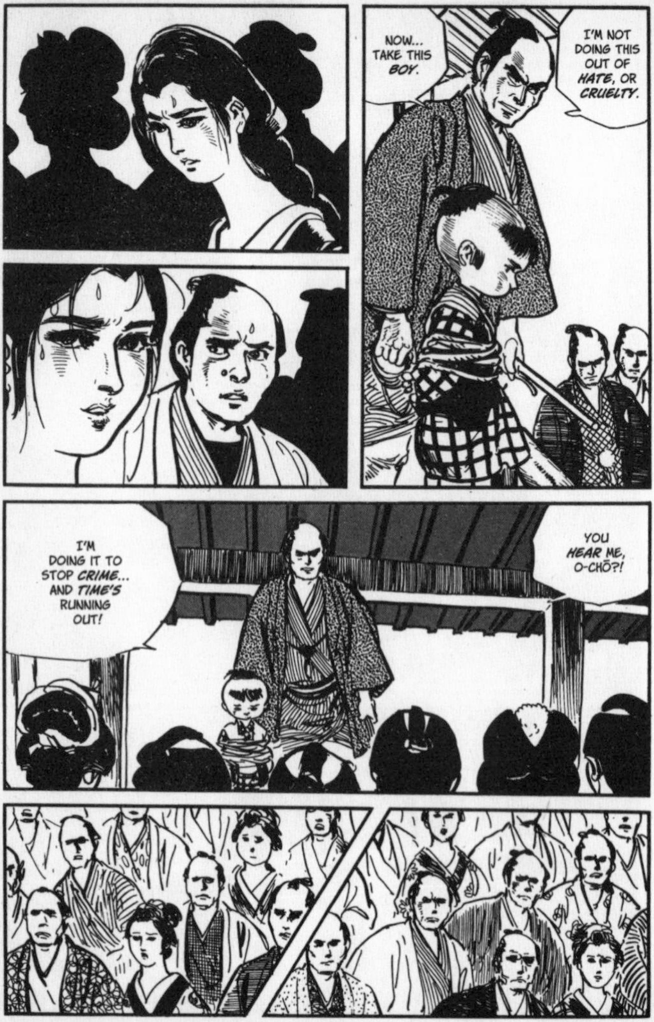
NOW... TAKE THIS BOY.
I'M NOT DOING THIS OUT OF HATE, OR CRUELTY.
I'M DOING IT TO STOP CRIME... AND TIME'S RUNNING OUT!
YOU HEAR ME, O-CHŌ?!

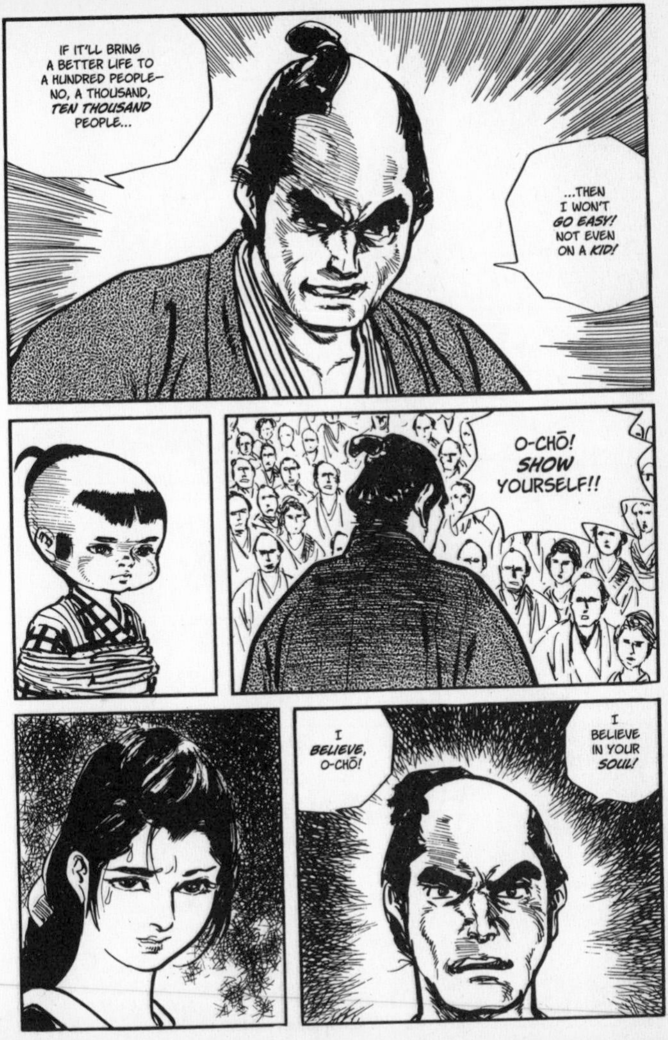
IF IT'LL BRING A BETTER LIFE TO A HUNDRED PEOPLE—NO, A THOUSAND, *TEN THOUSAND* PEOPLE...
...THEN I WON'T *GO EASY!* NOT EVEN ON A *KID!*
O-CHŌ! **SHOW** YOURSELF!!
I *BELIEVE,* O-CHŌ!
I BELIEVE IN YOUR *SOUL!*

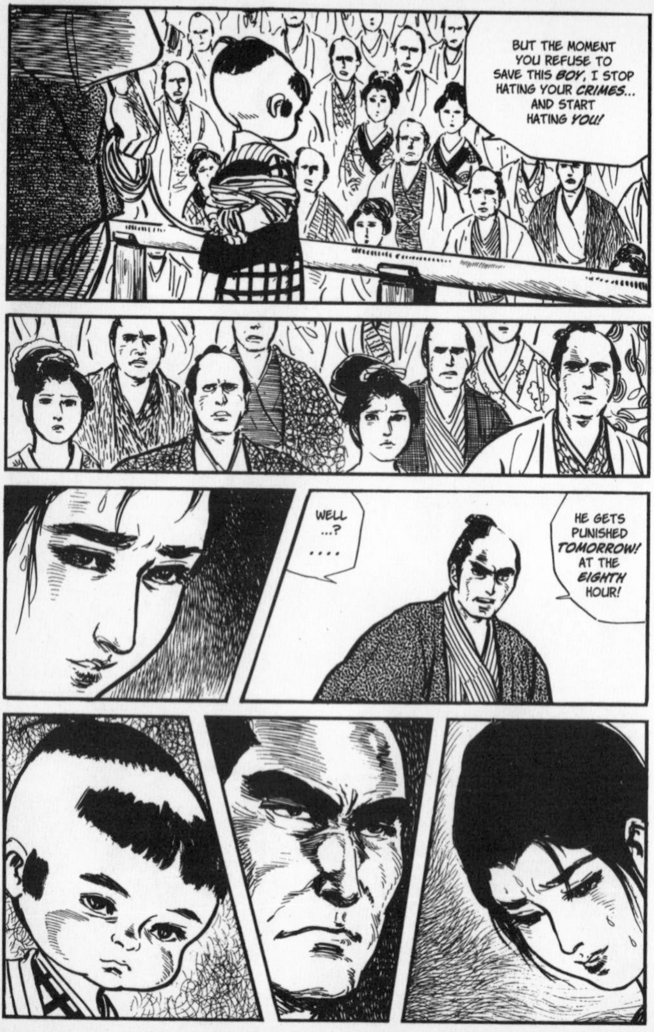
BUT THE MOMENT YOU REFUSE TO SAVE THIS *BOY*, I STOP HATING YOUR *CRIMES*... AND START HATING *YOU!*
WELL ...? ....
HE GETS PUNISHED *TOMORROW!* AT THE *EIGHTH* HOUR!

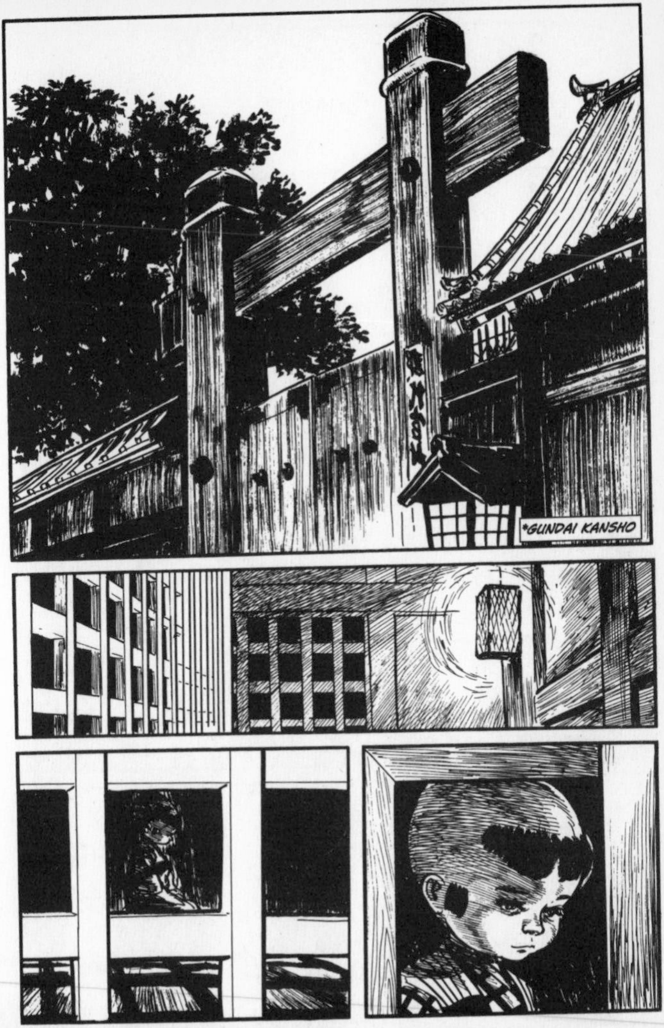
*GUNDAI KANSHO

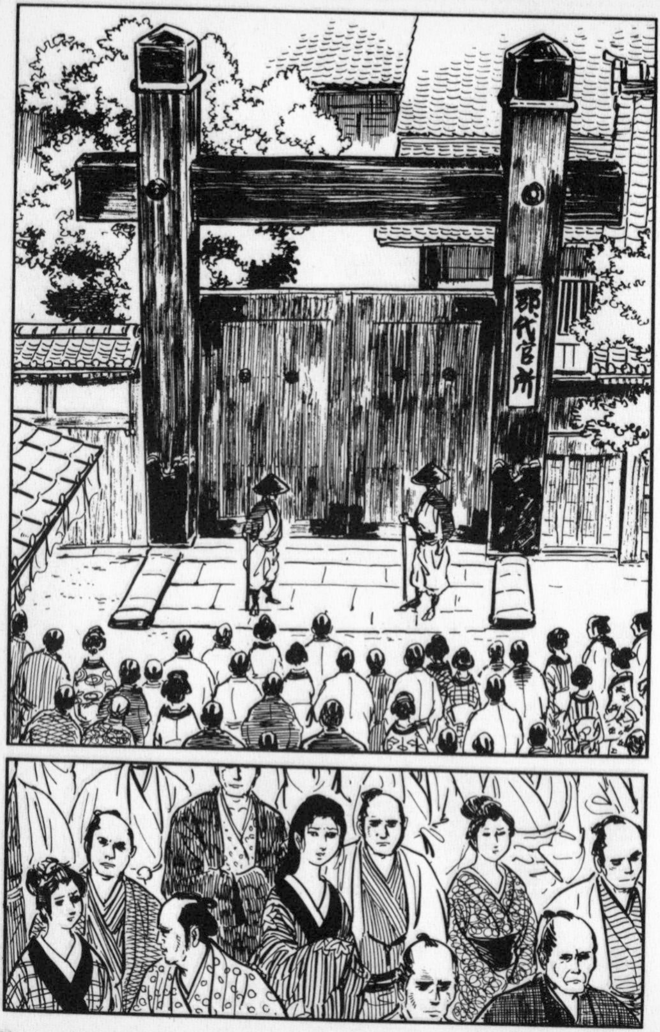
郡代官所

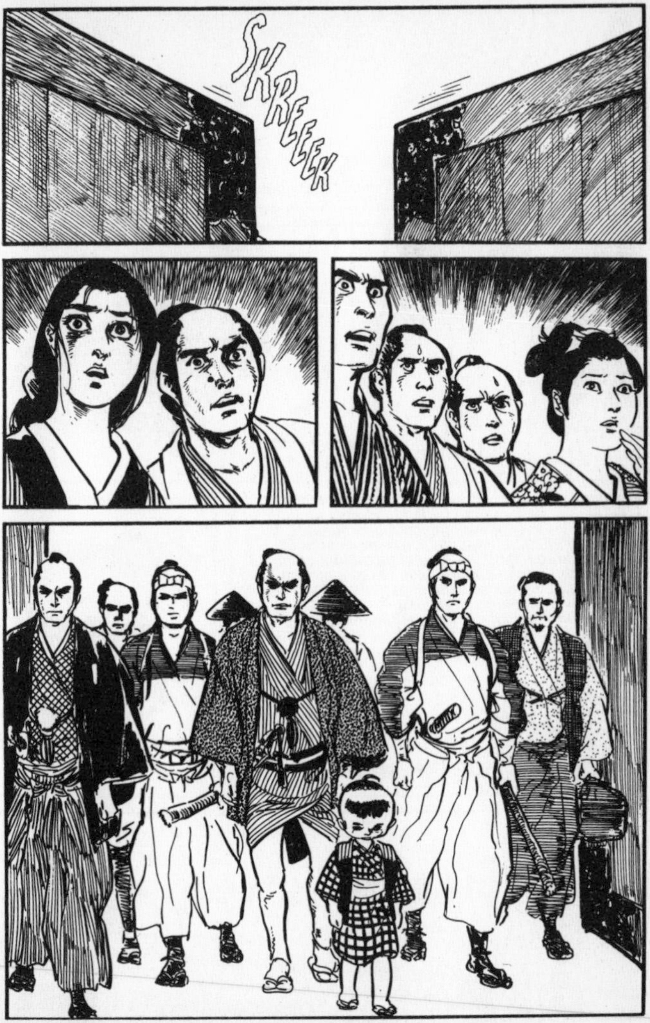
SKREEEK

THE FLOGGING TOOK PLACE BEFORE THE *KANSHO* GATES. A LIGHT FLOGGING WAS FIFTY LASHES, A HEAVY FLOGGING, ONE HUNDRED. THE CRIMINAL WAS PLACED ON HIS STOMACH, AND WAS BEATEN ABOUT THE SHOULDERS, BACK AND BUTTOCKS. THE STROKES CONTINUED UNTIL LOSS OF CONSCIOUSNESS, THEN RESUMED AFTER THE PRISONER RECOVERED. THE STICK USED FOR A FLOGGING MEASURED ONE *SHAKU* NINE *SUN* IN LENGTH AND FOUR *SUN* FIVE *BU* IN CIRCUMFERENCE, AND WAS MADE OF BUNDLED CANE, WRAPPED TIGHT WITH LONG STRIPS OF PAPER.

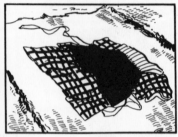

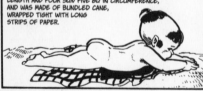

THAT *POOR* CHILD...!

BUT HAVE YOU EVER *SEEN* SUCH A TOUGH LITTLE GUY? AMAZING!

REALLY! HE ISN'T EVEN *PALE!*

294

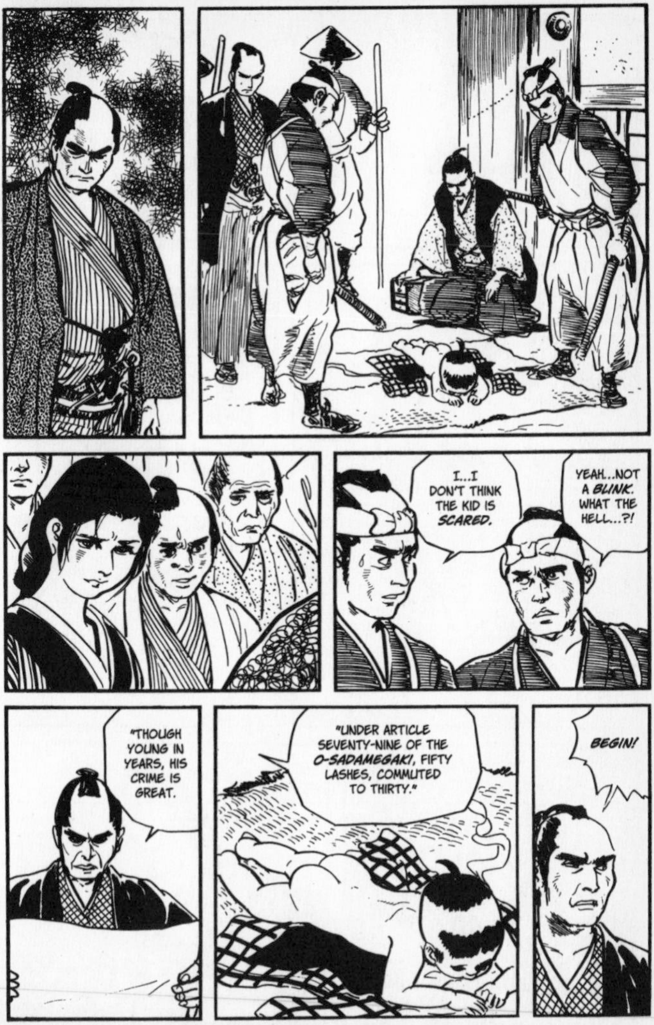
I...I DON'T THINK THE KID IS SCARED.
YEAH...NOT A BLINK. WHAT THE HELL...?!
"THOUGH YOUNG IN YEARS, HIS CRIME IS GREAT.
"UNDER ARTICLE SEVENTY-NINE OF THE O-SADAMEGAKI, FIFTY LASHES, COMMUTED TO THIRTY."
BEGIN!

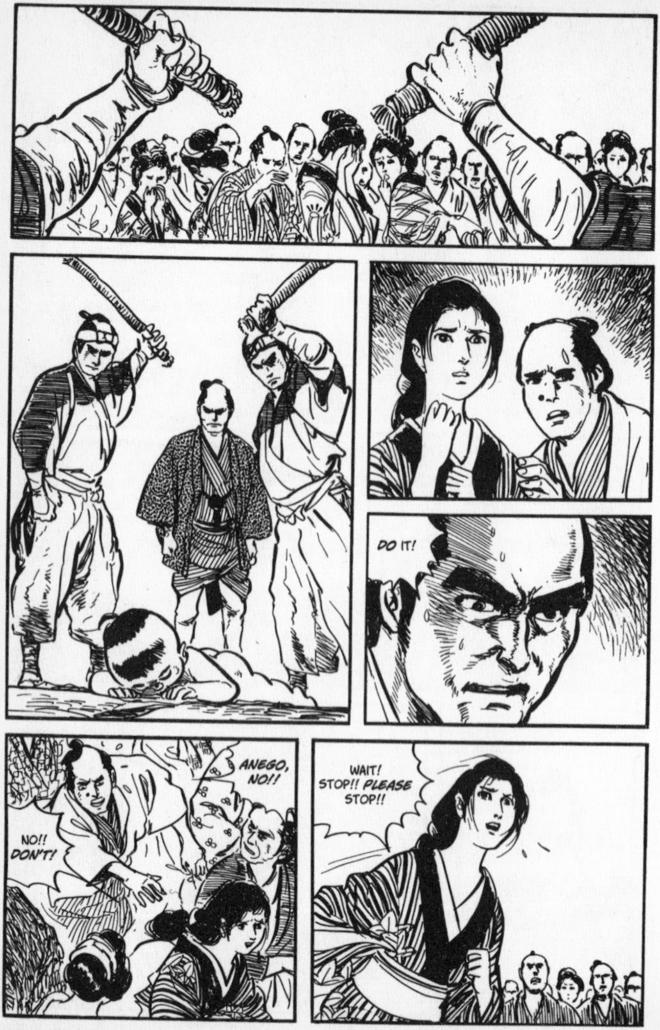
DO IT!
NO!!
DON'T!
ANEGO,
NO!!
WAIT!
STOP!! PLEASE
STOP!!

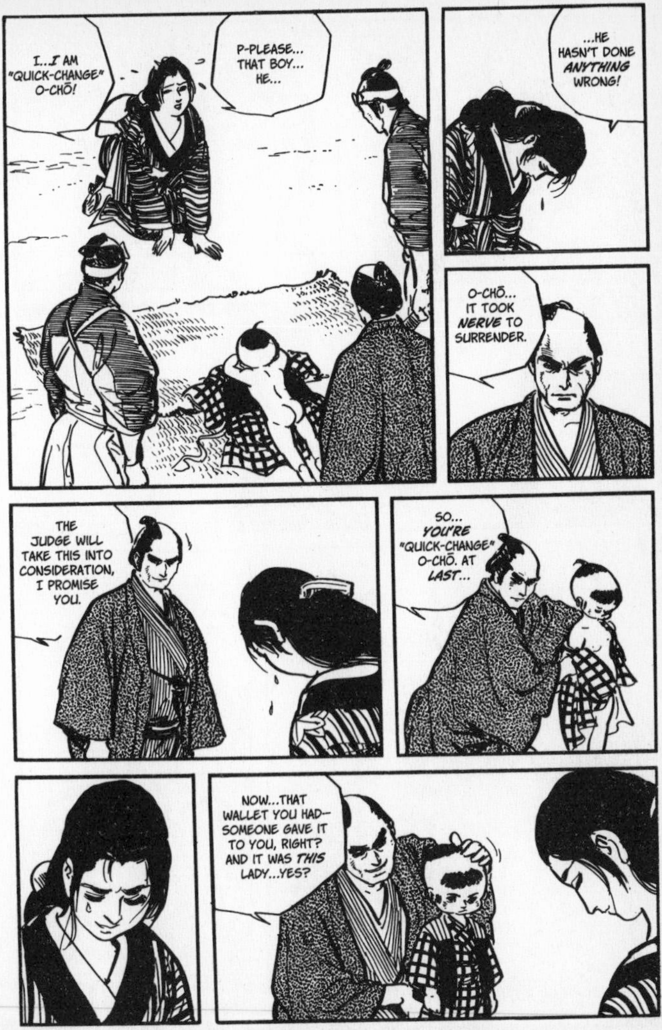
I...I AM "QUICK-CHANGE" O-CHŌ!
P-PLEASE... THAT BOY... HE...
...HE HASN'T DONE *ANYTHING* WRONG!
O-CHŌ... IT TOOK *NERVE* TO SURRENDER.
THE JUDGE WILL TAKE THIS INTO CONSIDERATION, I PROMISE YOU.
SO... *YOU'RE* "QUICK-CHANGE" O-CHŌ. AT *LAST*...
NOW...THAT WALLET YOU HAD—SOMEONE GAVE IT TO YOU, RIGHT? AND IT WAS *THIS* LADY...YES?

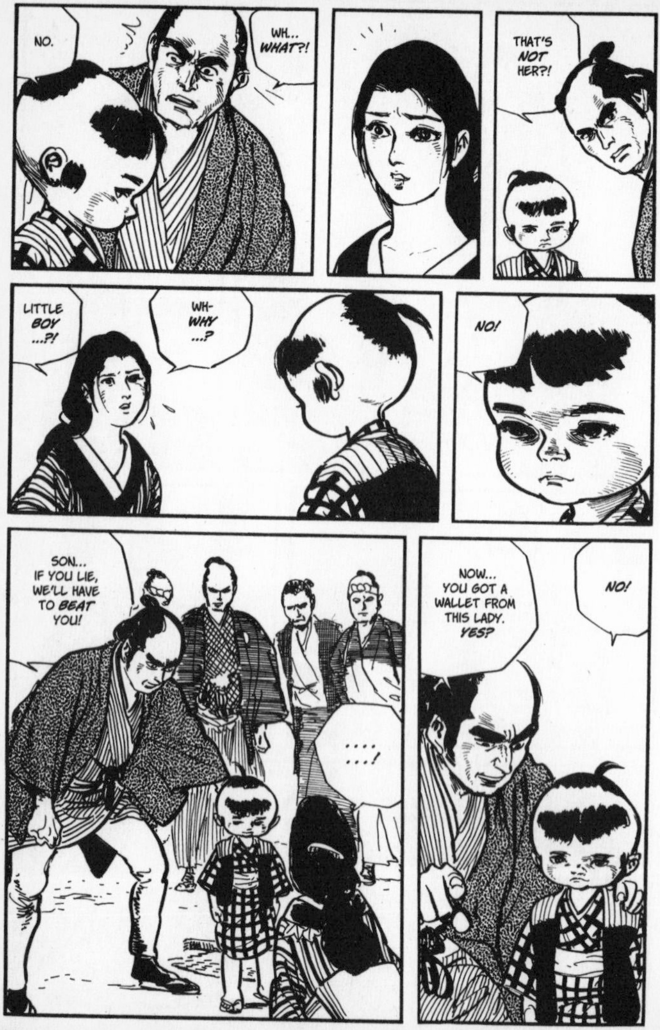
NO.
WH... WHAT?!
THAT'S NOT HER?!
LITTLE BOY ...?!
WH- WHY ...?
NO!
SON... IF YOU LIE, WE'LL HAVE TO BEAT YOU!
....
...!
NOW... YOU GOT A WALLET FROM THIS LADY. YES?
NO!

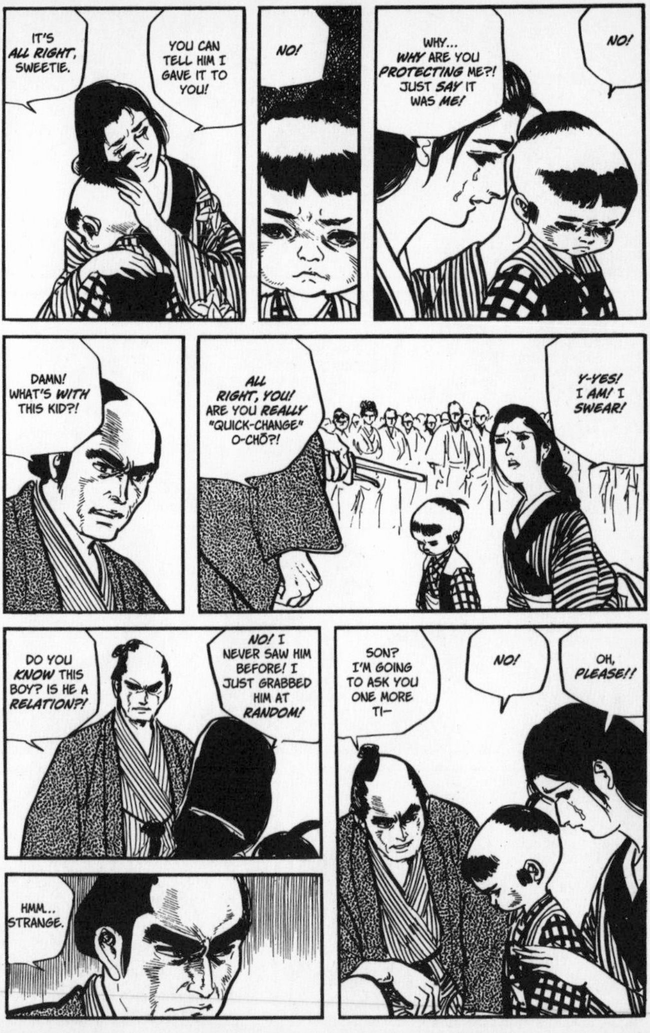
IT'S ALL RIGHT, SWEETIE.
YOU CAN TELL HIM I GAVE IT TO YOU!
NO!
WHY... WHY ARE YOU PROTECTING ME?! JUST SAY IT WAS ME!
NO!
DAMN! WHAT'S WITH THIS KID?!
ALL RIGHT, YOU! ARE YOU REALLY "QUICK-CHANGE" O-CHŌ?!
Y-YES! I AM! I SWEAR!
DO YOU KNOW THIS BOY? IS HE A RELATION?!
NO! I NEVER SAW HIM BEFORE! I JUST GRABBED HIM AT RANDOM!
HMM... STRANGE.
SON? I'M GOING TO ASK YOU ONE MORE TI—
NO!
OH, PLEASE!!

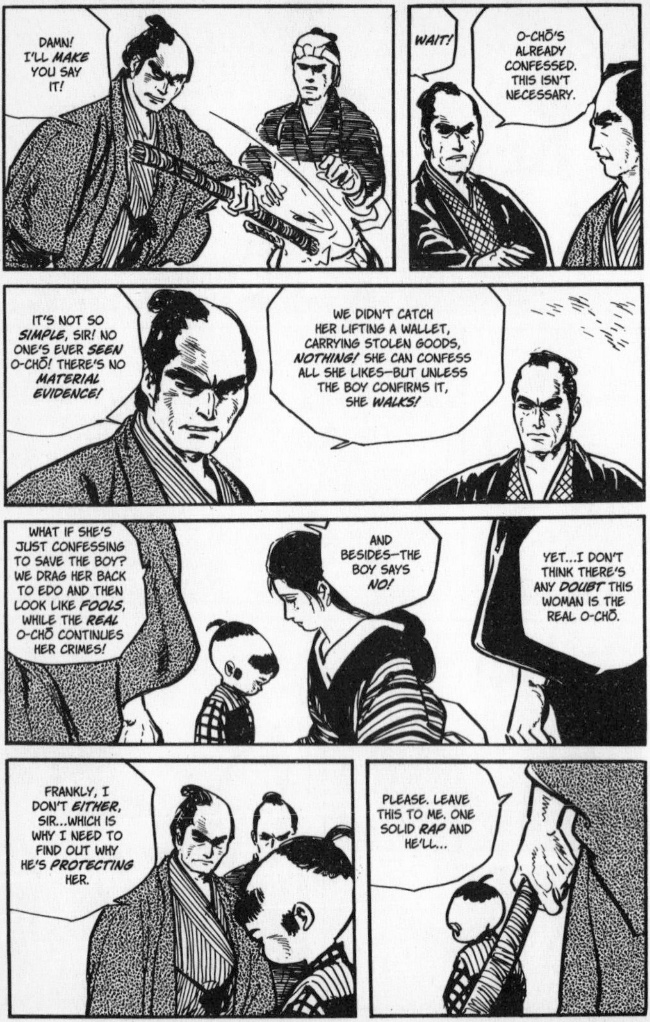
DAMN! I'LL MAKE YOU SAY IT!
WAIT!
O-CHŌ'S ALREADY CONFESSED. THIS ISN'T NECESSARY.
IT'S NOT SO SIMPLE, SIR! NO ONE'S EVER SEEN O-CHŌ! THERE'S NO MATERIAL EVIDENCE!
WE DIDN'T CATCH HER LIFTING A WALLET, CARRYING STOLEN GOODS, NOTHING! SHE CAN CONFESS ALL SHE LIKES—BUT UNLESS THE BOY CONFIRMS IT, SHE WALKS!
WHAT IF SHE'S JUST CONFESSING TO SAVE THE BOY? WE DRAG HER BACK TO EDO AND THEN LOOK LIKE FOOLS, WHILE THE REAL O-CHŌ CONTINUES HER CRIMES!
AND BESIDES—THE BOY SAYS NO!
YET...I DON'T THINK THERE'S ANY DOUBT THIS WOMAN IS THE REAL O-CHŌ.
FRANKLY, I DON'T EITHER, SIR...WHICH IS WHY I NEED TO FIND OUT WHY HE'S PROTECTING HER.
PLEASE. LEAVE THIS TO ME. ONE SOLID RAP AND HE'LL...

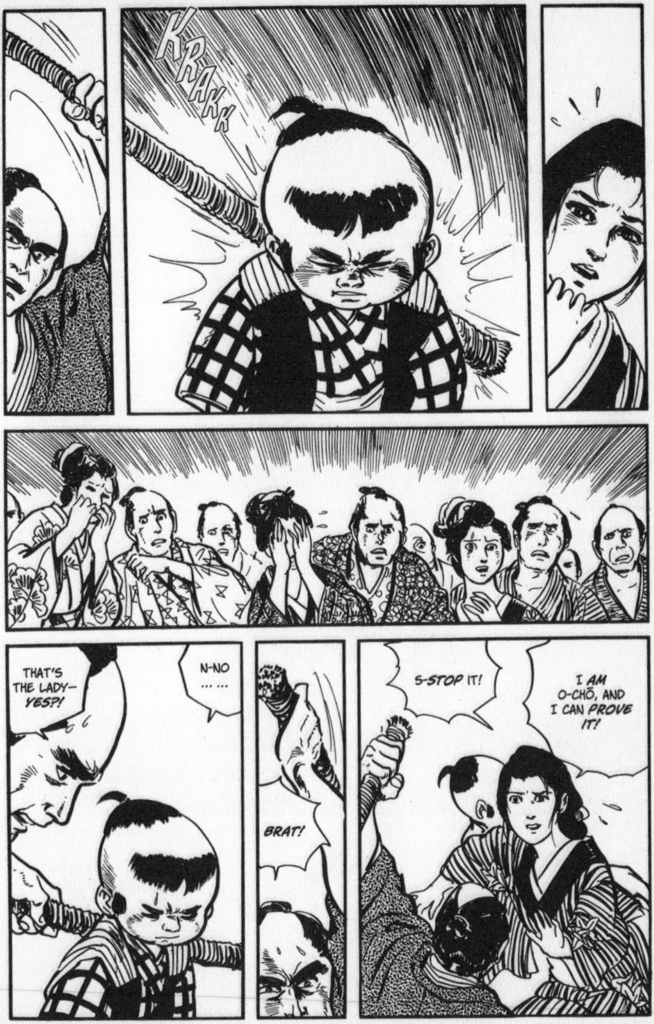
KRAKK
THAT'S THE LADY—YES?!
N-NO ... ...
BRAT!
S-STOP IT!
I AM O-CHŌ, AND I CAN PROVE IT!

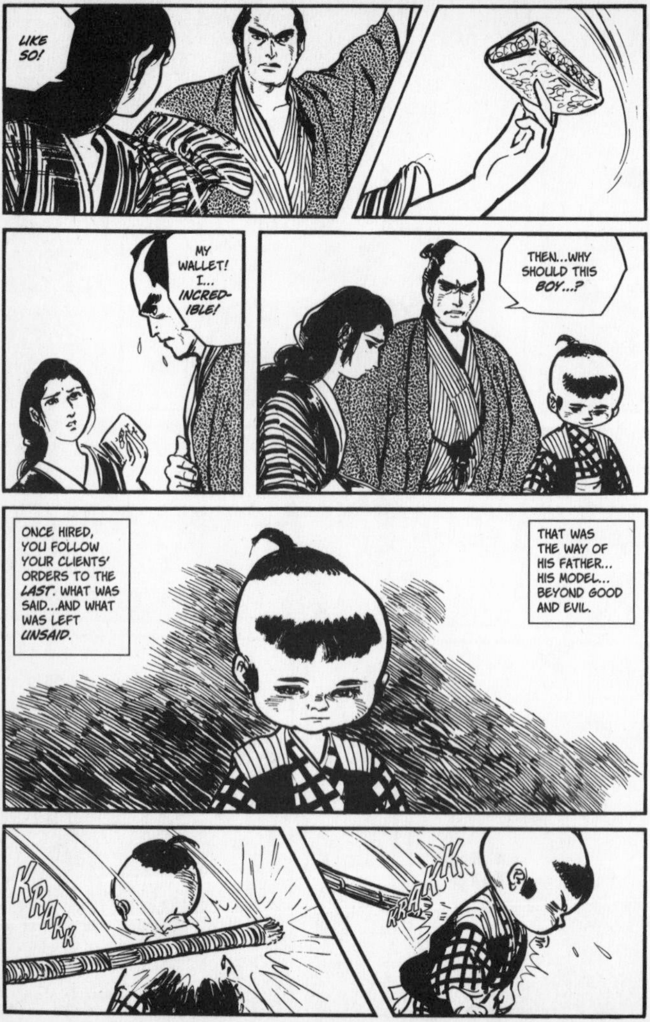
LIKE SO!
MY WALLET! I... INCRED-IBLE!
THEN...WHY SHOULD THIS BOY...?
ONCE HIRED, YOU FOLLOW YOUR CLIENTS' ORDERS TO THE LAST. WHAT WAS SAID...AND WHAT WAS LEFT UNSAID.
THAT WAS THE WAY OF HIS FATHER... HIS MODEL... BEYOND GOOD AND EVIL.
KRAKK
KRAKK

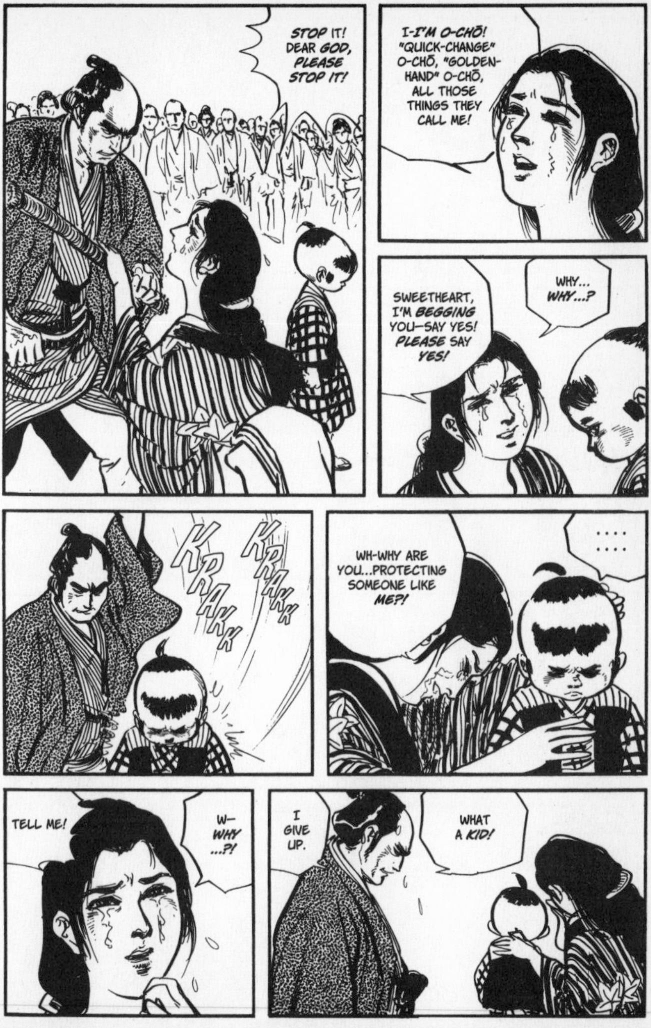
STOP IT! DEAR GOD, PLEASE STOP IT!
I-I'M O-CHŌ! "QUICK-CHANGE" O-CHŌ, "GOLDEN-HAND" O-CHŌ, ALL THOSE THINGS THEY CALL ME!
SWEETHEART, I'M BEGGING YOU—SAY YES! PLEASE SAY YES!
WHY... WHY...?
KRAKK KRAKK
WH-WHY ARE YOU...PROTECTING SOMEONE LIKE ME?!
....
....
TELL ME!
W-WHY ...?!
I GIVE UP.
WHAT A KID!

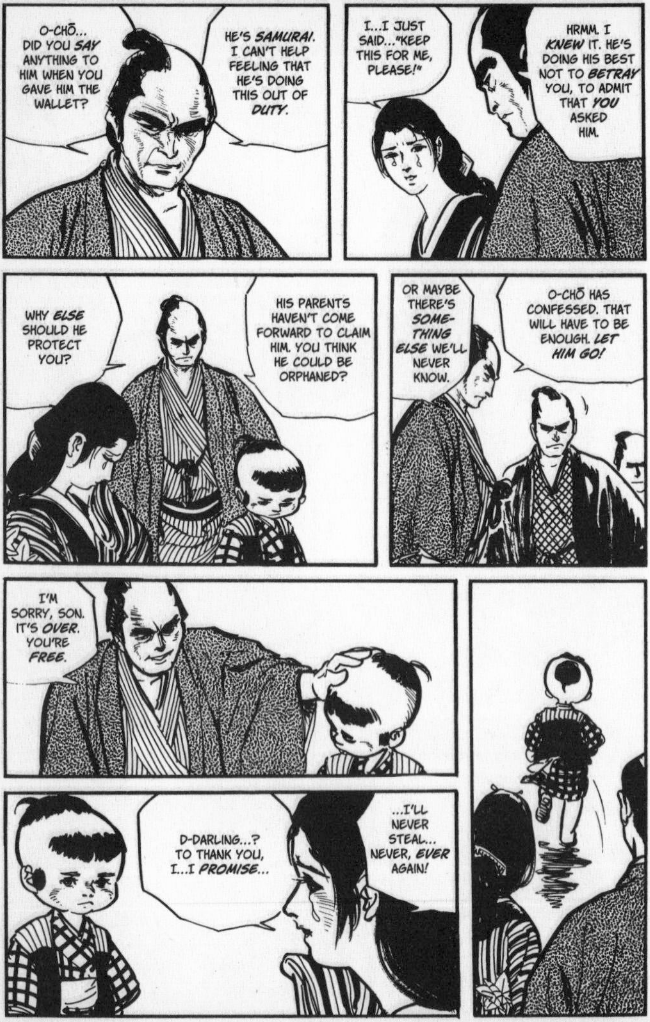
O-CHŌ... DID YOU SAY ANYTHING TO HIM WHEN YOU GAVE HIM THE WALLET?
HE'S SAMURAI. I CAN'T HELP FEELING THAT HE'S DOING THIS OUT OF DUTY.
I...I JUST SAID..."KEEP THIS FOR ME, PLEASE!"
HRMM. I KNEW IT. HE'S DOING HIS BEST NOT TO BETRAY YOU, TO ADMIT THAT YOU ASKED HIM.
WHY ELSE SHOULD HE PROTECT YOU?
HIS PARENTS HAVEN'T COME FORWARD TO CLAIM HIM. YOU THINK HE COULD BE ORPHANED?
OR MAYBE THERE'S SOME-THING ELSE WE'LL NEVER KNOW.
O-CHŌ HAS CONFESSED. THAT WILL HAVE TO BE ENOUGH. LET HIM GO!
I'M SORRY, SON. IT'S OVER. YOU'RE FREE.
D-DARLING...? TO THANK YOU, I...I PROMISE...
...I'LL NEVER STEAL... NEVER, EVER AGAIN!

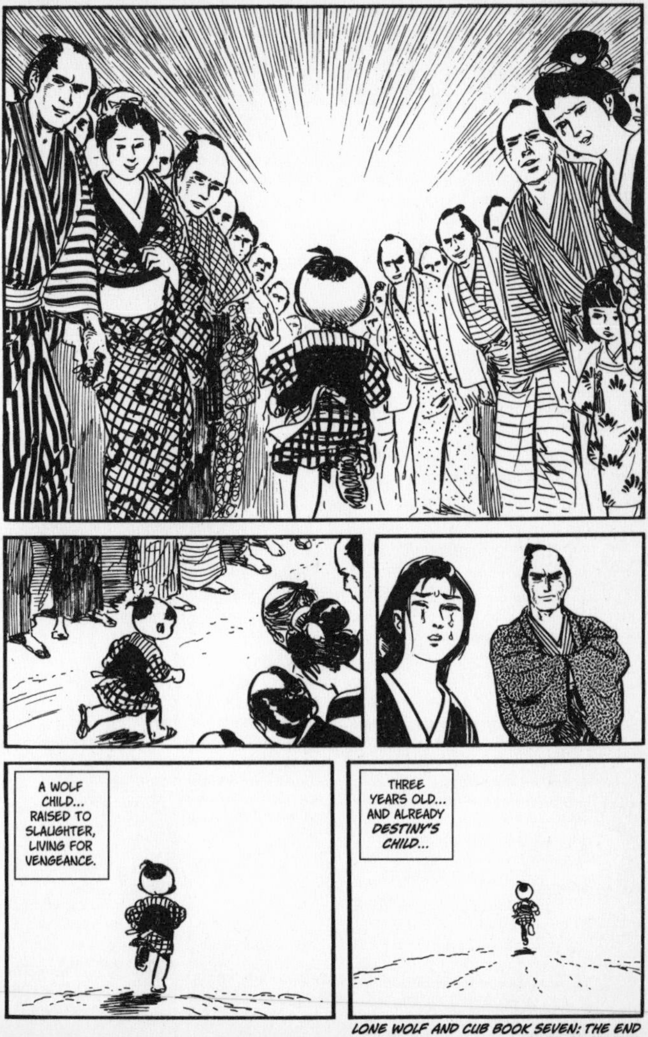
A WOLF CHILD... RAISED TO SLAUGHTER, LIVING FOR VENGEANCE.
THREE YEARS OLD... AND ALREADY *DESTINY'S CHILD*...

LONE WOLF AND CUB BOOK SEVEN: THE END
TO BE CONTINUED

GLOSSARY

anego
Underworld slang for a woman crime boss, or the wife of a crime boss. A derivation of *ane*, or elder sister.

bantō
The chief clerk in charge at inns, bathhouses, and other establishments, similar to today's hotel managers.

bu
Approximately 3 millimeters.

bushi
A samurai. A member of the warrior class.

bushidō
The way of the warrior.

cho
Old unit of measurement. Approximately 109 meters (119 yards).

crucifixion
One form of punishment in the Edo period was to be nailed or tied to an "X"-shaped wooden frame fixed in the ground and exposed to the elements until death.

currency
bu – A small coin, worth 1/4th of a *ryō*.
mon – A copper coin.
kan – A bundle of 1,000 *mon*.
monme – A silver piece.
ryō – A gold piece, worth 60 monme or 4 *kan*.
shu – Edo-period coin. Worth 1/16th of a *ryō*.

daikan
The primary local representative of the shōgunate in territories outside of the capital of Edo. The *daikan* and his staff collected taxes owed to Edo and oversaw public works, agriculture, and other projects administered by the central government.

daikansho
The office of the *daikan*.

daimyō
A feudal lord.

"the five lusts"
Goyoku. The Buddhists describe five primal human lusts: the lust for wealth, for eros, for food, for social advancement, and for sleep.

funai
The inner wards of Edo, home to the samurai class.

go-daishi-biraki
A traditional folk festival (later loosely linked to Buddhist teachings) held in late January.

go-dō
The five levels in the cycle of Buddhist reincarnation: heaven, human, beast, starvation, hell.

go-yō
Official business. As a lantern carried by the officers of the *daikan* magistrate, the equivalent of today's national police, or as the shout of the police apprehending a criminal, "*go-yō*" was one of the most dreaded words in the world of Edo Japan's criminal elements.

gundai
Commissioner. In areas administered directly by the shōgunate rather than by a local *han*, the *daikan* magistrate was superseded by the *gundai*, who performed the taxation and law-enforcement duties of the *daikan* but over a larger territory.

gundai kansho
Office of the commissioner.

han
A feudal domain.

hanshi
Samurai in the service of a *han*.

Ando Hiroshige
One of the most famous woodblock artists of all time. The depicted panel is Kojima's homage to a scene from Hiroshige's series of scenic sights along the Tōkaidō byway from Edo to Gojusantsugi, the ancient capital of Kyoto.

honjin
The lodgings for *daimyō* and senior shōgunate officials.

honorifics
Japan is a class and status society, and proper forms of address are critical. Common markers of respect are the prefixes o and go, and a wide range of suffixes. Some of the suffixes you will encounter in *Lone Wolf and Cub*:
chan – for children, young women, and close friends
dono – archaic; used for higher-ranked or highly respected figures
sama – used for superiors
san – the most common, used among equals or near-equals
sensei – used for teachers, masters, respected entertainers, and politicians

hōzuki
The Chinese lantern flower. Its boxy, crimson-orange seed pods never lose their color, even after the plant has died. Japanese children like to chew on the round, rubbery seeds, and sometimes blow through the pods like whistles.

jitte-mon
A policeman. The street cops of the Edo period carried *jitte*, a specialized weapon about 18 inches long, with no cutting edge — just two prongs designed to catch and snap off an opponent's sword blade.

kaishaku
A second. In the rite of *seppuku*, a samurai was allowed death with honor by cutting his own abdomen. After the incision was complete, the second would perform *kaishaku*, severing the samurai's head for a quick death. The second was known as a *kaishakunin*.

kenkyaku
Swordsman, *kenshi*.

kōgi kaishakunin
The shōgun's own second, who performed executions ordered by the shōgun.

koku
A bale of rice. The traditional measure of a *han's* wealth, a measure of its agricultural land and productivity.

Meireki
The reigns of the emperors were given special, felicitous names, or *nengo*. Sometimes there were several such *nengo* during a single emperor's reign. Meiriki is one such *nengo*.

metsuke
Inspector. A post combining the functions of chief of police and chief intelligence officer.

ō-bangashira
The supreme commander of a *han's* standing guard (or *ban*) of samurai, charged to protect the lord and castle.

ō-metsuke
Chief inspector. The senior law-enforcement officer of the shōgunate, reporting directly to the *rōjū* senior councilors who advised the shōgun.

O-Sadamegaki
Short for Kujigata O-Sadamegaki. The concordance of shōgunate laws, compiled in 1742.

ri
Old unit of measurement. Approximately 4 kilometers (2.5 miles).

rōjū

Senior councilors. The inner circle of councilors directly advising the shōgun. The *rōjū* were the ultimate advisory body to the Tokugawa shōgunate's national government.

Rongo

The *Analects* of Confucius.

rōnin

A masterless samurai. Literally, "one adrift on the waves." Members of the samurai caste who have lost their masters through the dissolution of *han*, expulsion for misbehavior, or other reasons. Prohibited from working as farmers or merchants under the strict Confucian caste system imposed by the Tokugawa shōgunate, many impoverished *rōnin* became "hired guns" for whom the code of the samurai was nothing but empty words.

ryū

Often translated as "school." The many variations of swordsmanship and other martial arts were passed down from generation to generation to the offspring of the originator of the technique or set of techniques, and to any *deishi* students that sought to learn from the master. The largest schools had their own *dōjō* training centers and scores of students. An effective swordsman had to study the different techniques of the various schools to know how to block them in combat. May *ryū* also had a set of special, secret techniques that were only taught to school initiates.

Sado island

Sado-jima, a cold and desolate island in the Japan sea off the coast of northern Honshu, has been a place of exile in Japan dating back to the eighth century A.D. After the discovery of gold on the island, labor in the gold mines of Sado was a virtual death sentence.

sengoku

Warring states. For two centuries between the old central rule in Kyoto and the rise of Oda Nobunaga (1534-1582), the first unifier of Japan, the country was in a state of anarchy, riven by constant civil war between rival warlords.

seppuku

The right to kill oneself with honor to atone for failure, or to follow one's master into death. Only the samurai class was allowed this glorious but excruciating death. The abdomen was cut horizontally, followed by an upward cut to spill out the intestines. When possible, a *kaishakunin* performed a beheading after the cut was made to shorten the agony.

shaku

10 *sun*, approximately 30 centimeters.

Shikyō

"Shi King," in Chinese. The oldest poetry collection in Chinese literature.

shinjū

A double-suicide. Given Edo-period Japan's strict caste structure, star-crossed lovers often found suicide a tragic last resort. *Shinjū* were one of the staples of Edo-period theatre and literature, not to mention the scandal sheets.

sokushitsu

The concubine of a *daimyō*. There was no stigma in old Japan to powerful men having mistresses in addition to their wives, and an *o-sokushitsu* shared the respect and influence of her powerful patron. *O-sokushitsu* literally means "the room next door" — for obvious reasons.

suemono-giri

Cutting through a stationary object.

sun

Approximately 3 centimeters.

Tsukuda

Tsukada-jima, a small island near the mouth of the Sumida River in old Edo. Now surrounded by landfill, it was a fishing port and a center for unskilled labor.

zanbatō

The mythical horse-slicing stroke used by Ōgami Ittō.

KAZUO KOIKE

Though widely respected as a powerful writer of graphic fiction, Kazuo Koike has spent a lifetime reaching beyond the bounds of the comics medium. Aside from co-creating and writing the successful *Lone Wolf and Cub* and *Crying Freeman* manga, Koike has hosted television programs; founded a golf magazine; produced movies; written popular fiction, poetry, and screenplays; and mentored some of Japan's best manga talent.

Lone Wolf and Cub was first serialized in Japan in 1970 (under the title *Kozure Okami*) in *Manga Action* magazine and continued its hugely popular run for many years, being collected as the stories were published, and reprinted worldwide. Koike collected numerous awards for his work on the series throughout the next decade. Starting in 1972, Koike adapted the popular manga into a series of six films, the *Baby Cart Assassin* saga, garnering widespread commercial success and critical acclaim for his screenwriting.

This wasn't Koike's only foray into film and video. In 1996, Crying Freeman, the manga Koike created with artist Ryoichi Ikegami, was produced in Hollywood and released to commercial success in Europe and is currently awaiting release in America.

And to give something back to the medium that gave him so much, Koike started the *Gekiga Sonjuku*, a college course aimed at helping talented writers and artists — such as *Ranma 1/2* creator Rumiko Takahashi — break into the comics field.

The driving focus of Koike's narrative is character development, and his commitment to character is clear: "Comics are carried by characters. If a character is well created, the comic becomes a hit." Kazuo Koike's continued success in comics and literature has proven this philosophy true.

GOSEKI KOJIMA

Goseki Kojima was born on November 3, 1928, the very same day as the godfather of Japanese comics, Osamu Tezuka. While just out of junior high school, the self-taught Kojima began painting advertising posters for movie theaters to pay his bills.

In 1950, Kojima moved to Tokyo, where the postwar devastation had given rise to special manga forms for audiences too poor to buy the new manga magazines. Kojima created art for *kami-shibai*, or "paper-play" narrators, who would use manga story sheets to present narrated street plays. Kojima moved on to creating works for the *kashi-bon* market, bookstores that rented out books, magazines, and manga to mostly low-income readers. He soon became highly popular among *kashi-bon* readers.

In 1967, Kojima broke into the magazine market with his series *Dojinki*. As the manga magazine market grew and diversified, he turned out a steady stream of popular series.

In 1970, in collaboration with Kazuo Koike, Kojima began the work that would seal his reputation, *Kozure Okami* (*Lone Wolf and Cub*). Before long the story had become a gigantic hit, eventually spinning off a television series, six motion pictures, and even theme song records. Koike and Kojima were soon dubbed the "golden duo" and produced success after success on their way to the pinnacle of the manga world.

When *Manga Japan* magazine was launched in 1994, Kojima was asked to serve as consultant, and he helped train the next generation of manga artists.

In his final years, Kojima turned to creating original graphic novels based on the movies of his favorite director, Akira Kurosawa. Kojima passed away on January 5, 2000 at the age of 71.

THE RONIN REPORT

by Tim Ervin-Gore

The Women of *Lone Wolf and Cub*

As Ratti and Westbrook state in *Secrets of the Samurai*, "the frequently myopic views of chroniclers of later ages and periods, bent upon reinforcing the preconceived notions of their patrons, tend largely to either denigrate woman's role in the military history of early civilizations or ignore it entirely." In the depths of feudal Japanese history, women are often poorly represented, as if their contributions were erased from the books in order to propel the advances of men. This is an activity observable in just about every culture throughout history. But women have refused to stay down, and continue to resist patriarchal societies, which might prefer to keep them in a subservient role. Pushing their ideas and leadership abilities to the fore, women have always been major players in society, albeit occasionally in backroom roles. Increasingly, history books are being rewritten to bring a focus back to women's roles in every realm of society. In Japan, there are numerous examples of women rising above society's restrictions, and Koike and Kojima do a fair job of giving women their deserved attention.

The pages of *Lone Wolf and Cub* present women in numerous societal roles: poor, rich, powerful, weak, young, old, fat, skinny, sexy, not so sexy, mean, kind, etc. And, aside from the roles that some historians would have you believe women filled, Koike and Kojima chose to place women in prominent positions, often heading a group of assassins here, running a Yakuza brothel over there, and performing the arts of war just about everywhere. Not only does this better help the reader to understand and sympathize for the whole of feudal Japanese society, but it also makes for a far more interesting (and sexually charged) read.

For instance, as early as the second story of the *Lone Wolf and Cub* continuum, the reader is pulled into the ruthless and shady scheme of Lady O-Sen, a woman of unbounded aspiration in her quest to be the behind-the-scenes ruler of her clan and, therefore, her *han*. Like the governors of states, *han* lords held bountiful power, collecting taxes from the commoners, and reporting directly to the Shogun. In "A Father Knows His Child's Heart, as Only a Child Can Know His Father's" (Vol. 1), the Lady O-sen uses her sexuality and guile to lure samurai into her evil plot, offering her body and receiving their loyalty in return. In the end, of course, O-Sen winds up on the wrong side of Ogami's sword, politics being the means to her abrupt end.

But the ambitious woman is not the predominant female image in *Lone Wolf and Cub*. In fact, only two chapters later, in the story "Baby Cart on the River Styx," Ogami and Daigoro meet a group of Yakuza who employ little Daigoro to suckle the breast of an ailing woman. In this story, Koike positions the woman as a sword-carrying equal amongst Yakuza brothers. Though much of the Yakuza business centers around female trades (prostitution in particular), current studies suggest that women's roles in Japanese organized crime were limited, with a few exceptions, such as an instance when a leader's wife makes decisions for the family in the event of his death. The reasons cited for this exclusion are usually based on an assumed weakness of women. However, Koike wrote women into leadership roles within feudal organized-crime families in numerous stories.

In the eighteenth chapter, "The Virgin and the Whore" (Vol. 3), a woman who heads a brothel hunts a girl who killed one of her procurers in self-defense. Ogami stands in the way of "floating world" business dealings, and the situation becomes immediately tense. However, the madam's bearing and wisdom suggest a deep understanding of samurai politics and a firm grip on her underlings within the organization. It could be assumed that, in feudal times, women had a better understanding of the samurai culture, and, having a coincidental impression of honor and desire to continue the bloodline, they were likely more adept in leadership of crime families. This logical path makes Koike and Kojima's stories more believable, and the reader's interest is piqued by the commanding, intelligent, and often martially skilled women populating the stories.

It is in the wielding of weapons that Koike and Kojima best expressed the fury of the female. Both women mentioned in the last paragraph carried weapons in their respective stories but never used them. However, as early as the seventh chapter of *Lone Wolf and Cub*, "The Eight Gates of Deceit" (Vol. 1), women take up arms against our protagonist and use them in an attempt to kill him. In fact, eight women using different ferocious techniques try to kill the unstoppable Ogami. The eight make up the main guard of their *han*, one being the captain of the guard and main martial instructor. Placing the women willfully behind the sword makes for a remarkably dramatic plot and dissolves any expectation of timid helplessness in women. In another moving story, "The Performer," a woman rises from the lower caste to become the female martial arts trainer, or *besshiki-onna*, of a *han*. The tale winds down to eventual tragedy, but not before the woman exacts her revenge upon a man with her superior technique. According to some scholars, the act of a woman taking up arms was not such a rare thing. Ratti and Westbrook note that there were notable woman warriors in Japanese history, such as Tomoe Gozen, wife of General Kiso no Yoshinaka. She was described as exceptionally strong and hauntingly beautiful and was the subject of many plays and poems. In a particularly historic incident, Tomoe beheaded an enemy general for tearing the sleeve of her kimono. Indeed, women were often the last defense for a village in times of war, so their martial skills tended to be quite important, if not celebrated.

Not to weave too far from the perceived truth, Koike and Kojima also cast many women into roles considered traditional, romantic, or expected. There are many sympathetic common women throughout the *Lone Wolf and Cub* series, such as the rice-planting women in "Black Wind" (Vol. 5), shown as a positive work force in the face of hard times. Ogami looks upon their country wisdom with respect, adapting their beliefs into his role as an assassin. In "Wings to the Bird, Fangs to the Beast" (Vol. 1), Ogami receives and returns the respect of a sympathetic and wise prostitute. In this story, the prostitute shows more honor and bearing than one samurai in the same predicament. Imprisoned by a band of brigands who demand to witness a sex act as entertainment, the prostitute defends Ogami's honor, and in return, he has sex with her to keep her from being murdered. Not much of a sacrifice, you might think, but as the prostitute says to the less honorable samurai a few panels after the consummated act, "when you're shaking and peeing in your pants that you're going to die, could you satisfy a woman?" This reiterates Ogami's virility and capabilities (now as a lover as well as a fighter) and places a woman of questionable honor in an air of higher respect than all of the men (save Ogami) around her.

Though it is explained a few chapters later that the prostitute had once lived a better life, a prostitute in feudal Japan might have earned such strong character and understanding of honor due to her occupation. According to George Scott's *The History of Prostitution*, "in no other country on the face of the earth has the woman of easy virtue received the respect accorded to her in Japan." Indeed, the Japanese courtesan, geisha, and/or prostitute largely carried the responsibility of creating and passing culture amongst society. Also, since the samurai were a large part of the customer base for courtesans, their culture passed through the ladies, probably finding refinement along the way.

Encompassing some of the aforementioned elements, the story "The Performer" features a woman who rose from the low caste of a street performer to become the *besshiki onna*, training the other women of a *han* court on the skills of war. As explained in the story, such a rise was unlikely, so her story is one of great pride and honor. However, as the tale turns tragic, the woman must defend her honor the only way she knows how, with the cold blade of vengeance.

Similarly, in "Inn of the Last Chrysanthemum," from this very volume, a young girl works at an inn, patiently awaiting her opportunity for revenge. As stated in the story, the girls working the inns commonly served as prostitutes. In fact, as Oliver Statler wrote in his charming tome *Japanese Inn*, "prostitutes were almost indispensable to a Japanese inn." He went on to discuss some of the very elements seen in the above story: girls competing in the streets for the attention of weary travelers and nervous managers worried about the caste of their clientele. In this chapter of *Lone Wolf and Cub*, the young girl would be of a lower caste of prostitutes, but it's what she's hiding that sets her apart. That classic samurai desire for revenge boils within her, and only one as sharp as Ogami can sense it. Vengeance may not have been exclusively a samurai element, but they certainly seemed to corner the market. A family's place in Japanese society seemed so important that if a samurai lost face by means of another's dishonesty, a baby not yet born might be expected to eventually find the existing head of the offending samurai's family and kill him (or her, as the case may be).

The combination of samurai sister and innocent prostitute serves as an excellent example of Koike and Kojima's artful use of feudal Japanese women in *Lone Wolf and Cub* — a girl passing into womanhood, of samurai birth, yet lost to the painful world of a roadside inn *de-onna*. The balance of the honorable society with the common and the retention of sensational emotion make for a well-developed character, and the element of vengeance not only motivates the character, but connects her to the underlying theme of *Lone Wolf and Cub*. The women Ogami meets on his journeys are the only people who share his dedication to revenge. If Koike and Kojima were to be credited with one thing, character development would be at the top of the list. As it says in his biography, Koike believes that "comics are carried by characters." And the colorful, intense flavor of female characters in *Lone Wolf and Cub* certainly reflects that philosophy.

BIBLIOGRAPHY:

Ratti, Oscar and Adele Westbrook. *Secrets of the Samurai: The Martial Arts of Feudal Japan.*
    Boston: Charles E. Tuttle Co., 1973.
Statler, Oliver. *Japanese Inn.* New York: Random House, 1963.
Scott, George Ryley. *The History of Prostitution.* Guernsey: The Guernsey Press Co. Ltd., 1968